Collins

Complete British Wildlife

Paul Sterry

I am extremely grateful for the shared enthusiasm and knowledge of a number of people who have helped me develop my interest in natural history over the years. In particular, Andrew Cleave has acted as my mentor on a wide range of subjects and I am also indebted to Andy Clements, Peter and Claire Henderson and Lee Morgan for their company and various expertises.

HarperCollins*Publishers* Ltd.
77-85 Fulham Palace Road
London
W6 8JB

The Collins website address is:
www.collins.co.uk

First published in 1997

10 09 08
10 9 8 7 6 5 4 3 2 1

ISBN: 978-0-00-781482-4

Colour reproduction by Colourscan, Singapore
Printed in Hong Kong by Printing Express Ltd.

CONTENTS

Introduction .4
Mammals .46
Birds .58
Reptiles .130
Amphibians .132
Fish .134
Insects • Butterflies and Moths .142
Insects .168
Spiders .198
Molluscs .202
Terrestrial and Freshwater Crustaceans .212
Seashore Crustaceans .214
Other Terrestrial and Freshwater Invertebrates .218
Other Seashore Invertebrates .220
Trees and Shrubs .224
Wild Flowers .236
Grasses, Rushes and Sedges .322
Lower Plants .332
Fungi .344
Glossary .354
Further Reading .357
Picture Credits .359
Index .360

INTRODUCTION

The British Isles may be comparatively small and in parts overcrowded but nevertheless the land harbours a diverse and fascinating array of wildlife. As a child, it was probably the wealth of insect and other invertebrate life that first aroused my interest in natural history. Over the years, this fascination has broadened to embrace all spheres of British wildlife and the species included in this book in part reflect my interest in the subject in all its forms. *Complete British Wildlife* will, I hope, cater for the needs of anyone with a general interest in natural history.

How to use this book

The book has been designed so that the text and photographs for each species are on facing pages. An easy to use series of grids, placed next to each species description, clearly identifies which photograph corresponds to the appropriate text. The text has been written to complement the information conveyed by the photographs.

At the start of each species description the most commonly used and current English name is given followed by the scientific name of the plant or animal in question; this comprises the species' genus name first followed by its specific name. There then follows some measure of the species' size. In the case of mammals, and many birds, this is often the length but in the case of birds or insects usually seen in flight or with their wings spread, wingspan was felt to be a more useful indicator of absolute and relative size. With other animals, the most appropriate dimension, be that height, length or width has been used, this being clearly indicated alongside the dimension itself. Similarly with the plants, overall height, or sometimes flower length or width has been employed as appropriate.

The text has been written in a condensed manner so that as much information as possible could be included. It begins with a description of the species in question. With some groups, for example, birds, this is broadened to cover male, female and juvenile, and summer or winter plumages where necessary. For insects, stages in the life cycle not illustrated are sometimes mentioned when these are conspicuous and distinctive.

An indication is also given in the text of where and when a species may be found in the British Isles together with an idea of its relative abundance or scarcity

The choice of species

This book is intended to serve the needs of the keen amateur naturalist or indeed anyone with even a passing interest in our wildlife. It is not intended to satisfy the needs of experts in any given field and a book of this size could never hope to achieve this aim. The choice of species had, therefore, to be made carefully. It was the intention from the outset to create an overall list which covered almost every commonly encountered, widespread or distinctive species of plant and animal likely to be observed on a day out anywhere in the country. Particular emphasis has been given to groups that arouse special interest among British naturalists and these include mammals, birds, butterflies and flowering plants, especially orchids. Throughout the book, a number of more unusual but particularly striking species can be found, the reason for their inclusion being the degree of interest their discovery always arouses.

Wildlife photographs as aids to identification

There is some disagreement among field guide users as to the way in which these books are best illustrated; some favour artwork while others prefer photographs. For many people, however, the argument is not cut and dry, and each has merits and disadvantages. For me, photographs are an ideal medium for illustrating general books on natural history. When used appropriately, they reproduce faithfully the structures and colours of the subject in life and can, under certain circumstances, convey more information about the species' habitat than would be the case with artwork. The selection of photographs for this book was undertaken with their role as identification aids in mind but also with an eye to their visual impact. If nothing else, they should serve as a photographic celebration of our varied British wildlife.

Thrift carpeting a cliff on the west side of Lundy, Devon

WILDLIFE PHOTOGRAPHY

Taking wildlife photographs is an obvious progression both for the keen naturalist and serious general photographer alike. The subjects found in nature are often stunning and colourful and many present a challenge to capture on film. For the natural historian in particular, photographing wildlife provides an ideal way of documenting sightings and satisfying the collector instinct that lurks in all of us. It can also serve as a great aid to identifying new species and committing them to memory: taking wildlife photographs requires a focused mind as well as a camera lens.

A wealth of experience, not to mention a full range of expensive equipment, may be needed for some avenues of nature photography. For most purposes, however, taking wildlife shots has never been easier. Many modern cameras are relatively inexpensive and are foolproof enough to generate correct exposures time after time; some makes and models even focus the lens as well. By understanding the limitations of your camera and by observing a few basic rules, stunning wildlife photographs can be taken by almost anyone.

Equipment

Someone on the point of buying a camera is faced with a bewildering choice of models and a spectrum of prices ranging from the modest to the frightening. It is impossible to recommend any one make and model and the purchaser would be well advised to visit a camera shop to try out several in their price range. Choose from the range of 35mm SLR cameras and pick one that feels good in the hand and that has a good reputation for sturdiness. You should also consider the extent of lenses available to fit the camera in question since additional lenses will undoubtedly be wanted at a future date.

When you buy a camera body, it is often sold with a standard (50mm) lens which is fine for most everyday subjects. If your photographic interests are more specific, however, you should consider your options. If you intend to take close-up pictures of insects or flowers, for example, a macro lens with a focal length of say 55mm might be a better option and would double as a standard lens too; a wide-angle lens (28mm or 35mm, for example) as an accompanying lens would be useful for scenic shots and landscapes. Bird photographers, on the other hand, will want to opt for a telephoto lens and 300mm is perhaps the minimum focal length needed for this type of photography. Many of the best bird photographs are taken with 500mm or 600mm lenses but the best of these are in the price range of a new small car.

For almost all types of wildlife photography a tripod is invaluable if not essential although there is no one tripod that is ideal for all purposes. For close-up work, a model which will allow photography down to ground level and with a ball-and-socket head is best; for telephoto lenses, a sturdy, heavy model with a pan-and-tilt head should be chosen.

THE BASICS OF TAKING A PICTURE

The amount of light reaching the film in the camera, otherwise known as the exposure, is determined by two factors, the shutter speed and the lens aperture. Modern cameras invariably have automatic light metering and so almost every shot you take should be perfectly exposed. The way in which this is achieved, ie. the ratio of aperture to shutter speed, however, can have a strong bearing on the success or otherwise of the photograph as a pleasing image. An understanding of how shutter speed and aperture affect photographic images can greatly improve your chances of achieving a successful result.

The faster the shutter speed used when taking a photograph the less the chances are that the picture will be spoilt either by camera shake, if you are hand-holding the camera, or by subject movement and blurring during the exposure. So why not use a fast shutter all the time? Fast shutter speeds often necessitate wide lens apertures to allow sufficient light for correct exposure. While this is fine under some circumstances, the lens aperture affects the depth of field in the photograph, a large lens aperture creating a small depth of field and vice versa. Aperture settings are indicated by a number (called the 'f' number) shown on the ring on the lens; these might range, on a typical lens, from f4 to f22. Small f numbers correspond to wide apertures and reduced depths of field.

As a rule of thumb, cameras with a standard or wide-angle lens can usually be hand-held without camera shake at shutter speeds down to 1/60th second although much slower speeds can be employed when using a tripod. Even when using a tripod, you would be well advised to use a shutter speed that corresponds roughly with the focal length of the lens; for a 300mm lens, therefore, a speed of 1/250th second should be used.

Long-winged conehead

Active wildlife subjects obviously require faster shutter speeds than static ones: a minimum of 1/250th second might be needed to 'freeze' the movement of a feeding wader while 1/30th or 1/60th second would suffice for a toadstool where a tripod was being used. Always contemplate the effect you want to achieve when selecting the aperture and hence the depth of field. If taking a close-up photograph of a flower, for example, you might want to have your subject sharp but the background thrown out of focus using an aperture setting of f 5.6 or f8. By contrast, a wide-angle shot placing the flower in the context of its habitat would by achieved by using an aperture setting of f16 or f22.

The choice of film is very much a matter of taste. Most serious photographers use slide film and ones with film speeds of between 50 and 100 ASA are usually best. Films with faster speeds, while useful under certain circumstances, produce results which are grainy and can have poor definition.

Lighting and composition

Under most circumstances, natural light produces entirely satisfactory results when it comes to illuminating a photograph. Experimentation with angle of light and time of day are, however, an essential part of developing your skills as a wildlife photographer. Generally speaking, the most effective way of using natural light is to photograph with the sun behind you; this reduces the risk of distracting shadows. At the other extreme, however, photographing into the light and backlighting your subject can achieve startling results when it works well.

On some occasions, the use of flash can enhance a photograph and, after dark, it is usually the only means by which a picture can be taken. The use of so-called fill-in flash can help brighten a subject in dull natural light or reduce the effect of harsh shadows under bright conditions. Specially designed macro flash systems are best for close-up work while larger flash guns, preferably ones which can be used away from the camera via long leads, are most suited for bird photography.

A migrant firecrest

Bird photography

Although a hide is a useful piece of equipment for photographing many wary bird subjects, it is by no means essential under all circumstances. Some species are seemingly indifferent to photographers and, if you happen to be in the right place at the right time, close views can be obtained simply by standing still. This approach is often particularly successful with migrating birds which are more concerned with feeding than with their human onlookers; for some species, this can be by far the best time to observe them. Firecrests, for example, are rare and elusive during the breeding season in Britain but occasionally turn up in good numbers in autumn at migration hotspots. Constantly active in search of insects, they will sometimes forage within a few feet of observers.

NATURE CONSERVATION

Although the British Isles still harbour a wealth of natural history and retain large tracts of land full of wildlife interest, few people would argue that many of our habitats and species are under threat. As elsewhere in the world, at the root of the problems faced by our environment is the scale of the human population and its quest for economic improvement in its many guises; these manifest themselves in issues such as pollution, the swallowing of land for housing, industry and road projects, and modern farming practices. Whatever the causes, the results have been fragmentation and degradation of habitats and the decline or loss of certain species.

Dormouse: under threat from habitat loss

But who is to blame for environmental and conservation problems today? Because of their economic power, arguably the most immediate threat to British wildlife comes from commerce. A few organisations and businesses do genuinely have an interest in nature conservation but it is probably fair to say that, for both industry and agriculture, environmental issues are very much secondary to their primary economic goals. As for the rest, some treat the subject with indifference; where legislation or public image is at stake, many pay lip-service to conservation; a few are even directly hostile to the aims of wildlife organisations. Government too is not without blame; conflicts of interest between different departments often seem to mean that British wildlife loses out to economic concerns. Ultimately, of course, commerce and government alone cannot shoulder the blame entirely for environmental problems: we as consumers and voters must also take our share.

Does conservation matter? For the unenlightened minority, the answer may be no but for the majority it is unquestionably yes. Membership figures for organisations such as the RSPB and The Wildlife Trusts testify to this. For most people, it is not just that diverse and species-rich habitats are likely to provide a healthy environment to live in but it is also that the prospect of unchallenged and often needless destruction of wildlife offends as being both unnecessary and akin to vandalism.

Fortunately, all is not doom and gloom and the need for active conservation measures is appreciated by many. A heartening array of organisations now exist to represent the interests of wildlife and its enthusiastic supporters. Statutory bodies concerned with conservation include English Nature, the Countryside Commission for Wales and the Nature Conservancy for Scotland. The umbrella of The Wildlife Trusts ensures that the county wildlife trusts, charitable status organisations representing the interests of counties, speak with one voice on matters of national interest. In addition to these, organisations such as the RSPB, Plant Life, Butterfly Conservation and the Marine Conservation Society, all represent the interests of naturalists. Although in the past, some of these organisations may have viewed each other as rivals, initiatives such as the Government sponsored Biodiversity Action Plan have engendered more of a spirit of co-operation and partnership.

Some of our best areas for wildlife have been designated Sites of Special Scientific Interest, a status which does not necessarily ward off development proposals. A range of other designated areas such as Nature Reserves and National Nature Reserves endeavour to protect especially good locations and ensure sympathetic habitat management. Our most endangered species are afforded special protection by law and threatened plants and animals are now the subject of study, their future hopefully ensured by Species Recovery Programmes.

THE COUNTRYSIDE CODE

As land-users, naturalists have just as much a moral duty as landowners to minimise their impact on our environment. By observing an unofficial countryside code, most elements of which are common-sense, we can all enjoy the countryside without unduly affecting the plants, animals and scenery we sought to study and appreciate in the first place. Among the more obvious guidelines for enjoying a day out are the following:

- Always keep to footpaths or other rights of way to avoid damaging fragile natural habitats and crops, even when walking on common-land, it is often good practice to keep to obvious paths, thus focusing the effects of trampling.
- Keep dogs under control and, if necessary, on a lead. Landowners are quite within their rights to shoot any dog which is out of control and worrying livestock. Badly trained dogs also cause considerable distress to wild animals including deer and ground-nesting birds.
- Avoid damaging fences, walls and property and be sure to close gates behind you.
- Do not leave litter behind you and above all do not drop lighted cigarettes, especially in fire-prone habitats such as heaths and woods.
- Do not pick wild flowers or collect animals: leave them in their natural habitat for others to enjoy. If you collect wild fungi in the autumn, consider the impact you are having on these organisms. While it may be true to say that limited harvesting has little impact on the underground part of the fungus organism, mushrooms and toadstools are the spore-producing part of the organism and their premature removal must have some effect upon dispersal to new sites.

PLANT AND ANIMAL GROUPS

Scientists and naturalists divide plants and animals into groups, members of which have characters in common with one another. The species included in this book have been organised into these widely accepted groups and the accompanying notes detail their most distinctive features. The coloured symbols to the left of the page correspond to those used throughout the book as thumbnail indicators of page subjects.

VERTEBRATE ANIMALS

Animals with backbones which comprise:

Mammals: warm-blooded animals which have hairy skins, give birth to live young which are subsequently suckled by the mother.

Birds: warm-blooded animals whose skins are covered with feathers, these aiding heat regulation and allowing flight; all birds lay eggs.

Reptiles: cold-blooded animals with scaly skins and which breathe air. The young develop inside eggs which, in some species, hatch within the body of the female.

Amphibians: cold-blooded animals with soft, moist skins capable of absorbing oxygen from water; also have lungs and can breathe air. Often found on land but always breed in water, laying eggs which grow as larval tadpoles before metamorphosing into miniature adults.

Fish: cold-blooded animals which live in water throughout their lives; all British species use gills to extract oxygen from water. In most species, the skin is covered with scales and fins facilitate swimming.

INVERTEBRATE ANIMALS

Animals without backbones which include:

Sponges: primitive, aquatic animals whose bodies have external vents and are covered in minute pores.

Coelenterates: radially symmetrical, soft-bodied creatures that include sea anemones, jellyfish and freshwater hydras.

Planarian worms: simple free-living flatworms which are relatives of tapeworms and flukes.

Molluscs: soft-bodied animals that occur on land, in freshwater and in the sea. Some molluscs protect their bodies by producing hard shells while this feature is absent or much reduced in slugs, sea slugs and octopuses.

Segmented worms: examples of which occur in soil, freshwater and in the sea. The body is soft, segmented and often bears bristles to aid movements as with earthworms and marine annelid worms; leeches have conspicuous suckers.

Arthropods: the most numerous group of animals and one which is characterised by the presence of an external skeleton and paired, jointed limbs. Members include Insects, Crustaceans, Spiders and allies, Millipedes and Centipedes. Insects groups dealt with in this book include butterflies and moths, mayflies, dragonflies and damselflies, grasshoppers and crickets, earwigs, lacewings, bugs, bees, wasps, ants and beetles; Crustacean groups covered include woodlice, crabs, shrimps, prawns, sandhoppers and barnacles; spider allies include harvestmen and pseudoscorpions.

Echinoderms: animals which are radially symmetrical, mostly organised into five rays. Some members have bodies protected by a hard shell comprising armoured plates with spines. Included in the book are sea urchins, starfishes and brittlestars.

Higher plants

Distinguished from animals by the presence of the green pigment chlorophyll which is used to manufacture food from sunlight energy, water and carbon dioxide; oxygen is produced as a by-product of this chemical reaction known as photosynthesis. Higher plants come in all shapes and sizes and are separated into two groups:

Flowering Plants: plants whose reproductive structures are borne in flowers; their seeds are enclosed in structures known as fruits, a term which, for botanists, is not confined to conspicuous and edible forms. Flowering plants covered in this book include deciduous and some evergreen trees, shrubs and wildflowers. For ease of interpretation, some characteristic aquatic flowering plants are featured separately alongside aquatic lower plants. Grasses, rushes and sedges, all flowering plants, are grouped separately.

Conifers: mostly sizeable, evergreen plants whose reproductive structures are borne in cones; the seeds are naked.

Lower plants

These lack the complex reproductive structures of higher plants and are generally smaller and less robust. Those included in this book include the following:

Algae: primitive aquatic plants. Many are microscopic and not covered in this book but the larger seaweeds are included.

Mosses: primitive land plants which lack roots and whose stems bear simple leaves.

Liverworts: primitive land plants which are usually broad and flattened, anchored to the substrate by root-like structures.

Lichens: unusual organisms that exist as a symbiotic relationship between a fungus and an alga. Usually for encrustations on rock or bark.

Clubmosses: small, simple plants with upright stems which bear numerous narrow leaves. Clubmosses bearing a passing resemblance to miniature conifers.

Horsetails: perennial plants that comprise an underground stem or rhizome from which arise upright stems bearing whorls of narrow leaves.

Ferns: easily recognised during their spore-producing stages which are large and robust and have a vascular system and roots.

Fungi

Although formerly considered to be part of the plant kingdom, many scientists now place fungi in a group separate both from plants and animals. They lack the photosynthetic pigment chlorophyll which characterises plants and are thus unable to make their own food; nutrition is obtained instead from organic matter via the thread-like hyphae which comprise the bulk of the fungal organism. The familiar mushrooms and toadstools are merely the reproductive structures of the fungi.

BRITISH HABITATS

Naturalists in Britain are indeed fortunate to live in an area so diverse in terrain. The varied appearance of the landscape is partly a reflection of the range of habitats found on these islands and the mosaic effect created by the often close juxtaposition of two or more different habitats contributes to the often surprising diversity of wildlife found within comparatively small areas.

Although a few species of plants and animals are rather catholic in their choice of habitat, any student of the British countryside will soon tell you that the majority are more specific in their requirements. In the case of animals, for example, their behaviour, feeding requirements, structure and tolerances having evolved to suit special niches in a particular habitat. Many plants will tolerate only certain types of soil and thrive best where other factors such as rainfall or degree of shade are to their liking. Learn how to recognise a given habitat and you may greatly improve your chances of finding a particular species or of identifying it correctly once discovered.

Although a species may be habitat-specific, it does not necessarily follow that it will be found in all examples of this habitat throughout Britain. In particular, climatic factors past and present have a strong influence on a species' current national distribution; temperature tolerance may determine whether a plant or animal favours southern England or northern Scotland while annual rainfall may influence its range from west to east.

The character of any given habitat is obviously influenced by, and in some cases determined by, the geography, geology and botany of the area. Arguably the most significant factor affecting the majority of them, however, is the influence of man. Only some of our coastal habitats and a few remote areas of the highest mountain tops can truly be said to have escaped human interference over the last few centuries.

Man's influence has not always been to the detriment of plant and animal diversity and indeed some habitats, such as heathland, owe their very existence to man's clearance of trees from the land. As an example of man's contemporary role, woodland management carried out in a traditional manner can exert a positive influence on plant and animal diversity. Land management is needed to maintain the quality of many of our habitats but, sadly, today these also have to contend with our seemingly insatiable desire to embark on new road and housing schemes.

The following pages detail all of our most characteristic and distinctive habitats. Contained within each habitat section is information about each one's vegetation and character, key species found there and examples of places to go to see the habitat in question.

THE COAST

In habitat terms, Britain's coastline is arguably its crowning glory. Although development has marred considerable stretches of the coast, particularly in southern England, those that remain unspoilt here and elsewhere in Britain are truly wonderful and harbour wildlife interest throughout the year. Plant and animal life is prolific near the sea and, bathed twice daily by an advancing and retreating tide, the marine life of our coastal waters is abundant and diverse.

The two photographs shown above illustrate the daily rhythms of the tide. At high tide (left), the seashore inhabitants are immersed in seawater; eight hours later they are exposed to the air (right).

CLIFFS AND COASTAL LAND

For breathtaking scenery and a sense of untamed nature, coastal cliffs offer unrivalled opportunities for the naturalist and outdoor enthusiast. Man has had minimal impact on these areas and wildlife is still found in profusion.

VEGETATION AND CHARACTER

Among the most characteristic plants of cliffs are thrift, sea campion, rock sea-spurrey and scurvy grass. Their presence is particularly striking on the west coast where prevailing, salt-laden winds tend to exclude most other plants from exposed sites. Visit one of these places in May and June and you will find a fantastic natural rock garden, the colours of the flowers being thrown in to contrast by orange and blue-green lichens which coat the rocks. Soil type has an influence on the other plants associated with clifftop habitats. Not surprisingly, therefore, downland flowers grow right to the edge of chalk cliffs in southern England while heathland plants such as bell heather and gorse favour acid rocks in the west.

Key animal species

Britain has some of the finest seabird cliffs in Europe with populations of birds such as razorbill and gannet being of global importance. The time to visit a seabird colony is between April and July when the sight, sound and smell of the birds will be at its height. Because each species has unique nesting requirements, not every seabird species will be found on every cliff. Where stable ledges occur, guillemots and kittiwakes can be abundant while puffins favour grassy slopes in which they can excavate burrows. Some seabirds are solitary nesters but many, such as cormorants and gulls, form loose colonies, their concentration due as much to the limited availability of nesting sites as to anything else. A fundamental requirement for any seabird colony is that it must be close to good feeding grounds.

Where to go

Views apart, the cliffs with the greatest wildlife interest are mostly found in the north and west. For coastal flowers, visit sites such as The Lizard Peninsula in Cornwall, Lundy off the north Devon coast and the Pembrokeshire coast in spring. For seabirds, Skomer Island in Pembrokeshire, The Farne Islands in Northumberland and Hermaness on Unst in Shetland offer easily accessible sites.

Seabird colony on Bass Rock

ESTUARY AND SALTMARSH

Mudflats and lugworm castes at Budle Bay, Northumberland

To the unenlightened eye, an estuary may seem like a vast expanse of mudflats and very little else. For the naturalist, however, this exciting habitat is full of interest throughout the year. Saltmarsh plants colonise the higher reaches of the estuary and waders and wildfowl feed in vast numbers from autumn to spring. The reason why estuaries can support so much birdlife lies buried in the mud itself. Incredible numbers of marine worms and tiny molluscs thrive in the oozing mud, their numbers in turn supported by the vast amount of organic matter deposited when river meets sea.

Vegetation and character

Estuaries are subject both to the influence of freshwater and to the daily tidal rhythms that affect all our coastline. The plants that colonise the higher reaches of the estuary have to tolerate periodic immersion in water of varying salinities as well as exposure to air. Characteristic saltmarsh plants include glasswort, common sea-lavender, sea-purslane and golden samphire; where conditions suit them, they grow in great abundance.

Key animal species

Evidence for the wealth of marine life found in mudflats and estuaries is not always easy to detect although the castes of lugworms and carpet of small molluscs on the surface gives some clue as to the productivity in the mud itself. Waders are perhaps the most characteristic group to exploit this resource, each species having bill lengths and feeding strategies adapted to suit a particular food source; this helps avoid undue competition with other species. Dunlin, for example, tend to feed on small surface-living animals while curlew and godwits use their long bills to probe deep for more substantial prey. Wildfowl too occur in huge numbers on many of our estuaries. Some, such as shelduck, feed in minute animals filtered from the mud with the bills while others, such as brent geese and wigeon favour plant material.

With the exception of a few bird species such as shelduck, most of these birds breed further north in Europe and the Arctic, visiting us from September to March. Britain's estuaries are globally important refuges for many bird species. Estuary waders and wildfowl feed most actively at low water when the mud is exposed or while following the progress of a rising tide. At high tide, their predatory role is replaced by fish such as bass, thick-lipped grey mullet and various flatfish species.

Where to go

Estuary wildlife can be seen at its best on the Exe estuary at Dawlish Warren in Devon, the Hayle estuary in Cornwall, Farlington Marshes in Hampshire, Pagham Harbour in Sussex, Blakeney Harbour in Norfolk, at Morecambe Bay and on the Solway Firth.

A typical saltmarsh

ROCKY SHORES

For the keen student of marine life, the intertidal zone on a rocky shore offers a wealth of opportunities for exploration. At low tide, rock pools and gulleys team with life and scores of crabs and small fish can be found simply by turning stones and seaweed. As when studying other habitats, it is vital to replace stones as you found them; by doing so you avoid killing anemones and other creatures attached to them and help recreate shaded, sheltered niches.

VEGETATION AND CHARACTER

On the west coast of Britain in particular, where the tidal range is large, zonation of seaweeds can be seen to good effect. The degree of exposure to wave action has a marked effect upon the seaweed species that prosper but on most moderately sheltered shores the visitor could expect to find, working down the shore, clearly defined zones of channelled wrack, spiral wrack, egg wrack, bladder wrack and serrated wrack. Kelps are exposed only at low tide and grow down into much deeper water. Among these larger species of seaweed are numerous smaller species and, of course, an abundance of marine animals, many of which are themselves zoned on the shore.

KEY ANIMAL SPECIES

Barnacles and limpets are among the most distinctive animals on the upper shore. They can be found on most rocky shores although in different parts of Britain and at different zones on the shore they are represented by a range of superficially similar species. Among the rock pools anemones are conspicuous along with blennies, prawns and shore crabs. A careful search under stones may reveal other species of crabs, retiring hermit crabs often living in the empty shells of periwinkles and dog whelks. Many rocky shore animals are year-round residents but during the summer months more unusual species visit from deeper waters.

A rocky shore at low tide covered in seaweeds

Where to go
Almost any safe, sheltered rocky shore on the west coast of Britain offers good opportunities for the seashore enthusiast, but Wembury and Lundy (Devon) have the additional attraction of underwater nature trails for divers.

SANDY SHORES AND DUNES
Beloved of holidaymakers, sandy shores also have much to offer the visiting naturalist. Beneath the surface of the sand live an abundance of marine worms and molluscs whose presence would go largely undetected were it not for the feeding activities of birds and the profusion of dead shells found along the strandline. Above the high tide line, tough resilient plants colonise the shifting sands and help create fragile dune systems with their own unique flora. Although seemingly less inviting, shingle beaches nevertheless have a charm and flora all of their own.

Vegetation and character
Given the shifting nature of the substrate, it is perhaps not surprising that seaweeds find it almost impossible to gain a foothold on sandy beaches. Only a few metres above the high tide line, however, terrestrial plants such as marram grass, sea sandwort, sea-holly and sea milkwort soon become established and initiate the stabilising process which leads to the establishment of sand dune vegetation. In well established and relatively undisturbed dune systems, a progression of vegetation can be followed inland, leading eventually to the creation of scrub and woodland. Wet dune hollows, known as slacks, are particularly rewarding places to search and often support thriving populations of interesting plants including sea spurge, various species of marsh-orchids and adderstongue fern. Many of the plants found colonising sandy shores also grow on stabilised shingle. In addition, however, sea-kale, yellow horned-poppy and sea pea also favour this habitat.

Key animal species
Human disturbance has all but excluded birds such as ringed plovers and terns from nesting on many beaches in southern England. In a few protected areas, however, good colonies still persist in the south while in northern Britain these birds fare better. Outside the breeding season, sandy beaches are the haunt of black-headed and other gull species along with sanderling, delightful little waders which follow the line of breaking waves in search of small invertebrates.

Where to go
For superb areas of sand dune flora, visit Dawlish Warren in Devon, Kenfig and Newborough Warren, both in Wales and Holy Island in Northumberland. Nesting terns and other coastal birds can be seen in large numbers at Blakeney Point in Norfolk and are best in May and June. Slapton beach in Devon, Chesil Beach in Dorset and Shingle Street in Suffolk are among the finest examples of shingle systems.

FRESHWATER

For wildlife and naturalists alike, freshwater habitats have the same magnetic appeal as do coastal habitats. In Britain we are indeed fortunate in having a wealth of habitats from small ponds and streams to large lakes and river systems; few people have to travel excessive distances to visit one or more of these habitats.

RIVERS AND STREAMS

Flowing water has a charm all of its own and a trip to one of our rivers and streams will always yield interesting wildlife sightings. The margins are often cloaked with vegetation which, if lush enough, will provide a haven for insects and nesting birds. If the water is clean and sufficiently shallow, a rich growth of submerged aquatic plants can often be seen whose waving fronds harbour fishes small and large. Even the substrate of the river or stream is likely to harbour wildlife with freshwater molluscs or the nymphs of aquatic insects finding refuge there.

VEGETATION AND CHARACTER

Water chemistry and soil type have such a profound influence on the plant species found in or beside any given river or stream that it is difficult to generalise. In lowland southern England, however, marginal plants often include yellow iris, purple loosestrife and great willowherb. These plants grow wherever the soil remains damp throughout the year and often form dense stands where conditions suit them.

Permanent inundation in flowing water requires special adaptations and the water-crowfoots have responded well to the challenge. The group comprises numerous species each with different leaf shapes which suit them to the varied nature of our streams and rivers; the spectrum of water-crowfoot species is also adapted to life in water as varied as chalk streams and acid flows. The dense drifts of water-crowfoot leaves often persist for much of the year and in spring are adorned by white flowers raised above the surface of the water on short stems.

A chalkstream in southern England

Lowland chalk streams are also the favoured haunt of water-cress, a plant which is grown commercially where water supplies permit. Streams and river margins of all types are home to water starworts, easily recognised by the long tangles of submerged stems which end in floating, star-like rosettes of leaves. Muddy margins, even where trampled by livestock, are good places to search for water mint and lesser spearwort.

Key animal species

Invertebrate life abounds in most unpolluted rivers and streams in Britain. Many of these creatures, such as mayflies, stoneflies and damselflies, may be more familiar as their airborne adult stages but nevertheless occur in large numbers as larval or nymphal stages. To avoid the depredations of fish in particular, many species lurk among the silt and sediment at the bottom but some, such as caddisfly larvae, build camouflaged and strengthened cases in which to conceal and protect themselves.

The fish are the dominant force beneath the surface of the water. Depending on the depth and quality of the water and its water chemistry, species such as pike, perch, roach, gudgeon and minnow are all widespread. In common with most other freshwater systems, however, the selective stocking or removal of certain species means it is almost impossible to determine the natural distribution for many species. Shallow, fast-flowing streams are the haunt of sticklebacks, bullhead, stoneloach and brown trout while slow-flowing, deep waters harbour perch, roach, chub and many others.

Birdlife abounds on many rivers and streams, larger ones supporting populations of mute swans, mallards and grey herons. Small, lowland streams are favoured by kingfishers and little grebes while, in north and west Britain in particular, dipper and grey wagtail are characteristic species.

A Scottish loch with a rich growth of aquatic and marginal vegetation

Where to go

Almost any unpolluted stream is likely to be worth visiting and even rivers, where their course is not influenced by large towns or cities, will hold some interest.

LAKES AND PONDS

Bodies of standing water often harbour a strikingly different range of plants and animals from those found in flowing water. Many are man-made or at least man-influenced and within this category should also fall flooded gravel pits, reservoirs and canals.

Vegetation and character

By mid-summer, a rich growth of aquatic plants dominates many of our ponds along with the shallow margins of lakes. Water-lilies are arguably the most distinctive of these with the white water-lily being the largest and most widespread species. Rooted in the silt of the bottom, its large, kidney-shaped leaves often blanket the surface, although it frequently has to compete with one of several species of pondweed. Beneath the surface of the water these days, native species of water plant often have to contend with introduced Canadian pondweed which often flourishes at the expense of the others. In upland waters in the north and west, which are often more acid than their lowland counterparts, bogbean and bladderwort can often be found.

Where left to their own devices, the margins of ponds and lakes are soon encroached by stands of emergent plants such as reed sweet-grass, reedmace and common reed. Although found in a wide range of wetland habitats, the latter often forms extensive beds around larger lakes and, when well established, creates an important refuge for wildlife including many unique species.

Key animal species

The seasons have a marked influence on the wildlife found in and around ponds and lakes in Britain. These habitats are excellent for amphibians and in early spring common frogs and toads gather in large numbers to mate and spawn. The resulting abundance of tadpoles, along with those of newts, provide a feeding bonanza for the larvae and adults of predatory water beetles along with several species of water bugs and the nymphs of larger dragonfly species.

As the year progresses, fish spawn in the shallows and waterbirds such as great crested grebes and coots nest among the marginal vegetation. Sedge warblers and reed buntings nest in emergent vegetation of all types but arguably the most important species in this respect is common reed. Extensive reed-beds in eastern England in particular also hold communities of bittern, marsh harrier and bearded tit along with more widespread species such as reed warbler.

During autumn and winter, areas of open water become refuges for large flocks of waterbirds such as tufted duck, pochard, coot and great crested grebe. For many species, reservoirs and flooded gravel pits fulfil the same role as natural and semi-natural lakes with the added advantage to the naturalist that they are often within striking distance of urban areas.

Where to go

Excellent areas of open water include Bosherston Pools in Pembrokeshire and Loch Garten in Scotland while man-made waterbodies include Chew Valley Reservoir in Somerset and Rutland Water. Extensive reed-beds can be found at Stodmarsh NNR in Kent, Minsmere RSPB Reserve in Suffolk and Leighton Moss RSPB reserve in Lancashire.

MIRES, FENS AND BOGS

The encroachment of vegetation into areas of open water leads to the creation of habitats known as mires which are more popularly referred in a general context as marshes. Mires often form on neutral soils but where there is a base-rich element then the resultant habitat is called a fen. Conversely, acid soils encourage the formation of bogs.

VEGETATION AND CHARACTER

Among all the wetland habitats, wet, marshy meadows offer the best opportunities for the keen botanist. Factors such as soil chemistry, grazing regime, if any, and geographical location obviously influence the species found but among the more widespread flowers are ragged robin, yellow iris, marsh marigold, southern and early marsh-orchids, water avens and a range of species of sedges and rushes. Marshes and fens evolve as a progression from open water to dry land and so it is not surprising to find them in close proximity to lakes and reed-beds.

Even at first glance, bog vegetation comprises a completely different set of plant species and the gradation from surrounding heathland may be extremely gradual. The nodding heads of cotton-grass species offer distant indications of the presence of bogs and, at close range, fresh green bog moss is a further sign of acid terrain despite the nutrient-poor, waterlogged ground, resourceful plants such as sundews and butterwort can flourish thanks to their carnivorous tendencies.

Key animal species

Nesting birds such as snipe and reed bunting do make use of these wetland habitats in undisturbed areas but insect life, and in particular moths, beetles and hoverflies, are among the most characteristic animals to be found here. The large numbers of dragonflies often associated with southern bogs often attract feeding hobbies which nest in adjacent areas of heathland. Spiders too occur in vast numbers although the scale of their presence is often not appreciated until the first mists of late summer and early autumn highlight their webs with dew.

Where to go

Perhaps the most accessible fenland area is Wicken Fen in Cambridgeshire but Hickling Broad in Norfolk is also well worth visiting for its mosaic of wetland habitats. Almost every county has examples large and small of marshland habitat and wet bogs abound among the heaths of the New Forest in Hampshire.

WOODLAND

The vast forests that once cloaked much of Britain have long since gone, felled and cleared by man over the centuries. Fortunately for the naturalist, the countryside still harbours numerous pockets of woodland some of which are large enough to retain a wilderness feel and characteristic forest plants and animals. Even small wooded areas can be surprisingly good for flowers and birds, mammals and invertebrates are often found in abundance.

DECIDUOUS WOODLAND

Woodlands of deciduous trees are found throughout Britain and are the dominant natural forest type in all regions except in parts of Scotland where evergreen conifers predominate. As their name suggests, deciduous trees shed their leaves in the winter and grow a new set the following spring. The seasonality seen in these woodlands is among the most marked and easily observed of any British habitat. Almost every British deciduous woodland has been, and still is, influenced in some way by man. This might take the form of simple disturbance by walkers at one end of the spectrum or regular woodland management at the other. Man's influence is not always to the detriment of wildlife, however, and sympathetic coppicing of hazel and ash, for example, can encourage a profusion of wildflowers, butterflies and nesting warblers.

Vegetation and character

Our two native species of oak are the dominant species in much of England and Wales, the pedunculate oak favouring the east with the sessile oak predominating in the west. Depending on factors such as soil type, annual rainfall and altitude, other species such as ash, beech, birch or hornbeam may be dominant although selective planting and felling by man has confused the picture of natural distribution. Within a semi-natural woodland other species such as hazel, hawthorn, field maple or blackthorn may contribute to the understorey, the first species in particular often encouraged to do so by woodland management practices such as regular coppicing.

Where the canopy is not too dense, deciduous woodlands are sometimes carpeted in spring with flowers such as bluebell, wood anemone, wood sorrel, lesser celandine or ramsons; amongst their numbers, less frequent species such as early purple orchid or herb paris may put in an appearance in suitable areas and on appropriate soil types.

Prior to the leaves falling in early winter, the autumn colours seen in many of our deciduous woodlands are a sight to behold. It is at this time of year that colourful fungi also put in an appearance adding to the mosaic effect on the woodland floor.

Key animal species

Most of our deciduous woodlands are home to thriving populations of birds with both resident and summer visitors among their numbers. Many of the residents include insects in their diet for at least part of the year, turning to seeds and nuts during the winter months, while others feed on invertebrates throughout the year. Well represented are members of the tit family, familiar birds to most people. Chaffinches too are widespread and common although their relative, the hawfinch, is a much scarcer bird with a patchy distribution. Nuthatch, treecreeper and

An English oakwood in early summer (left) and the dead of winter (right)

three species of woodpecker add to the variety of our resident woodland birds with sparrowhawk and tawny owl the most typical predators across the region; buzzards are widespread only in the west and north. Spring sees the arrival of migrants such as chiffchaff, willow warbler and blackcap. Redstart, pied flycatcher and nightingale are also welcome arrivals, the first two showing a marked preference for western woodlands while the latter confined mainly to the south and south-east.

Small mammals are well represented in our woodlands although many, such as the wood mouse, also occur in other habitats as well. Its relative the yellow-necked mouse is more restricted to woodland while the dormouse is entirely dependent on this habitat and furthermore one with a continuous canopy and good supply of honeysuckle and hazel. Foxes and badgers commonly use woodlands in which to excavate underground homes and, in a few parts of the country, roe deer are a delightful addition to our woodland fauna. Less welcome, however, is the introduced grey squirrel which has effectively replaced the native red squirrel in most parts of Britain except in the north.

The abundance of birdlife in most deciduous woodlands is a reflection of the wealth of insects and other invertebrates that favour this habitat. In terms of diversity, oaks support the greatest number of insect species of all our trees with a gradation of importance through our other native tree species. Not surprisingly, introduced trees are of comparatively little value to native insects.

Butterflies are perhaps the most conspicuous and sought-after members of the woodland invertebrate community. Speckled wood, comma, orange tip and green-veined white are all species which are fairly widespread and common, especially in the south. Species such as white admiral, purple emperor and silver washed fritillary are, however, much harder to track down and see. The nocturnal counterparts of butterflies, the moths, are even more diverse although finding them during the daytime can be a challenge. Run a moth trap after dark, however, and you will be amazed by the diversity: it would not be unusual for an oak wood in southern England to harbour in excess of 300 species.

Search among leaves, bark and under fallen branches and you will find a wealth of beetles and bugs with representatives too numerous to mention here. Distinctive or striking species abound and a full complement of other invertebrates such as slugs, snails, centipedes and millipedes add to the interest.

Where to go

Almost any small pocket of deciduous woodland is likely to harbour natural interest but among the larger, rewarding sites are the New Forest and Selborne Hangers, both in Hampshire, and the Forest of Dean in Gloucestershire. In the autumn, the woods around Virginia Water in Berkshire are good for leaf colour and fungi, despite over-picking of the latter, and woodland birds, including nightingale, can be found in spring at Blean Woods near Canterbury in Kent.

CONIFER WOODLAND

Unlike our deciduous trees, conifers are, with the exception of a few species, evergreen and keep their leaves throughout the year. Instead of having broad, often rounded leaves, they have narrow ones which are called needles. Their flowers and seeds are borne in structures known as cones and the shape of the trees themselves are often conical in outline.

Areas of native conifer woodland are restricted to a few relict pockets of Caledonian pine forest in the Highlands of Scotland. Conifers seen

A Caledonian pine forest in the Scottish Highlands

almost everywhere else in Britain have either been planted or have seeded themselves from mature plantations. While our native conifer forests harbour an intriguing array of plants and animals, some of which are unique or nearly so to this habitat, plantation conifers are usually species poor. This is not to say, however, that they are devoid of wildlife and the keen naturalist will always be able to find something to capture his or her interest.

Vegetation and character

The tree which dominates our Caledonian pine forests and indeed which is largely responsible for their character and appearance is the Scots pine. Gnarled and ancient trees with their open crowns and peeling bark are a majestic sight, especially during the summer months when the ling, which often dominates the ground layer, is in flower. Birch often encroaches on, or mixes with, the conifers, adding to the spectrum of colours in autumn. Juniper forms an understorey in some areas and, in addition to the ling, bilberry often flourishes. Caledonian pine forests are famed for their intriguing ground flora which includes plants such as twinflower, cowberry and common wintergreen.

By contrast, plantation forests have a restricted ground flora. The dense canopy of close-planted trees and the thick carpet of slowly decomposing needles hinder the growth of most plants although, along rides and in clearings on acid soils, bilberry, ling and bracken can often be found. Among the most commonly planted species are European larch, Corsican pine, Douglas fir and western hemlock-spruce.

For many people, the greatest natural history interest yielded by conifer plantations comes from the autumn crop of fungi. Many of the species found here are restricted to conifer woods and the diversity of species is always a pleasant surprise.

Key animal species

Caledonian pine forests harbour the only species of bird unique to Britain, the Scottish crossbill. However, although widespread in Europe generally, crested tit and capercaillie are also restricted to this habitat in Britain. Clearings and widely spaced trees also encourage birds such as tree pipit and redstart, making a trip to central Scotland an extremely rewarding one.

Those keen on mammals will also find the prospect of a visit to a Caledonian pine forest a tempting one since red squirrel, pine marten and wildcat all survive here. Although the first species is comparatively easy to see and sometimes even rather bold, the latter two predatory species are far more retiring and a good deal of luck will be needed to secure a sighting.

For all their bad name, plantation forests still merit some attention from the naturalist. Mature plantations in Scotland, for example, often harbour a number of the species more usually associated with native Caledonian pine forests and, in upland parts of Britain, plantations in their first few years of existence, are ideal nesting sites for short-eared owl and hen harrier. In later years, the elusive goshawk may find these sites to its liking and mature plantations in lowland areas can be good for crossbills and a modest selection of woodland birds including coal tit, great spotted woodpecker and chaffinch.

Where to go

For the best areas of Caledonian pine forest, visit the Abernethy and Rothiemurchus forests near Aviemore in Scotland. The areas comprise both areas of native forest and mature plantations, the latter easily recognised by uniformity in size and appearance of the trees themselves. For mature pine plantations elsewhere in Britain, visit the Kielder Forest in Northumberland, the forests around Betws-y-Coed in north Wales and parts of the New Forest in Hampshire.

HEDGEROWS AND ROADSIDE VERGES

Once so much a feature of the British countryside, hedgerows have suffered a dramatic decline in recent decades, grubbed out by farmers keen to expand arable field size or wrecked by inappropriate cutting regimes. Fortunately, however, they are undergoing a resurgence of interest and their value, both in wildlife terms and as stock-proof barriers and windbreaks, is again appreciated by many. It is perhaps a sign of the times that roadside verges are also perceived as important havens for wildlife; despite the close proximity of cars whizzing by, they suffer little disturbance from man other than noise pollution and periodic cutting.

A Wiltshire hedgerow in summer

Vegetation and character

Hedgerows usually comprise the species, and acquire the character of, any woodland edge in the vicinity. Since, for many species of bird and insect, the margins of woodlands are more important than adjacent interiors, a good network of hedgerows can dramatically increase the availability of this habitat in a region. Hawthorn, blackthorn and field maple are important hedgerow shrubs in many parts of Britain but search hard enough or visit different areas and you may find, oak, spindle, hazel, elm, wayfaring tree, dogwood and crab apple. Many of our hedgerows are extremely old, their location perhaps defining the boundary between farms or parishes. As a rule of thumb, every species of woody shrub found in a 100 metre stretch of hedgerow is likely to correspond to a century of existence. Of course, this will only apply in areas where replanting schemes have not occurred. Depending on location and soil type, a number of less robust and often scrambling species may be present. Most typical of these is bramble, but hop, black bryony, white bryony, dog-rose, honeysuckle, ivy and old man's beard are also common in many parts.

Because of regular cutting in many areas, roadside verges often assume the appearance and species composition of adjacent areas of unimproved grassland. Flowers such as oxeye daisy, common knapweed, red bartsia and bugle are often common, with many verges boasting a good range of orchids too, including common-spotted and bee orchids and common helleborine. Verges on chalk are often particularly colourful and species-rich with marjoram, greater knapweed, kidney-vetch and pyramidal orchid being found beside some roads.

Key animal species

Most mature hedgerows are extremely good for songbirds although the exact species present depends on geographical location. Numbers of resident species such as robin, dunnock, wren, long-tailed tit, bullfinch and yellowhammer are boosted by summer migrants including lesser whitethroat and blackcap; these find dense hedges ideal for nesting. Autumn sees the appearance of fruits and berries in our hedgerows, conspicuous examples being found in rose hips and hawthorn, guelder-rose and sloe berries. Large numbers are taken by resident thrush species including blackbird and mistle thrush but their ripening often corresponds with the first arrivals of fieldfares and redwings, winter visitors from mainland Europe.

Berries, fruits are nuts are not, of course, the exclusive domain of hedgerows birds and small mammals such as bank vole, wood mouse and harvest mouse also take advantage of this autumn bonanza. Common and pygmy shrews are widespread and typical hedgerow mammals but, of course, concentrate their attentions on this habitat's invertebrate community.

Insects are perhaps the most conspicuous invertebrates found in hedgerows with flowering and fruiting periods for bramble offering the best opportunities for observation. Although comparatively few butterfly species actually breed in hedgerows, bramble flowers are visited by species such as gatekeeper, ringlet, comma and red admiral. Moths are extremely well represented with large numbers of caterpillars feeding on a wide range of hedgerow shrubs. Use a beating tray in spring and summer and you will also discover an amazing array of bugs and beetles along with other invertebrate groups such as spiders and harvestmen.

Although rabbits are often the most conspicuous roadside verge mammals, smaller species such as short-tailed vole are usually more abundant. Their numbers are reflected in the frequency with which kestrels are seen hovering beside busy roads, their keen sense of vision allowing them to detect the slightest movement of unsuspecting prey.

Meadow brown, small copper and common blue are among the more usual roadside verge butterflies but colonies of marbled white and small blue are recorded in a few parts of southern England. Other insect life is often abundant and includes meadow and common field grasshoppers and dark bush crickets. After dark, keen-eyed observers may even discover small colonies of glow-worms during the summer months.

Where to go

Although almost any part of Britain has hedgerow interest, parts of the West Country are particularly well endowed with mature examples surrounding the mosaics of small fields typical of the region. Good roadside verges, where they are sympathetically managed and of sufficient age, can be found in most regions; unsurprisingly, the less frequently a road is used, the more enjoyable will be an exploration of its verges.

Roadside verges are, in a sense, unofficial nature reserves

GRASSLAND AND FARMLAND

A flower-rich meadow in late summer

Full of wildflowers and native grass species, a good grassy meadow is a delight to the naturalist. Unfortunately, prime sites are comparatively few and far between these days, many areas having been 'improved' by farmers for grazing by seeding and the use of selective herbicides. These latter habitats are largely devoid of wildlife interest, as are most areas of intensively farmed land, whether the regime be arable or livestock.

Vegetation and character

Within the context of the British Isles, grassland is a man-made habitat and, indeed, needs the continual intervention of man to ensure its survival. The habitat arose as a result of woodland clearance for grazing in centuries past and continual grazing or cutting is needed to ensure that scrub regeneration does not occur. As with many other habitats, the species composition of an unimproved meadow depends partly on the geographical location of the site but perhaps more importantly on the soil chemistry: those on basic soils on limestone or chalk tend to have far greater floral diversity than those on neutral or acid soils.

Widespread grass species found in unimproved meadows include timothy grass, also widely sown as well, creeping bent and Yorkshire fog while characteristic grassland wildflowers include oxeye daisy, common knapweed, yellow rattle, red bartsia, creeping thistle, bird's-foot trefoil, red and white clovers, hogweed and meadow buttercup. Wet grazing meadows often support interesting plants such as marsh marigold, southern marsh-orchid, ragged robin and water avens although it is arguably our chalk downlands that are the crowning glory of British grasslands. Here, during the spring and summer months, a succession of striking and sometimes aromatic species can be found including cowslips, kidney-vetch, greater knapweed, thyme, marjoram, yellow-wort and autumn gentian. It is for its orchids, however, that chalk downland is best known. Although local and patchy, species such as bee, fly, man, pyramidal, fragrant, frog and musk orchids, and autumn lady's-tresses are comparatively widespread in southern England in particular.

Visit a glorious meadow at the peak of its flowering and it may be difficult to perceive the need for habitat management. Without an annual cut in the case of hay meadows, or without periodic grazing at certain times of year in the case of water meadows and chalk downland, however, and many of the more attractive flowers would soon be swamped by competition from more vigorous species. Brambles and shrubs would eventually take over and the meadow would revert to scrub and eventually woodland. Meadow management techniques do not always benefit wildlife, however, and in farming areas the seeding of species such as ryegrasses and timothy, and the use of selective herbicides is designed to exclude everything except those plants favoured perhaps for silage or hay by the farmer.

Although arable fields may fall loosely under the category of grasslands if the crops grown include species such as wheat, barley and oats, their interest in botanical terms is minimal. In the past, so-called cornfield 'weeds' such as corncockle, corn marigold and pheasant's-eye might have livened up an afternoon's stroll around their margins but today these species are decidedly rare. It remains to be seen how much long term positive impact set-aside regimes and the creation of unsprayed field borders and headlands will have on these declining plants.

Key animal species

Although for many naturalists, a meadow's main attraction is likely to lie in its flowers, unimproved examples harbour an interesting range of animals too. Butterflies such as small copper, meadow brown, marbled white, small and large skippers and common blue are widespread and, on chalk downland, chalkhill and adonis blues and silver-spotted skipper are among the highlights. As their name suggests, grasshoppers are also well represented in grassland habitats with common field, common green and meadow grasshoppers being the most widespread species. Once again, chalk downlands in southern England harbour more unusual species in the form of stripe-winged and rufous grasshoppers.

By their very nature, intensively farmed areas have all-but lost their wildlife interest: insecticides and molluscicides effectively wipe out all but the most resilient of invertebrates. A few species of birds are, however, able to survive in this terrain and so have even benefited. Where not unduly persecuted, partridges are resident and lapwings still nest among arable crops in spring. The jingling songs of corn buntings can still be heard in many cornfields and stone-curlews are the highlight of any trip to arable fields in southern England or the East Anglia.

Where to go

Classic water meadows can be found at English Nature's North Meadow NNR near Cricklade in Wiltshire while fine stretches of chalk downs occur at Wye Downs in Kent and Queen Elizabeth Country Park in Hampshire. Good quality hay meadows can be found in many parts of the Yorkshire Dales, on many of the Scottish Islands and across much of Ireland.

A traditional English country landscape in Wiltshire

HEATHLAND

Home to a number of rare and endangered animals, heathlands are themselves very much under threat and the focus of much attention from conservation bodies. The habitat is essentially restricted to southern England with the majority of heaths concentrated in Surrey, Hampshire and Dorset. Further isolated examples of heathland can be found further afield, in south Devon for example, and this scattered distribution adds to the problems faced by the habitat: 'island' populations of plants and animals have little chance of receiving genetic input from other sites. A few coastal areas of south-west Britain also boast a fringe of maritime heath. In Pembrokeshire, for example, this comprises most of the typical heathland plant species while on the Lizard peninsula in Cornwall there are species unique to this part of Britain.

Heathland habitat owes its existence to man and came about following forest clearance on acid, sandy soils. Regimes of grazing and periodic burning in the past have helped maintain the habitat and continued management is needed to ensure that scrub encroachment does not occur. Ironically, man is also the biggest threat to the habitat. Uncontrolled burns can cause damage that takes a decade or more to repair while the destruction of heathland under housing schemes, as has happened in Dorset, obviously means the loss of this unique habitat for good.

New Forest heathland in summer

Vegetation and character

The habitat's name is clearly linked to the presence, and often dominance, of members of the heath family. These include ling, cross-leaved heath and bell heather, all of which flourish on acid, sandy soils; the first two favour rather dry areas while cross-leaved heath prevails in damper terrain, often around the margins of bogs. For a truly splendid visual display, visit an area of heathland during July, August or September when the heathers are in bloom. Cornish heath is restricted to Cornwall's Lizard peninsula, thriving where the underlying rock is serpentine.

From a botanical point of view, equally characteristic of heathland habitats are the great swathes of gorse that cover many slopes. Of the three species found in the region, common gorse is the most widespread and at its most colourful in May and June when it fills the air with a heady smell of coconut; this species is also widespread on acid soils generally in north and west Britain and not restricted just to heathlands.

Valley bottoms and depressions on heathland are often characterised by the formation of bogs which can usually be detected at a distance by the lush green growth of bog moss. Bog myrtle and bog asphodel also favour this habitat along with sundews, insectivorous plants which supplement their diet on the nutrient deficient soil. Keen-eyed botanists may be lucky enough to come across small groups of diminutive bog orchids growing among the mosses.

Key animal species

The heathlands of southern England lure birdwatchers from far afield in search of specialities such as Dartford warbler and hobby. Although not entirely restricted to this habitat, nightjar and woodlark are often present in good numbers during the breeding season along with more widespread species including stonechat and linnet. During the winter months, the possibility of finding great grey shrike, hen harrier or short-eared owl is an incentive to visit our heaths.

Reptiles are extremely well represented on most heathlands and all six native species can be found on some sites. Adder and common lizard are widespread and often numerous with grass snake and slow-worm adding to the diversity in some parts. Our two heathland specialities, smooth snake and sand lizard, are found on a few heaths in Surrey, Hampshire and Dorset, the latter species have a few isolated colonies on sand dunes elsewhere in Britain.

Many of our heathland birds and reptiles depend upon the rich diversity of invertebrates found here. Common field and mottled grasshoppers are widespread while heath grasshopper is very much a speciality of a few Dorset heaths. Damp ground is the haunt of the bog bush-cricket while the bogs themselves are the domain of the large marsh grasshopper, the largest of its kind in Britain. Day-flying emperor moths are conspicuous when they appear on the wing in spring; they are followed by delightful silver-studded blues in mid-summer. Wherever there are streams and pools of standing water, insects with aquatic stages in their life cycles will be found. The most characteristic group of these are the dragonflies and damselflies, some species of which are effectively restricted to heathland habitats.

Spiders too are abundant on heathlands and contain among their number the impressive swamp spider, the largest spider in Britain. Most other heathland spiders are considerably smaller, their numbers only becoming apparent when mists and frost highlight their webs in autumn.

WHERE TO GO

There are large stretches of heathland in the New Forest in Hampshire, the area around Beaulieu Road Station being a good starting point for exploration. In Dorset, Studland Heath and the adjacent RSPB reserve at Arne are superb; in Surrey visit Thursley and Chobham Commons.

Maritime heath on the Pembrokeshire coast

UPLAND HABITATS

Together with more remote stretches of coastline, upland areas are perhaps the only parts of the British Isles that can provide the outdoor enthusiast and naturalist with a sense of isolation. Many of these areas appear wild and untamed. In most parts of upland Britain, however, this is often just an illusion and few can be said to be truly pristine.

In centuries gone by, all but the highest peaks would have been wooded. Clearance and often excessive grazing by sheep ensure that natural woodland was removed and cannot regenerate. In general terms, moorland is the dominant habitat in upland areas although the characteristic plants and appearance vary considerably from region to region. In a few parts of Wales, northern England and Scotland, mountains dominate the landscape. Sometimes rising to altitudes above the level at which trees would grow if they were allowed to do so, these harbour unique communities of plants.

Today we associate wide open vistas with our upland areas and many people assume this is what they should look like. It is perhaps ironic that blanket conifer plantations in these areas are often reviled for changing the appearance of the landscape when, in visual terms at least, a covering of trees may give a more faithful impression of what the landscape looked like several thousand years ago. Were that these regiments of conifers could be replaced by native tree species and naturally structured forests.

VEGETATION AND CHARACTER

Upland vegetation varies considerably from region to region, influenced by such factors as underlying soil type, rainfall and altitude. Arguably the least interesting from a botanical point of view are areas on neutral soils, dominated by grasses, such as purple moor-grass and deer grass, and rushes. Here the uniformity of the landscape is often maintained by the nibbling attentions of sheep which do a thorough job of ensuring that little other than tormentil or lousewort flourish. In areas where the underlying soil is acid, heather moors, reminiscent in appearance of lowland heaths, often develop. These are dominated by ling and bell heather and, in many parts of northern Britain, are managed as grouse moors by periodic burning which encourages new shoot growth. In areas where the underlying soil is lime-rich, a far more diverse flora develops with species such as spring gentian, mountain pansy and bird's-eye primrose being among the highlights.

In common with other upland habitats, mountain flora is strongly influenced by the chemistry of the underlying rock. Mountain slopes and ledges in Snowdonia, the Lake District and the Scottish Highlands, for example, generally support a decidedly poor range of flowers but if you come across a base-rich outcrop the increased floral diversity is instantly apparent. Comparatively widespread plants include cyphel, crowberry, roseroot and purple and starry saxifrages. On base-rich soils, look out for other saxifrage species, mountain avens and moss campion.

For serious botanists, the tundra-like appearance of plateau mountain-tops in the Cairngorms, dominated by lichens and mosses, has a charm unique in Britain.

Key animal species

Surely the most evocative sound of upland areas of the British Isles is the somewhat mournful call of the golden plover displaying in its breeding territory. As a nesting bird, this species is restricted to moorland habitats and is often found in close proximity to other breeding waders such as dunlin, redshank, curlew and snipe. Songbirds are comparatively thin on the ground in this habitat although twite do breed sparingly in northern Britain. The meadow pipit is, however, ubiquitous on the moors during the breeding season and its numbers are essential to the diet of predators, and in particular the merlin. Hen harriers and short-eared owls are widespread and often conspicuous where not persecuted, their diet also including small mammals as well as small birds.

Heather moors are perfect for red grouse and this species is widespread and often encouraged in many parts of northern Britain. Its cousin, the black grouse, also favours moorland habitat but usually occurs where grassland and small conifer plantations are sited side-by-side.

Keen birdwatchers make regular pilgrimages to our higher mountains in search of specialist birds. With the exception of a few remote spots,

A typical moorland view in northern Britain

Cairngorms: one of Britain's remaining wilderness areas

human disturbance largely excludes shyer species from most mountains in England and Wales but many Scottish mountain regions still have good populations of golden eagles and peregrines. Ptarmigan live unobtrusive lives on higher peaks in Scotland and even the confiding dotterel still breeds here.

Mammals such as fox and short-tailed vole, more usually associated with lowland districts, also have good populations in upland areas. The mountain hare, however, is effectively restricted to these regions and, like the ptarmigan, its appearance changes throughout the year to match the colour of its surroundings. Although present in good numbers, invertebrates tend to be less noticeable than in lowland areas. Two species of butterfly, however, are exclusive to upland regions in northern Britain and these are the Scotch argus and the mountain ringlet.

Where to go

Snowdonia and the Lake District are good places for walking and scenic views but their natural history interest is comparatively limited and localised. Many Scottish mountains harbour upland birds and flowers but the Cairngorms are perhaps the most accessible and rewarding.

THE URBAN ENVIRONMENT

For the majority of people in Britain, who live in towns and cities, the urban environment is the one with which they are most familiar. It is encountered on a day-to-day basis with trips to the countryside relegated to weekend visits or holiday excursions. It would be a mistake, however, to assume that the urban environment is without its wildlife interest. Many of our plants and animals are extremely adaptable and have successfully colonised this seemingly unpromising habitat. In part this is because many features associated with our buildings and gardens mimic special niches in natural habitats. Mature gardens with hedgerows and shrubs, for example, recall woodland margins while buildings are like man-made cliffs with roof spaces becoming artificial caves.

VEGETATION AND CHARACTER

By and large, the conspicuous trees, shrubs and herbaceous plants we see in our parks and gardens are not there by chance but are invariably planted and tended. While the range of species may be limited by factors such as soil type and drainage, the choice of species is largely a matter for the gardener.

Lawns are commonplace around the country. By intention, the species composition is limited to one or two species of grass and so there any similarities between lawns and flower-rich meadows end. Unless maintained badly, they usually blanket excellent soil for earthworms which in turn are food for a whole range of birds and mammals.

The intention of most flower gardeners is to create impact with colour and many of the flowers used in the gardening palette are also extremely good sources of pollen for bees and nectar for butterflies, moths and other insects. Indeed, more enlightened gardeners encourage flowers such as iceplant and buddleia, which are particularly attractive to insects, to flourish; a few even go so far as to leave areas of native plants such as nettle as foodplants for their larvae.

Gardening for wildlife has become a popular theme for many gardeners who encourage thick, thorny hedges for nesting birds and berry-laden bushes as supplies for winter food. For many wildlife gardening enthusiasts, however, the single most rewarding project is the installation of a garden pond. Even the smallest and most artificial of ponds will soon have its quota of aquatic insects and frogs and will be drunk from and bathed in by birds and mammals in both winter and summer.

Although most gardeners do their best to discourage them, a number of our native plants thrive in tilled and fertilised soils in the urban environment. Among these so-called weeds are common chickweed, ground-elder, common nettle and creeping buttercup and a constant battle is often waged to keep them at bay. A number of alien species also thrive in more derelict and neglected areas. Some of these, such as common evening-primrose and buddleia are primarily garden escapes while Oxford ragwort, often seen growing on or beside railway lines, has spread without any direct help from man.

KEY ANIMAL SPECIES

Visit any mature city park, such as Hyde Park or Richmond Park in London, and you find an array birds more usually associated with woodland or farmland. These include woodpigeon, jay, great spotted woodpecker, blue tit, great tit, blackbird and robin. A number of these also find town gardens much to their liking although the more informal the garden, the more species it is likely to attract. A number of birds, however, seem inextricably linked to the urban environment, in the British Isles at least. House sparrows and feral pigeons, for example, are seldom found far from human habitation and swifts rarely nest other than in the rooves of buildings. Starlings often feed in gardens and roost during the winter months in towns, sometimes in phenomenal numbers. The winter months can also herald the arrival of more usual visitors from the continent. Redwings and fieldfares, for example, will move into urban areas when driven by severe weather and the exhaustion of natural berry supplies in the hedgerows. One winter visitor in particular, however, is more associated with urban settings than any other and this is the waxwing. These delightful and often confiding birds are invariably reported from suburban streets and industrial estates where berries of planted rowan, whitebeam and hawthorn satisfy their hunger.

Although seen far less frequently than birds, a number of mammals thrive in our towns and cities. Wood and house mice often make their presence known during the winter months and rats are seldom far away. Hedgehogs are not uncommon in many areas and surprisingly high populations of foxes are often found, especially on the rural fringes of conurbation's. Bats add to the contingent of mammals with pipistrelle and long-eared bats roosting in the rooves and eaves of even the most modern of houses.

A number of butterfly species seem to do particularly well in flower-rich gardens and these include small tortoiseshell, peacock and red admiral, along with the less welcome small and large whites, whose caterpillars feed on the leaves of cabbage-related plants; where holly and ivy thrive in close proximity, look out for holly blues. The use of a mercury vapour lamp moth trap after dark will reveal an astounding array of moth species; garden tiger moth and privet hawk moth are among the more spectacular species often encountered in towns and cities.

As mentioned previously, the encouragement of wildlife has rightfully earned a place in the agenda of most enlightened gardeners. One seemingly

Wildlife can be found even in the heart of London, beside Regent's Canal

ever-present factor that is often overlooked, however, is the presence of the domestic cat in our urban environment. The fact that owners feed them in no way diminishes their predatory urges; countless millions of songbirds and untold numbers of small mammals, frogs and other creatures are killed each year by these efficient killers which we maintain at far higher densities than the environment would support were they not fed. It is up to individuals as to whether the destruction caused by these pets outweighs the benefits of owning them but, arguably, the best thing any gardener could do for wildlife is not to own a cat. Speaking as someone who is dedicated to wildlife but was formerly owned by a cat, however, the choice is not an easy one!

Where to go

Although not necessarily meriting a specific visit, almost any sympathetically maintained park or garden is likely to harbour some natural history interest, especially if it has the added interest of a pond or lake.

HEDGEHOG *Erinaceus europaeus* Length 16-26cm
Familiar and unmistakable nocturnal mammal. At home in urban settings and often seen as a road casualty. Will come to food in the garden. If alarmed, rolls into a ball, protected against most potential predators by its spines. Widespread and common throughout Britain except a few Scottish islands.

MOLE *Talpa europaea* Length 11-16cm
Molehills more often seen than the animal itself. Lives in burrows and feeds mainly on earthworms. Useful soil aerator but not always welcome by gardeners. Seen at surface only rarely, usually in spring or in wet weather. Widespread in England and Wales but absent from many Scottish islands and from Ireland.

PYGMY SHREW *Sorex minutus* Body length 6cm
Our smallest mammal. Continually searching for insects, spiders and snails. Favours hedgerows, field borders and woodlands. Tail length two-thirds that of the body length. Common and widespread in mainland Britain and Ireland; found on many islands but absent from Scillies and N Scottish islands.

COMMON SHREW *Sorex araneus* Body length 7.5cm
Larger than pygmy shrew with tail length roughly half that of the body. Utters high-pitched squeaks. Found in hedgerows, meadows, marshes and woods. Constantly active in search of insects and other invertebrates. Common and widespread except in Ireland, many N Scottish islands and Isle of Man.

WATER SHREW *Neomys fodiens* Body length 10cm
Largest British shrew with clearly defined dark upperparts and white underparts. Invariably seen near water and feeds on aquatic invertebrates. When swimming, looks silvery due to air trapped in fur. Seldom numerous but widespread in England, Wales and S Scotland; absent from Ireland.

DORMOUSE *Muscardinus avellanarius* Body length 8cm
Scarce and local. Seldom seen, even in summer, because of nocturnal habits; often sluggish during daylight hours. Hibernates from October to May depending on the season. Feeds mainly on flowers, nuts and fruits, especially honeysuckle and hazel. Isolated colonies found mainly in C and S England and Wales.

EDIBLE DORMOUSE *Glis glis* Body length 12-15cm
Considerably larger than dormouse with greyish coat and relatively long, bushy tail. In Roman times, reared and fattened to be eaten. Introduced into Britain to Hertfordshire in 1902 and now established in parts of Chilterns; more occasionally seen elsewhere. Hibernates underground during winter months.

BANK VOLE *Clethrionomys glareolus* Body length 9-11cm
Easiest to tell from short-tailed vole by its reddish brown coat and proportionately longer tail. Common in woods and hedgerows. Found mostly in mainland Britain but absent from most islands; in Ireland, only in SW.

SHORT-TAILED VOLE *Microtus agrestis* Body length 10-12cm
Similar to bank vole but with grey-brown fur and very short tail. Common in grassy habitats and can be seen by turning over sheets of wood or metal in grassland. Creates 'runs' along which it can sometimes be seen moving. Widespread in mainland Britain; absent from many islands and from Ireland.

WATER VOLE *Arvicola terrestris* Body length 18-22cm
Charming waterside mammal, now rather scarce, in part due to habitat loss and predation by mink. Often rather confiding but will dive into water if danger threatens. Swims well both at surface and underwater. Burrow complex usually has at least one submerged entrance. Found in England, Wales and S Scotland.

HARVEST MOUSE *Micromys minutus* Body length 6-7.5cm
Britain's smallest rodent. Has orange-brown fur. Prehensile tail almost as long as body and used when climbing among plant stems. Mainly nocturnal and presence usually indicated by tennis ball-sized nests of woven grasses constructed among plant stems. Absent from Ireland and commonest in C and S England.

YELLOW-NECKED MOUSE *Apodemus flavicollis* Body length 9-12.5cm
Similar to wood mouse but larger and with proportionately larger ears and yellowish collar on throat. Mainly a woodland species and competent tree-climber. Enters houses in autumn. Distribution patchy and local. Found only in Wales and C and S England; commonest along Welsh borders and in SE England.

WOOD MOUSE *Apodemus sylvaticus* Body length 7.5-11cm
Commonest mouse of woods, hedgerows and mature gardens and important prey item for many native predators. Fur lacks warm brown hue of yellow-necked mouse and does not have this species' complete collar. Mainly nocturnal and may venture indoors in winter. Found throughout Britain and Ireland including most islands.

HOUSE MOUSE *Mus musculus* Body length 7.5-10cm
Formerly common and widespread but now comparatively scarce and local. Usually associated with people, both on farmland and in towns. Grey-brown fur distinguishes it from other British mice. Mainly nocturnal and fairly vocal. Likely to be encountered in almost any urban site or arable farm in Britain.

BROWN RAT *Rattus norvegicus* Body length 22-27cm
Reviled by many because of association with disease and choice of habitat. In reality, numbers reflect wastefulness of modern society, rats thriving on refuse and discarded food. In this respect at least, could be said to be serving useful function. Burrows and swims well. Common and widespread throughout Britain.

RED SQUIRREL *Sciurus vulgaris* Body length 20-28cm
Our only native squirrel species. Easily told by orange-red fur and presence of ear tufts; tail usually paler than body, sometimes almost white. Has disappeared from much of former range. Now commonest in N England and Scottish Highlands. Isolated colonies elsewhere, for example, on Brownsea Island, Dorset.

GREY SQUIRREL *Sciurus carolinensis* Body length 25-30cm
Introduced from N America in 19th century and now our commonest squirrel. Occurs in woodland but also found in urban sites such as parks. Fur can look reddish during summer months, but never has ear tufts. Has economic impact in commercial forests. Widespread in England and Wales but local in Scotland and Ireland.

RABBIT *Oryctolagus cunniculus* Body length 35-40cm
Introduced in Middle Ages but now a common and conspicuous countryside mammal despite depredations of myxomatosis. Often numerous enough to cause serious damage to crops and natural vegetation. Lives socially in extended warrens. Most active from dawn to dusk. Found in most lowland areas of Britain and Ireland.

BROWN HARE *Lepus capensis* Body length 60-70cm
Formerly widespread and common but has declined in many areas, in part due to persecution but also because of changes in land use. Larger, longer legged and with longer, black-tipped ears than rabbit. Males chase and box one another in spring. Native to lowland Britain; present but scarce in Highlands.

MOUNTAIN HARE *Lepus timidus* Body length 50-65cm
Sometimes known as blue hare because of blue-grey summer coat(A); in winter (B), has white fur, tips of ears remaining black. Favours upland moors although descends to lower altitudes in harsh winter weather. Found in Scottish Highlands and locally in S Scotland, Pennines and Snowdonia. The only hare native to Ireland.

STOAT *Mustela erminea* Length 35-40cm
Superficially similar to weasel but appreciably larger and with distinctive black tip to tail. Coat colour orange-brown above with clear demarcation from white underparts. Some N individuals turn white in winter, retaining black tip to tail. Sometimes located by pinpointing anguished squeals of rabbit prey, a favourite food. Found throughout Britain and Ireland except some islands.

WEASEL *Mustela nivalis* Length 20-25cm
Smaller than stoat with proportionately shorter tail which lacks that species' black tip. Highly active and relentless in pursuit of prey which comprise mainly small mammals. Favours a wide range of habitats wherever prey common and found in woodland, hedgerows and grassland. Common and widespread in mainland Britain although not always easy to see. Absent from Ireland and many islands.

POLECAT *Mustela putorius* Length 45-55cm
Sometimes confused with dark forms of escaped polecat-ferret but true polecat always has appearance of dark mask on face. Body fur rather variable in colour but usually dark brown with paler flanks. Rather secretive and mainly nocturnal. Favours wooded areas. In the past, much persecuted by gamekeepers and now restricted mainly to C Scotland, border counties and C Wales.

AMERICAN MINK *Mustela vison* Length 42-65cm
An unwelcome alien which has become established after escaping from fur farms during past few decades. Dark brown fur makes confusion with otter possible but mink's smaller size, slimmer build and proportionately shorter tail help distinguish it. Invariably associated with water where it feeds on water birds, fish and waterside small mammals. Found throughout Britain and Ireland.

PINE MARTEN *Martes martes* Length 65-75cm
Truly arboreal, favouring coniferous forests. Excellent climber, ability and confidence shown to best effect when in pursuit of red squirrel prey among treetops. Recognised by reddish brown coat and creamy yellow throat and chest. Shy and largely nocturnal. Confined mainly to Scottish Highlands but locally also in N Wales and N England.

OTTER *Lutra lutra* Length 95-130cm
Superbly adapted to amphibious lifestyle, occuring in both coastal waters and on rivers and lakes. Dives may last for several minutes. Feeds mainly on fish but also eats sea urchins around coasts. Persecution from fishing interests, hunting and habitat destruction have caused a serious decline in numbers. Once widespread but now common only on Western Isles, Orkney, Shetland and Ireland.

WILDCAT *Felix sylvestris* Length 75-105cm
Superficially similar to tabby cat but appreciably larger with bushier, blunt-ended tail. Body is always well marked with dark stripes and tail shows several dark rings. Largely nocturnal but sometimes seen prowling at dusk. Mostly confined to Scottish Highlands but sightings suggest range expanding W and N.

FOX *Vulpes vulpes* Length 100-120cm
Common but justifiably wary of man given history of persecution of this species. Easily recognised by dog-like appearance, orange-red fur and bushy, white-tipped tail. Gives birth and spends much of daytime in underground 'earth'. Widespread in mainland Britain and Ireland. Has colonised urban areas in recent years.

BADGER *Meles meles* Length 80-95cm
Recognised by black-and-white facial stripes. Common, but unobtrusive and largely nocturnal habits make it easy to overlook. With care, easily watched emerging from underground sett at dusk. Very fond of peanuts but slugs and earthworms important in natural diet. Found in mainland Britain and Ireland.

LESSER HORSESHOE BAT *Rhinolophus hipposideros* Wingspan 22-25cm
Distinguished from other British bat species, apart from greater horseshoe, by horseshoe-shaped 'nose leaves' (fleshy outgrowths from side of nose) and absence of tragus (pointed inner ear outgrowth). During summer months, uses caves and cellars for daytime roost. Active for much of the night in search of moths. Wingbeats fast and fluttering. In winter, hibernates deep in caves, sometimes in considerable numbers. Found in W England, Wales and W Ireland.

GREATER HORSESHOE BAT *Rhinolophus ferrumequinum* Wingspan 34-39cm
Rare and endangered. Like its lesser relative, it has horseshoe-shaped 'nose leaves' and lacks the ear formation known as the tragus. Favours wooded terrain but roosts and hibernates in caves, cellars and abandoned mineshafts; in summer, found near entrance but in winter usually deeper where temperature even and constant and frosts cannot penetrate. Flies only when completely dark and has heavy, rather laboured wingbeats. Restricted to SW England and S Wales.

DAUBENTON'S BAT *Myotis daubentoni* Wingspan 23-27cm
Medium-sized bat with comparatively short ears. Frequently associated with water and seen flying low over lakes, ponds and canals just as dusk is falling. Also feeds along woodland rides. Chirps can be heard by those with good hearing. In summer, roosts, sometimes in colonies, in hollow trees and tunnel entrances. In winter, hibernates in caves, mines and cellars. Widespread and fairly common in Britain except the far N of Scotland and present in Ireland except the SW.

SEROTINE BAT *Eptesicus serotinus* Wingspan 36-38cm
Large bat with dark brown fur on upperparts but paler below. Ears comparatively large and tragus well developed. Flies at dusk on rather laboured wingbeats and seen hunting along woodland rides, sometimes rising to a considerable height. In summer, roosts during daytime in hollow trees, lofts and barns; usually found in small groups. In winter, hibernates in similar habitats but also in caves and mines. Rather local and restricted to S and E England; absent from Ireland.

NATTERER'S BAT *Myotis nattereri* Wingspan 25-30cm
Medium-sized bat with comparatively large ears and well developed tragus. Wings pale in flight. Has brownish fur and fringe of hairs on wing membrane between legs. Generally favours wooded habitats but also found near water and in towns. In summer, roosts during day in hollow trees, caves and sometimes even lofts and buildings; sometimes colonial. In winter, hibernates in caves, tunnels and mines. Widespread and fairly common in England, Wales, Ireland and S Scotland.

LONG-EARED BAT *Plecotus auritus* Wingspan 23-28cm
As name suggests, has very long ears with well developed tragus. Seen in silhouette, outline of ears can clinch identification. Found in a range of habitats including gardens, woods and farmland. Flies throughout night and sometimes in daytime. Will hover to pick insect off vegetation. In summer, roosts in hollow trees and lofts. In winter, hibernates in cellars and caves. Widespread in Britain and Ireland as far N as C Scotland.

NOCTULE BAT *Nyctalis noctua* Wingspan 32-39cm
Large bat with reddish brown fur and broad, lobed ears. Often seen flying just before sunset or even during the day. A woodland species which hunts above tree canopy. Direct flight pattern interrupted by occasional, rapid twists and turns. Roosts and hibernates in hollow trees. Found in England, Wales and S Scotland.

PIPISTRELLE BAT *Pipistrellus pipistrellus* Wingspan 19-25cm
The commonest British bat and also the smallest. Its brown fur is variable in tone. Common in woodland and farmland but also often seen in towns where it roosts in lofts and buildings. Emerges just after sunset and has jerky flight pattern and fluttering wings. Found throughout most of Britain and Ireland.

FERAL GOAT *Capra hircus* Shoulder height 50-60cm
Although not native to Britain and Ireland, domesticated goats have long been kept for milk, meat and skin. In many parts of Britain and Ireland, feral populations have become established as a result of escapes or deliberate releases from captivity. Populations have persisted in remote and rugged areas to which the animal is ideally adapted; these include Snowdonia, the Scottish Highlands, many parts of Ireland and Lundy. Goats are nimble-footed on crags and precipitous cliffs. Occurs in range of colours but coat usually a mixture of grey, black and brown. Both sexes have horns, larger in male than female.

FALLOW DEER *Dama dama* Shoulder height 85-95cm
Introduced from mainland Europe by Normans but now well established in many parts of Britain and Ireland except N Scotland. Kept as a parkland animal, becoming accustomed to man. Away from protection, often hunted and is wary and shy. Parkland animals often selected for pale, dappled coats but elsewhere animals with dark coats predominate. Prefers to live in medium-sized herds and favours wooded areas; sometimes on farmland in summer months. Young born in spring. Rut occurs in October accompanied by barking coughs of males. Male only has antlers which, in mature animals, have broad, flattened tips.

RED DEER *Cervus elaphus* Shoulder height 115-120cm
An imposing animal and Britain's largest native land mammal. Male (stag, A) is larger than female (hind, B) and has well developed, branching antlers. These are shed each February, reappear in the spring and become larger with each successive season. Summer coat is reddish brown but appears more grey-brown in winter. Lives in separate sex herds for much of year and spends much of daytime resting or wallowing in mud. Most active from dusk to dawn. Annual autumn rut accompanied by roaring, bellowing sounds from stags. Restricted to wild terrain in S Scotland and Highlands, Lake District, SW England and Ireland.

SIKA DEER *Cervus nippon* Shoulder height 75-80cm
Introduced to this country from its native range in Asia in latter half of 19th century. Now established as feral populations in several locations; also seen as parkland deer in some parts of England. In winter, appears uniformly grey-brown in colour but, in summer, acquires reddish brown coat beautifully marked with white spots. Head appears narrow and pointed compared to other deer species. Female lacks antlers. Those of male are narrow and poorly branched; these are shed in April. Favours areas of woodland and farmland and found in isolated populations in England, Scotland and Ireland; small herd lives on Lundy.

ROE DEER *Capreolus capreolus* Shoulder height 65-70cm
Arguably our most attractive deer and smallest of our two native species. Does not form herds but seen instead singly or in twos or threes depending on sex and time of year. Male (buck, A) has small, ridged and branched antlers which are shed in November; female (doe) lacks antlers. Fawn (B) is well camouflaged. Found in areas of scrub and woodland with brambles and dense undergrowth; sometimes in upland areas. Where not unduly persecuted, becomes bold in presence of people. If alarmed, however, will bark loudly and make off with leaps and bounds. Commonest in CS England, especially Hampshire, N England and Scotland. Absent from Wales and much of C England.

MUNTJAC DEER *Muntiacus reevesi* Shoulder height 45-48cm
The smallest British deer, barely the size of an Alsatian dog. Although established and fairly common in many parts of C and S England, all these animals are descendants of escapees from Woburn Park in Bedfordshire. Favours areas of dense undergrowth through which it can move with surprising ease and silence. Coat is reddish brown. If only part of animal is seen, for example flanks, could be mistaken for fox. Male has small antlers and long canines projecting as tusks; tusks of female are shorter. Generally silent but utters sharp bark if alarmed. Fond of ornamental shrub, tea-leaved willow.

MINKE WHALE *Balaenoptera acutorostrata* Length 8-10m
Smallest of the baleen whales and the only one regularly seen in British coastal waters. Locally common in fish-rich seas off W coast of Scotland and around Ireland. Possibly overlooked elsewhere. Often seen in comparatively shallow waters and can sometimes be seen from land. Best views obtained from boats to which species is accustomed in some areas, notably off Mull in Scotland. At close range, diagnostic white spot on flippers can be seen in clear water. Seldom breaches but occasionally lunge-fishes at surface. Usually encountered singly or in groups of two or three. Head rather triangular in outline with ridge from snout to blowhole. Fin pronounced and curved. Tail not raised prior to diving. Blow is small and easily missed except on very calm days.

COMMON DOLPHIN *Delphinus delphis* Length 1.8-2.5m
Despite name, now distinctly uncommon in British waters and rather difficult to see from land; seen regularly, however, from Strumble Head, Wales. Fortunately, it is often inclined to accompany boats, usually well away from land. Schools of 10 to 100 may be encountered and will often bow-ride with consummate ease for several minutes before dispersing *en masse* with determined speed. Nowadays, ferry crossings from Britain to Ireland, mainland Scotland to the northern isles, and Cornwall to the Scilly Isles, offer the best chances of observation. Seen well and at close range, attractively marked with wavy stripes of yellow, grey or brown on its flanks; beak long and narrow. Being a fish-eater its demise in recent years must partly be attributed to over-fishing.

BOTTLE-NOSED DOLPHIN *Tursiops truncatus* Length 2.8-4m
Larger and more robust than common dolphin and with uniformly dark back and flanks; underside paler but seldom seen. Short snout and steep forehead give 'bottle-nosed' appearance. Fin is tall, broad-based and strongly curved. Usually encountered in groups of five to ten, often quite close to land and in comparatively shallow water. Occasionally joins boats and will bow-ride, sometimes leaping clear of water in apparent playfulness. Regular and relatively easy to see, given sufficient observation time, off Land's End peninsula, in Cardiff Bay, around Shetland Islands and off Durlston Head, Dorset. Feeds mainly near the surface or in shallow dives but sometimes stays submerged for several minutes. Lone individuals of this species sometimes become attached to human company.

COMMON SEAL *Phoca vitulina* Length 1.8-2m
The smaller of our two seal species, females being appreciably smaller than males. Compared to grey seal, has rather rounded disc-like face with short snout. Coat colour is extremely variable but usually some shade of grey or white with darker spots. Effectively absent from S and W England. The species' strongholds lie on the E coast, from Norfolk to Orkney and Shetland; it also occurs around W Scotland and the E coast of Ireland. Favours shallow, sheltered coastal waters and estuaries. Arguably the best place to observe common seals is at Blakeney Point, Norfolk. Large numbers present here throughout year, often sunbathing on sandbars. Females give birth on land but pups can swim straight away. Dives well for fish and can remain submerged for up to ten minutes.

A B

GREY SEAL *Halichoerus grypus* Length 2.5-3m
A large mammal, streamlined in water but cumbersome on land. Frequently seen 'bottling', with head and neck clear of water. Males (A) up to 0.5m longer than females and much heavier. Both sexes have rather dog-shaped appearance to head; male has a particularly thick neck and convex profile. Coat colour extremely variable but usually some shade of blue-grey; background colour of male generally darker than that of female. Both sexes show irregular and individually unique pattern of blotches and spots on coat. Comes ashore to mate and give birth. Pups (B) born in late summer or autumn and generally remain on land for two to three weeks. Common off W coast of Britain and Ireland but persecuted by fishermen in some areas. Easy to see on Farne Islands and off W Pembrokeshire.

BLACK-THROATED DIVER *Gavia arctica* Length 60-70cm
Large, robust water bird which swims buoyantly. Dives well and often for fish. In summer, unmistakable with blue-grey head and nape, black throat and black and white stripes on side of neck. Belly and underparts white, wings and upperparts black with chequerboard of white spots on back. Sexes similar. In winter, has mainly blackish upperparts and white underparts; white 'thigh' patch often visible at water level. Rare breeding bird on lochs in W Scotland. In winter, more widespread in coastal waters around Britain; rarely on inland reservoirs.

RED-THROATED DIVER *Gavia stellata* Length 55-65cm
Slim, elegant build. Dives well in search of fish. Characteristically holds head and dagger-like bill uptilted. In summer plumage, elegant with blue-grey face and sides to neck, red throat and black and white streaks on nape. In winter, has mainly dark grey upperparts and pale underparts; delicate speckling of white spots on back visible only at close range. Breeds on small lochs and tarns in Shetland, Orkney, W Scotland and NW Ireland, always within flying range of sea for feeding. In winter, found in sheltered waters around much of British coast.

GREAT CRESTED GREBE *Podiceps cristatus* Length 46-51cm
Slender water bird with long, thin neck; the largest British grebe species. Looks strikingly black and white at a distance although upperparts mainly grey-brown and underparts white. In summer, both sexes acquire prominent orange-rufous ruff and show crest to dark cap. In winter, loses ruff but retains dark cap and suggestion of crest. Pairs perform elaborate ritual displays in spring. Builds floating nest among emergent vegetation on lakes and gravel pits. Breeds throughout Britain and Ireland to S Scotland. In winter, often around coasts.

RED-NECKED GREBE *Podiceps grisegena* Length 40-45cm
In winter plumage, superficially similar to great crested grebe but smaller and shows characteristic black-tipped yellow bill (bill of great crested is always pinkish). Red-necked grebe also lacks great crested's white eyestripe at this time of year. Although not a British nesting species, sometimes seen in breeding plumage with brick red neck, white cheeks and black cap. Most sightings, however, are of non-breeding plumage birds with records mainly from October to March. Favours sheltered coastal waters, mainly on E coast.

SLAVONIAN GREBE *Podiceps auritus* Length 31-38cm
A B
Dumpy and compact grebe with straight bill. Stunning in breeding plumage (A) with black face, striking golden-yellow ear tufts and plumes, brick red neck and underparts, and black back. In winter (B), looks black and white with dark cap, nape and back, and pale underparts. Beady red eye visible only at close range. Rare breeding bird in Scottish Highlands. In winter, Britain receives influx of continental birds and is then widespread and locally common in sheltered coastal waters. Dives well and often for small fish and crustaceans.

BLACK-NECKED GREBE *Podiceps nigricollis* Length 28-24cm
Distinguished in all plumages from slavonian grebe by uptilted bill and steep forehead. In breeding season has black head, neck and back with striking yellow ear tufts. In winter, looks rather black and white with dark cap, cheeks, nape and back, and pale underparts. Rare and erratic breeder in Scotland and N Ireland. In winter, species is widespread in sheltered, coastal waters.

LITTLE GREBE *Tachybaptus ruficollis* Length 25-29cm
Smallest British grebe. Common in most of Britain and Ireland except N Scotland. In breeding plumage, has chestnut on cheeks and neck with lime green spot at base of bill; plumage otherwise brownish except for white powderpuff of feathers at rear end. In winter, has mainly dark brown upperparts and buffish underparts. Nests on ponds, canals and slow-flowing rivers. Presence often indicated by whinnying call. In winter, also on reservoirs around sheltered coasts.

FULMAR *Fulmarus glacialis* Wingspan 105-110cm
Superficially gull-like but easily told by stiff-winged, gliding flight pattern. Expert aeronaut, riding updraughts off cliff faces and ocean gales with consummate ease. Back and upperwings blue-grey but plumage otherwise mostly white except for dark smudge behind eye. Often seen closely when resting or nesting on cliff ledge; tube nostrils and bill plates then apparent. Formerly restricted to St Kilda but range has expanded in past 100 years. Now common on most cliffed coasts around Britain and Ireland. Sociable at breeding colonies, birds uttering cackling, grunting calls. Ejects foul-smelling crop contents in defence of nest.

MANX SHEARWATER *Puffinus puffinus* Length 30-38cm
Distinctive, even at a distance. Flies low over water on stiffly held wings showing, alternately, almost black upperparts then white underparts as it banks and glides. Invariably seen in small to large groups, usually flying in long lines. Comes ashore to breed in rabbit burrows only after complete darkness has fallen. Breeding colonies found on remote islands off N and W coasts and presence indicated after dark by weird, wailing calls; colony on Skomer Island easiest to visit. Seen at sea from May to September off W coasts of Britain and Ireland; ferries to Scilly Isles and Ireland good for daytime sightings.

EUROPEAN STORM-PETREL *Hydrobates pelagicus* Length 14-18cm
Smallest British seabird. Sooty brown plumage looks completely dark except at very close range. White rump distinctive and gives passing resemblance to house martin. Storm-petrel's dangling legs, webbed feet and masterful use of even gale force winds soon dispel any confusion. Patters feet on water when feeding but otherwise employs strong, direct flight. Occurs in British waters from May to September. During daytime, always far out to sea and seen only from ferries or on pelagic birdwatching trips. Visits breeding colonies on islands off W and N British and Irish coasts only after dark when strange, purring calls heard.

GANNET *Morus bassanus* Wingspan 165-180cm
Largest British seabird. Distinctive flight silhouette with long, narrow wings and cigar shaped body. Adult recognised by pure white body with black wing tips. Juvenile has dark brown plumage speckled with white dots. Acquires white adult plumage with successive moults over subsequent four years. In strong winds, glides on stiffly held wings but in calm conditions uses deep, powerful wingbeats. Breeds colonially on inaccessible cliffs or rocky islands. Easiest colonies to visit are Bempton Cliffs, Yorkshire and Bass Rock. Otherwise, invariably seen at sea. In good feeding areas, groups of birds plunge-dive after fish.

CORMORANT *Phalacrocorax carbo* Length 80-100cm
Large, dark seabird with long, hook-tipped bill. At close range and in good light, plumage has oily sheen. In summer, adult has white patch on face and on thighs; in winter, thigh patch lost and face appears grubby. Juvenile has dark brown upperparts and whitish underparts. Large, webbed feet used to good effect when swimming at surface or underwater in search of flatfish and eels. Plumage lacks complete waterproofing and so often seen perched on posts with wings held out to dry. Breeds on cliffs and islands on sheltered coasts around Britain and Ireland except S and SE England. In winter, seen on estuaries, reservoirs and rivers.

SHAG *Phalacrocorax aristotelis* Length 65-80cm
Superficially similar to cormorant but smaller and with green, oily sheen visible at close range and in good light. Adult has narrow yellow patch at base of bill, most apparent in breeding season when crest on forehead also seen. Juvenile has dark brown upperparts and pale but grubby underparts, these darker than on juvenile cormorant. Found throughout year on rocky coasts around W and N Britain and Ireland. Seemingly indifferent to rough seas and dives often and for considerable periods; characteristically leaps out of water as it dives. Frequently seen perched on rocks with wings outstretched to dry.

GREY HERON *Ardea cinerea* Length 90-98cm

A familiar large, long-legged wetland bird. Adult has dagger-like, yellow bill and black crest of feathers. Head, neck and underparts otherwise whitish except for black streaks on front of neck and breast. Back and wings blue-grey. In flight, wings are broad and rounded with black flight feathers; employs slow, flapping wingbeats and holds neck folded in hunched 's' shape close to body. Juvenile similar to adult but markings less distinct and plumage more grubby in appearance. Often seen standing motionless for hours on end on long, yellow legs, sometimes with neck hunched up. Will occasionally actively stalk prey which comprise mainly amphibians and fish, especially eels. Call a harsh and distinctive 'frank'. Nests in loose colonies mainly in trees but sometimes in reedbeds. Favours river margins, lakes and marshes for feeding but sometimes seen on coasts in winter. Breeds commonly throughout Britain and Ireland but absent from smaller offshore islands and Shetland Islands.

BITTERN *Botaurus stellaris* Length 70-80cm

Seldom seen on account of retiring nature and excellent camouflage afforded by streaked, buffish brown plumage in reedbed habitat. Presence in an area usually indicated by male's loud booming call, uttered at dusk and through night from April to June. When seen resting, bird has dumpy, hunched appearance. If alarmed, however, adopts upright, sky-pointing posture with neck outstretched and dagger-like bill held vertically. Occasionally seen briefly in flight, flying low over tops of reeds on broad, rounded wings and with legs trailing. Invariably associated with extensive, undisturbed reedbeds although harsh winter weather occasionally forces birds into more open wetlands. Only a few breeding pairs remain in Britain, these easiest to glimpse or hear at RSPB's Leighton Moss Reserve, Lancashire, or on reedbed reserves in N Norfolk. Wintering birds in Lea Valley regularly yield excellent, but brief, views from well placed hides. Feeds mainly on fish and amphibians but will take waterside small mammals too.

SPOONBILL *Platalea leucorodia* Length 80-90cm

A scarce but regular visitor to coasts, mainly in E and S England. Often stands for extended periods with bill tucked under wings and then can be confused with resting little egret or even mute swan if long, black legs not visible. Unmistakable at other times when long, flattened bill with spoon-shaped tip can be seen; bill is black with paler tip in adult but dull pinkish in juvenile. At all times has pure white plumage but breeding adult usually shows dirty yellow flush on breast and around base of bill. Feeds by wading through shallow water, sweeping bill from side-to-side. In flight, has long, bowed wings and keeps head and neck extended with legs trailing. Characteristically flies with shallow wingbeats and extended glides; wings of adult pure white but dark-tipped in juveniles. Nearest spoonbill breeding colonies are in Netherlands and so, not surprisingly, most British records are in E Anglia, mainly in spring. Food items include small fish, crustaceans, aquatic insect larvae and tadpoles.

LITTLE EGRET *Egretta garzetta* Length 55-65cm

Formerly classed as a rarity in Britain, this species is now a common and conspicuous year-round resident on many estuaries and coastal waterways in S England. Stragglers also turn up from time to time on coasts elsewhere in Britain and are occasionally seen on inland wetlands. Unmistakable, pure white, heron-like bird with black, dagger-like bill and long neck. Legs long and black with plastic-yellow feet, these often not visible if bird is wading. In breeding season, acquires head plumes and trailing plumes on back. In flight, trailing legs and yellow feet conspicuous; neck held in hunched 's' shape. Active feeder, often chasing after fish in shallow water and stabbing with great accuracy. At other times, may rest in hunched-up posture with head and bill hidden when can be confused with mute swan. Does not breed in Britain yet but may do so before long. Roosts in colonies, often in good numbers at places such as Little Sea on Studland Heath, Dorset and at Thorney Island on the Solent.

MUTE SWAN *Cygnus olor* Length 150cm
Large, distinctive water bird, the commonest swan in Britain. Adult has pure white plumage, black legs and orange-red bill; black knob at base of bill is smaller in female than male. Young cygnets often seen accompanying mother. Later in season, full grown juvenile has buffish brown plumage and dirty pink bill. When swimming, bird usually holds neck in elegant curve. In flight, has broad wings and shallow but powerful wingbeats which produce characteristic, throbbing whine; birds otherwise silent. Nests beside lakes and rivers. In winter, also on estuaries and sheltered coasts. Widespread in Britain and Ireland.

WHOOPER SWAN *Cygnus cygnus* Length 150cm
Almost exclusively a winter visitor to Britain and Ireland from breeding grounds in Iceland and Scandinavia but has bred in Scotland; seen mainly from October to March. Similar size to mute swan but has black and yellow bill, triangular in profile; yellow wedge extends beyond nostrils. Holds neck upright. Usually seen in medium-sized flocks comprising many family groups; juvenile birds have pinkish buff plumage and pinkish white bills. Feeds on arable land and in wetlands. Often returns to traditional sites and easy to see at Caerlaverock on Solway Firth. Occurs locally elsewhere in Scotland and in N England and Ireland.

BEWICK'S SWAN *Cygnus columbarius* Length 115-125cm
The smallest British swan. A winter visitor from October to March from Siberian breeding grounds. Adult pure white with black and yellow bill, triangular in profile; yellow on bill less extensive than on whooper swan and barely reaches nostrils. Juveniles have pinkish buff plumage and pinkish bill; arrive in Britain and remain together as family parties among larger flocks. Most birds return to traditional wintering sites such as Slimbridge WWT Reserve, Gloucestershire, and Welney Wildfowl Refuge, Norfolk. Harsh winter weather sometimes forces wintering birds from continent to move to S and E England.

BRENT GOOSE *Branta bernicla* Length 56-61cm
A small goose, barely larger than mallard. Winter visitor to Britain and Ireland from Arctic breeding grounds; present from October to March. Adult has black head and neck with small white collar; juvenile lacks collar in first half of winter. Dark-bellied race from Siberia winters mainly in S and E England while pale-bellied race from Spitsbergen and Greenland winters mainly in NE England and Ireland. Always found on estuaries and sheltered coasts. Diet mainly eelgrass but in late winter will feed on stubble or coastal grassland. Seen in large, noisy flocks, two important locations being Solent and N Norfolk coast.

BARNACLE GOOSE *Branta leucopsis* Length 58-69cm
Small, well-marked goose. Winter visitor from Arctic breeding grounds. Seen from October to March usually in large, noisy flocks which utter loud, barking calls. Vast majority of birds return to traditional wintering grounds. Adult has white face, black neck, barred dark grey upperparts and paler barred underparts; juvenile similar but markings less distinct. Flocks feed on coastal grassland and often roost on mudflats. Birds from Svalbard winter mainly on Solway Firth where best seen at Caerlaverock WWT Reserve. Greenland population winters mainly on Islay and in Ireland. Solitary birds likely to be escapees from captivity.

CANADA GOOSE *Branta canadensis* Length 95-105cm
Large, unmistakable goose with upright stance and long neck giving it a swan-like silhouette. As name suggests, true range is N America but introduced and now thoroughly established as common, resident breeding bird. Has white cheeks on otherwise black head and neck. Body mainly grey-brown except for white under stern; juvenile similar but markings less distinct. Nests beside wetlands and sometimes in nearby arable fields. Outside breeding season, seen in sizeable flocks on lakes and reservoirs; visits urban lakes and grazes parkland grass but seldom seen on coast. In flight, utters loud, disyllabic trumpeting calls.

GREYLAG GOOSE *Anser anser* Length 75-90cm
Largest of the so-called grey geese and the only one which breeds in Britain. Precise natural range confused by presence of numerous feral populations but Scottish birds presumed to be native. British population swollen in winter, from October to March, by migrants from Iceland which also occur in Ireland; these birds favour coastal grassland and farmland. Greylag goose has grey-brown plumage which is barred on back and belly; has white stern and dark, wavy feather ridges on neck. British birds have pink legs and orange-yellow bill; birds from E Europe have pink bills. In flight, has striking blue-grey panel on leading edge of inner wing. Rather noisy when in flocks, they sound identical to farmyard goose, the domesticated descendent of the greylag.

PINK-FOOTED GOOSE *Anser brachyrhynchus* Length 60-75cm
A small, compact goose. Bill rather small in comparison to other grey geese and shows variable pink band towards tip. Head and neck chocolate brown, grading to buffish brown on breast and belly. Stern white and back and wings grey. As name suggests, legs and feet pink. A winter visitor from Arctic breeding grounds, present from October to March; birds from Iceland and Greenland winter mainly in E Scotland while birds seen in E England come mainly from Svalbard. In flight, wings look quite pale; flies in extended 'v' formations uttering higher pitched calls than other grey geese. Usually seen in flocks comprising several hundred birds and favours areas of grassland and stubble fields; sometimes seen on wetlands or saltmarshes, usually after disturbance at favoured feeding areas.

BEAN GOOSE *Anser fabilis* Length 65-85cm
Superficially similar to pink-footed goose but much bulkier and with orange, not pink, band on more robust bill. Head and neck chocolate brown grading to paler brown on breast and belly. Stern white and back and wings dark brown; legs bright orange. Occasionally shows narrow white border at base of bill. A scarce winter visitor to Britain and Ireland from Arctic breeding grounds in Siberia and Scandinavia; present from October to March. Seen in small- to medium-sized flocks, usually grazing on areas of grassland or stubble fields. In flight, looks darker-winged than other grey geese and utters nasal cackling call. Occurs locally in C and SW Scotland; a small but regular flock of birds can be seen at Buckenham in Norfolk. Scarce but regular visitor to N and S Ireland.

WHITE-FRONTED GOOSE *Anser albifrons* Length 65-75cm
Distinctive grey goose. Winter visitor from Arctic breeding grounds, present from October to March. Has brown, barred plumage, darkest on head, neck and back. Stern white and belly has variable, thick black bars; legs orange-yellow. Adult has characteristic white blaze on forehead, absent in juvenile. Siberian birds have pink bills and winter mainly in S England. Birds from Greenland have orange-yellow bills and winter mainly in Ireland, W Wales and W Scotland. In flight, utters barking, rather musical calls. Although local, where it does occur it is usually common and seen in flocks of hundreds or even thousands. Perhaps easiest to see and most impressive at Slimbridge WWT Reserve, Gloucestershire, where hides afford excellent views of wild birds.

SHELDUCK *Tadorna tadorna* Length 58-65cm
A large, goose-sized duck with distinctive markings. Adult has glossy green head and upper neck which looks black in poor light. Plumage otherwise mostly white except for orange chest band and black on wings. Legs pinkish red and bill bright red, that of male having knob at base. In flight, looks very black and white. Juvenile has white and buffish brown plumage, the patterning reminiscent of that of adult. Favours coastal habitats including estuaries, mudflats and sheltered coasts where invertebrate food items common. A common breeding bird in undisturbed areas, nesting in burrows. After hatching, black and white ducklings follow parents onto mudflats. Common around coasts of Britain and Ireland. Many birds move to Bridgewater Bay, Somerset, for their summer moult.

MALLARD *Anas platyrhynchos* Length 50-65cm
Widespread and familiar duck. Colourful male (A) has yellow bill and green, shiny head and neck separated from chestnut breast by white collar. Plumage otherwise grey-brown except for black stern and white tail. Female (B) has orange bill and mottled brown plumage. In flight, both sexes have blue and white speculum (patch on trailing edge of inner wing). Resident throughout Britain and Ireland on wide variety of wetlands; often on urban ponds and lakes where usually tame.

GADWALL *Anas strepera* Length 46-56cm
Locally common dabbling duck. Breeds locally, especially E Anglia, but more widespread and numerous as winter visitor. Both sexes have white on speculum, best seen in flight. Male has dark bill and pale brown head. Plumage otherwise grey-brown except for diagnostic black stern, prominent when bird upends to feed. Female similar to female mallard and best identified by association with male or glimpse of white speculum. Favours lakes, reservoirs and gravel pits.

WIGEON *Anas penelope* Length 45-57cm
Scarce breeding species but locally common winter visitor to Britain and Ireland. Male has orange-red head with yellow forehead, pinkish breast and otherwise finely marked, grey plumage; characteristic black and white stern. In flight, male has bold white wing patch. Reddish brown female best told by association with male. Favours mudflats and saltmarsh; locally also on inland wetlands. Male's *wheeoo* call evocative of winter estuaries.

TEAL *Anas crecca* Length 34-38cm
Britain's smallest duck. Local and rather scarce breeding species, especially in N but widespread winter visitor from September to April. Male (A) has chestnut-orange head with yellow-bordered green patch through eye. Plumage otherwise finely marked grey except for black-bordered yellow stern. Grey-brown female (B) best identified by small size and association with male. Green speculum in both sexes. Favours freshwater marshes and estuaries. Rises almost vertically when alarmed.

SHOVELER *Anas clypeata* Length 44-52cm
Long, flattened bill characteristic. Male striking with green head, black and white on body and reddish chestnut flanks. Female mottled brown. Both sexes have green speculum and pale blue panel on forewing. Scarce breeding species but common winter visitor to Britain and Ireland. Favours wetlands and flooded grasslands.

GARGANEY *Anas querquedula* Length 37-41cm
Our only summer migrant duck. Arrives from African wintering grounds in March and stays until August. Male has reddish brown head and broad white stripe above and behind eye; breast brown but plumage otherwise greyish. Mottled brown female similar to female teal and best told by association with male or by blue forewing panel, seen in male as well. Breeds in small numbers in wetland habitats and also seen as passage migrant. Male has distinctive rattling call.

PINTAIL *Anas acuta* Length 51-66cm
Scarce breeding species but widespread and locally common winter visitor to Britain and Ireland. Male striking with chocolate brown head and nape, and white breast forming stripe up side of head. Plumage otherwise finely marked grey but shows cream and black at stern and long, pointed tail, often held at angle. Mottled brown female shares male's long-bodied appearance. Favours a range of wetland habitats in winter from estuaries to lakes and freshwater wetlands.

MANDARIN DUCK *Aix galericulata* Length 41-49cm
Introduced from native E Asia and feral populations now established in parts of S England such as Virginia Water. Male striking with mane of orange, white and brown feathers and orange 'sails' on back. Female grey-brown with white 'spectacle' around eye and large, pale spots on underparts. Nests in tree holes.

TUFTED DUCK *Aythya fuligula* Length 40-47cm
Familiar and distinctive diving duck. Widespread and common year-round resident in Britain and Ireland, numbers augmented in winter by continental birds. Male appears black and white but purplish sheen to head visible in good light; has tufted crest. Female has brown plumage, palest on flanks. Shows suggestion of crest and sometimes white at base of bill, this never as extensive as on female scaup. Both sexes show yellow eye and black-tipped grey bill. Favours lakes and gravel pits, sometimes in urban settings. Nests in waterside vegetation.

SCAUP *Aythya marila* Length 42-51cm
Locally common winter visitor to Britain and Ireland but rare breeding species. Superficially similar to tufted duck but larger. Male (A) has rounded, green-glossed head which lacks tufted crest; has dark breast, white belly and flanks, grey back and black stern. Female (B) has brown plumage, palest on flanks, and shows conspicuous white face patch. Usually seen in single species flocks in coastal waters, mainly N and E Britain and much of Irish coast. Occasionally on coastal lakes and reservoirs, particularly if forced to move by severe weather.

POCHARD *Aythya ferina* Length 42-49cm
Common winter visitor to Britain and Ireland but scarce breeding species. Male unmistakable with reddish orange head, black breast, grey flanks and back, and black stern. Female has brown head and breast and grey-brown back and flanks; usually shows pale 'spectacle' around eye. Bill of both sexes dark with pale grey band towards tip. In flight, wings of both sexes look rather uniformly grey-brown. Usually seen in medium- to large-sized flocks and often mixes with tufted duck. Dives well and often. Favours lakes, reservoirs and gravel pits.

EIDER *Somateria mollissima* Length 50-70cm
Distinctive and attractive seaduck with large, wedge-shaped bill forming continuous line with slope of forehead. Male (A) has mainly black underparts and white upperparts except for black cap, lime green on nape and pinkish flush on breast. Female (B) brown and barred. Immatures and moulting adults variably black and white. Found mainly on rocky shores where mussels and other molluscs common. In summer, females often accompanied by 'creche' of youngsters. Breeds mainly in Scotland, NE England and N Ireland. In winter, range extends further S.

COMMON SCOTER *Melanitta nigra* Length 44-54cm
Locally common winter visitor to coastal waters around Scotland, Ireland and Wales; scarce breeding species in Scotland and Ireland. Male is only all-black British duck; yellow ridge on bill visible only at close range. Female has mainly dark brown plumage but has noticeably pale cheeks. Invariably seen in flocks out to sea. Dives well and often after crustaceans and molluscs, especially mussels. In flight, often forms long lines of birds flying low over the water; migrating birds may gather into clustered flock in flight.

VELVET SCOTER *Melanitta fusca* Length 51-58cm
Appreciably larger than common scoter with which this species often mixes. Male has mainly all-black plumage but white eye, white patch under eye and yellow patch on bill visible at considerable distance. Female brownish but with pale patches at base of bill and on cheek. Both sexes have distinctive white wing patch, sometimes visible when swimming but most obvious in flight. Scarce winter visitor to Britain and Ireland mainly to N and E Scotland and England.

GOLDENEYE *Bucephala clangula* Length 42-50cm
Distinctive diving duck, male (A) with mainly black and white plumage; has rounded, green-glossed head with yellow eye and conspicuous white patch at base of bill. Female (B) has grey-brown body plumage separated from dark brown head by pale neck. Both sexes show white on wings in flight. Common winter visitor to Britain and Ireland on both lakes and coasts. Scarce breeding bird in Scottish Highlands.

LONG-TAILED DUCK *Clangula hyemalis* Length 40-47cm
Attractive diving duck. Winter visitor from northern breeding grounds between October and March. Male characterised by long, narrow tail and has mainly black and white plumage with buffish wash on face and pink band on bill in winter (A); occasionally seen in summer plumage (B) when head, neck and breast all-black except for pale patch on face. Female lacks male's long tail streamers and has brown and white plumage, darker on head and neck during summer months. Invariably found on coastal waters in restless flocks which dive frequently and take to wing often. Indifferent to rough seas and sometimes seen diving among crashing waves on sandy beaches. Small numbers occur off many coasts in Britain and Ireland but sizeable flocks seen only off Scotland, N England and N Ireland.

GOOSANDER *Mergus merganser* Length 58-66cm
Large, elegant sawbill duck, almost exclusively associated with freshwater. Male is unmistakable with red, serrated-edged bill, green-glossed head, white body and black back. Looks very white at a distance but close view reveals feathers to be flushed with delicate shade of pink. Female also has reddish bill but head is orange-red with shaggy crest; body plumage greyish, palest on breast. Both sexes show considerable amount of white on wings in flight. Nests in tree holes beside larger rivers in Scotland, N England and parts of Wales. In winter, seen in small flocks on lakes, reservoirs, flooded gravel pits and substantial rivers. Swims buoyantly and retains stately appearance even when moving at speed. Dives well and for long periods in search of fish.

RED-BREASTED MERGANSER *Mergus serrator* Length 52-58cm
Superficially similar to goosander but smaller and both sexes with shaggy crest on back on head. Male has narrow red bill, green head, white neck and orange-red breast; flanks grey and back black. Female has red bill, dirty orange head and nape except for pale throat, and greyish buff body plumage. Immature male resembles female. In flight, both sexes show white speculum broken by black line; male also has large patch of white on forewing. Nests in tree holes beside rivers in Scotland, N England and Ireland. In winter, widespread around sheltered coasts and estuaries of Britain and Ireland; seldom seen on freshwater at this time of year. Dives frequently for fish. Usually solitary but sometimes gathers in reasonable numbers if feeding conditions are good.

SMEW *Mergus albellus* Length 38-44cm
Small but stunning sawbill duck. Annual winter visitor in small numbers from Arctic breeding grounds in Scandinavia and Siberia. Recorded mainly between November and February but often only if severe weather affects mainland Europe forcing birds to move W. Unmistakable male (A) looks pure white at a distance but closer view reveals black patch through eye and black lines on breast and back. Female (B) and immature birds known as 'redheads' and have orange-red cap and nape contrasting with white cheeks and throat; body plumage grey-brown. Favours fish-rich waterbodies including reservoirs and flooded gravel pits. Unpredictable in appearance; can turn up almost anywhere in England and S Scotland but most often seen in E England. Seldom recorded as far W as Ireland.

RUDDY DUCK *Oxyura jamaicensis* Length 35-43cm
N American species but feral populations now established in parts of C England following escapes of captive birds from the WWT reserve at Slimbridge, Gloucestershire. Compact, dumpy diving duck with short, stiff tail often held cocked at an angle. Male has orange-chestnut body plumage, white stern, white cheeks and black cap; bill is a striking plastic-blue colour. Female has mainly grey-brown plumage with paler cheeks broken by dark line from base of bill; could possibly be mistaken for little grebe if only partial view obtained. Favours lakes and flooded gravel pits with well-vegetated margins. Spends much of time in cover of emergent and overhanging plants. Rarely seen in flight. In spring, male performs curious chest-beating display resulting in froth of bubbles forming on water.

OSPREY *Pandion haliaetus* Wingspan 145-160cm
Impressive fish-eating raptor, usually seen near water. Summer visitor, present from May to September. Formerly extinct but now breeds in Scottish Highlands. In flight, looks superficially gull-like with pale underparts and long, narrow wings; shows dark primary feathers and dark carpal patch. Upperparts brown except for pale crown. Catches fish by plunging into water, talons first. Breeds mainly in Scottish Highlands. Easily watched at RSPB's Loch Garten reserve and around Aviemore. On migration, occurs on lakes and reservoirs in England.

RED KITE *Milvus milvus* Wingspan 145-165cm
Easily told in flight by long, bowed wings and deeply forked tail, constantly twisted as aid to flight control. Seen perched (A), bird looks reddish with pale grey head; yellow feet and black-tipped yellow bill only visible at close range. Seen from below in flight (B), shows reddish chest, pale grey patches on wings and grey tail; from above, tail looks red and wings brown except for dark flight feathers. Has stronghold in C Wales but successfully reintroduced to several locations in England and S Scotland; population appears to be growing.

SPARROWHAWK *Accipiter nisus* Wingspan 60-75cm
Common and widespread raptor in much of Britain and Ireland. Recognised by relatively short, rounded wings and proportionately long, barred tail. Male appreciably smaller than female and has blue-grey upperparts and barred reddish brown underparts. Female has grey-brown upperparts and pale underparts with narrow brown barring. Catches small birds in flight by low-level, surprise attacks. Formerly heavily persecuted by gamekeepers but now protected and numbers are recovering to former levels. Year-round resident of woodland and farmland.

GOSHAWK *Accipiter gentilis* Wingspan 100-115cm
Formerly extinct as breeding species but now present in small numbers in England, Wales and Scotland. Similar in silhouette to sparrowhawk but much larger. Male noticeably smaller than female but both sexes have grey-brown upperparts and pale underparts with dark barring. Staring yellow eyes, white stripe over eye and yellow legs only visible at close range. Usually seen circling high above when white undertail feathers often fluffed out. Favours extensive forests. Medium-sized birds such as woodpigeons caught in flight.

BUZZARD *Buteo buteo* Wingspan 115-125cm
The commonest large raptor seen in W and N England, Wales and Scotland. Formerly much persecuted despite fact that diet comprises mainly earthworms and carrion in many areas. Draws attention to itself in flight with mewing calls. Rides thermals with ease on broad, rounded wings, held in 'v' shape when soaring. Perches for long periods on posts and dead branches. Plumage colour extremely variable but usually some shade of brown; wings barred and tail uniformly banded. Prefers farmland for feeding with nearby woods for nesting.

HONEY BUZZARD *Pernis apivorus* Wingspan 135-150cm
Superficially similar to buzzard but underparts paler; shows dark carpal patches on wings. Tail proportionately longer with two broad bands near base and broad, dark terminal band; these features separate it from buzzard. In flight, head appears narrow, pointed and pale. Soars on flat wings. Rare summer visitor to S and C England, present from May to September. Favours areas of undisturbed woodland where wasp and bee colonies common: feeds on their larvae.

GOLDEN EAGLE *Aquila chrysaetos* Wingspan 190-25cm
Britain's largest raptor but size often difficult to gauge. Adult soars on long, parallel-sided wings which are constantly flexed as bird rides upcurrents. Tail relatively long. Against sky, adult looks uniformly dark. Immature shows white patch at base of tail and on wings. Brown plumage and golden-yellow mane seen only on perched birds at close range. Relatively common in N and W Scotland.

MARSH HARRIER *Circus aeruginosus* Wingspan 110-125cm
Associated with wetlands, particularly extensive reedbeds. Flies at slow speed just above tops of reeds, occasionally stalling to drop on prey. Long-winged and long-tailed. Male reddish brown except for blue-grey head and grey, unbarred tail; in flight, has grey and reddish brown areas on wings and black wingtips. Female dark brown except for pale leading edge to wing and pale cap and chin. Rare breeding bird in England, mainly E Anglia. Seen on migration elsewhere.

HEN HARRIER *Circus cyaneus* Wingspan 100-120cm
Scarce, but the most likely harrier species to be seen in Britain. Male has pale blue-grey plumage except for white belly, white rump and black wingtips. Female and immature brown with barring on wings and tail, and white rump. Favours expansive areas of heathland, moor and grassland. Flies low and at slow speed, often quartering ground in search of voles and mice. Breeds on northern, upland moors in N England, Scotland, Wales and Ireland. Winters mostly S of breeding range, numbers swollen by continental birds. Uses communal winter roosts.

MONTAGU'S HARRIER *Circus pygargus* Wingspan 100-120cm
Both sexes superficially similar in size and appearance to corresponding sex of hen harrier. Male (A) has blue-grey plumage but with less pronounced white rump than male hen harrier and with single dark bar on upperwing and two dark bars on underwing. Female (B) has pale brown plumage with barring on wings and tail. Rare summer visitor from May to August, mainly S England. Seen on migration but occasional pair stays to breed, sometimes returning in successive years to same site. Recent nesting records have occurred in arable fields and on heaths.

PEREGRINE *Falco peregrinus* Wingspan 95-115cm
Britain's most impressive falcon. Formerly rare but now rather widespread. Adult has dark blue-grey upperparts and pale, barred underparts; face shows characteristic dark mask. Juvenile has browner plumage with streaked underparts. Sometimes seen perched on rocky crag but more usually spotted in flight with broad, pointed wings and relatively long tail. Soars with bowed wings but stoops on prey such as pigeons with wings swept back. Locally common on cliffed coasts of SW England, Wales, Scotland and Ireland; less so on upland areas inland.

HOBBY *Falco subbuteo* Wingspan 70-85cm
Small but elegant falcon. A summer visitor, mainly to S England, from May to August. Adult has dark blue-grey upperparts and pale, dark-streaked underparts. At close range, dark moustachial markings, white cheeks and reddish orange 'trousers' visible. In flight, has anchor-like outline with narrow, swept-back wings and long tail. In spring, hunts dragonflies over lakes and flooded gravel pits. Later in season, catches birds such as swallows on wing. Favours heathland but also farmland with clumps of trees for nesting.

MERLIN *Falco columbarius* Wingspan 60-65cm
Britain's smallest raptor. Male (A) has blue-grey upperparts and buffish, streaked and spotted underparts. Female (B) has brown upperparts and pale underparts showing large, brown spots. Seldom soars but more usually seen flying low over ground in dashing flight, in pursuit of prey such as meadow pipit. Perches on rocks and fencepost for long periods. Breeds on upland moors in Wales, N England, Scotland and Ireland. In winter, many birds move S to heaths and coastal marshes.

KESTREL *Falco tinnunculus* Wingspan 65-80cm
Britain's commonest and most familiar raptor and the only one which habitually hovers and hunts along motorway verges. Male has spotted, orange-brown back, blue-grey head and blue-grey tail with terminal black band. Female has barred, brown plumage. Nests in trees and on cliff ledges but also in man-made settings such as window ledges on office blocks. Feeds primarily on small mammals but takes insects in summer months. Widespread in Britain and Ireland.

RED GROUSE *Lagopus lagopus ssp scoticus* Length 37-42cm
Familiar gamebird of heather moorland. Male has chestnut-brown plumage and conspicuous red wattle over eye. Female has marbled, grey-brown plumage affording excellent camouflage when sitting on nest. Takes to the air explosively and, in flight, both sexes show uniformly dark wings; wingbeats rapid but interspersed with long glides on bowed wings. *Go-back go-back go-back* call evocative of moorland terrain. In Britain, found only in N and W but more widespread in Ireland. Feeds mainly on young shoots of heather.

PTARMIGAN *Lagopus mutus* Length 34-36cm
A mountain species, in Britain restricted to Scottish Highlands. In summer (A), male has marbled grey-brown plumage with white underparts and red wattle above eye. Female has mainly buffish brown plumage and white underparts. In flight, both sexes show conspicuous white wings. In winter (B), both sexes mainly white except for black in tail and at base of bill in male. Rarely below 700m even in winter. Easy to see on Cairngorm and often rather confiding. Presence indicated by piles of droppings like cigarette ash and by croaking call of male.

BLACK GROUSE *Tetrao tetrix* Length 40-55cm
Rather local and declining species. Associated with moorland habitats but specifically favours areas where woodland (often conifer plantations) adjacent to open land. Male (A) larger than female (B) and looks all-black at distance; close range reveals red wattle above eye and remarkable white-centred, lyre-shaped tail seen on birds at communal, traditional leks. Displaying birds best found in early morning. Female has orange-brown plumage; in flight shows forked tail and faint wingbar. Restricted to Wales, C and N England and Scotland.

CAPERCAILLIE *Tetrao urogallus* Length 60-90cm
Huge gamebird, male almost half as big again as female. Formerly extinct but reintroduced in 19th century to former range in Scottish Highlands. Now locally common here in native Caledonian pinewoods and in mature conifer plantations. Male (A) looks all dark at distance but at closer range has greenish sheen on breast, brownish wings and red wattle above eye. Displaying male fans tail out. Female (B) has grey-brown plumage with orange-brown patch on breast. Birds often perch in surprisingly small trees. Forages on ground for shoots and buds.

PHEASANT *Phasianus colchicus* Length 53-59cm
Introduced from native Asia but now well established and numbers continually boosted by release of captive-bred birds for shooting. Adult male (A) familiar and unmistakable with red wattle, blue-green sheen on head, orange-brown body plumage and long, orange tail; some birds show white collar. Female (B) is mottled buffish brown with shorter tail than male. Feeds on shoots, seeds and invertebrates and no doubt has impact on native plants and ground-dwelling insects where numerous. Widespread and common in mainland Britain and Ireland.

RED-LEGGED PARTRIDGE *Alectoris rufa* Length 32-34cm
True range SW and W mainland Europe but introduced to Britain and now well established, mainly in S and E England but locally further N and W. Sexes similar with red bill and legs, and white throat, bordered with gorget of black spots; plumage otherwise mainly blue-grey and warm buff except for black and white barring on flanks. Seen in small parties (covies), usually in arable fields. Male utters loud *chuka-chuka-chuka* call, sometimes from fencepost.

GREY PARTRIDGE *Perdix perdix* Length 29-31cm
A native gamebird, much persecuted but still common in many areas. Seen at close range, grey plumage is finely marked. Male has orange-buff face, dark chestnut mark on belly, maroon stripes on flanks and streaked back. Female similar but markings less distinct. Usually seen in small groups feeding mainly in arable fields. When disturbed, birds take to air with whirring, noisy wings.

WATER RAIL *Rallus aquaticus* Length 23-28cm
Shy and retiring wetland species whose pig-like squealing calls are heard more than bird itself is seen. Has long, reddish bill, reddish legs and mainly blue-grey underparts and reddish brown upperparts; shows black and white barring on flanks. Surprisingly narrow body enables bird to pass through dense vegetation with ease. Favours extensive reedbeds, marshes and overgrown margins of watercress beds. Local and rather scarce breeding species but more widespread in winter in Britain and Ireland due to influx of continental birds.

CORNCRAKE *Crex crex* Length 27-30cm
Has declined catastrophically in recent years and now confined to small numbers of birds in Western Isles of Scotland and Ireland. Summer visitor from May to September. Sandy brown plumage; in flight, shows chestnut on wings and dangling legs. Favours hay meadows which are undisturbed during nesting season; early rolling of grassland or cutting for silage largely responsible for species' decline. Presence usually indicated by male's *crek-crek* call uttered tirelessly throughout night. Bird itself rather shy and difficult to observe.

MOORHEN *Gallinula chloropus* Length 32-35cm
Widespread and familiar wetland bird in most parts of mainland Britain and Ireland. Often wary but in urban areas can become rather tame. Adult has brownish wings but otherwise mainly dark grey-black plumage. Has distinctive yellow-tipped red bill and frontal shield on head, white feathers on sides of undertail and white line along flanks. Legs and long toes yellowish. Juvenile has pale brown plumage. Swims with jerky movement and with tail flicking; in flight, shows dangling legs. Occurs on all sorts of freshwater habitats.

COOT *Fulica atra* Length 36-38cm
Often found in similar habitats to moorhen but easily told by all-black plumage and white bill and frontal shield to head. Has lobed toes which facilitate swimming. Utters distinctive, loud *kwoot* call. Feeds by upending or making shallow dives in water but also grazes waterside grass. Builds mound nest of waterplants often in full view. Common year-round resident of lakes, flooded gravel-pits and reservoirs in most parts of Britain and Ireland. Numbers boosted in winter by influx of continental birds; then forms large flocks.

OYSTERCATCHER *Haematopus ostralegus* Length 43cm
Distinctive and noisy wader. Widespread around coasts of Britain and Ireland and sometimes inland in N. Favours undisturbed shores for nesting and therefore excluded from much of S England at this time. More widespread outside breeding season on beaches and estuaries; sometimes roosts in large flocks. Distinctive black and white plumage with white wingbars seen in flight; winter birds have white half-collar. Long pinkish legs. Stout red bill used to feed on molluscs.

AVOCET *Recurvirostra avosetta* Length 43cm
Easily recognised by black and white plumage, long, blue legs and long, upcurved bill swept from side-to-side through water when feeding. Very local breeding species, mainly in E Anglia and present there from April to September. Symbol of RSPB and easy to see at their reserve at Minsmere, Suffolk. Outside breeding season, flocks present on estuaries in S and SW England, notably Exe in Devon.

LAPWING *Vanellus vanellus* Length 30cm
Formerly more numerous but still common in many parts of Britain and Ireland. Breeds on undisturbed farmland and on moors and open country throughout. N birds move S outside breeding season and, in winter, British population boosted by influx of continental birds. Looks black and white at a distance but in good light has green, oily sheen on back; winter birds have buffish fringes to feathers on back. Spiky crest feathers longer in male than female. In flight, has rounded, black and white wings and flapping flight. Loud *pee-wit* call.

RINGED PLOVER *Charadrius hiaticula* Length 19cm
Small, dumpy wader associated mainly with coastal habitats. Breeds on sandy and shingle beaches around Britain and Ireland but excluded from many areas in S by human disturbance. Outside breeding season, found on estuaries, mudflats and beaches. Adult has sandy brown upperparts and white underparts with continuous black breast-band and collar. Black and white markings on face and white throat and nape. Legs orange-yellow and bill orange with black tip. Juvenile similar but dark markings less distinct and has dull legs and dark bill. Shows white wingbar in flight at all ages. Feeds in distinctive manner, usually running along beach as if powered by clockwork and then standing still for few seconds before picking food item from sand. Frequently utters soft *too-it* call.

LITTLE RINGED PLOVER *Charadrius dubius* Length 15cm
As name suggests, marginally smaller than ringed plover and with slimmer body but size alone is not a good guide to identity. Like its relative, little ringed plover has sandy brown upperparts and white underparts with black collar and breast-band and black and white markings on face. Close views of adult reveal black bill, yellow legs and characteristic yellow eyering. Juvenile similar to juvenile ringed plover but, in flight, wings lack wingbars; adults have similarly uniform wings, the best feature for distant identification. Summer visitor, seen on migration on coasts in spring and autumn. Breeds very locally on gravel workings and open fields, mostly in S and SE England and present there from early April to August. Calls include a loud *pee-oo*, uttered on rising.

GOLDEN PLOVER *Pluvialis apricaria* Length 28cm
Both sight and sound of this species are evocative of desolate upland areas favoured during breeding season. Male in breeding season (A) has spangled golden upperparts with white on underparts and black belly grading to greyish on neck and face; breeding birds from N Europe with black face, neck and belly sometimes seen on migration. Female has similar upperparts to male but less distinct dark markings on underparts. Winter birds (B) lose black on underparts. In flight, shows white 'armpits'. Nests on moorland in N and W, often favouring newly colonised areas of burnt ground. Winters throughout much of Britain and Ireland, mainly on farmland; flocks sometimes mix with lapwings. Numbers boosted at this time by influx of birds from continent. Flight call *peeoo*. Song haunting and fluty.

GREY PLOVER *Pluvialis squatarola* Length 28cm
Non-breeding visitor from high Arctic nesting grounds, present usually from September to April. Almost exclusively coastal, favouring estuaries and mudflats. In winter plumage (A), looks grey with upperparts spangled black and white and underparts whitish. Juvenile birds can have buffish wash to upperparts leading to confusion with golden plover. Stockier grey plover shows black 'armpits' in flight at all times. Birds in breeding plumage (B) sometimes seen in spring and autumn and have striking black underparts, separated by grey upperparts by band of white. Trisyllabic *pee-oo-ee* call is like human wolf-whistle. Generally solitary. Feeds in plover manner: runs for several yards, tilts forward and remains still before leaning forward to pick morsel from mud.

DOTTEREL *Charadrius morinellus* Length 22cm
A rare and beautiful mountain-top wader. As a nesting species, more or less confined to plateau mountain tops in Scottish Highlands, almost always above 1,000m. Summer visitor to breeding grounds from May to August but small groups, known as 'trips', also seen on spring migration on traditional hilltops and fields in S and E England in first week of May. Rather dumpy with pot-bellied appearance. Female is striking with reddish orange breast and belly separated from blue-grey throat by black-bordered white collar; has whitish face and striking white stripe above and behind eye. Male, who incubates eggs, is duller than female. Juvenile has buffish brown plumage with suggestion of pattern seen on adult bird; sometimes encountered on autumn migration near coasts.

DUNLIN *Calidris alpina* Length 17-19cm
A local but fairly common breeding species on N moors but an abundant, flock-forming winter visitor to most estuaries and mudflats in Britain and Ireland where generally the most numerous species of wader. Variable in terms of body size and bill length but bill usually long and slightly downcurved. Winter bird (A) has rather uniform grey upperparts and white underparts. In breeding season (B), shows chestnut-brown back and cap, streaked underparts and black belly. Juvenile has dark spots on flanks with grey, black and chestnut on back. Call *priit*.

CURLEW SANDPIPER *Calidris ferruginea* Length 19cm
Very similar to dunlin but has more markedly downcurved bill and conspicuous white rump, latter best seen in flight. Occurs in Britain and Ireland as scarce passage migrant mainly in autumn en route from Arctic breeding grounds to African wintering range. Most birds seen are juvenile with pale-edged feathers on back giving scaly appearance and white belly and buffish breast. In winter, adult bird has grey upperparts and white underparts. In breeding plumage, head, neck and underparts become orange-red; both adult plumages encountered in migrants.

LITTLE STINT *Calidris pusilla* Length 13cm
Tiny wader, recalling miniature, short-billed dunlin. Scarce passage migrant, most records of juvenile birds in autumn. Favours margins of freshwater pools mainly near coasts, especially S and E England. Constant and frantic activity a clue to identity. Juvenile has chestnut-brown upperparts and cap, white underparts, and distinctive buff patch on shoulder; usually shows white 'v' on back. Adult seen comparatively rarely. In winter, has grey upperparts and white underparts; acquires reddish orange wash to head and neck in breeding plumage.

TEMMINCK'S STINT *Calidris temminckii* Length 14cm
Scarce passage migrant, mainly to coasts of E England, but also very rare and erratic Scottish breeder. Adults mostly seen in spring but juveniles in autumn. Superficially similar to miniature common sandpiper with short, straight dark bill and yellowish legs. Adult has grey-brown upperparts and white upperparts with clear demarcation between dark breast and pale belly; in summer, shows dark centres to many feathers on back. Juvenile shows pale margins to feathers on back. White outer tail feathers seen in flight.

KNOT *Calidris canutus* Length 25cm
Non-breeding visitor to estuaries and mudflats around Britain and Ireland and present from September to April. Seen mostly in winter plumage with uniform grey upperparts and white underparts. Bill black and comparatively short; legs dull yellowish. Juvenile similar but buffish and pale feather margins on back give scaly appearance. Brick red breeding plumage birds sometimes seen in spring and autumn. In winter, forms large flocks which fly in tight formation. Abundant on The Wash and spectacular roosts seen at RSPB's Snettisham reserve nearby.

SANDERLING *Calidris alba* Length 20cm
Common winter visitor to sandy beaches around Britain and Ireland, present from September to April. At a distance, winter bird looks very white; at close range shows grey upperparts, white underparts, black 'shoulder' patch, and black legs and bill. Invariably seen in small flocks running at great speed and feeding along edge of breaking waves. Usually tolerant of human observers. Confusing, reddish brown breeding plumage birds sometimes seen in spring and autumn.

PURPLE SANDPIPER *Calidris maritima* Length 21cm
Very rare and erratic breeder in N Scotland but widespread, although local, winter visitor from September to April. Recalls dumpy dunlin but has yellow-based bill, yellow legs, blue-grey upperparts and white underparts. Favours rocky shores and headlands, feeding in small, unobtrusive flocks just where waves are breaking. In spring, acquires purple sheen to grey feathers; seen only at close range.

Redshank *Tringa totanus* Length 28cm
Local but fairly common resident breeding species but numerous winter visitor throughout Britain and Ireland, numbers being boosted by influx of continental birds. A nervous bird, the loud, piping alarm call alerting observer to its presence. Easily recognised by its red legs and long, red-based bill. Plumage mostly grey-brown above and pale below with streaks and barring; plumage more heavily marked in breeding season. In flight, shows characterisitic broad, white trailing margin to wing. In breeding season, favours flood meadows, marshes and moors. In winter, occurs in coastal habitats, especially mudflats and estuaries.

Spotted Redshank *Tringa erythropus* Length 30cm
In non-breeding plumage, superficially similar to redshank but larger and with proportionately longer red legs and red-based bill. Breeds in Scandinavia and seen in Britain and Ireland as passage migrant and occasional winter resident. Winter bird (A) has pale grey upperparts and whitish underparts; juvenile (B) similar but more heavily marked and generally darker. Breeding plumage adult sometimes seen on migration and easily recognised by almost all-black plumage; passes through northwards in May and begins return journey by early July. In flight, all plumages have uniform grey-brown wings. Flight call distinctive *chewit*.

Greenshank *Tringa nebularia* Length 30-31cm
Attractive, long-legged wader which looks very white at distance. Rare breeding species on moorland in C and N Scotland. More usually seen as passage migrant and local winter resident further S in Britain and Ireland. In all plumages, has yellowish green legs and long, slightly upturned bill with grey base. Winter adult pale grey above with white underparts; in breeding season, some feathers on back acquire dark centres. Juvenile has brownish upperparts. In flight, all birds show uniform wings and white rump and wedge up back. Feeds in deliberate, probing manner. Flight call a distinctive, trisyllabic *tchu-tchu-tchu*.

Green Sandpiper *Tringa ochropus* Length 23cm
Fairly common passage migrant throughout Britain and Ireland and local but regular winter visitor to S England from September to April. Always seen near water and often first observed when flushed from ditch or pond margin. Then looks black and white with striking white rump; flight usually accompanied by yelping, trisyllabic call. Migrants occur on variety of wetlands but wintering birds often on watercress beds. Has curious gait, constantly bobbing body up and down. Straight bill and yellowish green legs seen at close range. Upperparts dark and underparts white; tail shows three broad, dark terminal bands.

Wood Sandpiper *Tringa glareola* Length 20cm
Superficially similar to green sandpiper but more elegant and with longer, yellow legs. Seen mainly as rather scarce passage migrant to shallow wetlands in Britain and Ireland, mostly in August and September with juvenile birds predominating. Very rare breeding species in N Scotland. Has brownish, spangled upperparts, brightest in juvenile birds, and pale belly. In flight, shows conspicuous white rump. White tail has narrow terminal bars, these greater in extent than on green sandpiper. Underwings are mostly white whereas on similar green sandpiper these are black. Flight call a distintive *chiff-chiff-chiff*.

Common Sandpiper *Actitis hypoleucos* Length 20cm
Common nesting species to N and W, invariably seen near river or lake margins. Summer visitor to breeding range, seen mainly from April to August. Occurs elsewhere in Britain on passage, often on coasts or beside flooded gravel pits. Scarce wintering species, mainly on coasts in S and W England. Small, plump-bodied wader with rather elongate tail end. Upperparts warm brown and underparts white showing clear demarcation between dark breast and white belly. Usually adopts horizontal stance and constantly bobs body up and down. Flies on bowed, fluttering wings and seldom seen flying more than a few feet above water.

CURLEW *Numenius arquata* Length 53-58cm
Widespread year-round resident in Britain and Ireland with numbers boosted by influx of continental birds in winter months. The commonest large wader with a long, downcurved bill. Plumage mainly grey-brown with streaked and spotted underparts and pale belly. In flight, wings uniformly dark brown but shows white rump and wedge on lower back; tip of tail has dark, narrow barring. Breeds on damp grassland and moors, mainly in N and W. In winter, usually found on coasts, preferring estuaries and mudflats. Uses long, blue-grey legs to wade in deep water and bill to probe for worms. Utters *curlew* call and has bubbling song.

WHIMBREL *Numenius phaeopus* Length 41cm
Superficially similar to curlew but appreciably smaller and with distinctive head pattern comprising two dark lateral stripes on otherwise pale crown. Presence also detected by bubbling call, usually of seven notes descending slightly in pitch from start to finish. Breeds only on N Scottish islands but there not uncommon. Present from May to August and nests on open moorland. Seen in rest of Britain and Ireland as rather scarce passage migrant in spring and autumn, almost always on coasts and favouring both rocky shores and sheltered estuaries. Winters in Africa. Song rather confusingly similar to that of curlew.

BLACK-TAILED GODWIT *Limosa limosa* Length 41cm
Large, long-legged wader with incredibly long, very slightly upturned bill which is pinkish at base. In all plumages, recognised in flight by black tail, white rump and conspicuous white wingbars. In winter plumage, has rather uniformly grey-brown upperparts and pale underparts. In breeding plumage, acquires orange-red wash to head and neck with feathers on back having black centres. Juvenile has buffish wash on neck and breast. Rare breeding species favouring flood meadows, mainly in E England. Locally common, flock-forming migrant and winter visitor to mudflats and estuaries; in winter, widespread except in N.

BAR-TAILED GODWIT *Limosa lapponica* Length 38-42cm
Superficially similar in outline to black-tailed godwit but with more dumpy appearance. Easily told in flight in all plumages by uniformly dark wings and white rump grading to narrow-barred tail. Passage migrant and winter visitor from high Arctic breeding grounds. Juvenile and adult in winter have rather curlew-like plumages, grey-brown above and pale below; upperparts more strongly marked in juvenile birds. Breeding plumage birds, with brick-red on head, neck and underparts, sometimes seen in late spring or early autumn. Locally common on estuaries and coastal grassland, mainly from September to April.

TURNSTONE *Arenaria interpres* Length 23cm
Common, non-breeding visitor to coasts all around Britain and Ireland. Can be seen in most months but majority of birds arrive from August onwards and stay until late April. Unobtrusive and well camouflaged and so easily overlooked. Winter adult and juvenile variably marked with black, brown and white on upperparts, usually showing clear demarcation between dark breast and white underparts. In breeding plumage, has orange-brown feathers on back and black and white markings on head. Legs reddish orange. Bill short and triangular; effective when turning stones and tideline debris in search of sandhoppers.

RUFF *Philomachus pugnax* Length 23-29cm
Very variable wader; proportionately small head its most consistent character. Male in breeding plumage (A) has coloured facial warts, ruff and head plumes, used in communal display. Each male is slightly different but ruff feathers usually uniform black, white or chestnut. Outside breeding season, male recalls smaller female (reeve, B) with grey-brown upperparts, pale underparts, dark bill and dull orange legs. Buffish juvenile has pale feather margins on back giving scaly appearance. Rare breeding species, mainly E Anglia, on marshy meadows. Passage migrant elsewhere. Scarce winter resident near coasts of S England and Ireland.

GREY PHALAROPE *Phalaropus fulicarius* Length 20-21cm
Charming and unusual wader. Typically seen swimming, often spinning rapidly or picking insects off water surface. Scarce passage migrant, mostly in autumn, and very occasional winter visitor to Britain and Ireland. Oceanic outside breeding season and so most usually seen near coasts during or after severe gales. Small groups sometimes seen flying past headlands in W of Britain and Ireland; storm-driven birds may feed on coastal pools, sometimes further inland. Usually tame. Mainly seen in winter plumage with grey upperparts, white underparts and black 'panda' mark around eye. Brick-red breeding plumage birds seen only very rarely.

RED-NECKED PHALAROPE *Phalaropus lobatus* Length 18cm
In winter plumage, similar to grey phalarope and best told by needle-like bill and more black and white appearance. In breeding season, female has white throat and red neck; male similar to duller. Habitually swims. Nests in small numbers in N Scotland and N and W Scottish Isles; rare and erratic breeder in N Ireland. Present on breeding grounds from May to August. Favours coastal moorland pools; often difficult to see among emergent vegetation. Tame but easily disturbed at nest and protected by law. Oceanic outside breeding season and seen around British and Irish coasts as scarce passage migrant and rare winter visitor.

WOODCOCK *Scolopax rusticola* Length 34cm
Dumpy, short-legged, long-billed wader. Marbled chestnut, black and white plumage affords superb camouflage among fallen leaves. Large eyes placed high on head give bird almost complete all-round vision. Nests on ground in woodlands throughout Britain and Ireland; camouflage and habit of sitting tight make it difficult to see. Easiest to observe on spring evenings when male performs 'roding' display over treetops; presence also indicated by soft duck-like calls and explosive squeaks. Feeds mostly between dusk and dawn, probing damp ground for worms. Resident British birds joined by continental visitors in winter.

SNIPE *Gallinago gallinago* Length 27cm
Easily recognised, even in silhouette, by dumpy, rounded body, rather short legs and incredibly long, straight bill. Feeding method characteristic: probes vertically downwards with bill in soft mud, in manner of sewing machine. In good light, has buffish brown plumage, beautifully patterned with black and white lines and bars, has distinctive dark stripes on head. Locally common breeding species on marshy ground and moors in many parts of Britain and Ireland although absent from much of S England in summer months. More widespread in winter and found in a range of wetland habitats; resident British birds joined by visitors from N Europe. Utters one or two *kreech* calls when flushed. Performs 'drumming' display in breeding season, humming sound produced by vibrating tail feathers.

JACK SNIPE *Lymnocryptes minimus* Length 19cm
Appreciably smaller than snipe. Bill shorter than relative but plumage similar although stripes on head more distinctive. Fairly common winter visitor to marshes in Britain and Ireland from October to March. Easily missed because feeds unobtrusively among vegetation and very reluctant to fly, preferring to crouch motionless until danger passes. If flushed, however, rises silently and drops back into cover after short distance. Pumps body up and down as it walks.

STONE-CURLEW *Burhinus oedicnemus* Length 41cm
Rare and secretive breeding bird, present from March to September and found only in S and E England from Wiltshire to Norfolk. Can sometimes be seen during day but most active at dusk and throughout night when strange, curlew-like wailing calls indicate the species' presence. Favours large, open fields, often on chalk downs, where lack of hedges gives uninterrupted view of terrain. Seen at close range, has sandy brown plumage, yellow legs, black-tipped yellow bill and large yellow eyes. Dark wings and white wingbars most apparent in flight. Always a challenge to find, even among short vegetation.

BLACK-HEADED GULL *Larus ridibundus* Length 35-38cm
The most numerous small gull in Britain and Ireland. Plumage varies according to age and time of year but at all times easily recognised in flight by white leading edge to wings. Adult has grey back and upperwings, white underparts, red legs and a reddish bill. In winter (A), has dark smudges behind eye but in summer (B) acquires chocolate brown, not black, hood. Juvenile birds, seen in late summer, have marbled brown and grey upperparts; in first winter plumage, shows dark-tipped pinkish bill with grey and brown on upperwings. Breeds beside upland lakes and on coastal marshes. Outside breeding season, found on a wide range of freshwater habitats as well as around coasts. Will visit urban areas and frequents car parks and ornamental lakes; also follows ploughs on arable land.

MEDITERRANEAN GULL *Larus melanocephalus* Length 36-38cm
Scarce but increasingly frequent visitor to Britain and Ireland, mostly in S and E; also a rare but regular breeding species in S England among colonies of black-headed gulls. Superficially similar to black-headed gull but separable in all plumages with care and experience. Most consistent features of adult are pure white wings. In winter (A), has dark smudges around eyes but in summer (B) acquires black hood, eyes defined by white 'eyelids'. Blood-red bill is stouter than that of black-headed and has dark band near tip. In first winter, similar to first winter black-headed but dark streaks on head and white 'eyelids' give menacing look to face. In second winter, similar to winter adult but, at rest, shows dark tips to primaries. Outside breeding season, often found with black-headed gulls.

LITTLE GULL *Larus minutus* Length 28cm
The world's smallest gull. Has buoyant, tern-like flight and favours coastal and marine habitats outside breeding season. Does not nest in Britain but seen as an uncommon passage migrant in spring and autumn, particularly along coasts of E England. Also occurs as a scarce and erratic winter resident, mostly to S and W England and Ireland. Small size is always a good character when seen with black-headed gulls, but adult little gull's sooty black underwing is its most diagnostic feature; wings look rounded and have narrow, white trailing margin. In winter, has dark smudges on face but in summer, acquires dark hood; legs and bill reddish at all times. Juvenile has striking black bars along wings and black-tipped tail; can be confused only with juvenile kittiwake.

COMMON GULL *Larus canus* Length 41cm
Despite name, generally not our most numerous gull. Recalls small version of herring gull, adult having grey back and upperwings with body plumage. Otherwise white, although in winter back of head and nape have dark streaks. In flight, black wingtips show white spots. Legs greenish yellow and bill yellow in summer but duller in winter with dark band near tip. First winter bird has bands of grey, brown and black on upperwings. Breeds mainly in N Scotland and N Ireland, mostly on the coast but sometimes inland beside freshwater. In winter, widespread around most coasts and also feeds inland, sometimes following ploughs with black-headed gulls; outside breeding season, resident British birds joined by influx of migrants from N Europe. Calls include a nasal *heeow*.

KITTIWAKE *Rissa tridactyla* Length 41cm
Visit almost any British seabird colony and you will not need to be told this bird's name. Loud *kittee-wake kittee-wake* calls ring from the cliffs and are highly evocative of coasts in N and W Britain and Ireland. Adult (A) easy to recognise with blue-grey back and otherwise white body plumage; bill yellow and legs and feet black. In flight, recalls adult common gull but wingtips pure black, as if dipped in black ink. Immature (B) is striking in flight with black zigzag markings on upperwings, black nape band and black tip to tail. Arguably, our only true seagull, with non-breeding period spent entirely at sea; confident flight even in the roughest weather. Nests mostly on precipitous cliff ledges overhanging sea and rarely on coastal buildings, especially NE England.

HERRING GULL *Larus argentatus* Length 56-66cm

A familiar and noisy bird, generally the most numerous large gull species. Common around coasts in Britain and Ireland but also inland, especially at rubbish tips. Nests in loose colonies, mainly on sea cliffs but sometimes on rooftops in coastal towns. Adult has blue-grey back and upperwings with white-spotted, black wingtips; body otherwise white but sometimes has dark streaks on nape in winter. Legs pink and bill yellow with orange spot near tip. Juvenile mottled grey-brown with dark bill; acquires adult plumage with successive moults over subsequent two years. Follows boats and can become bold when regularly fed.

LESSER BLACK-BACKED GULL *Larus fuscus* Length 53-56cm

Similar proportions to herring gull but most adult birds easily told by dark grey back and upperwings. Because precise tone varies, yellow legs are best diagnostic features; bill yellow with orange spot near tip. In flight, upperwing colour usually a shade paler than black wingtips. Juvenile closely resembles other large gull juveniles with mottled brown plumage; acquires adult plumage over subsequent two years. A very locally common, colonial breeding species, mostly on W and N coasts of Britain and Ireland. A partial migrant, numbers in winter boosted by birds from N Europe. Mainly coastal but also inland on fields.

GREAT BLACK-BACKED GULL *Larus marinus* Length 64-79cm

Our largest gull. Superficially similar to lesser black-backed but always looks more bulky and has pink, not yellow, legs. Bill massive and upperwings appear uniformly black in flight. Immatures resemble other large gulls of similar ages and best told by size and bulk. Breeds in small numbers around coasts of Britain and Ireland; least frequent on E and SE coasts of England. Pairs usually widely spaced and nest sited close to seabird colony; prey on adults, chicks and young of smaller species. In winter, mostly stays near coast but will visit inland rubbish tips. Laughing call is noticeably deeper than that of other gulls.

GLAUCOUS GULL *Larus hyperboreus* Length 62-68cm

A winter visitor to Britain and Ireland from Arctic breeding grounds in variable numbers. Easiest to see in N with most records between November and February. Marginally smaller than great black-backed gull but adult close in appearance to herring gull except for diagnostic white wingtips; these noticeable both at rest and in flight. Legs pink and bill massive. Immature birds relatively easy to identify, having very pale buffish grey plumage, pale wingtips and dark-tipped pink bills. Seen mostly on the coast but birds occasionally visit rubbish tips inland. Iceland gull is similar but smaller and with more dainty-looking bill.

GREAT SKUA *Stercorarius skua* Length 58cm

Chocolate-brown plumage recalls that of immature gull but relatively large head, bulky proportions and dark legs and bill soon confirm identity. In flight, shows conspicuous white patches near wingtips. In good light, resting bird shows mane of golden-brown feathers on nape. Summer visitor to breeding grounds in N Scotland, Orkney and Shetland, present from May to August. At other times, found at sea S of region; observed around coasts on migration, most easily from headlands in W during onshore gales. Kills seabirds such as puffins but also parasitises birds as large as gannets by forcing them to regurgitate last meal.

ARCTIC SKUA *Stercorarius parasiticus* Length 46cm

Buoyant and graceful on the wing. Adult recognised in flight by deep, powerful wingbeats and narrow pointed wings with white patch near tip; also shows pointed tail streamers extending beyond wedge-shaped tail. Two different adult plumages: sooty brown dark phase and pale phase with dark cap, back and wings but plumage otherwise white except for yellow-buff wash to nape. Juvenile has chocolate-brown, heavily barred plumage and pointed, wedge-shaped tail. Breeds in N Scotland, Orkney and Shetland, present from May to August. Otherwise seen around coasts on migration in spring and autumn. Feeds by parasitising other seabirds.

SANDWICH TERN *Sterna sandvichensis* Length 41cm

Elegant seabird, looking pure white at a distance. Summer visitor, seen on coasts from April to September. Easily recognised in flight by powerful, buoyant flight on long, narrow wings and frequently uttered, harsh *churrick* call. Back and upperwing of adult pale grey but plumage otherwise white except for dark crest; in winter plumage, sometimes seen in birds in autumn, loses dark cap but retains black on nape. Legs black and bill black with yellow tip. Juvenile has scaly-looking back and dark bill. Breeds very locally in large colonies on undisturbed sand or shingle beaches around British and Irish coasts.

COMMON TERN *Sterna hirundo* Length 35cm

Common and widespread around coasts of Britain and Ireland from mid-April to late August; also seen on large inland lakes and flooded gravel pits. Appearance typically tern-like with pale grey back and upperparts and otherwise white plumage. Red legs relatively long compared to similar Arctic tern. Bill orange-red with black tip. Black cap present in summer adult but incomplete in winter plumage. In flight, outer primaries appear dark on upperwing. Juvenile has scaly appearance to back and dark leading edge to inner wing. Colonial nester on undisturbed shingle and sandy beaches. Plunge-dives for surface-feeding fish.

ARCTIC TERN *Sterna paradisaea* Length 35cm

Superficially very similar to common tern and told at close range by uniformly blood-red bill and very short, red legs. Underparts pale greyish, becoming paler on throat and cheeks. In flight, wings have a translucent look. Summer visitor to coasts of Britain and Ireland from wintering grounds in Antarctic seas. Present from April to September and most numerous in N and W. Breeds in large colonies, mainly on undisturbed shingle and sandy beaches. Easy to see on Farne Islands, Northumberland, where nesting birds can be viewed at very close range. Plunge-dives for fish. Utters harsh *krt-krt-krt* call at intruders near nest.

ROSEATE TERN *Sterna dougallii* Length 38cm

Rarest breeding tern in Britain and threatened throughout world range. Rather similar to Arctic and common terns but adult has red-based black bill, long tail streamers and pinkish flush to breast and underparts in summer. In autumn, birds usually lack long tail streamers. Looks rather short-winged in flight compared to other terns. Present from May to August at breeding colonies, mainly in Ireland, N Wales and Firth of Forth; a few pairs can be seen on Farne Islands each year. Seen on migration around other coasts. Sometimes parasitises other terns returning to colonies with fish. Utters distinctive disyllabic call.

LITTLE TERN *Sterna albifrons* Length 24cm

The smallest tern, easily recognised by size and colour alone. At close range, black-tipped yellow bill, yellow legs and white forehead of adult can be seen. Juvenile has dull legs and bill colour and scaly appearance to back. Present around coasts from April to August. A scarce breeding species with scattered colonies from Solent to E Anglia, also in Scotland, Wales and Ireland. Excluded from many potentially suitable shingle and sandy beaches by human disturbance. Flight buoyant and frequently hovers before plunge-diving into shallow water for small fish and shrimps. Utters raucous *crree-ick* and other calls.

BLACK TERN *Chlidonias niger* Length 24cm

Seen mainly as scarce passage migrant, mostly in May and August; rare and erratic breeder. Single birds usually seen but sometimes occur in small flocks. Adult in breeding plumage has black body, dark grey wings and white stern and tail. From mid-summer onwards, body plumage of adult white except for black on nape and crown. Juvenile similar to winter adult but feathers on back have pale margins and tail and rump grey. Occurs near freshwater, often flooded gravel pits, reservoirs and lakes. Hunts insects over water with buoyant flight. Could turn up almost anywhere in Britain and Ireland but most records S and E England.

Razorbill *Alca torda* Length 41cm

Easiest to see at breeding colonies where present from May to August. In summer, has black head and upperparts and white underparts. Bill large and flattened; at close range, vertical ridges and white lines can be seen. In winter, acquires partly white face; spends most of non-breeding period far out to sea and so this plumage seldom seen on healthy or live birds. Flies on whirring wings. Nests among boulders and in rock crevices on cliffed coasts, mainly in N and W Britain and Ireland. Because pairs are usually more spaced out, never as visibly numerous as puffin or guillemot. Perhaps easiest to see well at seabird colonies on Shetland Isles. Like other auks, suffers badly in oil-spill incidents. Feeds mainly on fish, including sandeels, these carried back to chick in bill.

Guillemot *Uria aalge* Length 42cm

A common auk among larger seabird colonies. Where cliff ledges are suitable, hundreds or even thousands of birds sometimes stand side-by-side. Only visits land during breeding season, from May to August, thereafter being found at sea, sometimes in comparatively inshore waters. In summer, can be recognised by chocolate-brown head and upperparts (darker in northern birds than southern ones) and white underparts; bill dagger-like and straight. Some birds show white 'spectacle' around eye. In winter, has white cheeks marked by dark line from eye. Lays single, pear-shaped egg, sometimes on narrowest of ledges. Tiny youngster flings itself into sea to join parents long before it is fully fledged. Breeding colonies mainly N and W Britain and Ireland. Easy to see at Elegug Stacks, Pembrokeshire, St Abb's Head and on Farne Islands.

Puffin *Fratercula arctica* Length 30cm

Endearing and unmistakable seabird, often allowing close and excellent views at colonies. Has mainly black upperparts but dusky white face and white underparts. Legs orange-red and bill huge and flattened, marked with red, blue and yellow. Winter adult and juvenile have grubby-looking faces and smaller, duller bills. Comes ashore only during breeding season from May to August. Nests in burrows on sloping, grassy cliffs and islands, usually in large colonies. In June and early July, returns to burrows carrying several fish, usually sandeels, in bill. Numbers and range reduced in recent years but still locally common in N and W Britain and Ireland. Spectacular colonies on Hermaness and Noss, both on Shetland, and on Skomer Island, Pembrokeshire. Utters strange, groaning calls.

Little Auk *Alle alle* Length 20cm

The smallest auk in Europe. Does not breed in Britain and Ireland but seen as a winter visitor, in variable numbers, from its high Arctic breeding grounds. Winters mainly far out to sea and so usually observed during or after severe gales or prolonged cold weather. In outline, remarkable for seeming to have almost no neck and for its tiny, stubby bill. In flight, body can appear almost spherical with short wings and whirring wingbeats. Winter plumage birds have black cap, nape and back, and white underparts; white lines on wings and tiny white crescent above eye visible only at extremely close range. Makes long, frequent dives and so can be very difficult to find or relocate.

Black Guillemot *Cepphus grylle* Length 34cm

Distinctive at all times of year. In summer, has mainly sooty black plumage except for striking white patch on wing, conspicuous both at rest and in flight. In winter, upperparts look scaly grey and underparts white; white wing patch still visible but black element of plumage restricted to wingtips and tail. At close range, red legs and orange-red gape can be seen. Usually seen singly or in small groups, often quite close to shore off rocky coasts and jetties. Rather local and scarce, and easy to see only in N Scotland and around Scottish isles. Also occurs on W coast of Britain S to Anglesey and around much of Irish coast. Dives well in search of bottom-dwelling fish such as butterfish. Breeds in fairly small and loose colonies on rocky coasts. Utters high-pitched call.

Feral Pigeon/Rock Dove *Columba livia* Length 33cm
A descendant of native rock dove, the feral pigeon is now widespread and common, mainly in urban areas. Rock dove now local and scarce, confined to rocky coasts mainly in N and W Scotland and parts of Ireland. In some other parts of Britain, feral pigeon has returned to its ancestral haunts on cliffs. True rock dove recognised by blue-grey plumage, two broad, black wingbars, white rump and black-tipped grey tail. A few feral pigeons show ancestral-type plumage but most exhibit wide range of additional or alternative colours and features.

Stock Dove *Columba oenas* Length 33cm
A fairly common bird of farmland and open country with scattered woodland. Found locally throughout Britain and Ireland in suitable habitats as far N as S Scotland. Plumage lacks any prominent features and species recognised by uniform blue-grey upperparts and lack of white rump and white barring on neck; shows two narrow black wingbars on upper surface of inner wing. Feeds in flocks in arable fields, sometimes with woodpigeon. Nests in tree holes and, during breeding season, utters diagnostic and repetitive *ooo-look* call.

Woodpigeon *Columba livia* Length 41cm
A plump, medium-sized pigeon, common and familiar on farmland and increasingly seen in urban areas too. Plumage mainly blue-grey with pinkish maroon on breast. Has distinctive white patch on side of neck and, in flight, shows prominent, transverse white wingbars. When disturbed, flies off with loud clattering of wings. During breeding season sings typical series of *oo-OO-oo, oo-oo* phrases. Builds twig nest on horizontal branches; despite apparent fragility, often still intact, and more visible, in winter. Feeds on seeds and shoots.

Collared Dove *Steptopelia decaocto* Length 32cm
Despite being first recorded in Britain in 1950s, now common and widespread in most parts of Britain and Ireland although seldom far from habitation. A common garden bird in many areas, feeding on lawns and coming to food; often seen in pairs. Has sandy-brown plumage with pinkish flush to head and underparts. Shows dark half-collar on nape. Black wingtips and white outer tail feathers most noticeable in flight. In display, glides on bowed wings. Somewhat irritating song comprises much repeated *oo-oo-oo* phrase. Feeds on seeds and shoots.

Turtle Dove *Streptopelia turtur* Length 27cm
An attractive summer migrant, present from May to August. Rather local and now almost confined to C and S England and Wales; absent from Ireland. Has proportions of collared dove but appreciably smaller. Body plumage mostly blue-grey and pinkish with chestnut-brown on mantle; dark feather centres give a scaly appearance to back. Long, mainly black tail appears wedge-shaped in flight due to white corners. At close range, black and white barring on neck can be seen. Presence often indicated by purring song. Favours arable land with hedges.

Cuckoo *Cuculus canorus* Length 33cm
Males's familiar *cuck-oo* call heard more often than bird itself is seen for six weeks or so after arrival in late April; female utters bubbling call. Secretive but sometimes perches on fenceposts. In low-level flight, recalls sparrowhawk. Male and most females have grey head and upperparts, underparts being white and barred. Juvenile and some females have brown, barred plumage, juvenile with pale nape patch. Widespread in Britain and Ireland. Nest parasite of songbirds.

Nightjar *Caprimulgus europaeus* Length 27cm
Nocturnal habits and cryptic markings make this a difficult bird to see in daytime. Brown, grey and black plumage resembles wood bark. Sits motionless on ground, even when closely approached. At dusk, takes to wing and hawks insects. Looks long-tailed and narrow-winged in flight; male has white on wings and tail. Male utters churring song for hours on end at night. Mainly heaths in S England.

BARN OWL *Tyto alba* Length 34cm

A beautiful owl, sadly decidedly scarce in most areas. Usually seen at dusk or after dark, caught in car headlights, when appears ghostly white; flight leisurely and slow on rounded wings. Only when seen perched can the orange-buff upperparts, speckled with tiny black and white dots, be appreciated; facial disc heart-shaped and white. Feeds mainly on small mammals located by quartering meadows, farmland and roadside verges; seen all too often as a road casualty. Sometimes nests in tree holes but, as name implies, often uses barns and other buildings and readily takes to nesting platform provided for this purpose. Blood-curdling call one of the most frightening sounds of the countryside at night. Widespread in Britain and Ireland although absent from many upland areas.

LONG-EARED OWL *Asio otus* Length 36cm

Active only in complete darkness but, fortunately for birdwatchers, sometimes conspicuous at daytime roosts in winter. Has dark brown upperparts and paler underparts, the whole body, however, being heavily streaked; underwings look very pale when seen in flight. At close range, staring orange eyes and long 'ear' tufts can be seen; these may be raised or lowered, depending on bird's mood. When alarmed, bird sometimes adopts strange, elongated posture. Often nests in dense conifer woodlands. Roosts in similar habitats and occasionally in hawthorn hedges or damp woodland. Widespread in Britain and Ireland throughout year although precise distribution poorly known due to difficulty in locating species. Rather silent but young utter calls like rusty gate hinge.

SHORT-EARED OWL *Asio flammeus* Length 38cm

A large and well-marked owl, often seen feeding in daylight. Favours areas of open grassland for hunting small mammals and birds and often perches on fenceposts providing good views for observers. Plumage mainly buffish brown but heavily marked with dark spots and streaks. Seen head-on, round facial disc, short 'ear' tufts and staring yellow eyes are noticeable. Flight is leisurely and slow on long rounded-tipped wings with pale undersides. Usually quarters ground at low level but displaying birds sometimes rise to considerable heights. Breeds mainly in N Britain and nests on ground among clumps of moorland grass or young plantation conifers. In winter, range extends to much of S Britain where often seen on downland and coastal grassland. Absent from Ireland.

TAWNY OWL *Strix aluco* Length 38cm

The most common and familiar owl in Britain, found mainly in woodlands but also in urban parks and gardens with mature trees. A year-round resident. Plumage colour rather variable but usually a rich chestnut-brown. At close range, streaked underparts look greyish and upperparts are well-marked with dark streaks; eyes black. Caught in car headlights, bird can look deceptively pale. Roosts unobtrusively during day among branches and foliage of trees although sometimes discovered and mobbed by small songbirds. Emerges after dark to hunt mainly for small mammals. Utters sharp *kew-ick* call but best known for male's familiar hooting calls. Most vocal in late winter and early spring when territorial boundaries under dispute. A frequent road casualty.

LITTLE OWL *Athene noctua* Length 22cm

Our smallest owl and also one which is often active in hours of daylight. Introduced from mainland Europe in 19th century but now widespread and fairly common in many parts of Britain to S Scotland; absent from Ireland. Size and small, dumpy appearance usually enough to allow identification. At close range, large, white spots can be seen on most parts of the grey-brown plumage and the staring yellow eyes glare back at observer. Perches on fenceposts and dead branches, often bobbing head and body. Favours farmland and areas of open country; feeds mainly on insects and earthworms. Nests in tree holes and occasionally in cavities in stone walls. Calls include a strange, cat-like *kiu*, uttered repeatedly and agitatedly in early evening.

KINGFISHER *Alcedo atthis* Length 16-17cm
Dazzlingly attractive bird but colours often appear muted when bird seen sitting in shade of vegetation. Has orange-red underparts and mainly blue upperparts; electric blue back seen to best effect when bird observed in low-level flight speeding along river. Invariably seen near water and uses overhanging branches to watch for fish. When feeding opportunity arises, plunges headlong into water, catching prey in bill; fish is swallowed whole, head first, and sometimes stunned by beating head on branch. Nests in holes excavated in river bank. Widespread and fairly common on fish-rich rivers, lakes and flooded gravel pits in much of Ireland and Britain, becoming scarce N of Scottish border. In winter, sometimes seen on sheltered rocky coasts, especially in cold weather.

GREEN WOODPECKER *Picus viridis* Length 32cm
Despite size and bright, colourful plumage, can be surprisingly difficult to see. Usually rather wary and often prefers to hide behind tree trunk rather than show itself. Sometimes seen feeding on lawn or area of short grass when green back, greenish buff underparts and red and black facial markings can be seen; uses long tongue to collect ants. If disturbed, flies off revealing bright yellow-green rump. Spiky tail gives support when climbing tree trunk. Presence often detected by loud and distinctive *yaffling* call. Stout, dagger-like bill used to excavate wood for insect larvae and to create nest hole. Fairly common and widespread resident breeding bird in England and Wales but becomes scarce towards Scottish border; absent from Ireland. Favours open, deciduous woodland.

GREAT SPOTTED WOODPECKER *Dendrocopus major* Length 23cm
The larger and commoner of our two black and white woodpeckers. Upperparts mainly black with white patches on wings and on face. Underparts whitish except for red on vent and undertail. Male (A) only has small red patch on nape but this not always easy to see; juvenile (B) has red cap. In typical undulating flight, birds show rounded, black and white chequered wings with conspicuous white shoulder patches. In spring, male drums loudly on tree trunk to advertise territory. Excavates hole in trunk for nesting and also uses bill to probe for insect larvae in decaying wood; in winter, sometimes visits garden peanut feeders. Favours deciduous woodland and parks. Widespread and often fairly common throughout mainland Britain except the far N; absent from Ireland.

LESSER SPOTTED WOODPECKER *Dendrocopus minor* Length 14-15cm
Small and unobtrusive woodpecker. Has barred, black and white upperparts creating ladder-backed appearance. Underparts whitish and shows black and white markings on head; male has red crown. Although not especially shy, difficult to locate, especially during summer months when feeding among canopy of leaves in treetops. Not very vocal but utters raptor-like call for a few weeks in spring at start of breeding season. Nests in holes excavated in branches. In winter, sometimes mixes with roving mixed flocks of woodland birds. Seldom particularly common but often overlooked. Widespread in England and Wales but common only in S; absent from Scotland and Ireland. Favours areas of deciduous woodland and often found among waterside alders and willows.

WRYNECK *Jynx torquilla* Length 16-17cm
An extraordinary member of the woodpecker family. The intricately marked grey, brown, buff and black plumage looks remarkably like tree bark and affords the bird superb camouflage. Name derived from occasional habit of twisting its neck round. Feeds mainly on the ground, especially on ants. Nests in tree holes. Formerly widespread and quite common in England and Wales but now only very rare and erratic breeder in S. Birds, thought to be Scandinavian in origin, have begun to colonise Scottish Highlands, favouring open, park-like woodland; present there from May to August. Seen elsewhere in Britain as a scarce passage migrant; majority of records on E coast of England in September. Mostly silent but, on breeding grounds, raptor-like piping calls uttered by territorial birds.

SWIFT *Apus apus* Length 16-17cm

A familiar summer visitor to most of Britain and Ireland except N Scotland, present from mid-May to early August. Spends winter months in sub-Saharan Africa. Invariably associated with man-made structures when breeding, nests being placed in loft spaces and church roofs. Otherwise spends its entire life in the air, feeding, sleeping and mating on the wing. Easily recognised in flight by its anchor-shaped outline and all-black plumage; has paler throat but this visible only at very close range. Tail slightly forked but this feature often not visible. Parties of swifts are frequently seen hawking insects above towns and over freshwater; large gape facilitates this method of feeding. Presence often indicated by loud, shrill screaming as birds chase one another through narrow streets or over rooftops. Claws on the tiny feet enable bird to cling to walls. Legs are useless for walking and, once grounded, bird stands very little chance of getting airborne again without assistance.

SWALLOW *Hirundo rustica* Length 19cm

A common summer visitor to most of Britain and Ireland including the northern isles. The arrival of the first birds in early April heralds the start of spring. Most birds depart for their African wintering grounds in August and September but small numbers often linger late into autumn, usually being found near coastal lakes and reservoirs. Recognised in flight by pointed wings and tail with long streamers; shorter in juvenile and female than male. Has blue-black upperparts and white underparts except for brick-red throat and forecrown. Frequently utters its *vit* call in flight and, when perched on overhead wires, male sings a twittering song. Nests under eaves and in barns and sheds, building half cup-shaped nest of mud attached to wall or rafter. Prior to migration in autumn, gathers in sizeable flocks which feed over marshes and lakes and roost in reedbeds in hundreds or thousands. At this time, also seen perched side-by-side on roadside wires along with house martins.

SAND MARTIN *Riparia riparia* Length 12cm

Following a catastrophic decline in numbers, attributed to drought conditions in African wintering grounds, species is beginning to return to its former population level. A widespread and fairly common summer migrant to most parts of Britain and Ireland except most N and W Scottish Isles. Often one of the first spring migrants to arrive, with small numbers appearing in March, and one of the last to leave, October sightings on coasts in S not being uncommon. Recognised in flight by its sandy-brown upperparts and white underparts with brown breast-band; tail short and slightly forked. Juvenile has pale margins to feathers on back giving scaly appearance. Breeds colonially, birds excavating nest burrow in sandy bank of river or pit. Usually seen feeding around lakes and reservoirs, hawking for insects low over the water, sometimes even picking them from the surface. In autumn, often gathers in large numbers over freshwater lakes and lagoons in S, feeding on insects prior to long autumn migration S.

HOUSE MARTIN *Delichon urbica* Length 12-13cm

A familiar and welcome summer visitor to most parts of Britain and Ireland; least numerous in N Scotland. Elsewhere often found breeding in surprisingly urban settings. Most birds present from mid-April to August. Adult easily identified in flight by white underparts and blue-black upperparts showing conspicuous white rump; juvenile similar to adult. As its name suggests, most birds breed on outsides of houses, constructing almost spherical mud nests under eaves and overhangs in loose colonies; in more natural settings, birds sometimes use cave entrances or cliffs as sites for nest construction. Soon after arrival in spring, birds can be seen gathering sticky mud from puddles; this is carried back to nest site and applied, mixed with saliva. Like other hirundines, often seen feeding over freshwater pools and lakes, catching insects in low-level flight. Frequently utters its *prrrit* call in flight. Usually delivers twittering song from overhead wire near to nest site.

SHORE LARK *Eremophila alpestris* Length 16-17cm
Does not breed in Britain but occurs as scarce winter visitor to coast, mainly E England; there favours shingle beaches and coastal grassland. Recognised by yellow and black facial pattern, colours pale in winter but brighter in breeding plumage birds which have short black tufts on head. *Tsee-tsee* flight call.

WOODLARK *Lullula arborea* Length 15cm
Small, short-tailed lark, best known for its wonderful, yodelling song often delivered in flight. Local and rather scarce resident breeding species, found on heaths, young conifer plantations and open woodlands in S England. Has sandy-brown, streaked plumage with chestnut ear coverts, pale supercilium and black and white marking at joint of leading edge to wing. Sometimes perches in trees.

SKYLARK *Alauda arvensis* Length 18cm
Incessant trilling and fluty song, delivered in flight, can be heard over areas of grassland throughout much of Britain and Ireland and in most months. Plumage rather nondescript with streaked, sandy-brown upperparts and paler underparts; has a short crest. Mostly resident but N birds move S in winter, forming flocks.

TREE PIPIT *Anthus trivialis* Length 15cm
Locally common summer visitor to open wooded areas in much of Britain but absent from Ireland. Very similar to meadow pipit but plumage has warm-buff tone, most noticeably on throat and breast. Best identified by song: an accelerating trill ending with thin, drawn out notes uttered as bird 'parachutes' down from tree.

MEADOW PIPIT *Anthus pratensis* Length 14-15cm
Has rather nondescript plumage with streaked brown upperparts and pale streaked underparts. A common resident on open, grassy areas throughout Britain and Ireland, in winter, numbers being boosted by influx of continental birds. Utters *pseet pseet pseet* call and has trilling, descending song which is delivered in flight but starting from ground or fence-post, not tree as in tree pipit.

ROCK PIPIT *Anthus petrosus* Length 16-17cm
Almost always found within sight of sea. Widespread around coasts of Britain and Ireland but generally a winter visitor to those of E and SE England. Larger and darker than other pipits and has greyish, not white, outer tail feathers. Utters single *pseest* call and meadow pipit-like song delivered in flight from outcrop on cliff. Breeds on rocky coasts but in winter also feeds along beach tidelines.

PIED WAGTAIL *Motacilla alba ssp yarellii* Length 18cm
Familiar bird of playing fields, farmland and coastal meadows. Name derives from black and white appearance and habit of pumping tail up and down. Often seen in bounding flight, uttering loud *chissick* call. Female differs from male by dark grey, not black, back. Juvenile has black element of plumage replaced by grey. Common throughout.

GREY WAGTAIL *Motacilla cinerea* Length 18cm
Despite name and bird's blue-grey upperparts, the lemon-yellow underparts are the species' most striking feature. Male has black throat, absent in female and winter male. Invariably associated with water, mostly fast-flowing streams and rivers. Perches on boulders, pumping tail up and down. Utters *chsee-tsit* call in flight. Widespread in Britain and Ireland but absent from much of E England.

YELLOW WAGTAIL *Motacilla flava* Length 16-17cm
Summer visitor to Britain from April to August. Breeds on marshes and water meadows and mainly confined to E and SE England; local elsewhere in England and Wales and absent from Ireland. Male has greenish yellow upperparts and striking yellow underparts; female has duller plumage. Perches on tall plants and barbed wire. Once learned, *tsree-ee* call will identify even distant birds in flight.

WAXWING *Bombycilla garrulus* Length 18cm
Winter visitor in variable numbers from October to March. If berry crop fails in NE Europe, birds forced to move W to Britain in large numbers. Can turn up almost anywhere but most records from SE and E England, often on berry bushes in towns and gardens. Plumage pinkish buff. Has prominent crest, black throat and mask, chestnut undertail and yellow-tipped tail. Wings have white and yellow margins and red, wax-like projections. Trilling call. Starling-like in flight.

RED-BACKED SHRIKE *Lanius collurio* Length 17cm
Almost extinct as breeding species but seen as scarce passage migrant in spring and autumn, mostly around coasts and especially in E Anglia. Striking male has reddish brown back, pale underparts flushed with pink and blue-grey cap with dark mask; tail black with white on sides at base. Female has much less distinct colours and markings, with crescent markings on underparts. Juvenile looks scaly due to crescent markings on plumage. Feeds on insects and small birds.

GREAT GREY SHRIKE *Lanius excubitor* Length 24cm
Scarce and irregular winter visitor mainly to E and S England from October to March. Favours heaths and open country with trees and bushes, these used as lookouts. Almost annual in New Forest and on Surrey heaths. Recalls small bird of prey and, at a distance, looks very white. At close range, grey cap and back, and black mask and wings can be seen. Catches small mammals and birds, sometimes impaling them to assist with dismembering or as larder.

STARLING *Sturnus vulgaris* Length 22cm
Familiar urban bird in Britain and Ireland, also common in rural areas. Outside breeding season, forms huge flocks which roost in trees or on buildings. Numbers boosted in winter by influx of continental birds. Adult's dark plumage is iridescent in summer (A); in winter (B), acquires numerous white spots. Bill yellow in summer but dark in winter. Juvenile buffish brown. Varied song includes clicks and whistles; also imitates other birds and man-made sounds such as car alarms.

GOLDEN ORIOLE *Oriolus oriolus* Length 24cm
Seen as scarce passage migrant around coasts but also established as breeding species in E Anglia, present there from May to August. Male has bright yellow and black plumage and red bill; female duller and with streaked underparts. Despite bright colours, difficult to see among dappled leaves. Often first detected by male's fluty *wee-lo-weeow* song. Favours mature poplar plantations; easiest to see when flying between adjacent groves.

DUNNOCK *Prunella modularis* Length 14-15cm
Common but unobtrusive resident breeding bird in Britain and Ireland, except on Shetland. Adult has chestnut-brown back, blue-grey underparts, streaked flanks and needle-like bill. Feeds quietly, often on ground, searching for insects and seeds. Most noticeable in early spring when male sings lively, warbler-like song from exposed perch. Call a thin *tseer*. Favours woods, hedgerows and gardens.

WREN *Troglodytes troglodytes* Length 9-10cm
A tiny bird, recognised by dumpy proportions, mainly dark brown plumage and habit of frequently cocking tail upright. Generally widespread and common throughout Britain and Ireland although numbers plummet during cold winters. Creeps through low vegetation in search of insects and can look rather mouse-like. Song loud, and warbling, ending in trill and has rattling alarm call.

DIPPER *Cinclus cinclus* Length 18cm
Most likely dumpy, black and white bird seen perched on boulders in fast-flowing stream or river. Bobs body up and down and plunges into water to feed on aquatic insects. Chestnut on breast seen at close range. Flight fast and low over water. Favours upland regions of W and N Britain; more widespread in Ireland.

GRASSHOPPER WARBLER *Locustella naevia* Length 13cm
Widespread but local summer visitor to Britain and Ireland from May to August. Insect-like, almost mechanical song delivered mainly at dawn and dusk and heard far more often than bird itself seen. Olive-brown, streaked plumage and skulking habits combine to make bird difficult to see among favoured habitat, usually scrubby grassland often with abundant rushes. Occasionally sings in open.

REED WARBLER *Acrocephalus scirpaceus* Length 12-13cm
As name suggests, almost always associated with reedbeds. Locally common summer visitor, from May to August, to suitable habitats mainly in C and S England and Wales. Singing birds clamber up reeds or occasionally use bush to deliver grating, chattering song that includes some mimetic elements. Has rather nondescript sandy-brown upperparts, paler underparts and dark legs. Constructs woven, cup-shaped nest attached to upright reed stems. Feeds on insects.

MARSH WARBLER *Acrocephalus palustris* Length 12-13cm
A scarce passage migrant, mostly in spring, and rare breeding species, mainly in counties bordering Severn valley. Very similar to reed warbler and best told by choice of habitat, namely rank waterside vegetation such as stinging nettles, and by song. An amazing mimic whose repertoire includes both other European songsters and species from African wintering grounds. Sometimes sings in the open when paler throat, yellowish buff underparts and pinkish legs can be seen.

SEDGE WARBLER *Acrocephalus schoenobaenus* Length 13cm
A well-marked summer visitor whose harsh, scratchy song is a familiar sound in many wetland habitats. Widespread and fairly common in Britain and Ireland, present from May to August. Has noticeably streaked plumage with sandy-brown upperparts and paler underparts; head shows distinctive dark and pale stripes. Favours marshy scrub and reedbeds but also found along surprisingly small ditches if vegetation cover is sufficiently dense. Utters *chek* alarm call.

CETTI'S WARBLER *Cettia cetti* Length 14cm
An unobtrusive wetland warbler whose loud, explosive song is often the first indication of its presence. A recent addition to British list but now a firmly established resident in many suitable reedbed and marshland locations in S England. Plumage rather nondescript comprising dark brown upperparts and pale greyish buff underparts; rounded tail adds to impression of outsized wren. Song *chee-chippi-chippi-chippi* heard in spring.

WILLOW WARBLER *Phylloscopus trochilus* Length 11cm
Widespread and common summer visitor throughout Britain and Ireland, present from April to September. Adult has olive-yellow upperparts and pale, yellowish white underparts; juvenile has brighter, more yellow plumage. Flesh-coloured legs distinguish silent birds from similar chiffchaff. Song comprises a tinkling, descending phrase, endlessly repeated by newly-arrived birds. Favours birch woodland but can be found in almost any wooded or partly-wooded habitat.

CHIFFCHAFF *Phylloscopus collybita* Length 11cm
Similar to willow warbler and distinguished by its song (which gives it its name), dark legs and drabber plumage. Widespread summer visitor to Britain and Ireland; early birds arrive in March. Most birds migrate S in autumn but small numbers overwinter in S England. Found in woods and scrub. Call *hooeet*, similar to willow warbler.

WOOD WARBLER *Phylloscopus sibilatrix* Length 12-13cm
Larger than superficially similar chiffchaff or willow warbler and with brighter plumage comprising olive-green upperparts, yellow throat and white underparts. Distinctive song, likened to coin spinning on a plate, starts with ringing notes which accelerates into silvery trill. Favours mature woodlands, often beech, with open understorey. Widespread in Great Britain but absent from Ireland.

GOLDCREST *Regulus regulus* Length 9cm
Our smallest bird, common in suitable habitats throughout most of mainland Britain and Ireland. Has leaf warbler appearance with needle-like bill, large dark eyes and proportionately large head with seemingly short neck. Upperparts greenish with two pale wingbars and underparts yellowish buff. Adult male has black-bordered orange crown, that of the female being yellow; juvenile lacks adult's crown markings. During breeding season, found in areas of mixed woodland, conifer forests and sometimes in gardens with conifer hedges. In winter, becomes more widespread and then seen in deciduous woodland as well.

DARTFORD WARBLER *Sylvia undata* Length 12-13cm
A resident warbler, in breeding season confined to heathland in S England, mainly in Surrey, Hampshire (particularly New Forest) and Dorset; in winter, some birds move to scrub on S coast. Usually seen as a distant, dark bird perched on top of gorse bush with small body and long tail cocked up at an angle. In good light, male shows blue-grey upperparts, reddish underparts and white belly; female similar but plumage duller. Reddish eyering and leg colour seen only at close range. Male sings scratchy song. Rather shy, often detected by *tchrr-tche* call. Locally common but decimated in cold winters.

WHITETHROAT *Sylvia communis* Length 14cm
Locally common summer visitor to many parts of mainland Britain and Ireland, present from May to September. A characteristic bird of scrub, overgrown hedgerows and heaths, usually especially numerous and noticeable on sunny gorse- and bramble-covered coastal cliffs. Male often perches on exposed perch revealing white throat, blue-grey crown, rufous back and wings, and pale underparts with buffish tone on breast. Female drabber. Scratchy song often delivered in dancing song flight. Alarm call a harsh *chek*. Numbers recovering following decline in 1960s due to drought in African wintering quarters.

LESSER WHITETHROAT *Sylvia curruca* Length 13-14cm
Superficially similar to whitethroat but distinguished by plumage, song and choice of habitat. Summer visitor, mainly to C and S Britain, from May to September and only locally common; absent from Ireland. Good view reveals blue-grey crown, dark mask, grey-brown, not rufous, back and wings and white throat and underparts. Favours mature hedgerows and woodland with dense undergrowth from cover of which male sings characteristic song comprising a tuneless rattle, sung on one note. Has rather retiring habits and utters harsh *chek* call when alarmed. Feeds mainly on insects but also on berries in early autumn.

GARDEN WARBLER *Sylvia borin* Length 14cm
A rather nondescript warbler to look at with uniform grey-brown upperparts and paler, buffish underparts. At times, can resemble a blackcap without the cap colour; has also been likened to a robin without the red breast. Lack of distinguishing plumage features is more than made up for by song which is one of the most attractive of all British birds; can be confused with blackcap's song but is even more musical. A summer visitor to Britain from May to August. Common only in S and C England and Wales; scarce and local in S Scotland and Ireland. Favours wooded areas with dense undergrowth and mature gardens.

BLACKCAP *Sylvia atricapilla* Length 14cm
Overwinters in S England in very small numbers but seen mainly as a summer visitor, present from April to September. Then widespread in Britain and Ireland and common in suitable habitats except in N. Breeds in deciduous woodland with dense undergrowth and in areas of scrub and bushes. Male has grey-brown upperparts, paler underparts and distinctive black cap; female is similar but has chestnut-brown cap. Male's song attractive and musical with chattering and fluty elements; similar to song of garden warbler but usually shorter and without that species' blackbird-like tone to elements in its repertoire.

SPOTTED FLYCATCHER *Muscicapa striata* Length 14cm
Fairly common summer visitor to mainland Britain and Ireland, present from May to August. Adult has rather undistinguished plumage with grey-brown upperparts, streaked on crown, and paler underparts, heavily streaked on breast; juvenile similar but with spotted breast. Easily identified by upright posture and habit of using regular perch from which to make insect-catching aerial sorties. Often breeds around habitation.

PIED FLYCATCHER *Ficedula hypoleuca* Length 13cm
Distinctive male (A) is aptly named with black upperparts, white underparts and bold white band on otherwise black wing. Female (B) has black elements of male's plumage replaced by brown. Locally common summer visitor from May to August. Favours open oakwoods. Restricted mainly to SW and NW England, Wales and S Scotland; absent from Ireland. Breeds in tree holes and readily takes to hole-fronted nestboxes. Forages and fly-catches in tree canopy. Male has sweet, ringing song.

STONECHAT *Saxicola torquata* Length 12-13cm
Small, distinctive resident of heaths and commons, often numerous on gorse- and bramble-covered slopes near coasts. In breeding season, male (A) is handsome with black head, white on side of neck, dark back, reddish orange breast and pale underparts. Female (B) and winter male have duller plumage. Often perches openly, flicking tail and announcing presence with harsh *tchak* call, like two pebbles being knocked together. Whitethroat-like song sometimes delivered in flight.

WHINCHAT *Saxicola rubetra* Length 12-13cm
Superficially similar to stonechat but male has brown, streaked upperparts and conspicuous pale stripe above eye. Female has similar stripe but plumage otherwise similar to that of female stonechat. A summer visitor, present from May to September. Widespread but local. Common only in W and S Scotland and Wales; very scarce in Ireland and SE England. Favours rank grassland and scrubby slopes. Perches on low wires and bushes. Has *tik tik* call and chattering song.

WHEATEAR *Oenanthe oenanthe* Length 14-15cm
Summer visitor present from March to September. Breeds on coastal grassland, moors and heaths, common only in W and N; very local in E and SE England. Seen on migration around coasts generally. Male (A) has blue-grey crown and back, black mask and wings, and pale underparts with orange-buff wash on breast. Female (B) has mainly sandy-brown plumage. Both sexes show white rump in flight. Perches low and nests in burrow. *Chak* alarm call like pebbles being knocked together.

REDSTART *Phoenicurus phoenicurus* Length 14cm
Male is particularly attractive bird with black and grey on head and back, and red breast. Female has grey-brown upperparts and orange wash to pale underparts; both sexes have striking red tail, continually pumped up and down. A summer visitor to Great Britain, common only in W and N and absent from Ireland; present from April to September. Favours open woodland and wooded heaths, and nests in tree holes. Has ticking alarm call and tuneful, melancholy song.

BLACK REDSTART *Phoenicurus ochrurus* Length 14cm
Striking red tail in all plumages. Very scarce breeder when male's plumage mainly black and slate-grey. More often seen as passage migrant or winter visitor when male and female both grey-brown. Breeding records mainly from urban locations in S England. In winter, found on coasts of S and W England and Ireland.

ROBIN *Erithacus rubecula* Length 14cm
Adult (A) is familiar red-breasted bird of gardens and woodland. Brown juvenile (B) has streaked upperparts and underparts with crescent markings. Widespread resident throughout mainland Britain and Ireland. Alarm call a sharp *tic*. Male sings variation of melancholy song at most times of year. Highly territorial.

NIGHTINGALE *Luscinia megarhynchos* Length 16-17cm
Summer visitor to S and SE England, present from mid-April to August. Heard more easily than bird itself is seen. Famed for its powerful, musical song, which is delivered both by day and at night and is audible over long range. Has rich brown upperparts which contrast with chestnut-red lower back and tail; underparts pale grey-buff. Favours woodland with dense scrub layer and mature coppiced hazel; several neighbouring pairs usually found in suitable habitats.

BLACKBIRD *Turdus merula* Length 25cm
Familiar garden bird in much of Britain and Ireland but also found in woodland, farmland and on moors. Mostly resident but N European birds add to numbers in winter. Male (A) easily identified by thrush-like appearance and all-black plumage; yellow eyering and bill usually conspicuous. Female (B) and juvenile have brown plumages. Harsh *tchak* alarm calls often heard at dusk or if prowling cat located. Male is excellent songster. Feeds on worms, insects, fruit and berries.

RING OUZEL *Turdus torquatus* Length 24cm
A summer visitor to upland districts of N and W Britain from late March to September; scarce and local in Ireland. Superficially similar to blackbird but black male has striking white crescent on breast; at close range, pale margins to feathers can be seen along with pale patch on wing. Female has brown plumage, the feathers with conspicuous pale margins giving scaly appearance; pale crescent on breast less striking than on male. Alert and wary, found on slopes with broken ground and rocky outcrops. Has loud, fluty song and *tuk* alarm call.

FIELDFARE *Turdus pilaris* Length 25-26cm
A large thrush, seen mainly as a winter visitor from October to March, although a few pairs breed in Britain. Seen in large, flighty flocks, often mixed with redwings. Recognised by grey head, chestnut back and pale, spotted underparts with yellow wash on breast; pale grey rump and white underwings noticeable in flight. Occurs mainly on farmland. Could turn up almost anywhere in Britain and Ireland. Chattering calls often heard, sometimes from night-migrating flocks.

REDWING *Turdus iliacus* Length 21cm
A small but attractive thrush with grey-brown upperparts, prominent white stripe above eye, neatly spotted pale underparts and orange-red flush on flanks and underwings. Seen mainly as a winter visitor to almost all parts of Britain and Ireland from October to April; rare breeder in Scottish Highlands. Flocks are nomadic and numbers vary from year to year but usually a very common winter bird. Feeds on farmland and in woodland where it searches for worms and invertebrates. An opportunistic feeder, particularly in cold weather, and will feast on fallen apples and berries. Has high-pitched *tseerp* call.

SONG THRUSH *Turdus philomelos* Length 23cm
Familiar bird of gardens and grassland but numbers have declined markedly in recent years. Easily told from mistle thrush by smaller size, more dainty appearance and orange-red underwing. Upperparts warm brown with hint of orange-buff wingbar and pale underparts well marked with dark spots and with buff flush to breast. Song loud and musical, phrases repeated two or three times; often sung at dusk. Flight call a thin *tik*. Widespread resident in Britain and Ireland.

MISTLE THRUSH *Turdus viscivorus* Length 27cm
Distinctly larger than song thrush and with white, not orange-buff, underwings. Upperparts grey-brown with suggestion of white wingbar. Pale underparts with large, dark spots; in flight, white tips to outer tail feather noticeable. Juvenile has white, teardrop-shaped spots on back. Widespread and fairly common in Britain and Ireland but never numerous. In winter, individual birds often guard their own berry-bearing bush or tree. Has loud, rattling alarm call. Loud song contains brief phrases and long pauses; often sung in rain or dull weather.

BLUE TIT *Parus caeruleus* Length 11-12cm
Familiar garden resident in most of mainland Britain and Ireland, often coming to bird feeders in winter months; a common woodland species as well. Has elements of blue, green and yellow in its plumage with striking dark markings on head; juvenile similar to adult but lacking blue in plumage. Utters familiar, chattering *tserr err err err* call and has whistling song. Nests in tree holes and readily takes to hole-fronted nestboxes. In summer, feeds mainly on insects.

GREAT TIT *Parus major* Length 14cm
Common woodland and garden species, appreciably larger than blue tit alongside which it is often seen at bird feeders. Has bold black and white markings on head and black bib forming line running down chest, broader in male than female. Underparts otherwise yellow and upperparts mainly greenish. Juvenile has sombre plumage with no white on head. Song is extremely variable but a striking *teecha teecha teecha* rendered by most males. Feeds mainly on insects in summer months.

COAL TIT *Parus ater* Length 11-12cm
A small resident bird which can sometimes look rather warbler-like. Widespread and fairly common throughout most of mainland Britain and Ireland. Has black and white markings on head with conspicuous white patch on nape. Back and wings slate-grey with two white wingbars, and underparts pale pinkish buff. Found in both coniferous and deciduous woodland and will visit garden bird feeders in winter. Song *teecha teecha teecha*, higher-pitched and weaker than great tit.

MARSH TIT *Parus palustris* Length 11-12cm
Recognised by black cap and bib, brown upperparts and whitish underparts. Very similar to willow tit and best told by loud *pitchoo* call. At close range, smaller bib and glossier cap of marsh tit can be seen. A fairly common resident, restricted mainly to England and Wales; scarce in S Scotland but absent from Ireland. Found in deciduous and mixed woodlands and will sometimes visit garden feeders in winter. Sometimes feeds on ground in winter. Nests in tree holes.

WILLOW TIT *Parus montanus* Length 11-12cm
Has a similar distribution to marsh tit although range extends further N into Scotland. Precise distribution seldom overlaps with marsh tit, willow tit preferring more swampy woodland. Very similar in appearance to marsh tit and best told by nasal *tchay tchay tchay* call. Pale patch on wing not always distinguishable and dull black cap and larger bib only really reliable when both species present side-by-side. Fairly common but local resident.

CRESTED TIT *Parus cristatus* Length 11-12cm
Resident, restricted to native pinewoods and mature conifer plantations in Scottish Highlands but there not uncommon. Easily told by conspicuous black and white crest. Has black lines on otherwise white face; back brown and underparts pale. Usually feeds quite high in trees and presence often indicated by trilling call. Nests in holes in decaying tree stumps and feeds mainly on insects and invertebrates in summer months, supplemented by seeds at other times.

LONG-TAILED TIT *Aegithalos caudatus* Length 14cm
Charming resident of woods, heaths and hedgerows, feeding flocks resembling animated feather dusters. Plumage can look black and white but at close range has pinkish wash to underparts and pinkish buff on back. Has tiny, stubby bill, long tail and almost spherical body. Widespread in mainland Britain and Ireland.

BEARDED TIT *Panurus biarmicus* Length 16-17cm
Very local resident of large reedbeds in S and E England, particularly E Anglia. Has long tail and mainly sandy-brown plumage; male has blue-grey head and conspicuous black 'moustaches'. Usually seen in small groups, clambering up reeds or flying, one after the other. Utters distinctive pinging calls.

NUTHATCH *Sitta europaea* Length 14cm
Recognised by rounded, short-tailed appearance and habit of descending tree trunks head-downwards, a trait unique in Britain to this species. Has blue-grey upperparts, black eyestripe, white cheeks and orange-buff underparts. Chisel-like bill used to prise insects from tree bark and to hammer open acorns wedged in bark crevices. A woodland species, locally common in Wales and S and C England; scarce further N and absent from Ireland. Has falcon-like call. Nests in tree holes, often plastering entrance with mud to reduce diameter.

TREECREEPER *Certhia familiaris* Length 12-13cm
A widespread woodland resident in mainland Britain and Ireland. Unobtrusive and easily overlooked as it creeps up tree trunks; can look rather mouse-like. Has streaked brown upperparts, pale underparts and needle-like, downcurved bill. Spiky tail used as support when climbing. Has high-pitched *tseert* call. Typically feeds by spiralling round and up tree then dropping down to base of adjacent trunk to repeat process. Feeds on invertebrates, mainly insects, prised from bark crevices with bill. Often nests under flaps of peeling dead bark.

CORN BUNTING *Miliaria calandra* Length 18cm
A large but rather nondescript bunting with streaked, brown plumage and large but stubby bill. Best identified by its distinctive, jingling song, often likened to jangling keys and sung from fencepost or overhead wire. Also characteristically dangles legs in flight. Widespread but distinctly local, being found almost exclusively in areas of arable farmland. Consequently absent from large parts of W and N Britain and very scarce in Ireland. Forms often sizeable flocks in winter, sometimes mixing with other buntings and finches.

YELLOWHAMMER *Emberiza citrinella* Length 16-17cm
A familiar bird of farmland and open country throughout most of mainland Britain and Ireland. Male is particularly striking with mainly bright yellow head and underparts, and chestnut back and wings; female has more subdued colours and juvenile is sandy-brown and streaked. In spring, male sings well-known song, often rendered *a little bit of bread and no cheese*; also utters a rasping call. Feeds on insects and seeds, often on ground. In winter, forms flocks, sometimes with other species, and feeds in stubble fields or at grain spills.

CIRL BUNTING *Emberiza cirlus* Length 16-17cm
Although once fairly widespread, now more or less restricted to S Devon coast and sunny slopes inland. Superficially yellowhammer-like but male easily told by black throat and eyestripe, and olive-grey nape and breast-band. Female has paler yellow throat than female yellowhammer but best identified by olive-grey, not chestnut, rump or by association with male. In spring, male delivers tuneless, rattling song, similar to that of lesser whitethroat. Outside breeding season, forms small, single species flocks which feed in coastal stubble fields.

REED BUNTING *Emberiza schoeniclus* Length 15cm
Characteristic of wetland habitats but also in drier areas of farmland too. In breeding season, male has head black except for white moustachial stripes; underparts pale and upperparts chestnut-brown. Male in winter has less distinct black head; female has striking dark moustachial stripes at all times. In flight, all birds show conspicuous white outer tail feathers. Has chinking song.

SNOW BUNTING *Plectrophenax nivalis* Length 16-17cm
Very rare breeder in Scottish Highlands but also scarce passage migrant to coastal districts and local winter visitor, mainly to E coast of Britain and mountains in Scotland. Breeding male has unmistakable black and white plumage. In winter, all birds have variable amounts of buffish orange on breast and face, sandy-brown back and white underparts. Often unobtrusive when feeding on ground but in flight, black and white wings are conspicuous. Tinkling flight call.

CHAFFINCH *Fringilla coelebs* Length 15cm
One of the commonest and most widespread birds in Britain and Ireland, favouring a wide variety of habitats including gardens, parks and woodland; in winter, numbers of residents boosted by influx of N European birds. Colourful male (A) has reddish pink face and underparts, blue crown and chestnut back; female (B) is more uniformly buffish brown but, like male, has prominent white shoulder patch and white wingbar. Song comprises a descending trill with a characteristic final flourish. Call a distinct *pink pink*. Feeds mainly on insects during summer months but seeds taken in winter when often gather into sizeable flocks.

BRAMBLING *Fringilla montifringilla* Length 14-15cm
Very rare and occasional breeder in Scotland but common along E coast as autumn passage migrant and widespread and locally common as winter visitor to most parts of Britain and Ireland. In winter plumage, superficially similar to chaffinch but always shows orange-buff shoulder patch and on breast and flanks; white rump seen in flight. Female and immature birds have buffish grey face with characteristic dark, parallel lines down nape. Male has dark brown head which in breeding plumage becomes black. Calls including harsh *eeerp*. Seen in flocks, sometimes with chaffinches, and especially fond of fallen beech mast.

GOLDFINCH *Carduelis carduelis* Length 12cm
One of our most colourful birds and the only one with bright yellow wingbars and a white rump. Adult has red and white on face, black cap extending down sides of neck, buffish back, and white underparts with buff flanks. Juvenile has brown, streaked plumage but yellow wingbars as in adult. Common and widespread resident in Britain and Ireland except N Scotland. Favours wasteground and meadows where narrow, pointed bill is used to feed on seeds of thistles and teasels in particular. Usually seen in small flocks which take to the wing with tinkling flight calls. Male's song is twittering but contains call-like elements.

SISKIN *Carduelis spinus* Length 12cm
Charming little finch. Numerous and widespread during the winter months in Britain and Ireland, numbers being boosted by influx of continental birds. In breeding season, common in parts of Scotland but local elsewhere in Britain and Ireland, particularly so in S. Male in breeding plumage has striking yellow and green plumage with black bib and forehead. Female and winter male have more subdued colours but always show two yellow wingbars and yellow rump in flight. Breeds mainly in conifer forests but, in winter, forms flocks which feed mainly on cones of alder and birch. Often mixes with redpolls in feeding flocks.

GREENFINCH *Carduelis chloris* Length 14-15cm
Widespread throughout most of mainland Britain and Ireland although scarce N of C Scotland. A familiar bird of gardens, parks and farmland but absent from many wooded and upland areas with its range. In full breeding plumage, male is very bright yellow-green but for most of year colours are duller; female has grey-green plumage and juvenile is streaked. All birds show yellow wing patches and have yellow rumps and sides to tail. Bill pinkish and conical, used for feeding on seeds. Outside breeding season, forms flocks which feed on stubble fields and grain spills. Winter visitor to garden bird feeders. Has wheezy *weeeish* call.

BULLFINCH *Pyrrhula pyrrhula* Length 14-16cm
An attractive but unobtrusive resident throughout much of mainland Britain and Ireland. Often encountered in pairs. Easy to overlook in the dense cover it favours until its soft but distinctive, piping call is learnt. Male has rosy-pink face and breast, the colour unlike that of any other British bird; also shows black cap and blue-grey back. Female similar but with duller colours. Both sexes have characteristic white rump, seen as bird flies away. Found in woodland scrub, hedgerows and mature gardens. Uses stubby bill to feed on insects, seeds and berries; in spring, visits orchards to eat flower buds of fruit trees.

Hawfinch *Coccothraustes coccothraustes* Length 18cm

A blue-riband bird for many observers because of impressive appearance, local distribution and retiring nature. A very local resident with a scattered distribution from S England to S Scotland; absent from Ireland. Commonest in SE England in woodland with mature hornbeam or parks with flowering cherry; the hard-cased seeds of both trees are important sources of food. Distinctive even in silhouette because of large size (for a finch) and proportionately massive, conical bill. Has pinkish buff, orange-buff and chestnut elements to plumage, colours of male being brighter than those of female. Large white wingbar obvious in undulating flight. Commonest call a sharp, robin-like *tik*.

Redpoll *Carduelis flammea* Length 13-15cm

A small finch with rather variable plumage. Most birds can be recognised by yellowish conical bill, black bib and red patch on forecrown; latter feature absent in some juvenile birds. Has streaked, grey-brown upperparts and pale underparts, streaked on flanks; in breeding season, male has pinkish flush to breast. As a breeding species, occurs locally throughout much of Britain and Ireland but distinctly scarce in S. In winter, much more numerous and widespread, especially in S thanks to influx of birds from N Europe. Breeds in open woodland but winter flocks mostly in alder and birch, often with siskins.

Linnet *Carduelis cannabina* Length 13-14cm

Common and widespread resident throughout much of lowland Britain and Ireland although scarce or absent from parts of N and W Scotland. Male has grey head and chestnut back; in breeding season, acquires rosy-pink patch on forecrown and on breast but this feature absent in winter months when male is rather similar to streaked, grey-brown female. Breeds on gorse- or bramble-covered slopes, heaths and scrubby grassland. Male often perches prominently to deliver his twittering, warbling song. Has greenfinch-like flight call. Forms small flocks in winter.

Common Crossbill *Loxia recurvirostra* Length 16-17cm

Has evolved crossed-tipped mandibles to extract seeds from conifer cones, and in particular those of spruces; seldom seen away from mature specimens of these trees. Bizarre bill structure only visible, however, at close range. Male has mainly red plumage, that of female being yellowish green. Often nests as early as February or March and thereafter seen as roving, single-species flocks. Feeds high in trees but visits woodland pools to drink. Flight call a sharp *kip kip*. Presence of feeding birds often indicated by sound of falling cones. Replaced in native pinewoods of Scottish Highlands by very similar Scottish crossbill.

House Sparrow *Passer domesticus* Length 14-15cm

Widespread in Britain and Ireland. Because of affinity for human habitation and farmyards, however, only locally common, being absent from large tracts of land. Male has grey crown, cheeks and rump, chestnut-brown nape, back and wings, pale underparts and black throat. Female rather nondescript with streaked buff and grey-brown plumage. Small groups of birds often encountered sitting on roofs, uttering familiar sparrow chirps. Frequently dust-bathes. Usually nests in roof spaces or holes in walls but occasionally builds large and untidy nest in bush. Where fed in urban parks, can become remarkably tame, taking food from hand.

Tree Sparrow *Passer montanus* Length 14cm

Widespread distribution in mainland Britain and Ireland but decidedly scarce and local. Occasionally found on outskirts of villages but more usually associated with untidy arable farms, taking advantage of frequent grain spills along with buntings and finches. Sexes similar and easily distinguished from house sparrow by chestnut cap and nape, and black patch on otherwise white cheeks; plumage otherwise streaked brown on back with pale underparts. Juvenile lacks black cheek patch. Utters house sparrow-like chirps but also a sharp *tik tik* in flight. Forms flocks in winter months and sometimes feeds in stubble fields.

JAY *Garrulus glandarius* Length 34cm
Colourful bird but wary nature ensures that colours seldom seen to best effect. Woodland resident, widespread and common in most of England and Wales but scarce and local in Ireland and Scotland. Pinkish buff body plumage except for white undertail and rump, latter most conspicuous as bird flies away and emphasised by black tail. Wings have black and white pattern and chequerboard patch of blue, black and white. Utters loud, raucous *kraah* call. Buries acorns in autumn.

MAGPIE *Pica pica* Length 46cm
Familiar and unmistakable black and white bird. In good light, greenish blue sheen can be seen on rounded wings and long tail. Widespread and often common in much of Britain and Ireland but, in Scotland, absent from most upland areas. Builds large and untidy twig nest in bushes. Often seen in small groups outside breeding season, frequently uttering loud, rattling alarm call. An opportunistic feeder, taking insects, fruit, animal road kills, young birds and eggs.

CHOUGH *Pyrrhocorax pyrrhocorax* Length 40cm
A jackdaw-sized bird with glossy, all-dark plumage and bright red legs and long, down-curved bill. Almost exclusively coastal, favouring dry, grassy slopes in summer but sometimes visiting beaches in winter. A local and rather scarce species, found mainly in W Wales, Islay and Ireland. Often nests in sea caves. Outside breeding season, forms flocks. Recognised in flight by broad, 'fingered' wingtips and frequently uttered *chyah* call. Probes ground for insects.

JACKDAW *Corvus monedula* Length 33cm
The most familiar small crow. Widespread and common in much of Britain and Ireland, least so in NW Scotland. Equally at home on farmland or sea cliffs and often encountered in large flocks; aerobatic in flight, frequently uttering sharp *chack* calls. Has mainly smoky-grey plumage; at close range, pale eye and grey nape are obvious. Walks with characteristic swagger. Nests in tree holes and rock crevices, but also in buildings. Omnivorous, opportunistic diet.

RAVEN *Corvus corax* Length 64cm
Appreciably larger than carrion crow, with massive bill and shaggy, ruffled throat; plumage has an oily sheen in good light. Often seen in flight; distant bird bears a passing resemblance to buzzard but recognised by long, thick neck and wedge-shaped tail. Incredibly aerobatic, tumbling and rolling in mid-air. Utters loud, deep *cronk* call. A bird mainly of remote, untamed parts of N and W Britain and Ireland, common on rocky coasts.

CARRION CROW *Corvus corone corone* Length 47cm
Recognised by all-black, glossy plumage and stout bill; far less gregarious than superficially similar rook and lacking that species' pale, bare face. Widespread and often common in most of England, Wales and E Scotland; range overlaps only slightly with closely related subspecies, hooded crow. Found on farmland, moorland and on coasts. Utters harsh, croaking call. An opportunistic feeder, taking carrion, insects, young birds and eggs. Untidy twig nest built in tree.

HOODED CROW *Corvus corone cornix* Length 47cm
Distinguished from closely related carrion crow by grey and black, not all-dark plumage. Appearance and habits otherwise identical to carrion crow. Occurs mainly in NW Scotland, Isle of Man and Ireland. Where range overlaps with carrion crow, subspecies sometimes mix and intermediate birds occur.

ROOK *Corvus frugilegus* Length 46cm
A familiar bird of farmland throughout most of lowland, mainland Britain and Ireland. Often seen in large flocks feeding in fields or at colonial tree nest sites where noisy and active from early March to May. Glossy black plumage. Adult has bare, white facial patch at base of long bill; absent in immatures.

COMMON LIZARD *Lacerta vivipara* Length 10-15cm
Often seen sunbathing on sunny banks, sometimes several together. Colours and markings rather variable, but usually brown or grey-brown with patterns of dark blotches along length; throat and belly often whitish or reddish. Widespread throughout much of Britain and Ireland, favouring areas of dry, short grassland, especially on coastal cliffs, as well as heaths, moors and even warm embankments. Female produces eggs internally but young are born as tiny lizards, mainly during summer months. At all ages, feeds on invertebrates, especially insects. Hibernates from October to March. Can shed tail to fool predators.

SAND LIZARD *Lacerta agilis* Length 15-20cm
Bulkier and proportionately larger-headed than common lizard. Local and endangered species, confined to dry, sandy heaths in Dorset, S Hampshire (New Forest) and N Hampshire-Surrey borders; also sand dunes in S Lancashire. On heaths, favours mature, woody clumps of ling. Female is sandy-brown with rows of dark blotches along length but male has green flanks, brightest in breeding season. Often sunbathes on patches of bare sand. Hibernates from October to April. Feeds mainly on invertebrates such as insects and spiders. Female lays eggs in holes excavated in dry, sandy soil. Young seen from June to August.

SLOW WORM *Anguis fragilis* Length 30-50cm
Superficially snake-like but in fact a legless lizard. Head and neck barely distinguishable from rest of uniform-diameter body. Tail-end rather blunt-ended, sometimes very much so when tail itself has been shed to distract would-be predator. Most individuals are shiny golden-buff but a few, notably some coastal or island populations, are blue-spotted. Widespread in Great Britain but absent from Ireland. Favours hedgerows, grassland, heaths and woodland borders; also in rural gardens but easily caught and killed by domestic cats. Hibernates from October to March. Feeds on invertebrates such as slugs and insects.

GRASS SNAKE *Natrix natrix* Length 70-150cm
Attractively marked snake, often found near water. Widespread in England and Wales but has become decidedly scarce in recent years. Has greenish body with dark blotches along flanks. Best distinguishing features are yellow neck collar and round pupil. Found near ponds and canals, also in grassland and on heaths. Swims well and feeds on variety of prey including frogs, tadpoles and fish, sometimes even nesting birds; non-venomous. Emits foul-smelling odour if handled. Eggs laid in mounds of decaying waterside vegetation or in compost heaps; young hatch in summer months. Hibernates from October to March.

ADDER *Vipera berus* Length 50-60cm
Comparatively squat proportions and grey-brown body with diagnostic zigzag markings down back make identification easy in most individuals; reddish brown or all-black specimens are sometimes seen. Poisonous, but venom of little danger to healthy adult human; used to lethal effect, however, on small mammals, nestlings and lizards. Widespread but local in Great Britain but absent from Ireland. Found on heaths and moors and along woodland rides; sometimes in surprisingly wet areas in summer months. Hibernates from October to March. When newly emerged in spring, often sunbathes in groups. Eye has vertical pupil.

SMOOTH SNAKE *Coronella austriaca* Length 55-75cm
A rare and endangered species, confined to dry, sandy heaths in Dorset, S Hampshire (New Forest) and N Hampshire-Surrey border. Often found alongside sand lizard, upon which it preys; also feeds on slow worms, insects and nestlings, subduing and sometimes killing prey by coil constriction. Superficially similar to adder but distinguished by more slender appearance, round pupil and incomplete dark pattern down back. Ground colour of body usually grey-brown. Sunbathes on patches of bare, sandy soil sheltered by surrounding vegetation; will rest under corrugated iron to warm up. Hibernates from October to April.

SMOOTH NEWT *Triturus vulgaris* Length 8-10cm
Male is particularly well-marked and attractive. In breeding season, shows spotted flanks, undulating crest along back, and orange belly and pale throat with conspicuous spots. Brown female lacks crest and is similar to female palmate newt; distinguished by spotted, not unspotted, throat. Widespread and common across most of mainland Britain; the only newt species in Ireland but there rather scarce. Found in ponds, ditches and lakes from March to September; thereafter, leaves water and hibernates during winter months under fallen logs.

PALMATE NEWT *Triturus helvetica* Length 9cm
Outside breeding season, can be confused with smooth newt, and then best distinguished by unspotted throat. Breeding male has webbed hind feet and deep, coloured tail ending in thread-like filament; belly yellowish. Female similar to female smooth newt. Widespread in mainland Great Britain. Found in lakes, ponds and canals; often occurs in fairly acid pools on upland moors or near to coast. Spends much of year in water but hibernates on land between November and March, usually under logs or stones. Feeds on invertebrates but also frog tadpoles.

GREAT CRESTED NEWT *Triturus cristatus* Length 14cm
Our largest newt and also the most local; the legal protection it is afforded reflects its uncommon status. Widespread but extremely local in mainland Britain but absent from Ireland. Favours large, weedy ponds and small lakes; sometimes in dew ponds a considerable distance from other water bodies. Breeding male is striking with ragged crest down back, smoky-grey, dark-spotted flanks and orange, black-spotted belly. Female lacks crest but is otherwise similar. Like other newts, spawns in spring but often remains in water throughout year.

COMMON FROG *Rana temporaria* Length 6-9cm
Common and widespread native to mainland Great Britain but introduced to Ireland where distribution rather patchy. Colour variable but usually greenish brown or olive-buff with darker blotches; shows dark 'mask'. Male has hard swelling on first finger, used to grasp female during mating; throat often bluish in breeding season. Spawning takes place in December or January in West Country but not until March or April in N or upland districts. Mating pairs and masses of frogspawn are a common sight in most ponds. Males utter faint croaking song.

MARSH FROG *Rana ridibunda* Length 6-10cm
Introduced to Romney Marshes, Kent, in 1935 and now well established there and on Lewes Brooks, Sussex. Similar to common frog but usually distinctly greenish; head appears more pointed than common frog and lacks the dark 'mask' seen in that species. Spends most of year in water, favouring ditches and drainage channels. In spring, males are noisy, singing with inflated vocal sacs.

COMMON TOAD *Bufo bufo* Length 8-12cm
Easily told from common frog by warty, olive-brown skin and inclination to walk rather than hop. Visits ponds and lakes to breed in spring but at other times often found well away from water, sometimes in surprisingly dry areas. Common and widespread throughout mainland Britain but absent from Ireland. Often spawns in same ponds as common frog but usually active a few weeks after that species. Produces long strings of double-stranded spawn. On land, feeds on wide range of invertebrates including insects and slugs. Hibernates under logs and stones.

NATTERJACK TOAD *Bufo calamita* Length 6-8cm
Extremely local and endangered. Restricted to a few sites in S, E and NW England, SW Scotland and SW Ireland. Found on sandy heaths where it breeds in quite saline shallow pools; most of its coastal sites are areas of stabilised dunes. Body rather flattened with conspicuous yellow stripe down back. Gathers in pools to spawn in spring, often after heavy downpours. Most active at night when males are very vocal.

BROOK LAMPREY *Lampetra planeri* Length 12-15cm
Intriguing resident of unpolluted streams and shallow rivers. Most of three to five year lifespan spent as larva living unobtrusively buried in silt; filters organic matter. Adults seen in April and May after metamorphosing from larvae. These congregate in shallow, stony areas to spawn. Sucker used for attachment and to move stones to create egg-laying site. Adult does not feed; dies after spawning.

RIVER LAMPREY *Lampetra fluviatilis* Length 30cm
Migratory, adults moving upstream from sea in winter and spring to spawn on gravel beds in rivers. After spawning, adults die but eggs hatch into larvae which spend several years buried in river silt. Following metamorphosis to adult stage, they move to sea until maturity drives them to repeat cycle. Adult attaches to fish with toothed sucker to feed on blood; also eats carrion.

EEL *Anguilla anguilla* Length up to 1m
Snake-like body ideally suited to life spent among silt and debris at bottom of ponds, lakes and canals. Complicated life history. Spawns in Sargasso Sea and young larvae drift across the Atlantic in the Gulf Stream for three years or so. On reaching our shores, so-called elvers migrate up rivers; after several years, become familiar, yellow-bodied eels. Mature, silvery eels migrate to the sea and are sometimes found on estuaries.

GRAYLING *Thymallus thymallus* Length up to 50cm
An attractive fish of unpolluted, fast-flowing streams and shallow rivers. Widespread and locally common in England and Wales; absent from Ireland but introduced and established in S Scotland. Has large and diagnostic dorsal fin and small adipose fin, a character shared by members of salmon family. Apart from fin, outline streamlined and rather trout-like. Often lives in shoals.

ARCTIC CHARR *Salvelinus alpinus* Length up to 70cm
Member of salmon family. Relict species from last post-glacial era, now mostly confined to land-locked and isolated populations in deep, oligotrophic lakes in upland Britain and Ireland. Very local and confined to a few waterbodies in N Wales, Lake District, Scotland and Ireland. Also known as char; Welsh fish called torgoch. Body streamlined with small adipose fin. Male has greenish grey upperparts and bright red belly; colours on female much less intense.

ATLANTIC SALMON *Salmo salar* Length up to 120cm
Large and impressive when mature. Much of adult life spent at sea but returns to fast-flowing, healthy rivers in W England, Wales, Scotland and Ireland to breed. Moves upstream from November to February when rivers in full spate. Adult (A) jumps clear of water to overcome waterfalls. Spawns in shallow gravel beds after which most adults die. Young fish (B) migrate to sea after two years or so in freshwater.

TROUT *Salmo trutta* Length 50-80cm, often much smaller
A familiar and popular sport fish. Widespread and often common both in fast-flowing, unpolluted rivers and streams, and in stream-fed lakes. Known in two forms: brown trout which spends entire life in freshwater and sea trout which only ventures up rivers to breed. Both forms spawn in shallow water on gravel beds. Young spend first year or so in nursery stream before moving downstream to larger river (brown trout) or to sea (sea trout). Feeds mainly on invertebrates.

PIKE *Esox lucius* Length 30-120cm
Superb predator. Takes invertebrates when small but larger pike will tackle other fish and even young water birds. Marbled green and brown markings afford excellent camouflage when lurking among water plants. Streamlined shape and broad tail enable fish to perform lightning attacks on prey which are engulfed in huge mouth and retained by numerous sharp teeth. Favours weedy lowland lakes, flooded gravel pits and large, slow-flowing rivers. Widespread in Britain and Ireland.

CARP *Cyprinus carpio* Length 25-80cm
Introduced but long-established in lakes and gravel pits in Britain and Ireland. Ancestral form has golden-olive colour and even-sized scales; also seen as so-called leather and mirror carp. Feeds on bottom-living invertebrates and plants.

GUDGEON *Gobio gobio* Length 7-15cm
Bottom-dwelling fish of fast-flowing rivers and streams in England, Wales and Ireland; absent from Scotland. Has well-developed barbels which help detect invertebrate prey among sand and gravel. Shoal-forming during summer months.

ROACH *Rutilus rutilus* Length 10-25cm
Has silvery appearance and reddish fins; dorsal fin lies above pelvic fins. Common and widespread in England but less so in Wales and Scotland; rare in Ireland (where more numerous rudd is called roach). Favours lakes and rivers.

RUDD *Scardinius erythropthalamus* Length 20-35cm
Superficially similar to roach but usually has deeper body and golden tinge to flanks. Fins reddish, the dorsal fin lying behind point of origin of pelvic fins. Found in lakes and rivers in England, Wales and Ireland. Shoal-forming.

MINNOW *Phoxinus phoxinus* Length 4-10cm
Small but attractively-marked fish of fast-flowing streams but also lakes in N and W particularly. Widespread in mainland Great Britain but local in Ireland. Shoals seen in shallows in summer months but move to deeper water in winter.

DACE *Leuciscus leuciscus* Length 15-25cm
A streamlined, shoal-forming fish of fast-flowing rivers and streams. Widespread in England and Wales but local and scarce in Scotland and Ireland. Favours surface waters and can often be viewed well from river bank with patience.

CHUB *Squalius cephalus* Length 30-40cm
Similar to dace but appreciably larger when mature. Has plumper-looking body, often with golden hue; anal fin rounded rather than concave as in dace. Common in rivers in England and S Scotland but scarce in Wales and absent from Ireland.

STONE LOACH *Nemacheilus barbatus* Length 5-10cm
Charming and bizarre fish with well developed barbels around mouth. Widespread but often overlooked in gravel-bottomed, unpolluted streams and rivers throughout Britain and Ireland except N Scotland. Bottom-dwelling species.

PERCH *Perca fluviatilis* Length 25-40cm
Distinctive fish of rivers and lakes throughout Britain and Ireland except N Scotland. Greenish body shows broad, vertical dark stripes. Has two separate dorsal fins, the first very spiny; other fins usually red. Shoals when small.

BULLHEAD OR MILLER'S THUMB *Cottus gobio* Length 8-15cm
A bottom-dwelling fish of shallow, stony streams and rivers, often hiding under larger stones. Widespread in England and Wales but absent from Scotland and Ireland. Head proportionately large and broad; body fins with spine-tipped rays.

THREE-SPINED STICKLEBACK *Gasterosteus aculeatus* Length 4-7cm
Beloved of small boys and a familiar resident of both streams and brackish waters. Recognised at all times with the three dorsal spines. Silvery for most of year but, in breeding season, male acquires red belly and bluish dorsal sheen.

NINE-SPINED STICKLEBACK *Pungitius pungitius* Length 2-4cm
Recognised by its usually nine (sometimes ten) dorsal spines and elongated tail stock. Occurs both in freshwater and brackish conditions around coasts. Widespread in Britain and Ireland but absent from much of Scotland.

LESSER SPOTTED DOGFISH *Scyliorhinus canicula* Length up to 60cm
Common and widespread fish around the coasts of S Britain and Ireland. Occurs mainly in offshore waters but also sometimes in comparatively shallow seas off muddy shores and the mouths of estuaries. Well-marked with a rough skin. So-called 'mermaid's purses' (egg-cases of this species) often washed up on shores.

THORNBACK RAY *Raja clavata* Length up to 50cm
Has distinctive, diamond-shaped outline. Skin rough and with conspicuous spines down back and on dorsal surface of muscular tail. Common and widespread off coasts of S Britain and Ireland. Favours muddy and sandy seabeds and sometimes found trapped in pools at very low tide on expansive shores at estuary mouths.

CONGER EEL *Conger Conger* Length up to 2m, often shorter
Extremely muscular, snake-like fish whose skin lacks scales and is variable in colour. Favours rocky coasts, often in deep water but sometimes shallow enough seas to be found at extreme low water hidden among rocks. Upper jaw just longer than lower jaw. Common and widespread around coasts of Britain and Ireland.

WHITING *Merlangius merlangus* Length up to 50cm
Relative of the cod, often common in inshore waters over muddy or sandy seabeds. Body comparatively narrow and has upper jaw longer than lower jaw. First of two anal fins is long, starting mid-way along first dorsal fin and ending level with end of second dorsal fin. Sometimes seen while snorkelling but often in deeper water.

POLLACK *Pollachius pollachus* Length up to 1m
Common and widespread fish around rocky shores of Britain and Ireland. Easily seen while snorkelling off suitable coasts in summer months. Can also be viewed in clear water from jetties and piers, and in rocky gullies. Has cod-like appearance and lateral line which curves smoothly over pectoral fin.

FIVE-BEARDED ROCKLING *Ciliata mustela* Length up to 20cm
As name suggests, has five barbels around mouth. Body elongate with long dorsal and anal fins. Common and widespread around coasts of Britain and Ireland. Lives in shallow water on muddy and sandy shores, sometimes in intertidal zone. Can be found by turning over rocks and debris on estuaries and mudflats at low tide.

GREATER PIPEFISH *Syngnathus acus* Length up to 50cm
Bizarre little fish with worm-like body and elongate, snout-like mouth. One of several, similar species and best told by large size when adult and tapering, curved snout which is longer than length of rest of head. Common among seaweed and rocks in shallow water around coasts of Britain and Ireland.

THICK-LIPPED GREY MULLET *Chelon labrosus* Length up to 50cm
One of a complex of closely related grey mullet species. Body has grey, silver appearance and lip of upper jaw is very thick. A common fish of estuaries and shallow, sheltered coasts; congregates around outfalls of power stations and sewage treatment plants. Widespread around British and Irish coasts except in N.

BASS *Dicentrachus labrus* Length up to 60cm, often smaller
Common and widespread around coasts of Britain and Ireland. When small, often found in shoals near mouths of estuaries and in shallow, sheltered water. Larger specimens often solitary off shingle or rocky shores, sometimes in deep water. Young fish often show pinkish tinge but become more silvery-grey with age.

CORKWING WRASSE *Crenilabrus melops* Length up to 15cm
A beautiful fish. Variable colours and patterns but usually mainly blue with deep pink patterns and lines. Favours clean, rocky coasts. Sometimes found in rock pools but easy to see in calm water darting among seaweed in rocky gullies. Widespread around coasts of Britain and Ireland and common except in N.

BUTTERFISH *Pholis gunnellus* Length up to 15cm
Widespread around coasts of Britain and Ireland and commonest in N. A bottom-living species found among rocks and seaweed on otherwise sandy or muddy seabeds. Has elongate body with long dorsal and anal fins, continuous at tail-end. Sometimes found in pools at low tide. Important food of black guillemot.

COMMON BLENNY *Blennius pholis* Length up to 10cm
Delightful little fish of rocky shores. Common and widespread in suitable habitats around coasts of Britain and Ireland, particularly numerous in W. Found among stones and seaweed in rocky gullies on lower shore; sometimes trapped in rock pools at low tide. Colours variable but usually mottled greenish brown.

ROCK GOBY *Gobius paganellus* Length up to 19cm
A large-headed fish of rocky shores around coasts of Britain and Ireland. Often found among seaweed and stones at low tide and frequently trapped in rock pools at low tide. Characteristically has dark bands along length of otherwise usually pale brown body. Can be very difficult to see among rocks until it moves.

GREY GURNARD *Eutrigla gurnardus* Length up to 30cm
A distinctive fish with a tapering body and pectoral fins partly divided into three feeler-like rays, used in sensory detection. Usually lives near rocky outcrops on muddy or sandy seabeds and sometimes found near pier and jetty supports at very low tides. Widespread around British and Irish coasts, commonest in S.

FATHER LASHER *Myxocephalus scorpius* Length up to 15cm
Squat little fish with proportionately large, spiny head and tapering body. Body usually mottled grey-brown but often darker. Mouth rather large and gill covers spiny. Found among seaweed and stones on otherwise muddy or sandy seabeds. Common on suitable coasts around Britain and Ireland. A bottom-dwelling species.

LUMPSUCKER *Cyclopterus lumpus* Length up to 40cm, often much smaller
Curious, rather round-bodied fish. Young specimens typically mottled or marbled yellow-buff and brown but older fish rather grey above and reddish below. Usually found on rocky shores and can survive in turbulent waters, clinging to rocks with sucker formed by modified pelvic fins. Commonest on S coasts.

COMMON SEA-SNAIL *Liparis liparis* Length up to 10cm
A strange little fish with a rather tadpole-like appearance. Profile smooth with oval outline. Body colour variable but usually reddish grey. Anal fin fused with tail fin. Found mainly on muddy and sandy shores, often among rocky outcrops. Widespread around coasts of Britain and Ireland, commonest in SW.

CORNISH SUCKER *Lepadogaster lepadogaster* Length up to 6cm
Another strange-looking fish with flattened, tadpole-like appearance and rather pointed snout. Body colour usually reddish. Has two bluish, eye-like markings on back of head behind true eyes. Lives on rocky coasts, often in shallow water. Clings to rocks using sucker formed by modified pelvic fins. Commonest in SW.

SOLE *Solea solea* Length up to 25cm
One of the classic flatfish, easily recognised by its oval outline and very short tail whose fin is not separated from dorsal and anal fins by any distinct tail stock. Lives on sandy and muddy seabeds, often in shallow water in estuary and river mouths. Common and widespread around coasts of Britain and Ireland.

FLOUNDER *Platichthys flesus* Length up to 17cm
Flatfish with rounded-oval outline and long dorsal and anal fins separated from tail fin by distinct tail stock; dorsal fin starts near eye. Colour rather variable but usually mottled brown on upperside and pale on underside. Common and widespread on muddy and sandy seabeds around coasts of Britain and Ireland.

SWALLOWTAIL *Papilio machaon ssp britannicus* Wingspan 70mm
Large, unmistakable and rare, now confined to a few fens and marshes in E Anglia, mainly Norfolk Broads. Perhaps easiest to see at Hickling Broad. Flies May–June and again in August. Colourful caterpillars feed on rare milk parsley.

LARGE WHITE *Pieris brassicae* Wingspan 60mm
Underwings yellowish. Upperwings creamy-white with black tip to forewing; female also has two spots on forewing. Flies May–September. Foodplants of its black and yellow caterpillars include cabbages and other garden brassicas.

SMALL WHITE *Artogeia rapae* Wingspan 45mm
Smaller and commoner than large white. Underwings yellowish. Upperwings creamy-white with dark tip to forewing; female has two dark spots on forewing. Flies April–May and July–August. Caterpillars feed on cabbage and other brassicas.

GREEN-VEINED WHITE *Artogeia napi* Wingspan 45-50mm
Common wayside butterfly. Similar to small white but veins on upperwings dark and greyish green on underwings, particularly hindwing. Caterpillars eat garlic mustard and other wild crucifers. Double-brooded, seen in spring and mid-summer.

ORANGE-TIP *Anthocharis cardamines* Wingspan 40mm
Attractive spring butterfly, flying April–June. Male's orange patch on dark-tipped forewing absent in female; hind underwing of both sexes marbled green and white. Larvae feed mainly on cuckoo-flower. Widespread in S Britain and Ireland.

WOOD WHITE *Leptidea sinapis* Wingspan 40mm
Very local in S and SW England and S Ireland. Delicate-looking with rounded wings and feeble flight; forewings dark-tipped, most noticeably on upper surface. Flies May–July in two broods. Caterpillars eat plants of pea family.

BRIMSTONE *Gonepteryx rhamni* Wingspan 60mm
Herald of spring. Single-brooded. Summer adults hibernate and emerge from February onwards on sunny days. Uniquely-shaped wings. Male's brimstone-yellow colour unmistakable. Paler female can be mistaken for large white in flight

CLOUDED YELLOW *Colias croceus* Wingspan 50mm
Summer migrant in variable numbers. Sometimes breeds but does not survive winter. Fast-flying and active. Dark-bordered upperwings yellow in female, orange-yellow in male. Both sexes have yellow underwings with few dark markings.

SMALL TORTOISESHELL *Aglais urticae* Wingspan 42mm
Common and familiar garden and wayside species. Sun-loving. Seen on wing March–October with two or three broods. Upperwings marbled orange, yellow and black; underparts smoky-brown. Gregarious caterpillars feed on common nettle.

PAINTED LADY *Vanessa cardui* Wingspan 60mm
Summer migrant to flowering meadows in variable numbers; most numerous near coasts. Sometimes breeds but does not survive winter. Upperwings marbled pinkish buff, white and black. Underwing colour buffish, pattern as upperwing.

RED ADMIRAL *Vanessa atalanta* Wingspan 60mm
Adults hibernate in small numbers but seen mostly as summer migrant to Britain and Ireland, often in good numbers. Underwings marbled smoky-grey, upperwings black with red bands and white spots. Commonest July–August. Larvae on nettle.

PEACOCK *Inachis io* Wingspan 60mm
Common in Britain and Ireland except in N. Visits garden flowers. Adult flies July–September and again in spring after hibernation. Underwings smoky-brown but maroon upperwings have bold eye markings. Caterpillars feed on common nettle.

WHITE ADMIRAL *Ladoga camilla* Wingspan 50mm
Locally common woodland species in S England. Superb flier, seen June–July. Upperwings sooty-black with white bands; underwings chestnut with similar pattern of white. Visits bramble flowers along rides. Larvae on honeysuckle.

PURPLE EMPEROR *Apatura iris* Wingspan 65mm
Magnificent but rare; only in S C England. Favours oak woods with larval food, sallow. Flies July–August but seldom seen because of preference for tree canopy. Male only has purple sheen to brown upperwings. Underwings chestnut.

COMMA *Polygonia c-album* Wingspan 45mm
Has distinctive, ragged-edged wings. Underwings smoky-brown with white 'comma' mark; upperwings orange-brown with dark markings. Double-brooded and hibernates. Adults seen March–September. Caterpillars feed on common nettle, elm and hops.

PEARL-BORDERED FRITILLARY *Clossiana euphrosyne* Wingspan 42mm
Sun-loving butterfly of woodland glades. Widespread but local in British Isles, mostly in S; very local in W Ireland. Flies May-June. Underside of hindwing shows seven silver spots on margin and two in centre. Caterpillar feeds on violets.

SMALL PEARL-BORDERED FRITILLARY *Clossiana selene* Wingspan 40mm
Similar to pearl-bordered; shares seven silver marginal spots but has several silver central spots on underside of hindwing. Flies in June. Favours woods and grassland where larval foodplants, violets, common. Local. Absent from Ireland.

DARK GREEN FRITILLARY *Mesoacidalia aglaia* Wingspan 60mm
Widespread and locally common in Britain and Ireland. Flies July–August and seen on sand dunes and downs. Fast and powerful flier, visits thistles and knapweeds. Caterpillars feed on violets. Underside of hindwing has greenish scaling.

HIGH BROWN FRITILLARY *Fabriciana adippe* Wingspan 60mm
Scarce and rather endangered, found mainly in W and NW England. Flies July–August and favours meadows and open, grassy woodlands. Underside of hindwing has brownish scaling. Upperwings orange-brown with dark spots. Larvae on violets.

SILVER-WASHED FRITILLARY *Argynnis paphia* Wingspan 60mm
Locally common woodland species in S and SW England and Ireland. Upperwings well-marked orange-brown; underside of hindwing has silvery sheen. Sun-loving adult fond of bramble flowers; flies June–August. Larvae feed on violets.

MARSH FRITILLARY *Euphydryas aurinia* Wingspan 40-50mm
Widespread but very local in mainland Britain and Ireland. Flies May–June but only active when sunny. Beautifully marked wings. Favours damp heaths and moors but also dry chalk grassland. Larvae feed on devil's-bit scabious and plantains.

HEATH FRITILLARY *Mellicta athalia* Wingspan 45mm
Rare and local, mainly in SE and SW England. Favours woodland rides where larval foodplants, common cow-wheat, wood-sage or plantains, common. Flies June–July. Upperwings well-marked orange brown; underwings creamy-white and chestnut.

GLANVILLE FRITILLARY *Mellitaea cinxia* Wingspan 40mm
Confined to Isle of Wight but common there in grassland along S coast. Flies May–June and only active in sunny weather. Underwings creamy-white and orange-buff; upperwings orange-brown. Gregarious caterpillars feed on sea plantain.

DUKE OF BURGUNDY FRITILLARY *Hamearis lucina* Wingspan 25mm
Despite name, unrelated to other British fritillaries. Flies May–June and favours grassy places where larval foodplants, cowslip and primrose, common. Confined mainly to S England. Wings beautifully marked with orange and brown.

SPECKLED WOOD *Pararge aegeria* Wingspan 45cm
Widespread woodland butterfly but common only in S England; local further N and in Ireland and absent from much of Scotland. Double-brooded, flying April–June and July–September. Favours clearings and fond of sunbathing. Upperwings dark brown with pale markings; underwings rufous brown. Caterpillars feed on grasses.

WALL BROWN *Lasiommata megera* Wingspan 45cm
Range includes England, Wales and Ireland but local except in S. Has disappeared from many former haunts and now commonest on grassy heaths and coasts. Orange-brown colour gives fritillary-like appearance but shows small eyespots on wings. Double-brooded, flying April–May and July–September. Larva feeds on grasses.

SCOTCH ARGUS *Erebia aethiops* Wingspan 40mm
An upland butterfly, found very locally in N England and S and C Scotland. Favours woodland margins and moors where larval foodplant, purple moor-grass, common. Flies July–September but only active in sunny weather. Superficially ringlet-like but rich brown upperwings marked with orange band and eyespots.

MOUNTAIN RINGLET *Erebia epiphron* Wingspan 32mm
Small and surprisingly delicate butterfly given the inhospitable nature of its upland moorland and mountain slope habitat. Flies June–July but only when sunny; remains hidden among vegetation in dull weather. Very local and restricted to Lake District and C Scottish Highlands. Caterpillar feeds on grasses.

MARBLED WHITE *Melanargia galathea* Wingspan 50mm
Restricted to SE and CS England. Although local within this range, often common in suitable habitats. Favours flower-rich, grassy meadows, often on chalk downs but also on neutral soils. Distinctive black and white patterns on wings. Flies July–August and visits knapweed and thistle flowers. Larva feeds on grasses.

GRAYLING *Hipparchia semele* Wingspan 50mm
Favours warm, dry places including sea cliffs, heaths and dunes. Widespread in Britain and Ireland as far as S Scotland but commonest near coasts. Invariably sits with wings folded and angled to cast the least shadow. Flies June–August

RINGLET *Aphantopus hyperantus* Wingspan 48mm
Widespread in Britain and Ireland as far as S Scotland and found in grassy places. Flies June–July. Has smoky-brown wings, darker on males than females, with variable numbers of small eyespots. Caterpillars feed on various grasses.

GATEKEEPER *Pyronia tithonus* Wingspan 40mm
Wayside and hedgerow butterfly, flying July–August. Found in C and S England and Wales and S Ireland. Often feeds on bramble flowers. Upperwings smoky-brown with orange markings and paired eyespot on forewing. Caterpillars feed on grasses.

MEADOW BROWN *Maniola jurtina* Wingspan 50mm
Common and widespread butterfly, least so in N Scotland and Ireland. Favours all kinds of grassy places; flies June–August. Upperwings brown; male has small orange patch on forewing containing eyespot; orange patch larger in female (A). Pupa (B) among grasses.

LARGE HEATH *Coenonympha tullia* Wingspan 38mm
Found on acid moors where larval foodplant, white beak-sedge, common. Occurs N from C Wales and locally in Ireland. Flies June–July in sunny weather. Underside of hindwing grey-brown; forewing orange-brown with small eyespot.

SMALL HEATH *Coenonympha pamphilus* Wingspan 30mm
Widespread in Britain and Ireland but common only in C and S England and S Wales. Caterpillars feed on grasses and adult invariably found in meadows and on downs and dunes. Double-brooded, flying mainly May–June and August–September.

PURPLE HAIRSTREAK *Quercusia quercus* Wingspan 38mm
Locally common in S England and Wales; scarce further N and rare in S Scotland and Ireland. Flies July–August around tops of oaks on which caterpillars feed. Has purple sheen on upperwings. Underwings grey with hairstreak line.

WHITE-LETTER HAIRSTREAK *Strymondia w-album* Wingspan 35mm
Widespread death of larval foodplants, elms, from Dutch elm disease has caused decline. Now very local in S and C England. Flies July–August, usually around treetops but also visits bramble flowers to feed. White 'w' on hind underwing (A). Larva (B) is flattened.

BLACK HAIRSTREAK *Strymondia pruni* Wingspan 35mm
Scarce, very local, restricted to parts of E Midlands, mainly in Oxfordshire and Buckinghamshire. Favours woods bordered by thickets of larval foodplant, blackthorn. Adult (A) seen July. Visits privet flowers or feeds on honeydew on leaves. Pupa (B) resembles bird dropping.

BROWN HAIRSTREAK *Thecla betulae* Wingspan 40-50mm
Very local in S and C England and Wales. Favours areas where larval foodplant, blackthorn, forms thickets. Adult seen August. Sluggish and walks among foliage. Upperwings dark brown, male (A) with orange patch on forewing. Underwings (B) orange-brown.

GREEN HAIRSTREAK *Callophrys rubi* Wingspan 25mm
Small, highly active species, flying May–June. At rest, invariably has wings closed showing bright green underwings; brown upperwings seldom seen. Favours heaths, cliffs and downland scrub. Larva feeds on gorse, heathers and trefoils.

SMALL COPPER *Lycaena phlaeas* Wingspan 25mm
Attractive, open country species. Flies May–September in two or three broods. Variable orange and dark brown on upperwings. Underwings have similar patterns to upperwings but dark brown replaced by grey-buff. Larva feeds on sheep's sorrel.

COMMON BLUE *Polyommatus icarus* Wingspan 32mm
Common in grassy places and widespread in mainland Britain and parts of Ireland. Flies April–September in successive broods. Male has blue upperwings, female's being generally brown. Underside grey-brown with dark spots. Larva feeds on trefoils.

CHALKHILL BLUE *Cupido minimus* Wingspan 40mm
Told by pale sky-blue upperwings of male, female's being dark brown with orange submarginal spots. Underwings grey-brown with spots. Restricted to chalk and limestone grassland in S England. Flies July–August. Larva feeds on horseshoe vetch.

ADONIS BLUE *Lysandra bellargus* Wingspan 32mm
Male has iridescent blue upperwings with black and white margins; female's upperwings brown with orange submarginal spots. Flies May–June and July–August in two broods. Local in S England on chalk downs. Larva feeds on horseshoe vetch.

HOLLY BLUE *Celastrina argiolus* Wingspan 30mm
Silvery in flight. Violet-blue upperwings seldom seen well. Rests showing white, black-dotted underwings. Mainly S England and Wales and S Ireland. Two broods, flying April–May, laying eggs on holly, and August–September, laying eggs on ivy.

SMALL BLUE *Cupido minimus* Wingspan 25mm
Small and highly active. Local in England, Wales and S Ireland. Occurs where larval foodplant, kidney vetch, common, often on chalk grassland. Flies June–July. Upperwings smoky-brown, male with purplish iridescence. Underwings grey.

SILVER-STUDDED BLUE *Plebejus argus* Wingspan 25-30mm
Confined mainly to heaths in S England; also locally further N in places where larval foodplants, gorse and ling, occur. Flies June–July. Male has violet-blue upperwings, those of female brown. Grey underwings have orange and black spots.

BROWN ARGUS *Aricia agestis* Wingspan 25mm
Recalls female common blue but smaller and orange submarginal spots on brown upperwings (A) much more prominent. Local in S and C England. Larva on common rock-rose and storksbills. Closely related species, northern brown argus, is similar but has white spot on forewing; occurs very locally in N England and Scotland.

SMALL SKIPPER *Thymelicus sylvestris* Wingspan 25mm
A meadow species, flying July–August. Upperwings orange-brown and underwings orange-buff. Brown underside to tips of antennae the best feature for separation from very similar Essex skipper. Common and widespread in S England and Wales. Typically rests with wings held at an angle. Has active, buzzing flight and fond of visiting flowers of thistles and daisies. Larva feeds on various grasses.

ESSEX SKIPPER *Thymelicus lineolus* Wingspan 25mm
Very similar to small skipper but with underside to tips of antennae black not brown. Rather local but often overlooked, being passed by as the more common and widespread small skipper. Favours grassy meadows and restricted to SE England. Fond of visiting knapweed and thistle flowers. Buzzing, active flight. Flies mainly June–July. Caterpillar feeds on various grasses.

LULWORTH SKIPPER *Thymelicus acteon* Wingspan 28mm
Very local and found only in coastal grassland in S England from Purbeck in Dorset to E Devon. Upperwings typically khaki brown, forewing with crescent of pale spots like paw-print; markings on female brighter than those on male. Flies June–July. Active, buzzing flight. Caterpillar feeds on grasses.

LARGE SKIPPER *Ochlodes venatus* Wingspan 34mm
Common and widespread in England and Wales but absent from Scotland and Ireland. Favours grassy places of all kinds and flies June–July. Upperwings dark brown and orange-brown with pale markings. Underwings buffish orange with paler spots. In common with most other skippers, at rest often holds wings at an angle and can look rather moth-like. Caterpillar feeds on various grasses.

SILVER-SPOTTED SKIPPER *Hesperia comma* Wingspan 34mm
Superficially similar to large skipper but dark brown upperwings have distinctive pale spots; greenish brown underwings show the silvery-white spots which give the species its name. Very local and found only on chalk downland in S England. A late species, flying August–September. Larva feeds on grasses.

DINGY SKIPPER *Erynnis tages* Wingspan 25mm
Moth-like appearance with buzzing flight and dark grey-brown upperwings; underwings reddish brown. Sexes similar. Flies May–June and favours meadows and rough ground, sometimes in grassy woodland rides. Locally common in England and Wales but scarce in Scotland and Ireland. Caterpillar's main foodplant is bird's-foot trefoil but will also eat various species of vetch.

GRIZZLED SKIPPER *Pyrgus malvae* Wingspan 20mm
An attractive little butterfly. Has dark grey-brown upperwings marked with conspicuous white spots; underwings reddish brown but also showing numerous pale spots. Flies May–June. Confined mainly to S England and S Wales but there locally not uncommon. Favours rough grassland and woodland rides where larval foodplants, which include wild strawberry and cinquefoils, are common.

CHEQUERED SKIPPER *Carterocephalus palaemon* Wingspan 25mm
Formerly found in C England but extinct there and now restricted to open birchwoods in NW Scotland where very local. Flies May–June. Upperwings rich brown with orange-yellow spots; underwings paler but also well marked with pale spots. Caterpillars feed on various grasses. Flight active and fast but fond of sunbathing; difficult to locate in dull weather.

BROWN HOUSE MOTH *Hofmannophila pseudospretella* Length at rest 10mm
A frequent and unwelcome visitor to houses and can be found at almost any time of year. Adult usually found in vicinity of stored natural fabrics and foods on which eggs are laid and larvae feed. Seldom flies but prefers to scuttle along floor into crevice or cupboard. Extremely destructive if left unchecked.

MOTHER OF PEARL *Pleuroptya ruralis* Wingspan 35mm
Flies June–August and frequently comes to light. Flight weak. Has mother of pearl sheen to wings at certain angles. Common and widespread throughout much of mainland Britain and Ireland. Found in meadows, wasteground and overgrown hedgerows. Larva feeds on common nettle and lives inside rolled up leaf.

WHITE PLUME MOTH *Pterophorus pentadactyla* Wingspan 28mm
Attractive and distinctive moth with white, dissected, feather-like wings. Often seen resting among low vegetation in daytime. Flies from dusk onwards and often attracted to light; sometimes comes indoors. Flies May–August. Caterpillar feeds on hedge bindweed and lives inside rolled up leaf. Common and widespread.

GHOST MOTH *Hepialus humuli* Length at rest 25mm
Favours meadows and grassy hedgerows where larvae live underground and feed on roots of various plants. Groups of pure white males engage in dancing display flights at dusk. Female has buffish yellow wings with orange streaks. Widespread and often common throughout much of Britain and Ireland. Flies June–August.

5-SPOT BURNET *Zygaena trifolii* Wingspan 35mm
Distinctive, day-flying moth with red hindwings and five red spots on otherwise metallic greenish blue forewings. Favours damp meadows and common and widespread in Britain and Ireland. Flies July–August. Larva feeds on greater bird's-foot trefoil. Similar 6-spot Burnet has six spots on forewing and favours drier ground.

LAPPET MOTH *Gastropacha quercifolia* Length at rest 40mm
Superb camouflage when resting among fallen leaves on ground. Reddish wings have scalloped margins and head has pronounced 'snout'. Flies June–August and comes to light. Caterpillar feeds on hawthorn and also has amazing camouflage when resting lengthwise along twig. Commonest in S England and Wales.

THE LACKEY *Malacosoma neustria* Length at rest 17mm
Common and widespread in S England and S Ireland. Often found along hedgerows but can turn up in almost any habitat where larval foodplants, which include hawthorn and blackthorn, are common. Adult flies June-August. Colourful larvae live in communal silken tents spun on branches and are especially conspicuous.

PUSS MOTH *Cerura vinula* Length at rest 35mm
Attractive, furry-looking moth (A) with pale grey and white wings. Flies May–July and sometimes found resting on branches. Equally well known as caterpillar (B) which is squat and green with two whip-like tail appendages; larval foodplants include willows and poplars. Common and widespread in much of Britain and Ireland.

SALLOW KITTEN *Furcula furcula* Length at rest 20mm
A charming little moth which flies May–August in two broods. Comes to light and sometimes rests on walls during day. Has grey band across otherwise white forewing. Larva resembles miniature puss moth larva with two tail appendages; main foodplant sallow. Common and widespread throughout most of Britain and Ireland.

LOBSTER MOTH *Stauropus fagi* Length at rest 32mm
Named after its bizarre-looking caterpillar which has a fanciful resemblance to a lobster. Adult has reddish grey wings, usually with pinkish flush. Colours and markings give superb camouflage when resting on tree bark. Flies May–July and favours oak and beech woods, both of which are foodplants for the caterpillar.

EMPEROR MOTH *Saturnia pavonia* Wingspan 50-60mm
Large and impressive day-flying moth seen April–May. Favours heaths and moors where larval foodplant, ling, is common; bright green larva, which has black markings and tufts of hairs, also eats bramble. Spins pear-shaped silken cocoon in which it pupates. Widespread and locally common in Britain and Ireland.

LIME HAWKMOTH *Mimas tiliae* Wingspan 65mm
Adult is well camouflaged when resting among dappled leaves. Wing colour variable but usually olive-green with darker markings. Flies May–June. Pale green larva has diagonal stripes and numerous white dots; feeds mainly on lime and so found in gardens. Common only in S England, becoming scarce further N.

POPLAR HAWKMOTH *Laothoe populi* Wingspan 70mm
At rest, grey-brown forewing obscures the reddish mark on hindwing; this is exposed if moth becomes alarmed. Rests by day among leaves and easy to overlook. Seen May–August in two broods. Bright green larva has 'horn' at tail end and diagonal stripes along body; feeds on poplar and willows. Common and widespread.

EYED HAWKMOTH *Smerinthus ocellata* Wingspan 80mm
Marbled grey-brown forewings obscure the hindwings at rest. When disturbed, arches body and wings to expose striking eyespots on hindwings. Bright green larva has diagonal stripes and 'horn' at tail end; feeds on willows and apple. Flies May–August in two broods. Common in S England; scarce further N and Ireland.

PINE HAWKMOTH *Hyloicus pinastri* Wingspan 80mm
Grey-brown forewings with darker streaks and dots afford moth superb camouflage when resting on pine bark. Buffish orange hindwings seldom seen at rest. Green larva has stripes along body length and dark 'horn' at tail end; feeds on conifer needles. Once rare but now locally common in S England. Flies June–July.

PRIVET HAWKMOTH *Sphinx ligustri* Wingspan 100mm
Moth (A) is well-camouflaged when at rest but when disturbed exposes pink-striped abdomen and pale pink stripes on hindwing. Flies June–July. Bright green larva (B) has purple and white diagonal stripes and dark-tipped 'horn' at tail end; feeds on privet and lilac, often in gardens. Widespread but common only in S England.

ELEPHANT HAWKMOTH *Dielephila elpenor* Wingspan 70mm
Beautiful moth with pink and olive-green markings on wings and body. Flies May–June and visits garden flowers such as honeysuckle. Head end of larva fancifully resembles elephant's trunk; eyespots used to deter would-be predators; feeds on willowherbs. Widespread but common only in S and C England and Wales.

SMALL ELEPHANT HAWKMOTH *Dielephila porcellus* Wingspan 50mm
Attractive moth with pink and yellow-buff wings. Flies June–July and sometimes seen on wing at dusk. Favours heaths and downs where larval foodplants, bedstraws, are common. Larva is grey-brown with eyespots near head end; lacks a 'horn' at tail end. Widespread but always rather local and seldom common.

BROAD-BORDERED BEE HAWKMOTH *Hemaris fuciformis* Wingspan 43mm
Wings have covering of scales when newly emerged from pupa. These are soon lost when moth becomes strikingly similar to bumblebee. A day-flying species seen May–June, often hovering at flowers of bugle to feed. Favours sunny woodland rides. Larva feeds mainly on honeysuckle. Common only in S England.

HUMMINGBIRD HAWKMOTH *Macroglossum stellatarum* Wingspan 45mm
A migrant visitor to S England from mainland Europe during summer months. Occurs in variable numbers and not common every year. A day-flying species which hovers with audible hum and feeds on nectar of red valerian and other flowers using long tongue. Larva, which feeds on bedstraws, is seldom seen in Britain.

BUFF-TIP *Phalera bucephala* Length at rest 30mm
Buff head and silvery grey wings with buff tips give resting moth a broken twig appearance. Flies May–July and found in a variety of wooded habitats including mature gardens. Gregarious larvae are yellow and black and feed on a range of deciduous trees including oak and lime. Widespread and common in most areas.

CHOCOLATE-TIP *Clostera curtula* Length at rest 17mm
A charming little moth seen May–September in two or more broods. Grey-brown forewings have a chocolate-maroon tip; when alarmed, sometimes exposes brown-tipped abdomen. Usually associated with wooded areas. Widespread but only locally common. Comes to light. Larva feeds on aspen, poplars and willows.

IRON PROMINENT *Notodonta dromedarius* Length at rest 26mm
Forewings smoky-brown but richly marked with rusty-brown and yellow; in profile, tuft of hairs on hind edge of forewing shows as distinct prominence. Favours woodland and larva feeds on birch, oak, alder and hazel. Adult flies May–August with two broods in S. Widespread and often locally common. Comes to light.

MAPLE PROMINENT *Ptilodonta cuculina* Length at rest 22mm
An attractive species with distinct prominences when seen in profile. Wings are marbled brown but with whitish patch on outer margin of forewing. As name suggests, larva feeds mainly on field maple and so moth occurs in old hedgerows and woodland borders. Local and only common in S England. Flies May–July.

GREAT PROMINENT *Peridea anceps* Length at rest 30mm
Marbled brown and grey-brown wings and hairy legs and head afford the moth excellent camouflage when resting on bark of oak, the larval foodplant. Flies May–July and mostly found in mature oak woodland. Green larva has diagonal stripes along body.

LESSER SWALLOW PROMINENT *Pheosia gnoma* Length at rest 27mm
Has pale grey-buff wings with dark stripes; distinct white wedge on outer margin of forewing separates this species from similar swallow prominent. Flies May–June and August as two broods. Widespread in woods with larval foodplant, birch.

PEBBLE PROMINENT *Eligmodonta ziczac* Length at rest 25mm
Buffish brown forewings have grey-brown fingernail-like mark near tip and white patch on leading edge. Larva feeds on sallow, willow and aspen. Adult flies May–June, sometimes August as second brood. Widespread and often common in woodlands.

PALE PROMINENT *Pterostoma palpina* Length at rest 30mm
In profile, greyish brown wings show prominences along back; palps project at head end and tufted tip to abdomen protrudes beyond wings. Flies May–August. Favours woodlands and hedgerows where larval foodplants, sallow and aspen, grow.

PALE TUSSOCK *Calliteara pudibunda* Length at rest 30mm
Attractive, hairy moth (A) with grey or greyish buff wings. Associated with wooded areas where yellow and black, hairy larva (B) feeds on birch, oak, lime and other deciduous trees. Locally common in England, Wales and S Ireland. Flies May–June.

THE VAPOURER *Orgyia antiqua* Length of male at rest 16mm
Male has chestnut forewing with conspicuous white spot on trailing edge; flies July–September. Wingless female sometimes seen near clusters of eggs laid on bark of deciduous trees and shrubs. Larva has tufts of yellow and black hairs.

YELLOW-TAIL *Euproctis similis* Length at rest 24mm
Pure white moth exposes yellow-tipped abdomen when alarmed. Favours woods and hedges where larval foodplants, various deciduous shrubs, common. Flies June–August. Hairy larva is marked with black and red. Should be treated with caution since adult and larval hairs can cause serious irritation if handled or inhaled.

GARDEN TIGER *Arctia caja* Wingspan 65mm
Familiar and widespread moth, found in most habitats. Flies July–August. Often comes to outdoor lights around houses. Dark-spotted orange hindwings concealed by forewings unless moth disturbed. Hairy larva feeds on wide range of plants.

RUBY TIGER *Phragmatobia fuliginosa* Length at rest 22mm
Has reddish forewings which conceal pink or grey hindwings at rest. Widespread and often common. Adult flies May–June, sometimes August in second brood. Favours meadows and grassy hedgerows. Larval foodplants include dandelions and docks.

MUSLIN MOTH *Diaphora mendica* Length at rest 23mm
Male reddish buff, female white; both sexes have black spots on wings. Night-flying male comes to light; female often diurnal. Common and widespread in meadows. Larval foodplants include dandelions and plantains. Flies May–June.

WHITE ERMINE *Spilosoma lubricipeda* Length at rest 28mm
Attractive moth whose white wings bear conspicuous black spots. Yellow and black abdomen usually concealed by wings at rest. Widespread and common in most habitats. Flies May–July and comes to light. Larva eats wide variety of plants.

THE CINNABAR *Tyria jacobaeae* Length at rest 22mm
Recognised by red and charcoal-grey wings (A). Flies May–July, usually at night but also during day. Widespread and common in meadows and on coasts. Orange and black striped larvae (B) feed mainly on ragwort; usually seen in small groups.

COMMON FOOTMAN *Eilema lurideola* Length at rest 25mm
Widespread and locally common in Britain and Ireland. Flies July–August and favours wooded habitats. Larva eats lichens on the bark of trees and shrubs. Moth rests with wings rolled lengthways in somewhat caddisfly-like manner.

ROSY FOOTMAN *Miltochrista miniata* Length at rest 14mm
Attractive little moth with rosy-orange forewings bearing black spots. Rests with wings pressed close to surface on which it is clinging. Favours wooded areas; larvae feed on lichens on tree bark. Common only in S England and Wales.

HEART AND DART *Agrotis exclamationis* Length at rest 20mm
So-called because of dark markings on forewings. Widespread and extremely common; often the most numerous moth recorded at traps. Flies May–July. Larva eats a wide range of plants and adult found in gardens, meadows and woodland.

TRUE LOVER'S KNOT *Lycophotia porphyrea* Length at rest 16mm
Small but well-marked moth but with ground colour of forewing rather variable. Flies June–August. Favours heathy places and open woods where larval foodplants, ling and bell heather, grow. Widespread in Britain and Ireland but rather local.

BROAD-BORDERED YELLOW UNDERWING *Noctua fimbriata*
Length at rest 25mm. At rest, variably marked forewings obscure yellow and black hindwings. Moth is easily disturbed, however, needing little encouragement to fly even in daytime. Seen July–September. Widespread and common. Larva eats wide range of plants.

LARGE YELLOW UNDERWING *Noctua pronuba* Length at rest 25mm
Similar to *N.fimbriata* but forewings more marbled and yellow hindwings with only narrow black border. Flies June–September. Common and widespread in Britain and Ireland in gardens, meadows and woods. Larva eats almost any herbaceous plant.

BROOM MOTH *Ceramica pisi* Length at rest 22mm
Ground colour of forewing rather variable. Has characteristic pale spot on hind edge of forewing, the spots on both wings meeting when moth at rest. Widespread and fairly common. Flies May–June. Larva feeds on broom and many other plants.

HEBREW CHARACTER *Orthosia gothica* Length at rest 20mm
Common and widespread in Britain and Ireland. Flies March–April and comes to light. Recognised by dark mark on wings having semi-circular section removed as if by a hole-punch. Found in woods and gardens. Larva feeds on variety of plants.

BROWN-LINE BRIGHT-EYE *Mythimna conigera* Length at rest 21mm
Markings on reddish brown wings accurately described by name. Flies June–August. Widespread and often common in much of Britain and Ireland. Found in meadows and grassy hedgerows, the larva feeding on various species of grasses.

COMMON WAINSCOT *Mythimna pallens* Length at rest 20mm
Has straw-coloured forewings, the veins of which are white; white hindwings usually hidden at rest. Widespread and locally common. Flies June–October in two broods. Favours meadows and hedges. Larva feeds on various grass species.

THE SHARK *Cuculia umbratica* Length at rest 32mm
Unusually shaped moth sometimes found resting on frayed wooden surfaces in daytime. Flies May–July. Locally common in S England, Wales and S Ireland; less so further N. Favours rough meadows and wasteground. Larva eats sow-thistles.

POPLAR GREY *Acronicta megacephala* Length at rest 20mm
Has grey forewings well-marked with darker lines and well-defined pale circle; pale hindwings usually hidden at rest. Favours parks, gardens and woods. Flies May–August. Larva eats poplars and willows. Common in S England and Wales.

GREY DAGGER *Acronicta psi* Length at rest 23mm
Easily recognised by pale grey forewings bearing distinctive black dagger-like markings. Common and widespread in England, Wales and Ireland. Flies June–August and favours woodland. Colourful larva feeds on deciduous shrubs and trees.

THE MILLER *Acronicta leporina* Length at rest 20mm
Ground colour of forewing varies from pale to dark grey and typically shows jagged black transverse line from leading edge. Flies April–June and found in woodland. Hairy larva feeds mainly on birch but also on other deciduous trees.

NUT-TREE TUSSOCK *Colocasia coryli* Length at rest 18mm
Forewing has variable ground colour but always has rich-brown transverse band containing small eye-like marking outlined in black. Flies May–July in woodland. Larva feeds on hazel. Locally common only in S England, Wales and Ireland.

OLD LADY *Mormo maura* Length at rest 32mm
Marbled brown forewings held flat when resting and afford superb camouflage when sitting on tree bark or wooden fence. Flies July–August and found in gardens, parks and woodland. Larva found on various trees and shrubs including birch.

LUNAR-SPOTTED PINION *Cosmia pyralina* Length at rest 15mm
Attractive moth which holds its wings in a tent-like manner when at rest. Flies July–August. Locally common in S England but becoming scarce further N. Favours woodland edge and hedgerows. Larval foodplants include hawthorn and blackthorn.

STRAW UNDERWING *Thalpophila matura* Length at rest 22mm
Dark-bordered pale yellow hindwings usually concealed by well marked forewings at rest. Flies July–August. Widespread and fairly common in most of Britain and Ireland. Favours meadows and rough ground. Larva feeds on various grasses.

ANGLE SHADES *Phlogophora meticulosa* Length at rest 27mm
Recognised by forewing having ragged margin and with leading edge rolled in at rest. Wing colour variable but often olive-green or pale brown, showing pinkish triangular mark. Widespread. Common May–October, less so in other months.

GREEN SILVER LINES *Pseudoips fagana* Length at rest 17mm
Has bright green forewings with hindwings white in male and yellowish in female. Widespread but local in England and Wales but scarce in Ireland and Scotland. Flies June–July and found in woodland. Larval foodplants include oak and hazel.

SCARCE SILVER LINES *Bena prasinana* Length at rest 22mm
Despite name, not uncommon in many parts of England and Wales. Flies July–August and found in mature woodland where larva feeds on oak. At rest, green forewings, which bear two white, transverse lines, held in tent-like manner over body.

BURNISHED BRASS *Diachrisia chrysitis* Length at rest 21mm
A stunning moth with golden metallic areas on forewings. Flies June–July and August as second brood in S. Common and widespread in Britain and Ireland. Found in gardens, hedgerows and on rough ground. Larval foodplants include common nettle.

THE HERALD *Scoliopteryx libatrix* Length at rest 20mm
Brick-red forewings have ragged margins and transverse white lines. Flies August–November and, after hibernation, March–June. Widespread in England, Wales and Ireland. Found in gardens, woods and hedges. Larva feeds on various shrubs.

SILVER Y *Autographa gamma* Length at rest 21mm
Migrant visitor May–October from S Europe in variable numbers. Forewing bears distinctive white 'y' marking. Moth flies during day in hot weather and visits gardens flowers at dusk. Sometimes produces second brood but cannot survive winter.

BEAUTIFUL GOLDEN Y *Autographa pulchrina* Length at rest 21mm
Superficially similar to silver Y but forewings marbled brown not grey and 'y' marking is broken. Widespread and common in Britain and Ireland. Flies June–July and found in woodland and hedgerows. Larval foodplants include dead-nettles.

MOTHER SHIPTON *Callistege mi* Wingspan 23mm
Fanciful profile of eponymous witch appears on forewing. Flies May–July. Locally common in England, Wales and Ireland but scarce in Scotland. Found in meadows, woodland rides and on rough ground. Larva feeds on various species of clover

THE SPECTACLE *Abrostola triplasia* Length at rest 18mm
When viewed from head on, shows distinctive 'spectacle' markings. Forewings grey with dark central band. Flies May–August. Widespread and often common on rough ground, commons, verges and along woodland rides. Larva feeds on common nettle.

RED UNDERWING *Catocala nupta* Wingspan 65mm
Black-barred red underwings usually concealed at rest by marbled grey and brown forewings; they are revealed when moth is disturbed. Flies August–September. Common only in S England. Favours open woodland. Larva found on willows and poplars.

BEAUTIFUL HOOKTIP *Lasypeyria flexula* Length at rest 14mm
Has hooked-tipped, purplish grey forewings, these stippled with black dots and with two pale transverse lines. Flies July–August and locally common in S and SE England and Wales. Favours woods and hedges. Larva found on various trees and shrubs.

PEBBLE HOOKTIP *Drepana falcataria* Wingspan 28mm
Not closely related to previous species. Variable ground colour to hooked-tipped forewings which show dark transverse line. Flies May–June. Widespread and locally common in woodland and on heaths. Larval foodplant mainly birch.

PEACH BLOSSOM *Thyatira batis* Length at rest 17mm
Attractive moth whose brown forewings bear conspicuous pinkish spots and blotches. Flies June–July and found along woodland rides and in hedgerows. Widespread and fairly common. Larva feeds on bramble. Moth comes to light.

FIGURE OF EIGHTY *Tethea ocularis* Length at rest 24mm
Distinct white markings on forewing resemble figure 80. Locally common only in S and E England and E Wales. Flies May–July and favours wooded habitats where larval foodplants, aspen and poplar, occur. Frequently attracted to light.

LARGE EMERALD *Geometra papilionaria* Wingspan 42mm
Beautiful moth, brightest when newly emerged. Flies July–August and found on heaths and in woods. Larval foodplants include birch and hazel. Locally common in England, Wales and Ireland but scarce in S Scotland. Comes to light.

BLOTCHED EMERALD *Comibaena pustulata* Wingspan 30mm
Has bright green wings the margins of which show brown and white blotches. Flies June–July. Locally common only in S and C England and E Wales and restricted to mature woodland containing oak, the larval foodplant. Comes to light.

GREEN CARPET *Colostygia pectinataria* Wingspan 20mm
Sometimes found resting on lichen-covered tree bark in daytime. Flies May–August. Widespread and generally common in much of Britain and Ireland. Favours meadows, heaths and open ground. Larva feeds on various species of bedstraw.

SILVER GROUND CARPET *Xanthothoe montanata* Wingspan 22mm
Sometimes disturbed from wayside vegetation in daytime and also seen flying at dusk. Whitish forewing marked with darker central transverse band. Flies May–August. Widespread and common in grassy areas. Larva feeds mainly on bedstraws.

FOXGLOVE PUG *Eupithecia pulchellata* Wingspan 18mm
Attractive little moth with colourful forewings. Widespread and often common in many parts of Britain and Ireland. Flies May–July and found on heaths, along woodland rides and on coasts in W and N. Larva feeds in foxglove flowers.

THE MAGPIE *Abraxas grossulariata* Wingspan 38mm
Easily recognised by patterns of black spots and yellow on otherwise white wings. Flies July–August. Widespread and fairly common in England, Wales and Ireland. Favours woods, hedgerows and gardens. Larva feeds on various shrubs.

CANARY-SHOULDERED THORN *Ennomos alniaria* Wingspan 35mm
Recognised by bright canary yellow thorax; wings variable in colour but usually yellow-buff. Flies August–September and favours wooded areas. Larva feeds on birch, hazel and other trees and shrubs. Widespread but seldom numerous.

PURPLE THORN *Selenia tetralunaria* Length at rest 24mm
Rests with wings raised above body. Wings marbled purplish brown and buff; spring brood darker than summer brood. Flies April–May and July–August. Favours woods and heaths. Widespread but common only in S and C England and Wales.

LILAC BEAUTY *Apeira syringaria* Wingspan 40mm
Resemblance to dead leaf enhanced by creased leading edge to forewing. Flies June–September. Widespread and locally common in England, Wales and Ireland; absent from Scotland. Favours wooded areas. Larva eats honeysuckle and privet.

SCALLOPED OAK *Crocallis elinguaria* Length at rest 17mm
Colour of forewing rather variable but often buffish yellow with broad, transverse brown band containing single dark spot. Flies June–August. Widespread and fairly common in woodland. Larva feeds on most deciduous trees and shrubs.

SCORCHED WING *Plagodis dolabraria* Wingspan 23mm
Fairly common in England, Wales and Ireland but scarce in Scotland. Flies May–June and favours wooded habitats. Larval foodplants include oak, birch and other deciduous trees. At rest, base of wings and tip of abdomen look scorched.

BRIMSTONE MOTH *Opisthographis luteolata* Wingspan 28mm
Recognised by bright yellow wings marked with chestnut blotches. Widespread and often common. Flies April–October in several broods in S and favours hedgerows, wooded areas and mature gardens. Larval foodplants include blackthorn, hawthorn and other shrubs. Sometimes disturbed from low vegetation during daytime.

ORANGE MOTH *Angerona prunaria* Wingspan 40mm
Attractive moth, male of which has orange-brown wings, those of female being yellowish. Forewings of both sexes marked with numerous short, transverse lines. Locally common in S and C England, S Wales and S Ireland. Flies June–July and favours woodland and heaths. Larval foodplants include birch, hawthorn and ling.

SPECKLED YELLOW *Pseudopanthera macularia* Wingspan 30mm
Wings have deep yellow ground colour and grey-brown blotches. Fairly common day-flying moth often disturbed from wayside vegetation. Flies May–June and locally common in S England, Wales and Ireland. Favours woodland rides, rough ground and hedgerows. Larval foodplants include wood-sage and yellow archangel.

SWALLOWTAILED MOTH *Ourapteryx sambucaria* Wingspan 52mm
Attractive moth (B), easily recognised by pale yellow wings, angular tip to forewing and short tail streamer on hindwing. Flies June–July and widespread and locally common in England, Wales, S Scotland and Ireland. Found in woodland and gardens and along hedgerows. Comes to light. Foodplants of larva (A) include ivy and hawthorn.

WINTER MOTH *Operophtera brumata* Wingspan of male 28mm
Flies October–February and often seen in car headlights on mild winter nights. Widespread and often extremely common along hedgerows and in woodland and gardens. Wingless female, sometimes coupled with male, can be found by searching twigs after dark by torchlight. Larva feeds on most deciduous trees and shrubs.

MOTTLED UMBER *Erannis defoliaria* Wingspan of male 40mm
Forewings of male vary from pale to dark brown; pale central band, bordered by black line and containing black dot, usually visible. Female wingless. Flies October–December and comes to light. Widespread and often common. Favours woods, hedgerows and gardens. Larva feeds on wide range of deciduous trees and shrubs.

PEPPERED MOTH *Biston betularia* Wingspan 48mm
Colour varies but usually one of two extremes: all-black melanic form and normal form with white ground colour well-marked with black which is camouflaged on bark. Flies May–August. Common and widespread in England, Wales and Ireland; local in Scotland. Favours woods and gardens. Larva eats a wide range of plants.

OAK BEAUTY *Biston strataria* Length at rest 23mm
Attractive moth with good camouflage on tree bark. Flies March–April. Widespread and often common in England and Wales but rather local and scarce in Ireland and Scotland. Favours wooded areas, hedgerows and gardens. Larval foodplants include deciduous trees such as oak, hazel, alder and elm. Male comes to light.

BRINDLED BEAUTY *Lycia hirtaria* Wingspan 40mm
Colour rather variable but usually grey-brown; forewings also show black lines and stippling, with yellow-buff suffusion. Flies March–April and male comes to light. Widespread and often common in S England and Wales; scarce and local in Scotland and Ireland. Favours wooded areas. Larva feeds on deciduous trees.

MOTTLED BEAUTY *Boarmia repandata* Wingspan 38mm
Ground colour of wings usually pale grey-brown but sometimes darker. Wings always have fine black lines and stippling which produce superb camouflage on tree bark. Widespread and often common in Britain and Ireland. Flies June–July and found in woods and gardens. Larval diet includes birch, oak and bramble.

BRISTLETAIL *Petrobius maritimus* Body length 10mm
A curious little insect which is found on rocky shores above the high tide line and in sea caves; widespread around the coasts of Britain and Ireland. The body is elongate and it lacks wings. It has long antennae and three filaments at the tail end. Moves rapidly but in a curious scuttling manner. Feeds on detritus.

SPRINGTAIL *Order Collembola* Length 2-3mm
One of several common species, all of which are tiny, primitive insects that lack wings. They are characterised by their ability to leap using a sprung projection on the underside of the abdomen. Members of the Order are found in damp areas such as leaf litter and compost heaps where they feed on detritus.

Ephemera danica Body length 20mm
A familiar mayfly, widespread in Britain and Ireland. The orange-brown nymph has tapering, snout-like projection and three tail appendages; it lives buried in the silt and sand at the bottom of alkaline rivers and lakes. Like all mayflies, a winged sub-imago emerges from the nymphal skin in the spring and shortly afterwards moults again into the full adult stage which has spots on the wing.

Ephemera vulgata Body length 20mm
Superficially similar to *Ephemera danica.* Adult has a yellowish body but dark markings on upper surface of abdomen are usually triangular rather than oblong. Although, like all mayflies, the adult stage is short-lived, the period of emergence extends May–August. The orange-brown nymph lives in burrows in sand at the bottom of slow-flowing rivers. Only common in S and C England.

Cloeon dipterum Body length 5mm
A common and widespread mayfly in Britain and Ireland. The nymph can be found in a range of standing water habitats including ponds, streams and canals; it has long, hairy tail appendages and can swim well with a wriggling motion. The adult is seen in spring and summer. It lacks hindwings and the forewings are clear but have a beautiful sheen at some angles. The body colour is yellowish brown.

MAYFLY NYMPH *Order Ephemeroptera* Body length 8mm
Like all mayfly nymphs, this typical nymph shows the three tail appendages which are characteristic of the group. Representative species can be found in all types of freshwater from fast-flowing streams to the still waters of lakes and streams. Some mayfly nymphs are capable of sustained swimming while others tire easily. Pollution sensitive.

Perla bipunctata Body length 16mm
The nymph of this stonefly shows the two tail appendages typical of the group. It is found in stony rivers, mainly in N and W Britain. Nymphs are sometimes seen clinging to stones in the water and shed nymphal skins can be found among waterside vegetation from May–July after adult has emerged. Adult's yellowish body is shrouded by smoky wings at rest; two appendages project beyond wingtips.

Nemoura cinerea Body length 10mm
A widespread and fairly common stonefly seen May–July. The adult is sometimes disturbed from vegetation growing beside clean, fast-flowing streams and rivers. It prefers to creep away from danger and has rather sluggish flight. The wings are smoky-brown and, at rest, appear to be rolled lengthways around the body; the tail appendages are very reduced and do not project beyond wings at rest.

Dinocras cephalotes Body length 22mm
A large and robust stonefly, common in parts of N and W Britain. Nymph lives in fast-flowing stony, upland rivers and streams and adult is sometimes found among waterside vegetation from May–July. Body of adult is mostly dark brown and shows two long tail appendages which project beyond smoky-grey wings when at rest.

FIELD CRICKET *Gryllus campestris* Body length 24mm
An impressive cricket, sadly now rare and restricted to a few locations in S England. Favours short grassland and lives in burrows. Adults seen May–June and nymphal stages July–April. Male sings from burrow entrance in warm weather.

WOOD CRICKET *Nemobius sylvestris* Body length 7mm
Local and only found in a few sites in S England. Easiest to see in New Forest where found in small colonies among leaf litter. Two year life cycle so either nymphs or adults seen at most times of year. Male produces soft, warbling song.

MOTTLED GRASSHOPPER *Myrmeleotettix maculatus* Body length 16mm
Ground colour varies from green to brown but body always has marbled appearance. Tips of antennae clubbed in male and swollen in female. Has inflected, angular lines on pronotum. Favours dry places including dunes, heaths and chalk downs.

COMMON FIELD GRASSHOPPER *Chorthippus brunneus* Body length 18-24mm
Common and widespread except for N Scotland and N Ireland. Found in all kinds of dry, grassy places. Shows bulge at base of forewing. Pronotum inflected and angular; black wedge markings do not reach hind edge. Female larger than male.

MEADOW GRASSHOPPER *Chorthippus parallelus* Body length 17-23mm
Widespread and common in Great Britain but absent from Ireland. Both sexes recognised by short forewings which do not reach tip of abdomen; proportionately shorter in female. Hindwings absent. Pronotum gently incurved. Favours meadows.

HEATH GRASSHOPPER *Chorthippus vagans* Body length 15-18mm
Known only from heaths in Dorset and New Forest. Superficially similar to common field grasshopper but usually mottled grey. Black wedge markings on pronotum reach hind edge. Favours clumps of ling into which it retreats if alarmed.

LESSER MARSH GRASSHOPPER *Chorthippus albomarginatus* Body length 21mm
Restricted to S and E England, W Wales and SW Ireland but seldom found inland. Pronotum gently incurved. Forewing long but still does not reach tip of abdomen; shows bulge near base on anterior margin. Favours coastal grassland and dunes.

COMMON GREEN GRASSHOPPER *Omocestus viridulus* Body length 17-20mm
Widespread and often common in Britain and Ireland. Favours all kinds of grassy places. Body colour usually pure green. Shows keel on top of head; pronotum distinctly incurved. Forewings do not have a bulge near base on anterior margin.

WOODLAND GRASSHOPPER *Omocestus rufipes* Body length 15-18mm
Has proportionately large head, conspicuous white tips to palps and tip and underside of abdomen bright red; head and thorax often almost black. Rather local and restricted to open woods and grassy heaths in S England and S Wales.

STRIPE-WINGED GRASSHOPPER *Stenobothrus lineatus* Body length 17-19mm
Ground colour of body and wings usually greenish. Forewing has white comma-like mark and white stripe along anterior margin. White stripe usually continues along pronotum and around head. Found only on dry chalk and limestone grassland.

LARGE MARSH GRASSHOPPER *Stethophyma grossum* Body length 28-32mm
Our largest grasshopper. Local and restricted to floating acid bogs in S and E England and W Ireland where bog moss flourishes. Body and wings well marked with lime green, yellow and black. Hind legs marked with black and yellow bands.

RUFOUS GRASSHOPPER *Gomphocerippus rufus* Body length 16-18mm
Easily recognised by rufous-brown colour and white-tipped, clubbed antennae. Rather local and restricted to chalk and limestone grassland in S England and S Wales; favours S facing slopes. Adults appear late in season, August–September.

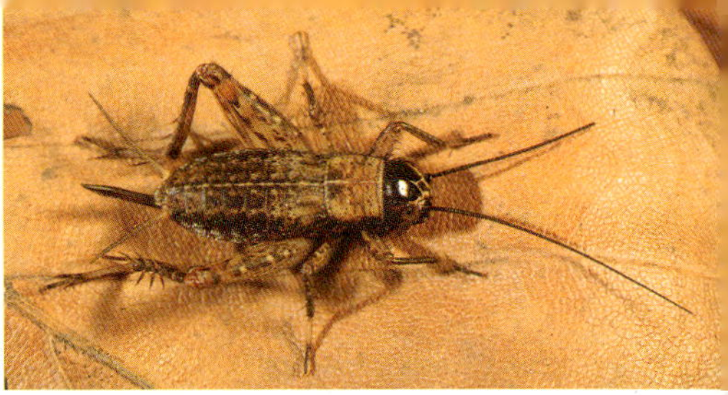

SPECKLED BUSH-CRICKET *Leptophyes punctatissima* Body length 14mm
Body green, speckled with black dots and rather compact, that of female bearing scimitar-shaped ovipositor. Legs long and spindly. Common in S England and S Wales but scarce elsewhere. Favours hedges and scrub. Often on bramble leaves.

OAK BUSH-CRICKET *Meconema thallasiniuim* Body length 15mm
Slender green body, that of female having narrow, slightly upcurved ovipositor. Legs long and spindly. Most active after dark and attracted to lighted windows. Fairly common only in S and C England and Wales. Favours woodland and gardens.

DARK BUSH-CRICKET *Pholidoptera griseoaptera* Body length 15-17mm
Body marbled dark brown, female with upcurved ovipositor. Forewings vestigial in female and reduced to flaps in male; used to produce chirping song. Widespread and common in S and C England and Wales. Favours hedgerows and rough grassland.

GREY BUSH-CRICKET *Platycleis denticulata* Body length 24mm
Body marbled grey-brown but yellow on underside of abdomen; female has upcurved ovipositor. Favours S facing chalk slopes, mostly near coasts. Restricted mainly to S England and S and W Wales. Difficult to locate during daylight hours.

BOG BUSH-CRICKET *Metrioptera brachyptera* Body length 17mm
Invariably found on bogs and wet heaths. Body brown except for bright green underside to abdomen. Top of pronotum and wings either brown or bright green. Has pale line on hind margin of pronotum side-flap. Local in England and Wales.

ROESEL'S BUSH-CRICKET *Metrioptera roeselii* Body length 15-18mm
Formerly found only near coasts of SE and E England but has spread further and inland in recent years. Body marbled brown with pale margin to entire pronotum side-flap. Forewings reach halfway along abdomen. Favours damp meadows.

LONG-WINGED CONEHEAD *Conocephalus discolor* Body length 17-19mm
Slender body bright green except for brown stripe on dorsal surface of head and pronotum; brown wings extend full length of abdomen. Female has upcurved ovipositor. Found among rushes and grasses. Found in S England; mainly coastal but range expanding inland.

SHORT-WINGED CONEHEAD *Conocephalus dorsalis* Body length 16-18mm
Green body has brown dorsal stripe; forewings reduced. Female has straight ovipositor. Found among rushes and grasses. When alarmed, aligns body, antennae and legs along stems. Common only in S England and S Wales. Mainly coastal.

WARTBITER *Decticus verrucivorus* Body length 35mm
Bulky, impressive bush-cricket. Body and wings marbled green and brown. Female has long, upcurved ovipositor. Restricted to a few sites on chalk grassland in S England. Despite size, easily overlooked. Male's song loud and mechanical.

GREAT GREEN BUSH-CRICKET *Tettigonia viridissima* Body length 46mm
Our largest bush-cricket. Bright green except for brown dorsal stripe. Female has long, straight ovipositor. Male's song loud but difficult to pinpoint. Found in scrub in S England and S Wales; commonest on S coast from Dorset to Cornwall.

COMMON GROUNDHOPPER *Tetrix undulata* Body length 10mm
Unobtrusive little insect, easily overlooked because of camouflaged appearance and small size. Colour variable but usually marbled brown. Wings shorter than pronotum which extends length of abdomen. Widespread in Britain and Ireland.

CEPERO'S GROUNDHOPPER *Tetrix ceperoi* Body length 10mm
Similar to common groundhopper but wings extend beyond tip of pronotum. Usually found on damp ground near water. Can fly for short distances; swims well both at and below surface. Very local and restricted to coasts of S England and S Wales.

SOUTHERN HAWKER *Aeshna cyanea* Length 70mm
Large, active species. Associated with ponds, lake and canals. Patrols regular patch of water when hunting but also seen hawking along woodland rides well away from water. Shows broad green stripes on thorax and abdomen with markings of similar coloration on abdomen except for last three segments of male where markings are blue. Widespread and generally common in S and C England. Scarce in Wales and absent from Scotland and Ireland. Flies from June–October.

BROWN HAWKER *Aeshna grandis* Length 74mm
Easily recognised, even in flight, by brown body and bronze wings. At rest, blue spots on second and third segments of male's abdomen can be noticed; these are absent in female. Widespread in S and C England but commonest in SE; local in Ireland and absent from Scotland. Found on well-vegetated ponds, lakes and canals. Patrols regular hunting territory around margins which is vigorously defended against intruders. Flies mainly July–September. Nymph mostly black and white.

EMPEROR DRAGONFLY *Anax imperator* Length 78mm
A large dragonfly. Recognised by dark dorsal line running length of abdomen; colour of abdomen sky blue in male (A) but greenish blue in female. Extremely active and wary. Associated with lakes, ponds and canals and characteristically hunts over open water, away from margins. Confined mainly to S England but there locally common. Flies from June–August. Head of nymph (B) rounded in outline.

GOLDEN-RINGED DRAGONFLY *Cordulegaster boltonii* Length 78-80mm
A striking dragonfly, easily recognised by its dark body marked with bright yellow rings on the abdomen. Favours clean, fast-flowing rivers and streams and squat nymphs live buried in silt and sediment at bottom. Fast-flying and active in sunny weather but on dull days often lethargic and can be watched at close range. Widespread in W of England, Wales and Scotland and often associated with uplands; also occurs locally further E on moors and heaths. Flies June–August.

BROAD-BODIED CHASER *Libellula depressa* Length 43mm
Has broad, flattened abdomen with wings which are dark brown at base. Abdomen of mature male is sky blue with small yellow spots on sides of segments; in female and immature males, abdomen is brown with conspicuous yellow spots on side. Favours ponds and canals. Actively hawks for insects but also uses regular perches from which aerial forays are made in pursuit of prey. Flies May–August. Common only in S England. Squat nymph lives buried in silt at bottom of pond.

BLACK-LINED SKIMMER *Orthetrum cancellatum* Length 50mm
Found only S and E of line from Severn to Wash but there locally common. Mature male has blue eyes and black-tipped blue abdomen with orange-yellow spots on sides. Female and immature male yellow-brown with black lines on abdomen. Wings of both sexes clear even at base. Flies June–August. Skims low over water and frequently uses regular perch. Favours marshes, lakes and flooded gravel pits.

COMMON DARTER *Sympetrum striolatum* Length 36mm
Often the commonest dragonfly in England and Wales; also occurs in Ireland but scarce in N England and absent from Scotland. Mature male (A) has blood-red abdomen but in immature male and female this is orange-brown. Nymph (B) found among pondweeds and debris. Frequently rests on ground but also uses perches. Flies June–late autumn; often the latest-flying species of dragonfly.

RUDDY DARTER *Sympetrum sanguineum* Length 35mm
Both sexes and all ages similar in size and colour to common darter. Male, however, is easily recognised by marked constriction towards front of abdomen. Locally common in S and E England and SE Ireland. Favours ponds, marshes and lakes. Frequently perches with wings depressed slightly. Flies July and August.

DOWNY EMERALD *Cordulia aenea* Length 48mm
Attractive dragonfly (A) with green head and thorax and bronze-green abdomen with metallic sheen. Thorax coated with hairs and base of wings yellowish. Front of abdomen constricted in male. Flies in June and July. Very locally common in SE England and scattered colonies elsewhere in C and S England. Flies fast and low over water but perches high in overhanging tree or bush. Very alert. Nymph)B) found in ponds, lakes and canals.

CLUB-TAILED DRAGONFLY *Gomphus vulgatissimus* Length 50mm
Male has tip of abdomen swollen and both sexes show eyes spaced wide apart. Body of both sexes mainly black but with conspicuous yellow markings in immature specimens, these becoming lime-green when mature. Very local, being restricted today to stretches of Rivers Severn and Thames and a few sites in Sussex. Nymphs live in silt on river bed; empty nymphal skins can often be found among riverside vegetation. Adult emerges in late May and flies throughout June.

BANDED DEMOISELLE *Calopteryx splendens* Length 45mm
An attractive damselfly, often found resting among waterside vegetation. Males seen in small, fluttering groups hovering over water; flight of female rather feeble. Favours clean streams where nymph lives partly buried in muddy sediment. Male has blue body with metallic sheen; smoky wings show a conspicuous blue 'thumbprint' mark. Female has green body with metallic sheen and greenish brown wings. Flies May–August. Locally common in S and C England, Wales and Ireland.

BEAUTIFUL DEMOISELLE *Calopteryx virgo* Length 45mm
Superficially similar to banded demoiselle but wings of male bear much more extensive areas of dark bluish brown; those of female are duller brown than in female banded demoiselle. Body of male is bluish, that of female being green; metallic sheen seen in both sexes. Prefers fast-flowing clear streams where nymph lives buried in sand or gravel bottom. Flies from May–August. Locally common in S and C England and Wales; local in Ireland and absent from Scotland.

COMMON COENAGRION *Coenagrion puella* Length 33mm
Male is sky blue with black bands along length of abdomen and black 'U' marking on segment two of abdomen; female is mostly black but with tip of abdomen blue. Favours marshes, canals and ponds and nymph (B) lives in still water. Widespread and generally common in England and Ireland; local in Wales and very scarce in Scotland. Flies May–August and often found resting among waterside vegetation.

COMMON BLUE DAMSELFLY *Enallagma cyathigerum* Length 32mm
Can be confused with common coenagrion. Marking on segment two of male's abdomen usually resembles dot attached to stalk but rather variable in shape. Green and black female is similar to females of other small damselflies but can be identified with certainty by ventral spine on segment eight of abdomen. Widespread in Britain and Ireland and generally common. Favours well-vegetated lakes, ponds and canals and flies from May–early September, often resting on emergent plants.

BLUE-TAILED DAMSELFLY *Ischnura elegans* Length 32mm
A common and widespread species in much of England, Wales and Ireland; in Scotland, rather scarce and restricted mainly to S. Both sexes easily identified by mainly black body with segment eight of abdomen sky blue. Favours ponds, lakes, canals and ditches; tolerant of slightly polluted waters. Flies May–August.

LARGE RED DAMSELFLY *Pyrrhosoma nymphula* Length 35mm
A distinctive, bright red damselfly; abdomen marked with black, more extensive on female than male. Common and widespread across much of Britain and Ireland. Found in a wide variety of freshwater habitats including ponds, lakes, streams, canals and bogs. Flight rather weak and frequently settles on waterside vegetation. Often the first damselfly seen in spring and flies May–August.

DUSKY COCKROACH *Ectobius lapponicus* Length 9mm
A small native cockroach. Mainly ground-dwelling and easy to overlook in scrub, grassland and woodland habitats it favours. Body dark grey-brown except for pale translucent margin to pronotum and forewing. Adults seen during summer months and fly in warm weather. Found only in S England but locally common there.

COMMON EARWIG *Forficula auricularia* Length 13mm
Common and widespread earwig. Found in leaf litter and under stones or logs during daytime. Most active after dark and emerges to feed mainly on detritus and dead organic matter. Easily recognised by chestnut-brown, shiny body and pincer-like cerci at tail end; these are curved in male but rather straight in female. Flightless. Found throughout year.

HAWTHORN SHIELD BUG *Acanthosoma haemorrhoidale* Length 13mm
Shiny green with black and deep red markings; wings pale and membranous at the tip. Feeds mainly on hawthorn berries and consequently seldom found where this shrub is absent. Also feeds on leaves of other deciduous trees when berries not available. Favours hedgerows and woods. Autumn adults hibernate and appear again April–July; larvae seen June–August. Widespread in England, Wales and Ireland.

SLOE BUG *Dolycoris baccarum* Length 12mm
Dark reddish brown and stippled with black dots; segments of abdomen banded reddish yellow and black and these visible beyond outer margin of wings. Pronotum lacks pronounced lateral projections seen in some other shield bugs. Widespread and common in Britain and Ireland although scarce in N. Associated with blackthorn and other hedgerow shrubs and feeds on sloe and other berries.

GREEN SHIELD BUG *Palomena prasina* Length 13mm
Rather oval in outline. Mainly green but stippled with tiny black dots; tip of wing dark. Overwintering adults usually dull but bright green when newly emerged from hibernation in May. Larvae seen during summer months and new generation of adults appear in September. Widespread and often common in England, Wales and S Ireland; rather scarce further N. Feeds mainly on hazel but also other shrubs.

PIED SHIELD BUG *Sehirus bicolor* Length 7mm
Oval in outline with black and white markings on wings and abdomen. Larvae similarly pied but lack fully formed wings. Following hibernation, adults from the previous autumn emerge in May and are seen until July. Feeds on low-growing plants, particularly white dead-nettle and black horehound. Favours hedgerows and waysides. Widespread in England and Wales; absent from Scotland and Ireland.

FOREST BUG *Pentatoma rufipes* Length 14mm
Shield-shaped in outline, the pronotum having prominent lateral processes. Reddish brown and shiny with legs, mark on scutellum and tip of wings orange-red; abdominal segment banded orange-red and black. As name suggests, found in woodlands where main food, oak, occurs; also feeds on other deciduous trees. Overwintering larvae appear in April; adults seen August–October. Widespread.

Deraeocoris ruber Length 7mm
A common capsid bug in S England and Wales; scarce or absent further N and in Ireland. Colour variable but usually dark reddish brown; forewings show orange-red lateral patch near tip. Feeds on developing fruits and seeds of numerous plants but also on aphids and other small insects. Adult seen July–August.

Campyloneura virgula Length 5mm
A tiny capsid bug, the adults of which are seen July–October. Colour of body and wings buff and dark brown but shows orange-yellow patch on pronotum and near tip of forewing on lateral margin. Common and widespread, usually found in deciduous trees and shrubs. Beneficial predator, feeding on aphids and red spider mites.

POND SKATER *Gerris lacustris* Body length 10mm
Widespread and common on ponds and lakes. Skates over water surface with body supported on tips of legs. Responds to distress movements of insects trapped in surface film; feeds on these using proboscis. Adults hibernate away from water.

LESSER WATER BOATMAN *Corixa punctata* Length 10mm
Common and widespread in weedy ponds and lakes. Can be found all year in water but adults occasionally fly in warm weather. Swims the right way up using fringed hind legs as paddles. Feeds on algae and detritus on bottom of pond.

WATER BOATMAN *Notonecta glauca* Length 14mm
Swims upside down in ponds and lakes using fringed hind legs as paddles. Often looks silvery due to air bubble trapped on ventral surface of body. Predator of other aquatic creatures and insects trapped in surface film. Common all year.

SAUCER BUG *Ilyocoris cimicoides* Length 12mm
Oval in outline, yellowish brown and stippled with numerous tiny dark dots. Widespread and found in most clean, weedy ponds and lakes. Fierce predator of aquatic creatures. Handle with caution since capable of causing a painful bite.

WATER SCORPION *Nepa cinerea* Length 30mm
Easily recognised by leaf-like body outline, long breathing siphon at tail end and pincer-like front legs. Common in weedy ponds and lakes year-round. Predator of tadpoles, small fish and other aquatic insects. Movements slow and creeping.

WATER STICK INSECT *Ranatra linearis* Length 50mm
Easy to overlook in pond samples since remains motionless and stick-like when out of water. Adopts mantid-like pose when submerged and captures passing aquatic creatures. Fairly common and widespread in S in weedy ponds and lakes.

COMMON FROGHOPPER *Philaenus spumarius* Length 6mm
Adult is oval in outline; colour variable but usually marbled brown. Jumps well. Nymph is green and, like adult, feeds on plant sap; creates frothy mass known as 'cuckoo-spit' in which it lives. Common and widespread from June–August.

Cercopis vulnerata Length 9mm
Distinctive, shiny red and black froghopper. Found resting on low vegetation and jumps well to escape danger. Common and widespread in hedgerows, woodland rides and meadows; seen from May–August. Feeds on plant sap. Nymphs found on roots.

RHODODENDRON LEAFHOPPER *Graphocephala fennahi* Length 9mm
Introduced from N America but now firmly established on rhododendrons in S England. Recognised both by plant preference and by red forewing stripes on otherwise green body. Widespread and fairly common where foodplant flourishes.

Ledra aurita Length 14mm
Despite size and being fairly common, this camouflaged leafhopper is easily overlooked. Favours oak woodland and feeds on lichen. Brown, winged adult has thoracic projections. Oval shaped nymph is pale, squat and strangely flattened.

BLACK BEAN APHID *Aphis fabae* Length 2mm
Widespread and at times extremely abundant. Eggs overwinter on spindle. Wingless females appear on beans in spring; huge colonies form by summer when winged adults appear. Eaten by ladybirds but guarded and 'milked' for honeydew by ants.

ROSE APHID *Macrosiphum rosae* Length 2mm
The familiar garden 'greenfly'. Can be either green or pink but has two black horn-like projections towards end of abdomen. Widespread and often extremely abundant. Found in colonies on roses in spring but on other plants by summer.

ALDER FLY *Sialis lutaria* Length 14mm
Adult (A) superficially lacewing-like but has broad, brown wings with clearly defined black veins forming a relatively simple network. Wings held in tent-like manner at rest. A poor flier, often found resting on waterside vegetation May–June. Aquatic larva (B) is predatory; its brown, tapering abdomen is fringed with gills.

LACEWING *Chrysoperla carnea* Length 15mm
Familiar insect of house and garden with transparent, well-veined wings. Found among vegetation during summer months and attracted to lighted windows. In autumn, often comes indoors to hibernate, turning from green to pink. Larva feeds mainly on aphids and creates camouflaged home from their empty skins.

SCORPION FLY *Panorpa communis* Length 14mm
A strange-looking insect, the male of which has a scorpion-like, upturned abdomen. Flight weak and at rest holds wings flat. Head has beak-like downward projection used in feeding; scavenges dead animals, including contents of spiders' webs, and ripe fruit. Seen May–July in hedgerows and among brambles.

SNAKE FLY *Raphidia notata* Length 14mm
Elongated thorax enables head to be raised in a bizarre and fancifully snake-like manner. Transparent wings resemble those of lacewings. Associated with mature oak woodlands and seen May–July. Adult feeds mainly on aphids. Larva found in decaying wood and under bark; also eats small insects. Locally common.

Agapetes fuscipes Length 9mm
A relatively small caddis fly, associated with fast-flowing streams with stony bottoms. Often extemely common in chalk streams and larval cases, built from small stones, often cover larger pieces of flint. Adult has light brown, hairy wings; emerges in spring and masses often congregate on waterside vegetation.

Glyphotaelius pellucidus Length 16mm
A widespread and often common caddis fly found in standing waters of ponds and lakes. The larva constructs a case from dead leaves and is difficult to detect in pond samples until occupant decides to move. Adult appears April–June and has marbled brown and white wings, the forewing having a notched outer margin.

Limnephilus rhombicus Larval case length 18mm
A common caddis fly; widespread in a wide range of waterbodies from ponds to slow-flowing stretches of chalk streams and watercress beds. Larval case constructed from stems and leaf stalks of water plants. Considering size of case, larva is fairly agile. Adults have mottled brown, rather narrow forewings.

Phryganea striata Length 25mm
One of our largest caddis flies and a species which sometimes comes to light. Widespread and perhaps commonest in N and W regions. Wings are marbled brown and buff; female has broken black line on forewing. Larva builds case made from leaves, stems and other plant material, arranged spirally to form a cylinder.

Limnephilus elegans Length 12mm
A well marked caddis fly with grey-brown, hairy wings bearing black lines on forewings. Like all caddis flies, at rest the antennae are held out in front of head. Rather cumbersome larval case constructed from plant material. Adult seen from May–July. Usually associated with upland pools and slow-flowing rivers.

Limnephilus marmoratus Length 13mm
Associated with well-vegetated upland and northern tarns and lakes and locally common in suitable habitats. Adult has well-marked forewings and is seen resting among emergent vegetation from May–July. Larva constructs case from fragments of plant material; sometimes observed moving around in clear, shallow water.

Tipula maxima Body length 30mm
A large and impressive crane-fly with wings conspicuously marked with patches of brown. Widespread and fairly common, adults seen in spring and summer. Found in damp woodland and beside wooded streams; leathery larva lives in watery margins.

DADDY-LONG-LEGS *Tipula paludosa* Body length 16mm
A familiar insect of garden lawns and grassland with weak flight and dangling legs. Adults most common August–October, especially after wet weather. Larva live in soil and eat roots and stems of plants; often known as 'leatherjackets'.

PHANTOM MIDGE *Chaoborus crystillinus* Body length 16mm
Common, non-biting fly (A) associated with all sorts of standing freshwater. Male has plumed antennae and wings that do not reach tip of abdomen. Transparent aquatic larva (B) sometimes known as 'ghost worm'; feeds on small aquatic animals.

Culex spp Larval length 6mm
Adult (A) is familiar mosquito; female sucks blood while male feeds on nectar. Larval (B) and pupal stages found in all kinds of standing water including stagnant water-butts; easily disturbed from water surface and swim with wriggling motion.

Chironomus plumosus Body length 10mm
A common, non-biting midge seen from spring to autumn. Males have wings shorter than abdomen and plumed antennae; form large swarms. Females have relatively longer wings and simple antennae. Aquatic larvae often known as 'bloodworms'.

ST MARK'S FLY *Bibio marci* Body length 11mm
Adult often appears around St Mark's Day (April 25th). Antennae are short and body is black and hairy. Rather sluggish when resting on vegetation. Male flies with dangling legs. Found in areas of short grass and larva lives in soils.

Chrysops relictus Body length 10mm
An attractive horse-fly with patterned wings, yellow markings on abdomen and iridescent green eyes. Seen June–August and can inflict a painful bite. Associated with damp ground in woodland and on heaths; larva lives in wet soil.

CLEG-FLY *Haematopota pluvialis* Body Length 10mm
Common horse-fly, seen May–September. An unwelcome and attentive follower of human visitors to damp woodland. Has grey-brown body and mottled brown wings held in roof-like pose at rest. Eyes are iridescent and head is rather compressed.

Haematopota crassicornis Body length 10mm
A common and widespread horse-fly, sometimes also called a 'cleg'. Seen in close-up, eyes are amazingly iridescent. Feeds on blood and inflicts a painful bite. Approaches victim silently and creeps over skin unfelt until ready to bite.

Tabanus bromius Body length 14mm
Robust horse-fly. Abdominal segments show yellowish brown and black markings. Flies July–August and commonly found around cattle and ponies; can also inflict a painful bite on humans. Carnivorous larva lives in damp soil. Widespread.

BEE-FLY *Bombylius major* Body length 10mm
Recognised at rest by hairy, bee-like body and long proboscis. In flight, even more bee-like and produces high-pitched hum. Flies April–May. Visits flowers to feed on nectar. Larva feeds on grubs of solitary bees. Widespread; common in S.

Empis tesselata Body length 11mm
A small, dark empid or assassin fly, seen April–July. Visits flowers for nectar but also catches other flies; these are sometimes carried in flight and then sucked dry using long, downward pointing proboscis. Abdomen strongly downcurved.

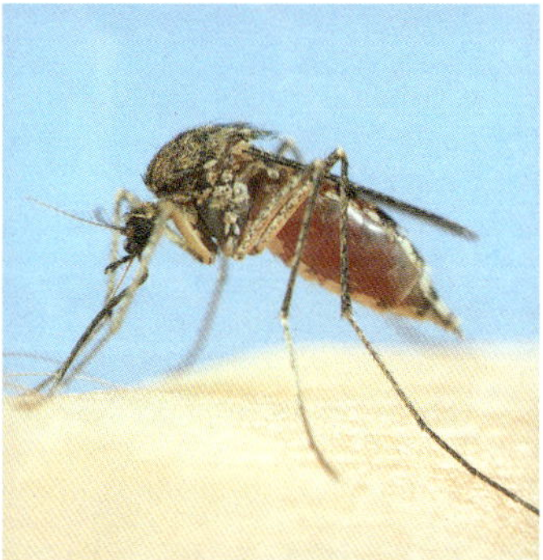
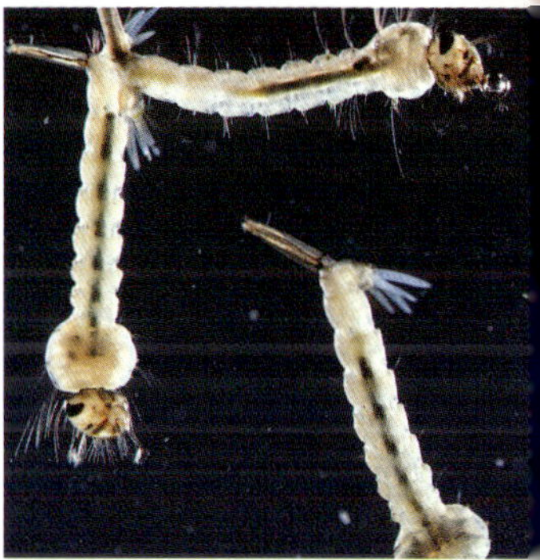

SNIPE-FLY *Rhagio scolopacea* Body length 12mm
Common and widespread, seen May–July. Often sunbathes on vegetation but also sits head-down on tree trunks and will sometimes suddenly fly straight at observer. Adult feeds on nectar; larva is carnivorous and lives in leaf litter.

DRONE-FLY *Eristalis tenax* Body length 12mm
Superficially very similar to honey bee drone but close inspection reveals relatively large eyes and body not 'waisted' between thorax and abdomen. Visits flowers to feed on nectar. 'Rat-tailed maggot' larva lives in stagnant water.

Helophilus pendulus Body length 10mm
A common hover-fly often seen visiting garden flowers and wayside species such as hogweed and ragwort. Favours damp, wooded sites and male often hovers over water. Flies May–September. Frequently sunbathes. Larva lives in stagnant water.

Sericomyia silentis Body length 16mm
A striking, wasp-like hover-fly, widespread in Britain and Ireland. Favours wet meadows, moors, heaths and damp woodland and frequently visits flowers to feed on nectar. Adult seen from May–August and larva lives in damp, peaty soil.

Syrphus ribesii Body length 12mm
Extremely common hover-fly, widespread in Britain and Ireland. Found in gardens, hedgerows and woodland rides and visits flowers to feed on nectar. Multiple-brooded, adults seen April–October. Larva found on leaves and feeds on aphids.

Volucella bombylans Body length 14mm
Extremely good bumble bee mimic. Some individuals have white-tipped abdomen while in others it is red. Frequent visitor to flowers in gardens, hedgerows and woods and seen May–September. Larva scavenges in nests of bumble bees and wasps.

GREENBOTTLE *Lucilia caesar* Body length 9mm
Has shiny green or bronzy-green body and red eyes. Common and widespread in Britain and Ireland. Found in all sorts of habitats. Attracted to flowers, dung and carrion. Larvae found in rotting carcasses and sometimes attracted to open wounds.

FLESH-FLY *Sarcophaga carnaria* Body length 15mm
Common and widespread. Adult has greyish body but with chequered markings on abdomen; eyes red and feet proportionately large. Attracted to carrion and carcasses on which female gives birth to live young. Seldom ventures indoors.

COMMON HOUSE-FLY *Musca domestica* Body length 8mm
Extremely common and widespread visitor to houses throughout Britain and Ireland. Has red eyes and mostly dark body except for orange patches on abdomen. Sharp bend in fourth long vein of wing. Attracted to rubbish where they lay their eggs.

LESSER HOUSE-FLY *Fannia canicularis* Body length 5mm
Superficially similar to common house-fly but smaller and fourth long vein of wing straight, without sharp bend. Often found indoors; males fly repetitive circuits beneath ceiling lights and fixtures. Larvae in putrefying corpses and dung.

BLUEBOTTLE *Calliphora erythrocephala* Body length 11mm
Extremely common visitor to homes. Found in most months but commonest in summer. Makes loud buzzing sound in flight. Female attracted to meat on which eggs are laid and larvae feed. Adult has blue, shiny body and reddish eyes and jowls.

YELLOW DUNG-FLY *Scatophaga stercoraria* Body length 9mm
Swarms of furry, golden males collect on cowpats and seen March–October. Arrival of female greeted with flurry of activity and mating pair subsequently seen. Adult preys on other flies. Larvae develop inside cowpat. Widespread and common.

BIRCH SAWFLY *Cimbex femoratus* Length 21mm
Adult is large and impressive with yellow-tipped antennae and yellow on base of abdomen. Wings are smoky and dark-bordered. Flies May–June and makes buzzing sound in flight. Favours birch woods; larvae feed on birch leaves. Rather local.

GIANT WOOD WASP *Uroceras gigas* Body length 30mm
Alternative name of this large sawfly is 'horntail', after female's long ovipositor; this is used to lay eggs in timber. Also recognised by black and yellow colours. Flies May–August. Widespread. Favours areas of pine forest.

MARBLE GALL Diameter up to 20mm
Clusters of marble galls on oak are caused by larvae of tiny gall wasp *Andricus kollari*; green then brown when mature. Emergence holes seen from autumn onwards. Parthenogenetic females overwinter and then lay eggs on oak buds in spring.

KNOPPER GALL Length up to 28mm
Deeply ridged outgrowths on acorns of pedunculate oak caused by larvae of tiny gall wasp *Andricus quercuscalicis*. Subsequent generation develops in galls induced in Turkey oak catkins. Cycle is then repeated in penduculate oak.

OAK APPLE Diameter up to 25mm
Irregularly shaped buffish brown gall on oak caused by larva of gall wasp *Biorhiza pallida*. Adults emerge in June and July, each gall containing a single sex. Subsequent asexual generation develops in spherical galls on oak roots.

ROBIN'S PINCUSHION Diameter up to 25mm
Spherical, seemingly fibrous growths on dog rose caused by larvae of gall wasp *Diplolepis rosae* which live in hardened centre of gall. Widespread and rather common. Green at first but acquires a reddish tint with maturity in autumn.

CHERRY GALL Diameter up to 10mm
Attractive spherical galls on the underside of oak leaves caused by larvae of gall wasp *Diplolepis quercusfolii*. Individual galls often grade from bright red to green. Adults emerge in winter and subsequent generation found in oak buds.

SPANGLE GALL Diameter up to 4mm
Disc-like galls on underside of oak leaves caused by larvae of gall wasp *Neuroterus quercusbaccarum*. Found on ground after autumn leaf fall. Subsequent generation causes currant galls on oak flowers in spring. Common and widespread.

YELLOW OPHION *Ophion luteus* Length 20mm
Has yellowish or orange-yellow body and constantly twitching antennae. Common and widespread July–September. Female lacks an ovipositor but is still able to parasitise caterpillars of larger moths inside which its own larvae develop.

Rhyssa persuasoria Body length 35mm
Our largest ichneumon fly and an impressive insect. Associated with mature pine woods and flies July–August. Female uses long ovipositor to parasitise larvae of giant wood wasp which are located deep in living timber. Locally common.

RUBY-TAILED WASP *Chrysis ignita* Length 11mm
Small but attractive insect with green, shiny head and thorax and ruby-red abdomen. Flies June–August. Female searches diligently on walls and banks for mason wasp nests which she enters, if owner is absent, to parasitise the larvae.

LEAF-CUTTER BEE *Megachile centuncularis* Length 13mm
A B
Well-known for the neat, semi-circular holes which are cut from the leaf margins of garden roses (B) and other plants by female bees; these are used to create nest walls. Underside of abdomen is orange. Common and widespread in June and July.

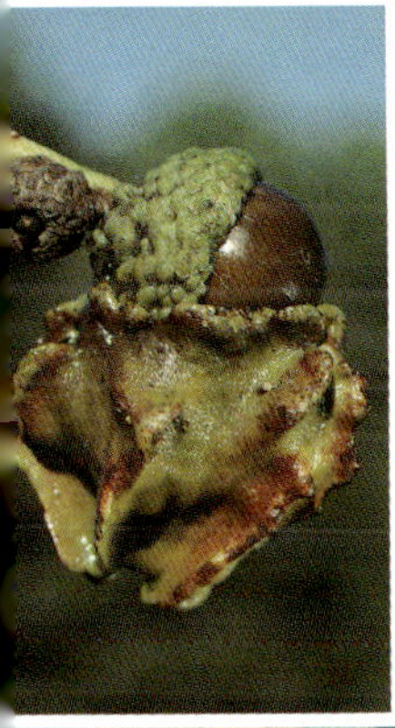

WOOD ANT *Formica rufa* Length 10mm
Forms large colonies in woodland clearings, these easily recognised by sizeable mounds of dry plant stems and leaves. Reddish brown workers seen collecting caterpillars and other insects. Can spray formic acid from rear end if alarmed.

BLACK GARDEN ANT *Lasius niger* Length 3mm
Widespread and common in a range of habitats but perhaps most familiar in gardens where nests are formed under paving stones and brickwork. Diet varied but 'milks' aphids for honeydew. Winged ants swarm in hot, humid weather.

RED ANT *Myrmica rubra* Length 4mm
Favours garden soil and lawns. Yellowish red workers can deliver surprisingly painful sting. Active throughout year but winged ants swarm in late summer, often during hot, humid weather. Diet varied and includes many garden pests.

FIELD DIGGER WASP *Mellinus arvensis* Length 12mm
Yellow and black colours recall those of true wasps but 'waisted' abdomen more pronounced. Excavates deep burrow in sandy soil. Breeding cells stocked with flies, immobilised by sting; these feed the developing young. Flies May–August.

SAND DIGGER WASP *Ammophila sabulosa* Length 20mm
Favours sandy areas, particularly coasts; commonest in S. Often seen dragging immobilised caterpillar larger than itself back to burrow in which eggs are laid; burrow entrance plugged with soil. Has narrow 'waist'. Flies May–August.

HORNET *Vespa crabro* Length 30mm
An impressive insect and our largest wasp. Local and common only in parts of S England. Recognised by size and by tawny brown and dull yellow colours. Favours wooded areas and usually nests in dead trees. Colony most active June–September.

GERMAN WASP *Vespula germanica* Length 18mm
Has typical wasp colours and markings and seen head on, face has three black dots. Common and widespread. Grey, papery nest built underground or sometimes in loft space. Beneficial since it collects large numbers of insects to feed its larvae.

COMMON WASP *Vespula vulgaris* Length 17mm
Similar to German wasp but, seen head on, face has black anchor mark. Common and widespread, active mainly June–September. Grey, almost spherical papery nest built underground or in buildings. Like other wasps, attracted to rotting fruit.

HONEY BEE *Apis mellifera* Length 12mm
Widely kept in hives for honey. In wooded areas, wild colonies nest in holes in trees. Network of wax cells form comb in which honey is stored and young are raised. Female workers comprise bulk of colony which is ruled by a single queen.

COMMON CARDER-BEE *Bombus agrorum* Length 13mm
A common and widespread species with buffish brown or reddish brown hairs on thorax and abdomen, the latter looking rather banded. Active from spring to autumn. Nests above ground, sometimes in old songbird nests or even nestboxes.

RED-TAILED BUMBLE BEE *Bombus lapidarius* Length 23mm
A large and familiar species. Appears all-black except for hairs at tip of abdomen which are bright orange-red. After hibernation, female emerges in May and looks for burrow in which to build nest. Common and widespread except in N.

BUFF-TAILED BUMBLE BEE *Bombus terrestris* Length 24mm
Common and widespread, except in N. After hibernation, female appears in April and visits flowers on sunny days. Builds nest in burrow. Recognised by broad, buffish yellow band at front of thorax and on abdomen; tip of abdomen buff.

GREEN TIGER BEETLE *Cicindela campestris* Length 14mm
An active, ground-dwelling beetle of sandy places including heaths and dunes. Upperparts usually green with pale spots on elytra; legs and thorax margins are shiny bronze. Widespread and locally common. Seen May–July. Active predator.

Pterostichus madidus Length 14mm
Very common ground beetle, usually found under stones or logs in daytime; often in gardens. Shiny black in appearance, elytra with fine grooves; legs typically reddish. Predatory but also feeds on plant material including fruit. Flightless.

Acilius sulcatus Length 16mm
A common water beetle in England but local elsewhere. Favours weedy ponds and canals. Swims well using fringed hind legs as paddles. Male has shiny, golden elytra which are finely marked; those of female are grooved. Active carnivore.

GREAT DIVING BEETLE *Dytiscus marginalis* Length 30mm
Large and impressive water beetle. Found in ponds and lakes. Widespread and generally common. Margins of elytra and thorax orange-brown. Male has smooth, shiny elytra; female's are grooved. Both adults and larvae are fierce predators.

GREAT SILVER BEETLE *Hydrophilus piceus* Length 40mm
Our largest water beetle. Extremely local and now confined to a few areas in S England; favours weedy drainage ditches. Upper surface shiny black and underside silvery in water due to air film. Adult vegetarian but larva eats water snails.

Nicrophorus humator Length 22mm
A large, all-black burying beetle sometimes found in the act of interring dead mouse or small bird. Female lays her eggs beside buried corpse which developing larvae use as source of food. Often covered in mites. Tips of antennae orange.

Nicrophorus vespilloides Length 16mm
A distinctive sexton beetle, recognised by orange-red markings on otherwise black elytra; has all-black antennae unlike other closely related species. Often found by turning over animal carcasses. Buries corpses of small mammals and birds on which eggs are laid and larvae feed. Attracted to light. Widespread.

DEVIL'S COACH-HORSE *Staphylinus olens* Length 24mm
An all-black, long-bodied beetle the abdominal segments of which are not covered by the elytra. If threatened, curls up abdomen and opens jaws. Shelters during daytime under stones and logs. Emerges after dark to feed on invertebrates. In autumn, may venture indoors. Common and widespread in hedgerows and gardens.

LESSER STAG BEETLE *Dorcus parallelipipedus* Length 28mm
Recalls female stag beetle but has all-black body and proportionately large and broad head and thorax. Rather local but widespread in S and C England, Wales and S Ireland. Larva found in rotting wood and adults feed on sap of deciduous trees including ash and willow. Adults seen May–September but commonest in spring.

STAG BEETLE *Lucanus cervus* Length 40mm
Large and impressive beetle with reddish brown elytra and black head and thorax. Male has enlarged, antler-like jaws, used for battling with rivals for right to mate with antler-less female. Depends on a large and undisturbed supply of rotting wood, especially oak, in which larvae live and feed. Consequently, now rather scarce and found locally only in S and C England. Adults seen May–July.

Sinodendron cylindricum Length 15mm
Male resembles a miniature rhinoceros beetle, having a horn-like projection on head. Rather local but widespread; occurs in mature woodland, especially beech or oak. Adult sometimes found in or under rotting wood in which larva lives.

ROSE CHAFER *Cetonia aurata* Length 17mm
A large and attractive beetle. Colour usually shiny bronzy-green, the elytra flecked with white lines and marks. Elytra parallel-sided and rather flattened. Moves in a rather cumbersome manner among vegetation and often found in flowers, including roses. Widespread and locally common in Britain and Ireland. Active in sunny weather and seen May–September. Larva lives in rotting wood.

COCKCHAFER *Melolontha melolontha* Length 35mm
Adults (A) are seen in May and June, hence alternative name of 'may-bug'. Easily recognised by hairy, rufous-brown elytra and pointed-tipped abdomen. In many areas, common enough to form large swarms at dusk; these often fly around tree tops and consume large numbers of leaves. Larva (B) lives in soil and spends several years feeding on roots of grasses, herbaceous plants and trees; sometimes occurs at sufficient densities in lawns and cultivated land to cause visible damage.

BEE BEETLE *Trichius fasciatus* Length 14mm
An extremely hairy beetle with wasp- or bee-like black and orange-yellow markings on elytra; thorax and abdomen buffish brown. Adults seen from June–September and visit flowers including thistles and thyme. Mostly associated with upland areas. Seldom common; occurs locally in N Wales, N England and Scotland.

Rhagonycha fulva Length 11mm
An extremely common soldier beetle. Body mostly orange-red except for tip of elytra which are dark. Very active in sunny weather and flies well. Frequently visits flowers, especially umbellifers, where it hunts for insect prey; often becomes dusted with pollen. Seen May–August; mating pairs are a common sight.

GLOW-WORM *Lampyris noctiluca* Length of female 14mm
Grub-like, wingless females (B) located after dark by greenish light emitted from underside of tip to abdomen; this serves to attract winged males. Females usually climb up grass stems and luminosity ceases temporarily if disturbed. Adults do not feed but larvae (A), which can also emit light, eat snails. Found in meadows and along forest rides and verges. Widespread but local; absent from N.

CLICK BEETLE *Athous haemorrhoidalis* Length 14mm
Extremely common and widespread; generally associated with woodland, scrub and hedgerows. Body appears relatively narrow with reddish brown elytra and darker head and thorax; body cloaked in downy hairs. Best known for ability to hurl itself into air when placed on back, this process accompanied by a loud click. Adults seen May–June and often found on leaves of hazel. Larvae in rotting wood.

Pyrochroa serraticornis Length 14mm
An attractive cardinal beetle, so-called because of scarlet colour of head, thorax and abdomen. Adult seen May–July and often found under flaking bark or in rotting timber; in sunny weather also visits flowers to hunt for small insects. Carnivorous larva lives in rotting wood. Rather local in England and Ireland.

Oedemera nobilis Length 10mm
Distinctive little beetle; body is shiny green and surprisingly slender. Elytra taper and splay towards tip of abdomen and do not completely cover wings. Male has distinctive swollen hind femora. Seen May–August. Common and widespread in S England and Wales. Favours grassy places and visits flowers to feed on pollen.

Meloe proscarabeus Length 26mm
An oil beetle, so-called because of pungent oil it produces when alarmed. Local and widespread in grassy places. Has shiny, bluish black body with small elytra that do not cover the swollen-looking abdomen. Adult seen April–June. After emerging from egg, young larva climbs flowers and attaches itself to passing solitary bee; then carried back to bee's nest inside which larva then develops.

EYED LADYBIRD *Anatis ocellata* Length 8mm
Widespread and locally common, usually associated with conifers. Elytra rich orange-red and marked with black spots, these usually ringed paler producing an eyed appearance. Adult seen during June and July and feeds mainly on aphids.

7-SPOT LADYBIRD *Coccinella 7-punctata* Length 6mm
Familiar ladybird; widespread and often abundant. Elytra are reddish orange and, at rest, show seven black spots; anterior spot embraces both elytra. Both adults and larvae feed on aphids. Adults hibernate and are active from March–October.

14-SPOT LADYBIRD *Propylea 14-punctata* Length 5mm
Black and yellow markings rather variable, but suture between elytra always black. Widespread and fairly common in S and C England, Wales and Ireland. Found on a wide variety of wayside plants and shrubs. Active from April–September.

WASP BEETLE *Clytus arietus* Length 16mm
Extremely wasp-like, both in terms of black and yellow appearance but also in its behaviour. Flies well in sunny weather and often visits hedgerow and garden flowers. Seen May–July. Widespread and often common in Britain and Ireland.

Strangalia maculata Length 16mm
Has somewhat variable yellow markings on elytra and legs but is otherwise black. Body elongate and elytra taper towards tail end. Frequently visits flowers to feed on pollen and found among leaves of trees and shrubs. Active June–August.

Rhagium mordax Length 21mm
A well-marked and rather downy longhorn beetle. Widespread and fairly common in mature woodlands, especially oak. Adults seen May–July. Sometimes seen foraging among flowers or foliage; sometimes in rotting wood and stumps alongside larvae.

TORTOISE BEETLE *Cassida rubiginosa* Length 7mm
An intriguing little beetle whose broad, flattened elytra and pronotum overlap body by a considerable margin and provide camouflage and protection when clamped down. Usually found on leaves of thistles and seen June–August. Fairly common.

POPLAR LEAF BEETLE *Chrysomela populi* Length 10mm
Striking, rounded beetle with bright red elytra and black head, thorax and legs. Superficially ladybird-like but elytra usually unmarked. Seen from April–August; often associated with poplars and willows. Widespread and fairly common.

MINT LEAF BEETLE *Chrysolina menthastri* Length 9mm
An extremely shiny, bronzy-green beetle which is usually found on mint leaves; sometimes also on hemp-nettles. Body extremely rounded. Seen from May–August. Favours damp, waterside meadows and hedgerows. Widespread and locally common.

BLOODY-NOSED BEETLE *Timarcha tenebricosa* Length 20mm
A lumbering, flightless leaf beetle, often seen plodding across paths or through grass. When disturbed, exudes drop of bright red, blood-like fluid from mouth. Widespread and fairly common in Britain and Ireland and seen from April–June.

Phyllobius pomaceus Length 9mm
A small weevil. The body is black but it is covered by greenish scales which are easily rubbed off. Usually found on leaves of common nettle but also on other wayside plants. Widespread and fairly common, seen mainly from April–August.

HAZEL WEEVIL *Curculio nucum* Length 6mm
Widespread and locally common wherever larval foodplant, hazel, occurs. Female bores through husk of embryo nut to lay egg. Larva feeds on developing nut inside case until it falls in autumn; pupates in ground. Adult seen April–June.

Araniella curcurbitina Body length up to 6mm
A small but attractive spider, the abdomen of which is lime green with yellow bands; the cephalothorax and legs are reddish brown. Spins a rather untidy orb-web among low wayside vegetation such as thistles and brambles. Favours rough meadows, hedgerows and gardens. Common and widespread from May–September.

GARDEN SPIDER *Araneus diadematus* Body length up to 12mm
Arguably our most familiar spider. Female considerably larger than male. Ground colour of body and legs rather variable but usually grey-brown or reddish brown. Abdomen has row of white dots down centre and transverse white streaks forming a distinct cross. Common in a wide range of habitats including gardens, hedgerows, rough meadows and woodland clearings. Spins a sophisticated web comprising radial and spiral silk threads. Widespread and seen as adult from July–October.

Araneus quadratus Body length up to 20mm
Superficially similar to garden spider but abdomen has four large white spots arranged almost in a square and a white anterior stripe. Abdomen colour varies from nut-brown to bright red; in mature females it can appear grotesquely swollen and almost spherical. Widespread and common in a wide range of habitats including gardens, scrub, hedgerows and meadows. Adults seen from July–October. Spins a large and sophisticated web. Female much larger than male.

WATER SPIDER *Argyroneta aquatica* Body length up to 14mm
The only truly aquatic spider. Very locally common in weedy lakes and ponds; also occasionally in slow-flowing streams. Looks silvery underwater due to film of air trapped around grey-brown abdomen; cephalothorax and legs reddish brown. Constructs domed, air-filled web among water plants in which it spends much of daytime; air periodically renewed by spider. Silk threads radiating from web alert occupant to passing prey. Adults can be found at most times of the year.

PURSE-WEB SPIDER *Atypus affinis* Body length 12mm
An extraordinary spider which lives inside a subterranean silken tube. A small part of the tube lies on the soil surface like the finger of a glove. When an insect walks over the tube, the spider rushes to the source of the disturbance and, walking upside down, thrusts its long fangs through the silk, thus grabbing the prey; damage to the tube is repaired after the meal has been consumed. Fairly common in dry, well-draining soil but silken tubes are easily overlooked.

Amaurobius similis Body length up to 12mm
A fairly common and widespread spider. Usually found on walls, behind bark and on fences where it constructs a rather tangled web of bluish white silk leading back to a crevice. It is into this that the spider retreats for much of the time. Abdomen usually buffish with paired dark markings on dorsal surface and chevrons towards the rear end. Cephalothorax and legs usually orange-brown.

SWAMP SPIDER *Dolomedes fimbriatus* Body length 25mm
Without doubt our most impressive spider. Body and legs chestnut-brown with yellow line around margins of cephalothorax and abdomen. Rather local; common only in parts of S England such as New Forest and Surrey heaths. Restricted to damp heathland and typically found on or beside boggy pools. Sits with front legs touching water surface and attracted to vibrations caused by distress movements of insects trapped in surface film. Can skate with ease over surface but will also submerge if alarmed. Seen May–August.

Dysdera crocata Body length 12mm
An attractive spider with reddish legs and cephalothorax and buffish brown abdomen. Fangs are huge relative to body size and are opposable; used to good effect when capturing woodlice. Hides under stones during daytime. Widespread and fairly common. Found in most habitats that support good numbers of woodlice.

Pardosa lugubris Body length 6mm
A common and widespread wolf spider found among leaf litter on woodland and forest floors. Adult has buffish brown band on carapace. Most active April–June when female can sometimes be seen carrying around egg sac attached to spinnerets at tip of abdomen. After the young hatch, they remain clinging to the mother's abdomen for several weeks. Actively hunts insect prey and does not spin a web.

Metellina merianae Body length 9mm
Sometimes referred to as a cave spider because of its preference for cave entrances, cellars and other dark, dank places; needs plenty of crevices into which it can retreat. Abdomen is marbled brown and black and shiny legs are marked with irregular bands of reddish brown and black. Widespread and fairly common in suitable habitats; often coastal. Seen mainly from May–July.

Misumena vatia Body length up to 10mm
A widespread and often common crab spider. Colour of female is variable and changeable but usually white, creamy yellow or pale green; sometimes has red lines on side of abdomen. Male much smaller than female and darker. Female usually found sitting on flowers that match her body colour such as gorse or ox-eye daisy. Catches insects that land on flower to feed. Seen from May–August.

DADDY-LONG-LEGS SPIDER *Pholcus phalangioides* Body length 8mm
A narrow-bodied, long-legged spider which is almost always associated with houses and buildings. Cannot survive in locations where temperature dips below 50°F and so commonest in homes with central heating in S England. Can be found at most times of the year but most active during summer months. The spider is typically found hanging upside down from ceilings; spins a tangled, untidy web.

Pisaura mirabilis Body length 14mm
A common and widespread hunting spider which is found in hedgerows, woodland rides and grassland. Body colour buffish brown but shows a dark-bordered, yellow stripe on carapace. Actively hunts prey on ground without the aid of a web. Female sometimes seen carrying egg sac underneath body, secured by mouthparts. Builds a nursery tent just before eggs are due to hatch. Seen from May–July.

ZEBRA SPIDER *Salticus scenicus* Body length 7mm
An intriguing little jumping spider named after its black and white stripes; body rather hairy. Usually seen restlessly moving up sunny fences and walls. Spots potential prey using large eyes and then stalks to within leaping range. Will even jump up vertical surfaces. Seen from May–September. Occasionally ventures indoors in warm weather. Common and widespread in most of Britain.

HOUSE SPIDER *Tegenaria domestica* Body length 10mm
A large, long-legged spider that is often found in and around houses. Body rather hairy and varies from pale to dark brown. Can look rather intimidating when trapped in bath or scurrying across floor. Spins untidy web in corner of room with tubular retreat. Female can survive for several years. Widespread.

Xysticus cristatus Body length 6mm
A common and widespread crab spider. Has pale stripes on thorax and patterns of pale and dark brown on abdomen forming series of overlapping triangles. Favours hedgerows and meadows and usually found waiting motionless with legs outstretched on bare stalk or flower for passing insect. Seen mostly from May–July.

Tetragnatha extensa Body length 10mm
A long-legged spider, the abdomen of which is elongate and sausage-like. Legs and cephalothorax reddish brown and abdomen marbled yellow, brown and white. Found in damp meadows and hedgerows. When alarmed, typically aligns itself along plant stem with legs outstretched. Widespread and common. Seen June–August.

LARGE RED SLUG *Arion ater* Length up to 12cm
Widespread and common throughout Britain and Ireland. Occurs in almost all terrestrial habitats. Body is uniform in colour but seen in two forms: orange-red form is commonest in S and in gardens while black form prevails in N and upland areas. When alarmed, contracts into an almost spherical ball and often rocks from side to side. Mucus colourless. Lays clusters of pale eggs under logs.

COMMON GARDEN SLUG *Arion distinctus* Length up to 3cm
A comparatively small slug, considered by some to be a form of *Arion hortensis*. Commonest in N England, lowlands of Scotland and parts of Ireland. Favours gardens and agricultural land and damages crops. Has yellowish orange sole and orange body mucus. Body usually striped and covered in tiny gold dots.

DUSKY SLUG *Arion subfuscus* Length up to 7cm
Common in most parts of Britain and Ireland but scarce in E England. Favours woodland and hedgerows but also found in gardens. Body pale brown but dark on dorsal surface and with single longitudinal dark stripe on each side. Often looks golden due to orange body mucus. Sole yellow but sole mucus colourless.

YELLOW SLUG *Limax flavus* Length up to 10cm
A large, yellowish slug, the body of which is marbled and mottled with olive-brown. Tentacles blue and mantle with thumbprint-like pattern of concentric rings typical of all *Limax* species. Common and widespread in England, Wales and Ireland but almost always associated with gardens and houses; ventures indoors after dark and into cellars. Feeds voraciously on seedlings and vegetables.

LEMON SLUG *Limax tenellus* Length up to 4cm
A small, bright yellow slug with dark tentacles. A distinctly scarce species, always associated with woodland and a good indicator of ancient sites. Extremely local in England, Wales and Scotland and absent from Ireland. Very difficult to find except in late summer and early autumn when usually seen feeding on fungi.

LEOPARD SLUG *Limax maximus* Length up to 16cm
A large and well-marked slug. Ground colour of body usually pinkish grey but is covered with numerous dark blotches and spots. Has pronounced keel running along rear part of body to tail. Mucus sticky and colourless. Sole whitish. Widespread and common throughout most of Britain and Ireland. Favours woodland and gardens.

ASHY-GREY SLUG *Limax cinereoniger* Length up to 25cm
Our largest slug when fully grown. Body colour ashy-grey but has pale yellowish keel along back from mantle to tail. Occurs locally throughout Britain and Ireland but restricted to mature and undisturbed woodland. Found under logs.

TREE SLUG *Limax marginatus* Length up to 7cm
A rather pale and translucent-looking slug. Body colour pale greyish buff but marked with two dark lines on both sides of body from mantle to tail. As name suggests, climbs trees, usually in wet weather. Produces copious quantities of watery mucus when disturbed. Widespread in woodland in W Britain and Ireland.

NETTED SLUG *Deroceras reticulatum* Length up to 5cm
An extremely common slug of gardens and agricultural land; widespread throughout lowland Britain and Ireland. Body colour variable but usually buffish brown with network of darker brown veins and blotches. Body often looks lumpy; keel is truncated at tail end. Produces large quantities of clear mucus when irritated.

SHELLED SLUG *Testacella scutulum* Length up to 10cm
A strange slug with a fingernail-like shell covering the mantle at the rear end. A predator of earthworms and spends much of its life underground; easiest to find in garden compost heaps. Occurs locally in SC and E England and SE Ireland.

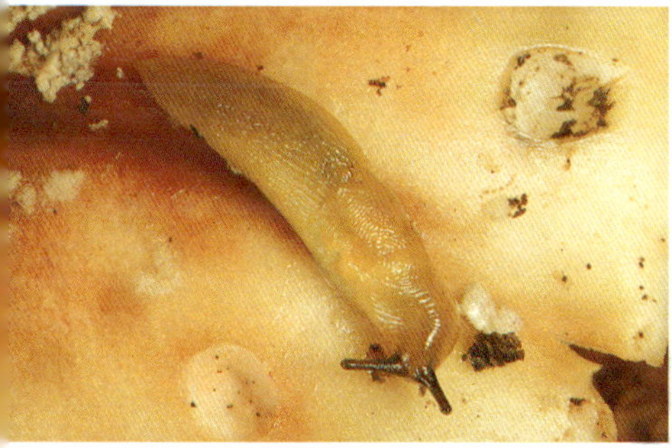

COPSE SNAIL *Arianta arbustorum* Shell diameter 25mm
A widespread but rather local snail in England, Wales and Scotland; scarce in N Ireland. Restricted to damp lowland areas including hedgerows, meadows and woods. Shell almost spherical and usually orange-brown with a dark spiral band.

WHITE-LIPPED SNAIL *Cepaea hortensis* Shell diameter 18mm
Shell colour extremely variable, ranging from uniform yellow to yellow with dark brown spiral bands; lip of shell almost always white. Locally common throughout Britain and Ireland. Favours wide range of habitats including woods and hedges.

BROWN-LIPPED SNAIL *Cepaea nemoralis* Shell diameter 21mm
Shell colour variable and often similar to white-lipped snail with which it may occur; shell lip almost always dark brown. Widespread and often common in much of Britain and Ireland except N Scotland. Favours woodland, hedgerows and dunes.

PLAITED DOOR SNAIL *Cochlodina laminata* Shell length 16mm
Long, narrow shell is distinctive. Colour usually orange-brown but becomes worn with age. Favours damp, shady woodland and typically climbs trees in wet weather and at night. Locally common in England; scarce in Wales, Scotland and Ireland.

GARDEN SNAIL *Helix aspersa* Shell diameter 40mm
A familiar garden resident but also found in woods and hedgerows. Common and widespread in lowlands of England, Wales and S Ireland; absent from much of Scotland. Shell marbled brown and black; often rather worn in older specimens.

ROMAN SNAIL *Helix pomatia* Shell diameter 50mm
Appreciably larger than garden snail. Shell usually more uniform buffish brown with darker spiral bands. Introduced to S England and now established in a few woodlands, mainly on chalk. Courting snails sometimes found in damp weather.

CELLAR SNAIL *Oxychilus cellarius* Shell diameter 12mm
Flattened, spiral shell is amber brown and rather translucent; body of snail is bluish grey. Widespread and generally common throughout Britain and Ireland but absent from most upland areas of Scotland. Favours gardens, woods and hedgerows.

GARLIC SNAIL *Oxychilus alliarius* Shell diameter 6mm
Similar to, but smaller than, cellar snail with orange-brown, translucent shell; snail body blackish. Emits strong smell of garlic when handled. Widespread and often common throughout Britain and Ireland. Found in most terrestrial habitats.

AMBER SNAIL *Succinea putris* Shell length 15mm
A delicate little snail with an orange-brown, translucent shell. Widespread in lowland wetland habitats throughout much of England, Wales and S Ireland. Often observed climbing among leaves of waterside vegetation such as yellow iris.

STRAWBERRY SNAIL *Trichia striolata* Shell diameter 12mm
Shell buffish brown in colour, rather flattened and shows growth ridges. Widespread and fairly common in England, Wales and Ireland but scarce and local in Scotland. Favours lowland habitats including gardens, woodland and hedgerows.

ROUNDED SNAIL *Discus rotundatus* Shell diameter 7mm
Shell rather flattened and has tightly-packed whorls; usually shows conspicuous ridges and is marked with bands. A widespread species throughout the whole of lowland Britain and Ireland. Common in gardens; also in woods and stony places.

COMMON BULIN *Ena obscura* Shell length 8mm
A snail of ancient and undisturbed woodland. Easily overlooked, especially when young since shell is often coated with mud. Very local in Britain and Ireland; commonest in S and E England. Found in leaf litter. Climbs trees in wet weather.

RIVER LIMPET *Ancylus fluviatilis* Shell length 8mm
A characteristic species of fast-flowing streams and rivers but also found in clear lakes and upland tarns; intolerant of polluted or disturbed waters. Widespread and locally common and can be observed throughout the year. Typically found attached to stones and rocks. The streamlined, flattened conical-shape of the shell aids the animal's ability to cling on in fast currents. Grazes algae.

SWAN MUSSEL *Anodonta cygnea* Shell length up to 12cm
A large and impressive bivalve mollusc which is found in slow-flowing rivers, canals and lakes. In sites where the animal is common, empty shells are often washed up on the shoreline and live mussels can sometimes be seen side by side in clear, shallow water from bridges and other overlooks. Lives part-buried in silt and filter-feeds organic particles. Breathes by passing large quantities of water through its body via siphon. Can alter its position using a large, powerful foot. If disturbed, muscles clamp the two shell halves tight. Widespread but local in England, Wales and Ireland; scarce in Scotland.

COMMON BITHYNIA *Bithynia tentaculata* Shell length 15mm
A rather conical, dark brown water snail. When moving among water plants, a small plate called an operculum can be seen on the upperside of the foot. If the animal is disturbed, it retreats into its shell and seals itself off with operculum. Favours ponds, canals and lakes. Fairly common and widespread in England, Wales and Ireland; local in S Scotland. Tentacles comparatively long and slender.

GREAT POND SNAIL *Lymnaea stagnalis* Shell length 45mm
A large water snail with a brown, conical shell. Sometimes seen moving among water plants or even at surface, gliding along underside of surface film. Also comes to the surface periodically to replenish air supply. Feeds on encrusting algae by rasping with tongue; feeding trails can sometimes be observed on sides of tanks if kept in captivity. Sausage-shaped gelatinous masses of eggs are often found on undersides of water-lily leaves. Widespread and common in ponds, lakes and canals in England, Wales and Ireland; extremely local in Scotland.

WANDERING SNAIL *Lymnaea pereger* Shell length 10mm
An extremely common and widespread water snail, found in ponds, lakes and ditches throughout lowland Britain and Ireland; sometimes found in slightly brackish conditions. The shell is rather oval or rounded with the last whorl relatively large and expanded; it is pale brown but has darker blotches. The tentacles are broad, flattened and ear-like. Egg masses are long and gelatinous.

GREAT RAMSHORN *Planorbis corneus* Shell diameter 25mm
Our largest spiral-shelled water snail (A) with a dark brown shell comprising five or so whorls; older shells are rather ridged. It favours ponds, lakes and canals and is common only in S and C England. Sometimes found in rather stagnant water; assisted in its uptake of oxygen by the presence of haemoglobin in blood. Eggs (B) in tight clusters.

THE RAMSHORN *Planorbis planorbis* Shell diameter 12mm
Appreciably smaller than the great ramshorn and with narrower, more tightly-packed whorls. Shell colour pale brown and seen sideways on, it is noticeably flattened on one side. Common and widespread in most lowland areas of Britain and Ireland. Favours ponds, ditches and lakes and, like its relative, can tolerate quite stagnant conditions. Grazes mainly algae which coat water plants.

PEA MUSSEL *Sphaerium corneum* 6mm
A tiny, fingernail-sized bivalve mollusc. When the two shell halves are clamped shut, almost spherical. Its shape, together with the pale brown colour, make it difficult to spot among gravel and sand on beds of ponds, streams and canals. Filter feeds and has two short, white siphons to assist this process. Muscular foot enables animal to adjust position. Common and widespread in lowland sites.

EDIBLE PERIWINKLE *Littorina littorea* Shell length 25mm
Extremely common among seaweed on which it feeds. Found on rocky shores from low- to high-tide levels. Shell is rather rounded but with a pointed, conical apex and a thick lip. Usually dark brown in colour and bearing concentric ridges and dark lines. Widespread on most suitable coasts around Britain and Ireland.

FLAT PERIWINKLE *Littorina littoralis* Shell diameter 10mm
A rounded, almost spherical mollusc with a smooth, shiny shell. Colour extremely variable but commonly bright yellow or reddish brown. Usually associated with egg wrack and bladder wrack and could be mistaken for these species' air floats. Often numerous at mid-tide level on rocky shores around Britain and Ireland.

PEPPERY FURROW SHELL *Scrobicularia plana* Shell length up to 50mm
A common bivalve mollusc. Shell rather rounded in outline but thin when viewed sideways on; marked with numerous, close-packed concentric growth ridges. Shell colour pale grey-brown. Widespread and often common in sand and mud on shores and estuaries around Britain and Ireland. Filter feeds using its long siphons.

LAVER SPIRE SHELL *Hydrobia ulvae* Shell length 6mm
Widespread and often abundant on mud of estuaries around Britain and Ireland and sometimes climbs glasswort at low tide on sunny days. Found mostly between low- and high-tide levels. Important source of food for many birds such as shelduck. Shell is dark brown and conical; apex appears blunt and usually rather worn.

TOOTHED TOPSHELL *Monodonta lineata* Shell diameter 24mm
Shell is marked with close-packed concentric ridges and bears beautiful purple zigzag patterns; older specimens are usually worn at the apex. Seen from below, mouth of shell has sheen of mother-of-pearl and 'toothed' lip. Widespread and common on rocky coasts of Ireland, SW England and Wales; favours mid-tide level.

COMMON OCTOPUS *Octopus vulgaris* Length up to 50cm
An intriguing and advanced mollusc, occasionally found in rock pools at very low tide off rocky coasts of SW Britain and Ireland. Easily recognised by bulbous, bag-like body, large eyes and eight arms bearing powerful suckers. Active predator of crabs and other invertebrates. Can change colour quickly and dramatically.

COMMON COWRIE *Trivia monacha* Shell length 11mm
A small, bean-shaped mollusc whose shell is marked with pinkish purple lines and has a slit-like opening on its lower side. In life, the animal's mottled mantle edges envelop the margins of the shell. The foot is beautifully striped and, at the head end, there is a conspicuous siphon. Widespread on the lower shore.

COMMON LIMPET *Patella vulgata* Shell diameter up to 6cm
Commonest of several similar limpet species and found on exposed rocky shores around Britain and Ireland; occurs between mid- and high-tide levels. Shell conical and ridged; older specimens usually encrusted with barnacles and algae. Grazes algae when covered by water; feeding trails usually visible at low tide.

SLIPPER LIMPET *Crepidula fornicata* Shell length 30mm
Accidentally introduced from N America and now widespread around coasts of S and E England and S Wales. Shell ear-shaped and greyish. Sometimes found in large enough numbers for empty shells to dominate debris on beaches. In life, attaches itself to mussels, oysters or other slipper limpets. Favours sheltered coasts.

BLUE-RAYED LIMPET *Patina pellucida* Shell length 15mm
A delicate little limpet. The brown, conical shell is marked with iridescent blue lines which radiate from the apex; young specimens are brightest. In life, invariably found attached to fronds, stalks or holdfasts of kelp; usually found inside excavated depression or cavity. Not normally visible until very low tide.

SEA-LEMON *Archidoris pseudargus* Length up to 6cm
A shell-less mollusc. Mostly found in fairly deep waters but in summer moves to lower rocky shores to spawn. Body yellowish but with olive-brown blotches; skin texture rather warty. When undisturbed, looks rather sausage-like with two tentacles at head end and frilly gills at rear. Contracts body when alarmed.

Greilada elegans Length up to 3cm
An attractive sea slug whose bright orange body colour and purple spots serve to indicate its unpleasant taste to potential predators. Intolerant of cold waters and restricted to SW Britain and Ireland. Mostly in fairly deep water but moves inshore in summer to spawn and sometimes trapped in rock pools at very low tide.

SEA-HARE *Aplysia punctata* Length up to 12cm
A bizarre-looking mollusc whose body encloses its soft shell. Body often appears rather lumpy and is blotched grey and brown; has four tentacles at head end. Slow-moving creature, found among seaweeds in rock pools on very low tides. Ejects a purple dye if alarmed. Widespread around S and W coasts of Britain and Ireland.

COMMON COCKLE *Cardium edule* Shell width up to 5cm
A common bivalve mollusc which is found buried in mud and sand in estuaries and on expansive beaches. Shell valves are identical; grey-buff outer surface scored with radiating ridges and inner surface shiny and white. Widespread and often common around suitable coasts of Britain and Ireland. Often grown commercially.

COMMON MUSSEL *Mytilus edulis* Shell width up to 9cm
A common and familiar bivalve mollusc. Found both on exposed rocky shores and attached to stones or posts in estuary mouths. Both shell valves identical; dark grey-brown on outer surface but with mother-of-pearl coating on inside. Forms large groups, each attached to rocks by tough threads. Common and widespread.

COMMON OYSTER *Ostrea edulis* Shell width up to 10cm
Formerly abundant and still fairly common bivalve mollusc in shallow water with gently shelving seabed. Lower shell valve is saucer-like and sits on sand or silt; upper valve is flattened. Outer surface of both valves rough and grey-brown; inner surface smooth with mother-of-pearl coating. Grown commercially.

POD RAZORSHELL *Ensis siliqua* Shell length up to 18cm
An elongated bivalve mollusc, seen mostly when shell from dead animal is washed-up. In life, lives buried deep in sand around low-tide level on beaches; siphons reach surface of sand when immersed thus enabling animal to filter feed. Outer surface of shell valves olive-brown and flaky. Widespread and generally common.

COMMON WHELK *Buccinium undatum* Shell length up to 8cm
Living animal sometimes found on sand or mud in shallow water at low tide. More usually encountered when shell of dead animal is washed-up on beach; empty shell often occupied by hermit crab. Shells of larger animals often coated with encrusting sponges and algae. Common and widespread around Britain and Ireland.

DOG WHELK *Nucella lapillus* Shell length up to 3cm
Has a rather oval, pointed shell the colour of which is influenced by diet: this includes barnacles and mussels. Both creamy white and grey-brown forms are seen and banded individuals are not uncommon. Favours rocky shores wherever prey is common; sometimes seen beside egg masses which are secured to rocks. Widespread.

COMMON PIDDOCK *Pholas dactylus* Shell length up to 12cm
An intriguing bivalve mollusc that bores into sandstone and other soft rocks. Shell is pale buffish brown and surprisingly fragile considering it is used to perform the boring process. In suitable substrates, often found at considerable densities on lower shore. Widespread and often common in SW Britain and Ireland.

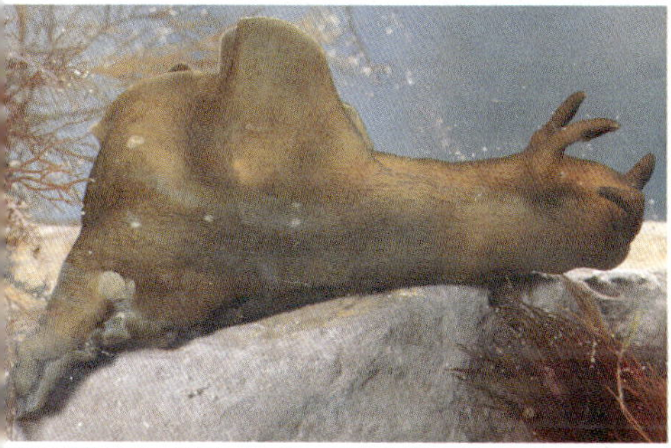

COMMON WOODLOUSE *Oniscus asellus* Length 14mm
A widespread and common woodlouse throughout most of Britain and Ireland. Often numerous in gardens but also found in woodland, and hedgerows on wasteground. Easily becomes desiccated and hides under stones and in crevices during daytime, especially during dry, hot weather. Forages for vegetable matter after dark.

PILL WOODLOUSE *Armadillidium vulgare* Length 11mm
An intriguing species, easily recognised by its ability to roll into a ball when disturbed. Body colour uniform slate-grey. Widespread and reasonably common, especially in S England. Usually found in mature woodland where it hides under logs and in rotting wood during daytime; also in hedgerows and rural gardens.

Porcellio scaber Length 10mm
An extremely common woodlouse which is widespread in most lowland regions of Britain and Ireland. Often numerous in gardens where it hides under stones and in compost heaps and crevices in walls. Also found in hedgerows, woodland and coastal dunes. Emerges after dark to feed on algae and other plant matter.

Trichoniscus pusillus Length 5mm
A small species of woodlouse. Body rather rounded in cross-section and elongate; usually pinkish purple in colour. Invariably found in damp locations and often common among leaves and debris that have collected in ditches or around the margins of woodland ponds. Widespread and fairly common but easily overlooked.

FRESHWATER LOUSE *Asellus aquaticus* Length 15mm
Widespread and often extremely common in ponds, lakes and slow-flowing streams. Rather woodlouse-like in appearance with flattened, segmented body but has very long antennae. Scuttles among water plants and scavenges organic matter from the sediment. In spring, female carries whitish eggs around with her in brood pouch.

FRESHWATER CRAYFISH *Astacus pallipes* Length up to 40mm
Formerly common and widespread but rather scarce and endangered today; numbers threatened by pollution and disturbance of favoured river and stream habitats and by competition from introduced N American species. Needs fast-flowing, well-oxygenated water and, during daytime, hides under stones and in holes in bank.

FAIRY SHRIMP *Chirocephalus diaphanus* Length 16mm
An enigmatic creature found in seasonal and temporary pools, puddles and cart-ruts. The eggs persist in dry mud after breeding pools dry up in summer. Hatch after autumn rains replace water. Extremely local but often abundant where it does occur. Sporadic in appearance and distribution. Swims upside down.

TRIOPS *Apus cancriformis* Length 30mm
Sometimes called the tadpole shrimp because of its appearance. More closely resembles a miniature horseshoe crab with its shield-shaped carapace; segmented abdomen has two tail-like projections. Sporadic in appearance; eggs can persist for long periods in dry mud. Known only from a few seasonal pools in New Forest.

WATER-FLEA *Daphnia sp* Length 1mm
Tiny crustacean which is present in phenomenal numbers in most bodies of still water at certain times of year. The body is almost transparent and internal organs can be seen through carapace. Swims through the water as if by hopping by beating second antennae. Body usually pinkish and has single dark compound eye.

FRESHWATER SHRIMP *Gammarus pulex* Length 11mm
Intolerant of polluted waters or ones with low oxygen content; favours fast-flowing streams and rivers but also found near inflows or outflows in stream-fed lakes. Body is laterally flattened and animal swims on its side. Often found under stones and around the bases of rooted water plants. Widespread and common.

EDIBLE CRAB *Cancer pagurus* Carapace width up to 15cm, often smaller
A familiar seashore animal, recognised by the 'piecrust' appearance to the margin of the carapace and its pinkish orange colour; the tips of the broad pincers are black. Widespread around the coasts of Britain and Ireland. Small specimens are found on the lower shores of rocky coasts and are often encountered in rock pools and among seaweeds; larger individuals live further offshore. Has a mainly scavenging diet and is attracted to decaying animals. Common throughout year.

SHORE CRAB *Carcinus maenas* Carapace width up to 5cm
Generally the commonest crab found around the coasts of Britain and Ireland. Favours all kinds of marine habitats from rocky shores to breakwaters on sandy beaches. Body colour is rather variable but usually greenish or olive-brown. Characteristically has three blunt teeth between the eyes. Found between mid- to low-tide levels on shoreline and usually hides beneath seaweed or stones. Quite aggressive when cornered but prefers to scuttle sideways away from danger.

MASKED CRAB *Corystes cassivellaunus* Carapace length 4cm
A bizarre-looking and distinctive crab which lives on sandy beaches. Sometimes found washed-up dead on shoreline but in life lives buried in sand, using its long antennae to create passage for seawater to gills. Carapace much longer than it is broad and pincer-bearing, front pair of legs are extremely long. Common on suitable beaches and fairly widespread around the coasts of Britain and Ireland.

HERMIT CRAB *Eupagurus bernhardus* Body length up to 9cm
Body size difficult to determine since animal lives inside empty shell of periwinkle, whelk or other mollusc; shell periodically exchanged for larger one as animal grows. Body colour reddish brown and right hand pincer larger than left; this serves to block entrance to shell when crab retreats inside in alarm. Mainly scavenging diet. Common on sheltered shores and often seen in rockpools.

SPIDER CRAB *Macropodia rostrata* Carapace length 10mm
Has long, spider-like legs and a roughly triangular carapace. Outline of body usually obscured, however, by covering of seaweeds and sponges; these afford the animal excellent camouflage among the seaweeds where it is usually found. Occurs on the lower shore and sometimes found in rock pools or among netted samples. Widespread and fairly common around Britain and Ireland but easily overlooked.

BROAD-CLAWED PORCELAIN CRAB *Porcellana platycheles* Carapace width 13mm
An extremely flattened crab with a rounded carapace and very broad pincers. Upper surface sandy-brown in colour and rather hairy, especially so on walking legs and front edge of pincers; hairs trap silt and add to the effect of the animal's camouflaged colour. The underside is white and porcelain-like. Found under stones where silt and debris collect on sheltered rocky shores. Widespread and common around coasts of Britain and Ireland.

VELVET SWIMMING CRAB *Macropipus puber* Carapace width 7cm
A distinctive crab with beady red eyes and reddish joints along the legs; there are 8–10 teeth between the eyes. The upper surface of the carapace is rather hairy and this collects silt, giving the animal a velvety appearance. Often easily told by its behaviour: when cornered, becomes aggressive and will lift itself up and brandish its pincers which can deliver a painful nip. Tips of back legs are flattened to form paddles. Widespread and often common on rocky shores.

COMMON LOBSTER *Homarus vulgaris* Carapace length up to 40cm
Large specimens are found in deep water but smaller individuals are sometimes discovered in rock pools at extreme low water. In life, body is blue and only turns red when boiled. Usually found in crevices and small caves and defends itself using powerful pincers. Has a scavenging diet. Widespread around Britain and Ireland. Generally common but, unsurprisingly, least so where exploited.

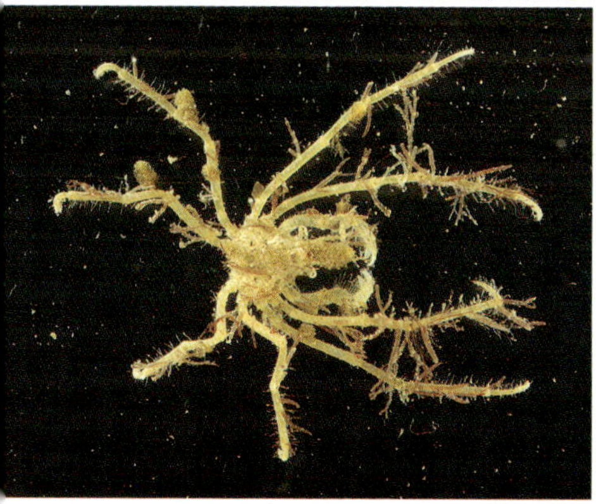

Chthalamus stellatus Shell width up to 10mm
A typical barnacle and a locally abundant member of the rocky shore community. Forms encrusting communities between the upper and middle shores. Its range extends further up the shore in exposed areas compared to sheltered ones but it always occurs at a higher level on the shore than *Semibalanus balanoides*. Body of animal protected by volcano-like shell comprising six calcareous plates. The central opening is oval and, when exposed to air, this is sealed by four plates; the sutures to these meet at right angles to one another. When immersed by seawater, extends feathery thoracic appendages to catch food. Only found on W coasts of Britain from SW England and S Ireland to N England.

ACORN BARNACLE *Semibalanus balanoides* Shell width up to 12mm
A common barnacle on the lower shores of rocky coasts. Sometimes forms large, close-packed colonies, so dense that the true colour of the rock to which they are attached is completely obscured. Body protected calcareous shell comprising six plates. Opening is diamond-shaped and sealed by four plates the sutures of which meet obliquely. Absent from SW England; widespread elsewhere and commonest in N.

Elminius modestus Shell width up to 10mm
Introduced from Australia to The Solent during 2nd World War. Has become firmly established and has spread widely along coasts of S England and Wales. Shell comprises four greyish white, smooth plates. Favours the middle shore in sheltered waters where it attaches to stones; not averse to the influence of freshwater.

GOOSE BARNACLE *Lepas anatifera* Shell length up to 4cm
An extraordinary animal. Normally pelagic but frequently washed-up on exposed beaches after onshore gales, mostly on W coasts. Typically found in sizeable groups attached to driftwood by 15cm long retractable stalk. Body of animal is protected by five translucent plates which are bluish white. Appearance of shell, and feathery appendages which often project, lead in the past to fanciful suggestion that goose barnacles were the embryonic stages of the barnacle goose.

COMMON PRAWN *Leander serratus* Length up to 6cm
Common on rocky shores around coasts of SW Britain and Ireland. Often trapped in rock pools at low tide but difficult to spot until it moves because of near transparent body; closer inspection reveals an array of purplish brown dots and lines. Has very long antennae and toothed rostrum extending forward between the eyes. Diet mainly scavenging. Uses fan-like tail to swim backwards when alarmed.

COMMON SHRIMP *Crangon vulgaris* Length up to 5cm
Found in shallow, sheltered waters including estuaries. Usually associated with sand and sometimes found in pools at low tide. Almost translucent body, stippled with dark dots, affords the animal superb camouflage when resting on sand or more especially when part-buried. Has long antennae but rostrum reduced to tiny tooth. Widespread around the coasts of Britain and Ireland and often abundant.

SAND-HOPPER *Talitris saltator* Length up to 15mm
Very common and one of several rather similar species of crustaceans known as sand-hoppers. Found among rotting seaweed and under stones along the strandline, usually on sandy beaches. Easily seen by turning over piles of tideline debris when it escapes from danger by hopping and crawling under cover. Body is shiny and laterally compressed. Widespread around most coasts of Britain and Ireland.

SEA-SLATER *Ligia oceanica* Length up to 25mm
A large relative of the woodlice, common under rocks in the splash zone and in sea walls. The body is greyish, segmented and flattened and carries two long antennae. Alert and rather fast-moving compared to its terrestrial relatives. Most active after dark when it scavenges for organic matter among the rocks and seaweed. Found in most suitable habitats on the coasts of Britain and Ireland.

Flat-backed Millipede *Polydesmus angustus* Length 24mm
A common and widespread invertebrate found in organic-rich soils, compost heaps and under the bark of rotting wood. Body is rather flattened and centipede-like but the presence of two pairs of legs per segment identifies it as a millipede.

Cylindrosulus punctatus Length 27mm
Widespread millipede in wooded areas and often found under the bark of rotting wood or among leaf litter. Body cylindrical in cross-section and pale reddish brown in colour. Feeds mainly on decaying plant matter but will also eat roots and bulbs.

Pill Millipede *Glomeris marginata* Length 20mm
Armoured body is shiny chestnut-brown and superficially rather woodlouse-like in appearance. When disturbed, however, quickly rolls into a protective ball and reluctant to emerge again for some time. Locally common in mature woodland.

Haplophilus subterraneus Length 35mm
A burrowing centipede which is widespread and often common in garden soils and compost heaps. One pair of legs per segment typical of centipedes as a whole. An active predator of soil animals and is distinctly beneficial to the gardener.

Lithobius variegatus Length 30mm
A common centipede and a familiar garden resident which also occurs in hedgerows and woods. Usually hides under stones or in compost heaps during daytime and emerges after dark to hunt invertebrates. Body shiny, flattened and orange-brown. Widespread.

Harvestmen *Order Opiliones* Body length up to 4mm
A common and widespread group of spider-like invertebrates with tiny bodies relative to the length of their spindly legs. Often found among wayside foliage, in bramble patches and grassland. Predatory and commonest in summer and autumn.

Common Earthworm *Lumbricus terrestris* Length up to 8cm
An abundant and invaluable member of the soil community, important for its role in aeration and the incorporation of leaves and other organic matter. Comes to surface in wet weather and at night. Deposits conspicuous digested soil casts.

Lumbriculus sp Length 30mm
An often abundant group of annelid worms found in freshwater habitats. Resemble miniature earthworms and live in sediment and silt at the bottom of ponds and lakes. Transparent body reveals many of the internal organs. Feed on detritus.

Fish Leech *Piscicola geometra* Length 10mm
A fairly common external parasite of freshwater fish, particularly small species such as sticklebacks. Body long, narrow and sinuous with suckers at both ends. Often looks rather banded. Usually attaches to gills and other soft body parts.

Dugesia lugubris Length up to 20mm
A common and widespread planarian worm found in slow-flowing streams and weedy ponds and lake. Body is grey-brown in colour with two pale spots at anterior end next to the eyes. Moves in a gliding manner. Predator of small invertebrates.

Hydra fusca Length up to 5mm
Freshwater relative of sea anemones and jellyfish. Found in ponds, canals and lakes, usually attached to stems of water plants. If disturbed or removed from water, contracts into a blob and difficult to see. Buds new animals in summer.

False Scorpions *Order Pseudoscopiones* Length up to 3mm
A common but often overlooked group of soil animals with representative species found in gardens, woodlands and on the seashore. Body is rounded and tick-like. Pincers borne on long front legs. Predators of mites and other small animals.

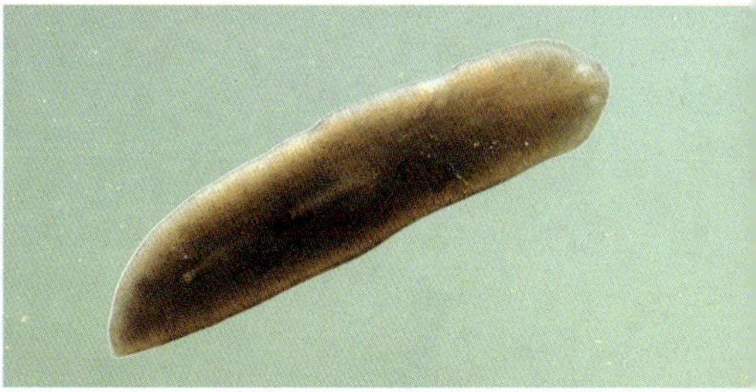
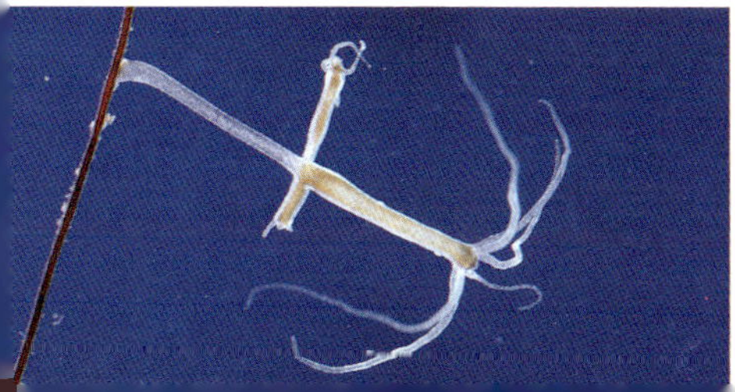

Chrysaora isosceles Diameter up to 25cm
A mainly pelagic jellyfish but sometimes seen in inshore waters from piers or boats during summer months; occasionally washed ashore during gales. Umbrella-shaped body is marked with dark central spot and dark red radiating lines. Long tentacles suspended from lobed margin. Mainly off S and W Britain and Ireland.

COMMON JELLYFISH *Aurelia aurita* Diameter up to 20cm
A pale, translucent jellyfish which is generally the commonest species around the coasts of Britain and Ireland; sometimes washed ashore in gales. Body colour pale yellowish brown but tinged with bluish purple as it pulsates through water. Underside of 'umbrella' has numerous short tentacles and four frilly mouth arms.

BEADLET ANEMONE *Actinia equina* Height up to 5cm
Widespread and often extremely common on middle and lower shores of rocky coasts around Britain and Ireland. Attaches itself to rocks with sucker-like base. Colour variable but commonly seen as either red or green forms. Tentacles extended when immersed (A). When exposed to air or disturbed, retracts tentacles to become a jelly-like blob (B).

SNAKELOCKS ANEMONE *Anemonia sulcata* Height up to 10cm
Rather squat and flattened sea anemone which is unable to retract its tentacles. Attached to rocks on middle and lower shores by sucker-like base. Body colour variable but commonly grey-brown or purplish green; tentacles same colour as body but often purple-tipped. Common on W and SW coasts of Britain and Ireland.

JEWEL ANEMONE *Corynactes viridis* Height up to 2cm
More closely related to corals than to true sea anemones. Found in small colonies attached to rocks on lower shore around SW and W coasts of Britain and Ireland; often in gullies or crevices. Body colour usually pale buffish white but sometimes pale grey-green; tentacles tipped with iridescent pinkish purple.

Amphitrite johnstoni Length up to 10cm, sometimes longer
A bizarre-looking marine annelid worm of sheltered muddy and sandy shores. The animal lives in a shallow burrow and this provides a degree of protection for its soft body; the burrow is often sited under, or close to, a stone. At the head end, there are numerous long tentacles and branched, blood-red gills.

LUGWORM *Arenicola marina* Length up to 18cm
A burrowing marine annelid which is common in muddy estuaries and sandy beaches from the middle shore downwards. Presence often indicated by holes and casts which mark the entrances to its U-shaped burrow. Widespread around British and Irish coasts; often common. Important food for birds such as curlew and godwits.

RAGWORM *Nereis diversicolor* Length up to 10cm
An active, predatory annelid worm which is often abundant in estuaries and on sandy or muddy beaches. Widespread around the coasts of Britain and Ireland. Close examination reveals a toothed proboscis and jaws at the head end with tufts of hair-like chaetae on each of the 100 or so segments. Burrows freely.

Spirorbis borealis Tube diameter up to 3mm
A curious little annelid worm which lives inside a spirally arranged, calcareous white tube. Small groups of these tubes can be observed on the fronds of various seaweeds such as serrated wrack; also found on rocks and mollusc shells on the lower shore. Common and widespread around the coasts of Britain and Ireland.

PEACOCK WORM *Sabella pavonia* Height up to 20cm
An intriguing marine annelid worm that lives in tube constructed of sand and mud particles glued together by mucus. These tubes stand proud of the substrate in which they are embedded; found in large colonies on beaches at low tide. When immersed, radiating gills appear allowing the animal to filter feed and breathe.

COMMON BRITTLE-STAR *Ophiothrix fragilis* Disc diameter up to 15mm
Often found at low tide among seaweeds and under stones, especially where silt and sediment collect. Body comprises a central, flattened disc and five, narrow and radiating arms; the surfaces of both disc and arms are rather spiny. Colour rather variable but usually purplish brown but with paler bands visible along arms. As its name suggests, legs are brittle and easily broken. Widespread.

CUSHION-STAR *Asterina gibbosa* Diameter up to 5cm
Identified by its distinctive shape and the five radiating arms projecting as short tips from the otherwise pentagonal outline. Upper surface is rather rough and usually blotched pinkish yellow and grey-brown; some specimens are greenish brown. Underside yellowish grey with numerous tube-feet. Widespread and often common off S and W British and Irish coasts. Found under rocks on lower shore.

COMMON STARFISH *Asterias rubens* Diameter up to 40cm
A familiar seashore inhabitant, recognised by its five radiating arms. Upper surface is orange-red and covered with pale warts; the underside, which bears rows of tube-feet, is paler. A predator of bivalve molluscs such as mussels, oysters and scallops and so only common where prey species are numerous. Also scavenges at corpses of dead marine animals, sometimes in considerable numbers.

SPINY STARFISH *Marthasterias glacialis* Diameter up to 30cm, sometimes larger
Has rather slender arms which are usually olive-brown in colour and bear large and conspicuous pink spines; the radiating arms are often upturned at the tip. The underside is much paler. Sometimes occurs in comparatively deep water but can also be found in rock pools at low tide. Widespread but commonest off W and SW coasts of Britain and Ireland. Favours exposed and sheltered rocky shores.

COMMON SEA-URCHIN *Echinus esculentus* Diameter up to 10cm
Common in deeper waters around the coasts of Britain and Ireland but also found in rock pools and among seaweeds at low tide; commonest off W and N coasts. Living animal is red and purplish brown; covered by spines and tube-feet. Dead animal loses spines to reveal rounded test which is reddish brown with radiating paler lines. A favourite food of otters where their range is coastal in N and W.

HEART URCHIN *Echinocardium cordatum* Length up to 8cm
A distinctive sea-urchin. Most familiar as the smooth, pale brown and potato-like test of the dead animal which is washed up on the tideline. In life, it is covered by a dense mat of fine spines, most of which are directed backwards. Burrows in sand and sometimes found near surface at low tide. Widespread and locally common around Britain and Ireland.

BREADCRUMB SPONGE *Halichondria panicea* Thickness up to 2cm
An encrusting sponge which often forms large patches on rocky overhangs or in shady crevices from the middle shore downwards on rocky coasts. Colour rather variable but often bright orange, sometimes greenish brown. Spongy surface is pitted with crater-like openings through which seawater passes. Widespread.

DEAD MAN'S FINGERS *Alcyonium digitatum* Length up to 15cm
Coral-like colonial animals which inhabit a branched, toughened skeleton. Colour rather variable but usually pale pink or yellowish white. When feeding, numerous tiny polyps emerge giving the surface a fuzzy appearance, fancifully resembling a decomposing hand. Widespread on rocky coasts from the lower shore downwards.

STAR ASCIDIAN *Botryllus schlosseri* Star diameter up to 5mm
An encrusting, colonial animal which forms tough mats on shaded surfaces of rocks on the lower shore. Individual animals are arranged in a star-like fashion around a common opening. Colour rather variable but usually seen as white stars on a purplish brown background. Widespread; particularly common off W coasts.

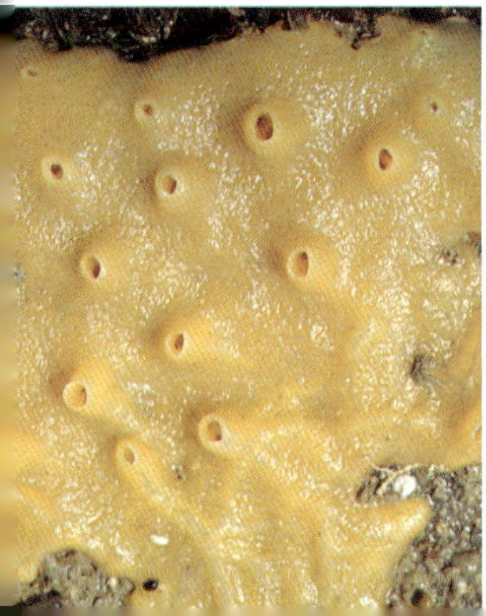
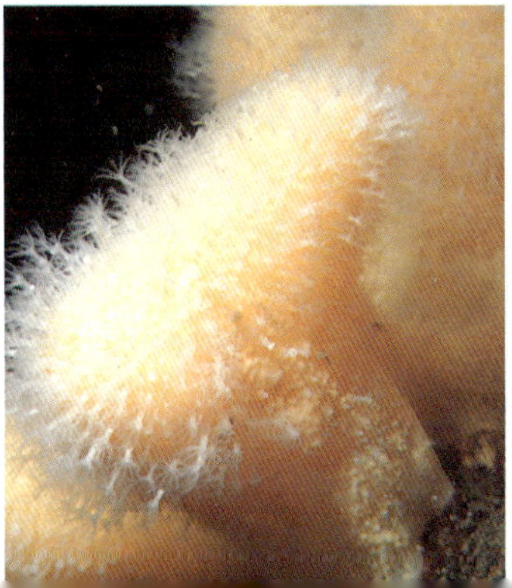

DOUGLAS-FIR *Pseudotsuga menziesii* Height up to 50m or more
Native to N America but widely planted in Britain. Crown conical and comprising whorls of branches. Thick, corky bark becomes purplish brown and encrusted with algae with age. Needles 25–30mm long, soft, dark green and pointed. Pendulous cones are 5–10cm long, oval in outline and with 3-pronged, protruding bracts.

NORWAY SPRUCE *Picea abies* Height up to 60m
The most familiar 'Christmas tree' species. Native to N Europe but widely grown in Britain. Has distinctly curved branches, the lower ones drooping. Needles are 15–25mm long, dark green and spreading; leave a peg on twig when they fall. Male cones red; 15cm long pendulous female cones are cigar-shaped and reddish brown.

SITKA SPRUCE *Picea sitchensis* Height up to 60m
Native to N America but widely planted. Evergreen foliage is blue-green. Needles 20–30mm long, flattened, stiff and pointed; radiate at first but pressed against shoot with age. Pendulous, cigar-shaped cones are reddish brown when mature.

EUROPEAN LARCH *Larix decidua* Height up to 35m
Native, deciduous conifer. In spring, needles are bright green but turn yellow in autumn before they drop. Has grey-brown, cracking bark and pendulous twigs. 15–20mm long needles borne in tufts of 30–40. Mature ovoid cones 2–3cm long.

SCOTS PINE *Pinus sylvestris* Height up to 35mm
Common native tree in Scotland and widely planted elsewhere in Britain. Mature tree domed and often rather lop-sided with bare lower branches; young tree is more conical. Bluish green needles are paired and 30–70mm long. Male cones are yellow; female cones are green when young but become grey-brown when mature.

CORSICAN PINE *Pinus nigra ssp laricio* Height up to 40m
A native of S Europe but often grown in plantations and coastal areas; favours poor, light soils. Straggly and sparse foliage with soft, grey-green needles seen in whorls and each up to 15cm long. 6–8cm long cones are borne in clusters.

WESTERN HEMLOCK-SPRUCE *Tsuga heterophylla* Height up to 65m
Native to N America but widely grown in plantations for its timber. Medium-sized specimens usually conical in outline and with drooping leading shoot. Needles of variable length, usually 7–18mm; dark green above with two white bands below. Male cones reddish purple, those of female are reddish brown, ovoid and pendulous.

LAWSON CYPRESS *Chamaecyparis lawsoniana* Height up to 45m
A native of N America but widely planted as an ornamental or hedging species. Mature tree is tall and conical but seldom allowed to reach this state and usually heavily pruned. Shoots form flattened sprays which carry the scale-like leaves. Male cones are dark red; female cones are blue-green and spherical.

LEYLAND CYPRESS *x Cupressocyparis leylandi* Height up to 35m
A hybrid cypress. Popular as a hedging plant in gardens. Usually heavily pruned and seldom acquires tree-like proportions. Several colour forms exist but sprays of foliage usually comprise dark green scale-like leaves. Female cones globular.

JUNIPER *Juniperus communis* Height up to 5m
Variable in size and shape, sometimes dwarf and almost prostrate. Stiff, bluish green, needle-like leaves arranged in whorls of three. Male and female flowers on separate plants. Those of female green and oval, ripening to blue-black berries.

YEW *Taxus baccata* Height up to 25m
Familiar evergreen tree, also used as a hedging plant. Dense foliage comprises pointed and flattened dark green needles. Bark reddish and flaking. Male flowers yellow. Female flowers on separate tree; green, maturing to bright red fruit.

BAY WILLOW *Salix pentandra* Height up to 6m
A typical shrub of upland regions in N Wales, N England and Scotland. Favours riversides and other wetland habitats. Leaves broad, glossy dark green and bay-like. Flowers May–June; male catkins are yellow and cylindrical, female green.

CRACK WILLOW *Salix fragilis* Height up to 25m
Usually has broad, rounded crown and leaning trunk although often pollarded. Twigs easily snap and trunk sometimes cracks open. Alternate leaves are 10–15cm long, narrow and dark glossy green above. Catkins appear April–May, with leaves.

WHITE WILLOW *Salix alba* Height up to 20m
Tree often appears silvery-white due to colour of alternate leaves which are narrow, pointed and silky when young. Tree has upswept branches and trunk often leaning. Flowers April–May. Yellow male catkins are 4–5cm long and cylindrical.

WEEPING WILLOW *Salix x chrysocoma* Height up to 12m
Distinctive hybrid. Popular ornamental tree and often grown beside water. Long, trailing branches with long, yellow twigs. Leaves long and narrow. Male catkins yellow; on separate trees from females. Flowers April–May, when leaves appear.

GREY WILLOW *Salix cinerea* Height up to 10m
Common in wet habitats; forms a broad crown in mature specimens. Broad, oval leaves and twigs softly hairy when young; leaves develop inrolled margins with age. Flowers March–April. 2–3cm long male and female catkins on different trees.

SALLOW *Salix caprea* Height up to 10m
Forms a rounded shrub or small tree. Leaves are rounded-oval and are green and hairy above but greyish and woolly beneath. Flowers March–April, before leaves have appeared. Yellow male catkins on separate trees from green female catkins.

OSIER *Salix viminalis* Height up to 5m
Undisturbed shrub is highly branched; often pollarded and then produces numerous long, straight twigs which are reddish brown. Leaves narrow and tapering; green above but silvery below. Flowers February–April. Often seen along river margins.

WHITE POPLAR *Populus alba* Height up to 20m
Native to S Europe but widely grown as an ornamental tree. A spreading tree, the trunk often leaning. Leaves dark green above but white below making tree look silvery. Catkins appear February–March, males and females on different trees.

HYBRID BLACK POPLAR *Populus x canadensis* Height up to 30m
Hybrid species with greyish, furrowed bark and spreading branches. Alternate leaves are triangular to oval with toothed margins. Flowers March–April with 3–5cm long male and female catkins on different trees. A popular timber tree.

ASPEN *Populus tremula* Height up to 20m
Easily distinguished in even dense woodland by its fluttering leaves which catch even the slightest breeze and reveal very pale undersides. Widespread, favouring damp areas. Flowers February–March, male and female catkins on separate trees.

SILVER BIRCH *Betula pendula* Height up to 30m
Common and widespread throughout Britain and Ireland. Silvery-grey bark cracks into rectangular plates with age and branches pendulous towards tips. 4cm long oval to triangular leaves turn yellow in autumn. Catkins appear April–May.

DOWNY BIRCH *Betula pubescens* Height up to 25m
Common in damp areas and upland sites with high rainfall, especially in N and W. Young twigs downy and 5cm long leaves have coarsely-toothed margins. Catkins appear February–April. Smooth, grey bark often covered with lichens and mosses.

ALDER *Alnus glutinosa* Height up to 20m
Common in damp habitats in most parts. Rounded leaves are bright green with shallow teeth. Flowers appear before leaves, February–March; male catkins are long and pendulous while those of female are ovoid and reddish. Cones brown.

BOG MYRTLE *Myrica gale* Height up to 1m
Characteristic woody shrub of boggy habitats, usually on acid soils. Brown stems bear aromatic, oval leaves which are grey-green. Orange, ovoid male catkins and pendulous brown female catkins appear in April on separate plants, before leaves.

COMMON WALNUT *Juglans regia* Height up to 30m
Widely planted tree with spreading crown. Grey bark becomes fissured with age. Alternate leaves pinnately divided into 7–9 leaflets. Pendulous male catkins and clustered female flowers appear May–June. Green fruit contains familiar walnut.

HAZEL *Corylus avellana* Height up to 12m
Common and widespread small tree or shrub. Often coppiced. 8cm long alternate leaves are almost circular with double-toothed margins. Male catkins and tiny red female flowers appear January–March, before leaves. Fruits ripen in autumn.

HORNBEAM *Carpinus betulus* Height up to 30m
Mature tree is impressive with spreading crown and often twisted trunk. Bark smooth and pale grey. 5–10cm long oval leaves are pointed with sharply double-toothed margins. Catkins appear April–May. 3-lobed fruits carried in clusters.

BEECH *Fagus sylvatica* Height up to 40m
Forms single-species stands, usually on chalky soils. Mature trees large and stately; dense canopy inhibits understorey plants. Leaf oval with wavy margin; bright green in spring but golden in autumn. Paired nuts borne in spiky fruit.

ENGLISH OAK *Quercus robur* Height up to 45m
Also known as penduncculate oak. Dominant tree in many woodlands in lowland Britain. Irregularly lobed, oblong leaves borne on very short petioles but clustered acorns carried on long stalks. Catkin-like flowers appear May–June.

SESSILE OAK *Quercus petraea* Height up to 40m
The typical oak in W Britain and upland areas. Irregularly and shallowly lobed oblong leaves are borne on short stalks and the clustered acorns are almost stalk-less; the acorn cups have downy scales. Catkin-like flowers appear in May.

HORSE-CHESTNUT *Aesculus hippocastanum* Height up to 35m
Well-known for its spreading habit, the pyramidal spikes of white flowers that cover the tree in April and May, and for its seed, the familiar conker. Bright green leaves divided into 5–7 oval leaflets. Introduced but widely planted.

SWEET CHESTNUT *Castanea sativa* Height up to 12m
An introduced species but widely planted both for its timber and its spiny-cased edible nuts. Bark fissured and spirally twisted around trunk. Shiny, dark green leaves are narrow and oblong-oval with toothed margins. Catkins flower in July.

ENGLISH ELM *Ulmus procera* Height up to 35m
Formerly common but mature trees now almost vanished from many parts due to Dutch elm disease. Still fairly common in hedgerows. Dark green oval leaves have toothed margins and asymmetrical bases. Tufted red flowers seen February–March.

WYCH ELM *Ulmus glabra* Height up to 40m
Mature tree has broad, spreading crown. Dark green oval leaves have 10–18 veins and asymmetrical bases, one side overlapping the short leaf stalk. Clustered red flowers seen February–March. Still common in N and W; fairly disease resistant.

LONDON PLANE *Platanus x hispanica* Height up to 35m
Tolerant of pollution and therefore widely planted along city streets. Grey bark flakes to reveal patchwork of yellow-buff. 5-lobed leaves have toothed margins. Flowers appear in June and comprise strings of spherical heads; ripen to brown fruits.

SYCAMORE *Acer pseudoplatanus* Height up to 35m
Introduced but widely planted and now firmly established. 5-lobed leaves have toothed margins. Flowers appear in April and comprise hanging, yellowish green clusters. Wings of paired fruits form angle of 90º. Tolerates salt-spray.

FIELD MAPLE *Acer campestre* Height up to 25m
A common hedgerow shrub, sometimes forming a small tree. 5-lobed leaves are dark green but turn orange-yellow in autumn. Yellowish green flowers appear in May, carried in upright spikes. Wings of paired fruits form an angle of 180º.

HOLLY *Ilex aquifolium* Height up to 10m
Familiar Christmas decoration, common and widespread in woods and hedges. Stiff, leathery leaves have spiny margins; dark green above but paler below. White, 4-petalled flowers appear May–July and clusters of red berries ripen in autumn.

ASH *Fraxinus excelsior* Height up to 40m
Widespread and common, especially in N England and on base-rich soils. Tall with unkempt, rounded crown. Bark grey and fairly smooth. Twigs bear large black buds before pinnate leaves appear, these divided into 7–12 leaflets. Seeds winged.

ROWAN *Sorbus aucuparia* Height up to 15m
Attractive, bushy tree sometimes known as mountain ash. Common in upland and waterlogged habitats; also planted as street tree. Leaves are pinnately divided into 5–10 leaflets. White flowers appear in May; ripen to red berries in August.

WHITEBEAM *Sorbus aria* Height up to 25m
Tree looks silvery due to downy white undersides to leaves; upper surface of leaf dark green. White flowers appear May–June and ripen to red, ovoid fruits by autumn; avidly eaten by birds. Favours limestone areas. Also grown ornamentally.

WILD SERVICE TREE *Sorbus torminalis* Height up to 25m
A rather scarce and local native tree and a good indicator of ancient woodland. Angular-oval leaves are divided into 3–5 pairs of toothed lobes; turn bright red in autumn. White-petalled flowers appear May–June and ripen to brown fruits.

WILD PEAR *Pyrus communis* Height up to 20m
The ancestor of the cultivated pear. A widespread hedgerow tree, commonest in S England. Leaves are 5–8cm long, oval and with finely-toothed margins. White, 5-petalled flowers appear in April and ripen to form hard, greenish brown fruit.

CRAB APPLE *Malus sylvestris* Height up to 10m
A familiar hedgerow and woodland tree or shrub. Alternate, finely-toothed leaves are oval, deep green and slightly hairy. Pinkish white, 5-petalled flowers appear in May and ripen to small, green apples by late summer. Commonest in S.

WILD CHERRY *Prunus avium* Height up to 30m
Recognised by its reddish brown bark which peels in horizontal bands. Alternate, oval leaves have short-toothed margins. Clusters of 5-petalled, white flowers appear in April–May and fruits ripen in summer, turning from green to dark red.

BIRD CHERRY *Prunus padus* Height up to 15m
Native to upland areas of Britain, often on limestone. Bark pungent-smelling and grey. Oval, green leaves have reddish stalks and finely-toothed margins. White, 5-petalled flowers appear after leaves have burst in May. Fruits shiny black.

BLACKTHORN *Prunus spinosa* Height up to 5m
Common, thorny hedgerow shrub which often forms dense thickets. Alternate, oval leaves are 2–4cm long and have toothed margins. White, 5-petalled flowers (A) appear March–April, before the leaves. Purplish fruits (sloes, B) have a powdery bloom.

CHERRY LAUREL *Prunus laurocerasus* Height up to 8m
A popular ornamental evergreen shrub whose leaves smell of almonds when bruised; they are glossy, elongate-oval and laurel-like in appearance. Spikes of white, 5-petalled flowers appear in April. 2cm long fruits ripen from red to black.

HAWTHORN *Crategus monogyna* Height up to 15m
The commonest hedgerow shrub, forming dense, thorny thickets in many areas. Shiny, roughly oval leaves are divided into 3–7 pairs of lobes. The 5-petalled, white flowers appear May–June and ripen to form bright red clusters of berries.

BOX *Buxus sempervirens* Height up to 5m
A familiar garden plant which is widely used in hedging and topiary. Grows wild on chalk in England but rather rare. Oval 1.5–3cm long leaves are leathery and have inrolled margins. Tiny, petal-less yellow-green flowers appear March–May.

SPINDLE-TREE *Euonymus europaeus* Height up to 6m
Native shrub or small tree found locally on limestone mainly in C and N England. Leaves are narrow-oval and pointed, with toothed margins; green in summer but turning reddish in autumn. Tiny greenish flowers appear May–June. Fruit is pink.

BUCKTHORN *Rhamnus catharticus* Height up to 8m
Native to lowland areas, mainly C and E England. Forms a thorny bush or small tree. Opposite leaves 3–6cm long, oval and finely toothed. Clusters of greenish yellow flowers appear in May and bunches of black berries are found in autumn.

ALDER-BUCKTHORN *Frangula alnus* Height up to 5m
A rather open, thornless bush, native to damp hedgerows and scrub in England and Wales. Oval leaves have wavy margins; dark green, turning yellow in autumn. Pale green, 5-petalled flowers appear in May. Berries ripen from green to black.

GOOSEBERRY *Ribes uva-crispa* Height up to 1m
Native but rather local bush in woods in S and C England and Wales. Spiny stems bear rounded and irregularly-toothed leaves. Small, yellowish flowers appear March–May. Green, hairy fruits eventually swell to form the familiar gooseberry.

SEA-BUCKTHORN *Hippophae rhamnoides* Height up to 10m
Native to stabilised, coastal dunes; also planted ornamentally inland. Forms a dense shrub with thorny twigs and narrow, greyish leaves. Small, greenish female and male flowers grow on separate plants. Orange berries form on female bushes.

COMMON LIME *Tilia x vulgaris* Height up to 45m
Widely planted ornamental hybrid. Mature trees often have a rather tall, narrow crown in proportion to width of the base. 6–10cm long heart-shaped leaves exude sap. Clustered flowers attached to a wing-like bract. Ovoid seed is hard-cased.

SMALL-LEAVED LIME *Tilia cordata* Height up to 30m
A rather local native tree, mostly in limestone areas. Forms a rather narrow tree. 3–9cm long leaf is heart-shaped, finely-toothed and with a pointed tip. Flower clusters appear in July attached to wing-like bract. Seed is hard-cased.

RHODODENDRON *Rhododendron ponticum* Height up to 5m
A popular ornamental shrub but naturalised and invasive in some areas. Shiny and leathery, evergreen leaves are elliptical and dark green. Clusters of stalked, pinkish red flowers appear May–June. Fruit capsule contains numerous flat seeds.

BUDDLEIA *Buddleia davidii* Height up to 4m
Common garden shrub, also widely naturalised on wasteground and around coasts. Has long, narrow leaves which are darker above than below. Showy, often drooping spikes of purple flowers appear June–September. Very attractive to butterflies.

DOGWOOD *Cornus sanguinea* Height up to 4m
Common hedgerow shrub in S England, mostly on chalk. Easily recognised, even in winter, by its red stems. The opposite, oval leaves have 3–5 veins and reddish stalks. Flat clusters of white flowers appear May–July. Ripen to black berries.

PRIVET *Ligustrum vulgare* Height up to 10m
Common hedgerow and wayside shrub, mostly on chalk in the S. Shiny, oval leaves are sometimes evergreen. Twigs carry terminal spikes of scented, white flowers which are 4-petalled and appear May–June. Berries are black and ripen in autumn.

ELDER *Sambucus nigra* Height up to 10m
Common shrub of hedgerows and waysides. Usually has outcurved main branches and corky bark. Unpleasant-smelling leaves divided into 5–7 leaflets. Flat-topped sprays of fragrant white flowers appear June–July. Berries black and luscious.

GUELDER-ROSE *Viburnum opulus* Height up to 4m
Large shrub or small tree. Found in hedgerows and fairly common except in the N. Leaves are divided into five, irregularly-toothed lobes. Flowers appear June–July in flat-topped heads, inner ones much smaller than outer ones. Berries are red.

WAYFARING-TREE *Viburnum lantana* Height up to 6m
Large shrub or small, spreading tree. Oval leaves have toothed margins; dark green above but paler below. Flowers April–June in flat-topped heads comprising small, even-sized flowers. Berries ripen from red to black, not simultaneously.

HONEYSUCKLE *Lonicera periclymenum* Height up to 5m
Common hedgerow and woodland climber which twines up other shrubs and trees. Leaves are grey-green, oval and opposite. Scented, trumpet-shaped flowers appear June–August; borne in whorled heads. Clusters of red berries ripen in autumn.

HOP *Humulus lupulus* Height up to 6m
Twining hedgerow climber. Common in England and Wales; introduced and scarce in Scotland and Ireland. Leaves divided into 3–5 coarse-toothed lobes. Male flowers seen in open clusters. Female flowers are green cone-like hops that ripen brown.

OLD MAN'S BEARD *Clematis vitalba* Length up to 20m
Scrambling hedgerow perennial found on chalky soils. Widespread and common in C and S England and Wales. Leaves divided into 3–5 leaflets. Clusters of creamy flowers appear July–August. Clusters of ripe fruits adorned with hairy plumes.

WHITE BRYONY *Bryonia cretica* Height up to 4m
Hedgerow perennial. Climbs using long, unbranched tendrils. Leaves divided into five lobes. Clusters of greenish, 5-petalled flowers appear May–August and arise from base of leaves; male and female on different plants. Berries red and shiny.

IVY *Hedera helix* Height up to 20m
An evergreen, self-clinging climber which also carpets the ground. Glossy, dark green leaves are 3- or 5-lobed with paler veins. Heads of yellow-green flowers appear September–November; ripen to black berries. Widespread and very common.

BLACK BRYONY *Tamus communis* Height up to 3m
A twining climber. Superficially similar to white bryony but it lacks tendrils. Leaves heart-shaped, glossy and net-veined. Yellow-green, 6-petalled female and male flowers appear on separate plants, May–August. Berries ripen bright red.

MISTLETOE *Viscum album* Diameter up to 1m
Woody, evergreen parasite. Forms large, spherical clumps among branches of host trees, mainly poplar and apple. Branches evenly forked with opposite pairs of oval yellowish leaves. Flowers are inconspicuous. Berries white and sticky.

COMMON NETTLE *Urtica dioica* Height up to 1m
The familiar stinging nettle. Oval leaves are toothed and pointed-tipped; borne in opposite pairs and covered with sharp hairs. Flowers appear June–October in pendulous catkins; male and female on separate plants. Favours disturbed soils.

PELLITORY-OF-THE-WALL *Parietaria judaica* Height up to 7cm
Spreading, downy perennial found typically on walls and rocky ground. Oval, long-stalked leaves are borne on much-branched, red stems. Clusters of flowers appear June–October, at leaf bases. Widespread in England, Wales and Ireland.

JAPANESE KNOTWEED *Reynoutria japonica* Height up to 2m
Fast-growing, invasive perennial, quick to colonise roadsides, riverbanks and other wayside places. Large, triangular leaves are borne on red, zigzag stems. Loose spikes of white flowers arise from leaf bases and appear August–October.

KNOTGRASS *Polygonum aviculare* Often prostrate
Widespread and common much-branched annual of bare soil, paths and open ground generally. Oval, rather leathery leaves, are alternate and have a silvery sheaf around leaf bases. Pale pink flowers appear June–October, arising in leaf axils.

BISTORT *Polygonum bistorta* Height up to 60cm
Medium-sized perennial of damp meadows, locally common in the N but rare in the S. Leaves oval or arrow-shaped; borne on unbranched, upright stems. 30–40mm long terminal cylindrical spikes of pink flowers appear June–August. Forms patches.

AMPHIBIOUS BISTORT *Polygonum amphibium* Height up to 40cm
Perennial seen both as a plant of pond margins and on dry land. Aquatic form has floating stems and oval leaves. Globular or cylindrical terminal spikes of pink flowers appear June–September on upright stems. Widespread and locally common.

ALPINE BISTORT *Polygonum viviparum* Height up to 30cm
Upright, unbranched perennial of upland and northern grassland; locally common northwards from N Wales. Leaves narrow and grass-like. Terminal flower spikes comprise pale pink flowers in top half and reddish brown bulbils in lower part.

WATER-PEPPER *Polygonum hydropiper* Height up to 70cm
Upright, branched annual, characteristic of damp, bare ground such as winter-wet ruts. Widespread and common except in N. Narrow oval leaves have peppery taste when chewed. Pale pink flowers borne in long spikes which often droop at tip.

REDSHANK *Polygonum persicaria* Height up to 60cm
Upright or sprawling annual which is widespread and common on disturbed ground. Narrow oval leaves typically show a dark, central mark. Reddish stems are much-branched. Pink flowers appear June–October and are borne in terminal spikes.

BLACK-BINDWEED *Bilderdykia convolvulus* Height up to 1m
A very common, clockwise-twining annual which both trails on ground and climbs among wayside plants. Arrow-shaped leaves are borne on angular stems. Clusters of dock-like greenish flowers appear July–October and arise from the leaf axils.

CURLED DOCK *Rumex crispus* Height up to 1m
A common and widespread perennial of rough meadows and disturbed soils. Narrow leaves are 25cm long and have wavy edges. Oval, flattened flowers appear June–October; borne in dense, leafless spikes which do not spread away from stem.

COMMON SORREL *Rumex acetosa* Height up to 60cm
An often short, upright perennial. Common and widespread everywhere in all sorts of grassy habitats. Deep green leaves are arrow-shaped, narrow and taste vaguely of vinegar. Reddish flowers appear May–July and are carried in slender spikes.

SHEEP'S SORREL *Rumex acetosella* Height up to 25cm
Short, upright perennial of bare, well-drained acid soils. Common and widespread in suitable open habitats. Leaves are arrow-shaped but the basal lobes point forwards. Flowers appear May–August and are carried in slender, loose spikes.

WATER DOCK *Rumex hydrolapathum* Height up to 1.5m
Large, branched perennial, associated with damp habitats such as ditches, river banks, canals and marshes. Widespread but absent from the N; commonest in S and E England. Leaves large and oval. Dense flower spikes appear July–September.

BROAD-LEAVED DOCK *Rumex obtusifolius* Height up to 1m
A widespread and often extremely common upright perennial of field margins and disturbed meadows. Leaves are large and broadly oval, heart-shaped at the base. Flowers appear June–October in loose spikes which are leafy at their bases.

WOOD DOCK *Rumex sanguineus* Height up to 1m
Upright, straggly and branched perennial. Widespread and often common but absent from much of Scotland. Favours grassy woodland rides and shaded meadows. Easily identified when flowers (June–October), leaf veins and stems turn red.

SPRING BEAUTY *Montia perfoliata* Height up to 30cm
Annual introduced from N America; now widely naturalised. Basal leaves oval and stalked. Flowering stems with fused pair of perfoliate leaves. White, 5-petalled 5mm diameter flowers appear April–July in loose spikes. Favours dry, sandy soil.

PINK PURSLANE *Montia sibirica* Height up to 30cm
Introduced annual or perennial from N America; now widely naturalised in damp woods. Basal leaves oval and stalked. Flowering stems carry pair of unstalked leaves. Pink, 5-petalled flowers are 15–20mm across and appear April–July.

FAT HEN *Chenopodium album* Height up to 1m
A very common and widespread plant of disturbed arable land and waste places. An upright annual. Green leaves look matt due to mealy coating; leaf shape varies from oval to diamond-shaped. Spikes of whitish flowers appear June–October.

RED GOOSEFOOT *Chenopodium rubrum* Height up to 60cm
Variable upright annual. Widespread and common in S England but rare elsewhere. Favours manure-rich soil. Leaves shiny, diamond-shaped and toothed. Leafy flower spikes appear July–October. Stems often turn red in old or parched specimens.

GOOD KING HENRY *Chenopodium bonus-henricus* Height up to 50cm
Introduced, upright perennial. Widely established and often common on disturbed arable land and wasteground. Lower leaves triangular; mealy when young but then green. Stems sometimes with red lines. Leafless flower spikes appear May–August.

BABINGTON'S ORACHE *Atriplex glabriuscula* Prostrate and spreading
Entirely coastal but widespread around Britain and Ireland on stabilised shingle and bare ground. Has triangular or diamond-shaped leaves. Stems usually reddish and whole plant often turns red in autumn. Flower spikes appear July–September.

SEA BEET *Beta vulgaris ssp maritima* Height up to 1m
Sprawling perennial, forming clumps on cliffs, shingle beaches and other coastal habitats. Leaves glossy, dark green and leathery, with reddish stems; leaf shape varies from oval to triangular. Spikes of green flowers appear July–September.

SEA PURSLANE *Halimione portulacoides* Height up to 1m
A spreading, often rather rounded perennial, all parts of which are mealy. Grey-green leaves are oval at the base but narrow further up stem. Yellowish flower spikes appear July–October. Grows on saltmarshes in England, Wales and Ireland.

GLASSWORT *Salicornia europaea* Height up to 30cm
A yellowish green, fleshy annual which fancifully resembles a miniature cactus. Usually much-branched and looks segmented. Tiny flowers appear August–September at stem junctions. Typical saltmarsh plant. Tolerates immersion in saltwater.

ANNUAL SEA-BLITE *Suaeda maritima* Height up to 50cm
Widespread annual of saltmarshes around the coasts of Britain and Ireland. Much-branched and forms small clumps which vary from yellowish green to reddish. Leaves are rather swollen and cylindrical. Tiny flowers appear August–October.

PRICKLY SALTWORT *Salsola kali* Height up to 50cm
Spiky-looking, prickly annual, typical of sandy beaches around most of Britain and Ireland. Leaves are swollen, flattened-cylindrical and spiny-tipped. Tiny solitary flowers appear July–October at the leaf bases. Often rather prostrate.

THYME-LEAVED SANDWORT *Arenaria serpyllifolia* Usually prostrate
Common in lowland areas of Britain and Ireland and favouring dry, bare soils. Slender, delicate stems bear oval leaves in opposite pairs. White, 5-petalled flowers are 5–7mm across; appear April–October. Green sepals longer than petals.

SPRING SANDWORT *Minuartia verna* Height up to 10cm
Characteristic plant of bare limestone soils or spoil from lead mines. Whorls of narrow, 3-veined leaves are carried on slender stems. White, 5-petalled flowers are 7–9mm across and appear May–September. Green sepals are shorter than petals.

MOSSY CYPHEL *Minuartia sedoides* Prostrate
An upland perennial of damp, stony ground on mountain tops in Scottish Highlands and on some Scottish islands. Narrow, fleshy leaves form dense cushions studded with yellow flowers June–August; these are 4mm across and often lack petals.

SEA SANDWORT *Honkenya peploides* Prostrate
Familiar coastal perennial found on stabilised shingle and sandy beaches. Often forms large mats which comprise creeping stems bearing opposite pairs of fleshy, oval leaves. The greenish white flowers are 6–8mm across and appear May–August.

GREATER STITCHWORT *Stellaria holostea* Height up to 50cm
Widespread and common in open woodland and along rides and hedgerows. Leaves are narrow, fresh green and grass-like. Easily overlooked among foliage until white flowers appear April–June. These are 20–30mm across and have notched petals.

LESSER STITCHWORT *Stellaria graminea* Height up to 50cm
Widespread and common in similar habitats to greater stitchwort; favours acid soils. Long, narrow and fresh green leaves found among grasses and other wayside plants. The white, 5-petalled flowers are 5–15mm across and appear May–August.

COMMON CHICKWEED *Stellaria media* Height up to 30cm
Common annual of flower beds, vegetable patches and other areas of disturbed ground. Often prostrate and spreading. Leaves oval, fresh green and in opposite pairs; upper leaves unstalked. White flowers are 5–10mm across; seen all year.

WATER CHICKWEED *Myosoton aquaticum* Height up to 1m
Straggling perennial of damp, grassy ground and river margins. Leaves are heart-shaped with wavy edges. Borne in opposite pairs; upper leaves lack stalks. Stems hairy. White flowers comprise five deeply divided petals and appear June–October.

COMMON MOUSE-EAR *Cerastium fontanum* Height up to 30cm, often shorter
Hairy perennial, widespread and usually common in gardens and grassland, and on disturbed ground. Grey-green leaves borne in opposite pairs. Non-flowering and flowering shoots occur, the latter with white, 5-petalled flowers April–October.

STICKY MOUSE-EAR *Cerastium glomeratum* Height up to 40cm
Stickily-hairy annual which is widespread and common on dry, bare ground. Leaves are pointed-oval and borne in opposite pairs. The white, 5-petalled flowers are 10–15mm across and are carried in clustered heads; they appear April–October.

CORN SPURREY *Spergula arvensis* Height up to 30cm
A stickily-hairy annual which is a widespread and fairly common weed of arable land with sandy soils. Narrow leaves are borne in whorls along straggling stems. Flowers are 4–7mm across and comprise five whitish petals; they appear May–August.

LESSER SEA-SPURREY *Spergularia marina* Usually prostrate
Annual plant associated with grassy upper margins of saltmarshes; widespread and locally common. Fleshy, narrow leaves are pointed and borne in opposite pairs on trailing stems. Deep pink flowers appear June–September and are 6–8mm across.

ROCK SEA-SPURREY *Spergularia rupicola* Height up to 20cm
A sticky perennial characteristic of rocky coastal habitats and found on cliffs, sea walls and stone walls. Sometimes forms clumps comprising branched stems with whorls of fleshy leaves. Pink flowers are 8–10mm across; appear June–September.

PROCUMBENT PEARLWORT *Sagina procumbens* Prostrate
Creeping perennial of damp, bare ground; common in Britain and Ireland. Forms mats comprising central rosette with radiating shoots bearing narrow leaves. The green, petalless flowers are borne on side shoots and are seen May–September.

ANNUAL KNAWEL *Scleranthus annuus* Height up to 10cm
Yellowish green annual. Locally common on dry, bare soil and arable land in most of Britain and Ireland. Narrow, pointed leaves borne in opposite pairs along the stems. Flowers comprise green, pointed sepals and no petals; appear May–August.

CORAL-NECKLACE *Illecebrum verticillatum* Prostrate
A charming annual of damp, sandy ground beside drying-up ponds. Only found in S England and mainly in the New Forest. Plant comprises reddish stems which bear opposite, bright green leaves and clusters of white flowers in summer months.

BLADDER CAMPION *Silene vulgaris* Height up to 80cm
Grassland perennial favouring well-drained soil, often on chalk. Widespread but common only in S. Upright stems bear opposite pairs of grey-green leaves. White flowers appear May–September and comprise five petals and a swollen sepal tube.

SEA CAMPION *Silene maritima* Height up to 20cm
A cushion-forming perennial. Confined to coastal habitats including shingle and cliffs but widespread and locally abundant. Leaves grey-green and fleshy. White flowers are 20–25mm across and have overlapping petals; appear June–August.

MOSS CAMPION *Silene acaulis* Diameter up to 20cm
A cushion-forming perennial associated with mountain tops and ledges from Wales to Scottish Highlands; also found nearer sea level in far N and on some Scottish islands. Leaves narrow and densely packed. Pink flowers appear June–August.

RED CAMPION *Silene dioica* Height up to 1m
Hairy biennial or perennial. Locally common except in E England, N Scotland and Ireland. Hairy leaves are borne in opposite pairs on upright stems. Pinkish red flowers are 20–25mm across and appear March–October; they comprise five petals.

WHITE CAMPION *Silene alba* Height up to 1m
Widespread and common hairy perennial which favours disturbed ground and grassy habitats including hedgerows and verges. Oval leaves are borne in opposite pairs on stems. White, 5-petalled flowers appear May–October and are 25–30mm across.

NOTTINGHAM CATCHFLY *Silene nutans* Height up to 50cm
A very local perennial, restricted to sites on calcareous grassland and shingle beaches. Stem leaves oval and unstalked. Nodding flowers 17mm across; pinkish white petals are inrolled during daytime but roll back at dusk; seen May–July.

RAGGED ROBIN *Lychnis flos-cuculi* Height up to 65cm
Widespread and common perennial of damp meadows and marshes. The narrow, grass-like leaves are rough, the upper ones in opposite pairs. The flowers comprise five pink petals each of which is divided into four lobes; they appear May–August.

MAIDEN PINK *Dianthus deltoides* Height up to 20cm
A hairy perennial of dry, sandy places. Widespread and locally common in the S. Leaves are narrow and grey-green. Flowers are 18–20mm across and appear June–September; the five pink petals show white basal spots and have toothed margins.

CORNCOCKLE *Agrostemma githago* Height up to 70cm
Formerly widespread and common as a cornfield weed but now scarce and erratic due to use of modern herbicides. Leaves narrow and grass-like. Flowers comprise five reddish pink petals and long, narrow radiating sepals; appear May–August.

STINKING HELLEBORE *Helleborus foetidus* Height up to 75cm
A local, strong-smelling perennial, restricted calcareous woodlands in C and S England and Wales. Leaves divided into toothed lobes; lower ones persist through winter. Green, bell-shaped flowers are 15–30mm across and appear January–May.

GREEN HELLEBORE *Helleborus viridis* Height up to 60cm
Scarce and local perennial, found in calcareous woodlands in C and S England and Wales. Leaves divided into bright green, elongate lobes; they are not evergreen. Green flowers have pointed sepals but no petals; they appear February–April.

WINTER ACONITE *Eranthis hyemalis* Height up to 10cm
An attractive perennial, introduced but now widely established in many parts of the region. Upright stems carry three spreading leaves, each divided into three lobes. Above these, flowers appear January–April, these comprising six yellow sepals.

MARSH MARIGOLD *Caltha palustris* Height up to 25cm
A familiar and widespread perennial of damp woodland, marshes and wet meadows. Plant is borne on stout stems. Leaves kidney-shaped and shiny. Flowers comprise five yellow sepals but no petals; they are 20–50mm across and appear March–July.

GLOBEFLOWER *Trollius europaeus* Height up to 60cm
Attractive perennial, absent from S but locally common from N Wales to Scotland and in NW Ireland. Leaves palmately divided into toothed lobes. Almost spherical flowers borne on long stems; comprise 10–15 yellow sepals and appear May–August.

MEADOW BUTTERCUP *Ranunculus acris* Height up to 1m
Widespread and abundant perennial of grassland habitats. Rounded leaves divided into 3–7 lobes; upper ones unstalked. The flowers appear April–October and are 18–25mm across; they comprise five shiny, yellow petals and have upright sepals.

CREEPING BUTTERCUP *Ranunculus repens* Height up to 50cm, often shorter
Often unwelcome perennial of lawns and other grassy places. Long, rooting runners assist its spread. Hairy leaves divided into three lobes, the middle lobe stalked. Yellow flowers 20–30mm across with upright sepals; appear May–August.

BULBOUS BUTTERCUP *Ranunculus bulbosus* Height up to 40cm
Widespread and often abundant hairy perennial. Favours dry grassland including chalk downs. Leaves divided into three lobes, each of which is stalked. The flowers are 20–30mm across and appear May–August. The sepals are folded back down stalk.

HAIRY BUTTERCUP *Ranunculus sardous* Height up to 40cm
A rather local hairy annual. Rcstricted to England, Wales and S Scotland and often found on coastal grassland. Lower leaves divided into three lobes. Pale yellow flowers are 15–25mm across and appear May–September. The sepals are folded back.

CORN BUTTERCUP *Ranunculus arvensis* Height up to 40cm
Formerly a common annual arable weed but now rare and local; seen regularly only in S England. Leaves divided into narrow lobes. Pale yellow flowers are 10–12mm across and comprise five petals; they appear May–July. Fruit is distinctly spiny.

GREATER SPEARWORT *Ranunculus lingua* Height up to 1m
Widespread but local perennial. Favours the shallow margins of ponds and lakes. Plant has long runners and upright stems bearing narrow, 25cm long leaves which are sometimes toothed. Flowers are 20–40mm across and appear June–September.

LESSER SPEARWORT *Ranunculus flammula* Height up to 50cm
Upright or creeping perennial. Sometimes roots where leaf nodes touch ground. Stem leaves are narrow and oval. Flowers are 5–15mm across and usually solitary; appear June–October. Widespread and common on damp ground, often beside rivers.

CELERY-LEAVED BUTTERCUP *Ranunculus scleratus* Height up to 50cm
Fresh-green annual. Favours marshes and wet grazing meadows; often on trampled ground. Lower leaves are celery-like and divided into three lobes. The flowers are 5–10mm across and are borne in clusters; they appear May–September. Mainly in S.

LESSER CELANDINE *Ranunculus ficaria* Height up to 25m
Common and widespread perennial of hedgerows, open woodland and bare ground, sometimes forming clumps or patches. Leaves are heart-shaped, glossy and dark green. Flowers are 20–30mm across and appear March–May; open only in sunshine.

COMMON WATER-CROWFOOT *Ranunculus aquatilis* Floating
Widespread and common annual or perennial found in both slow-flowing and still waters. Has both thread-like submerged leaves and floating ones which are entire but with toothed lobes. White flowers are 12–20mm across; appear April–August.

CHALK STREAM WATER-CROWFOOT *Ranunculus penicillatus* Floating
Local annual or perennial of fast-flowing chalk streams and rivers. Widespread except in N. Has lobed, rounded floating leaves and long, thread-like submerged ones which collapse out of water. Flowers 15–25mm across; appear May–July.

POND WATER-CROWFOOT *Ranunculus peltatus* Floating
A widespread and common annual or perennial of ponds, lakes and other areas of still water. Has lobed but rounded floating leaves and short, rigid thread-like submerged ones. The flowers are white, 15–30mm across and appear May–August.

ROUND-LEAVED WATER-CROWFOOT *Ranunculus omiophyllus* Floating
Creeping annual or biennial. Favours damp, muddy patches, often beside water seepages. Rather local and restricted mainly to S and W England and Wales and S Ireland. Leaves lobed and rounded. Flowers 8–12mm across and appear May–August.

COMMON MEADOW-RUE *Thalictrum flavum* Height up to 1m
Local plant of damp meadows, ditches and fens; favours basic soils and common only in the S and E. Leaves are pinnately divided two or three times into toothed lobes. Flowers have yellow anthers and are borne in dense clusters June–August.

LESSER MEADOW-RUE *Thalictrum minus* Height up to 1m, often shorter
Local plant of basic soils including rocky slopes or dunes; widespread but absent from much of S and E. Leaves pinnately divided three or four times into toothed lobes. Yellow flowers are borne in open sprays not dense clusters, June–August.

COLUMBINE *Aquilega vulgaris* Height up to 1m
A familiar garden perennial. Also native although local in many parts of Britain and Ireland. Grey-green leaves comprise three, 3-lobed leaflets. The nodding, purple flowers are 30–40mm long, the petals with hooked-tipped spurs; appear May–July.

WOOD ANEMONE *Anemone nemorosa* Height up to 30cm
Widespread and locally common woodland perennial. Sometimes forms large carpets. Long-stalked stem leaves are divided into three lobes, each being further divided. Solitary flowers comprise 5–10 white or pinkish sepals and appear March–May.

PASQUEFLOWER *Pulsatilla vulgaris* Height up to 25cm
Silky-hairy perennial of dry, calcareous grassland. Restricted to few sites in S and E England. Leaves divided two or three times and comprise narrow leaflets. Purple, bell-shaped flowers 50–80mm across, upright then nodding; appear April–May.

YELLOW WATER-LILY *Nuphar lutea* Floating
Water plant with oval, floating leaves up to 40cm across. Widespread and locally common except in N Scotland. Favours still or slow-flowing water and roots in mud in shallows. Flowers 50–60mm across, carried on stalks; appear June–September.

WHITE WATER-LILY *Nymphaea alba* Floating
Water plant with round, floating leaves, 20–30cm across. Widespread and common on still or slow-flowing water. Flowers comprise 20–25 white or pinkish white petals. They are 15–20cm across and appear June–August; open only in sunshine.

COMMON FUMITORY *Fumaria officinalis* Height up to 10cm
Spreading or scrambling annual arable weed favouring well-drained soil. Leaves much-divided, the flat lobes all in one plane. Crimson-tipped pink flowers are 6–7mm long, spurred and two lipped; appear April–October. Widespread and common.

CLIMBING CORYDALIS *Corydalis claviculata* Height up to 70cm
Delicate, climbing annual of woodland and scrub on acid soils. Widespread and common in W but rare in Ireland. The much-divided leaves end in tendrils which assist climbing. Creamy white flowers are 5–6mm long and appear June–September.

COMMON POPPY *Papaver rhoeas* Height up to 60cm
Hairy annual weed of arable land and disturbed ground. Widespread but commonest in S and E England; scarce in N and W. Leaves are much-branched. Flowers 70–100mm across with four papery, scarlet petals; appear June–August. Ovoid seed capsule.

YELLOW HORNED-POPPY *Glaucium flavum* Height up to 50cm
Blue-grey, clump-forming perennial of shingle beaches; locally common on most suitable coasts. Leaves pinnately divided, clasping upper ones having shallow, toothed lobes. Flowers 60–90mm across; June–September. Seed pods long and curved.

WELSH POPPY *Meconopsis cambrica* Height up to 50cm
Perennial of shady woods. Native to Wales, SW England and Ireland; naturalised as a garden escape elsewhere. Leaves pinnately divided and stalked. Flowers are 50–80mm across and comprise four overlapping, yellow petals; appear June–August.

GREATER CELANDINE *Chelidonium majus* Height up to 80cm
Tall, brittle-stemmed perennial with grey-green, pinnately divided leaves. Found in hedgerows and along woodland rides; native in most areas but also introduced. Flowers 20–30mm across; comprise four non-overlapping petals, appearing April–October.

TREACLE MUSTARD *Erysimum cheiranthoides* Height up to 85cm
A wasteground and arable land annual, common only in SE England. Shallowly-toothed, narrow leaves are borne on upright, angled stems. Topped with heads of yellow flowers, each 6–10mm across, appearing June–September. Seed pods long and slender.

MARSH YELLOWCRESS *Rorippa palustris* Height up to 50cm
Widespread annual of damp, marshy hollows, sometimes growing in shallow water. Upright stems carry lobed leaves. Terminal heads of yellow flowers, each one 3mm across, appear June–October; sepals as long as petals. Seed pods 4–6mm long.

HEDGE MUSTARD *Sisymbrium officinale* Height up to 70cm
Tough upright annual or biennial of wasteground and disturbed soil. Lower leaves deeply divided; stem leaves narrow. Unbranched upper part has cylindrical pods pressed close to stem and terminal head of small yellow flowers; appears May–October.

CHARLOCK *Sinapis arvensis* Height up to 1.5m
Widespread and common annual of arable land and wasteground. Dark green leaves are large and coarsely-toothed, the upper ones unstalked. Flowers appear April–October and are 15–20mm across. Seed pods are long, with a beaded appearance.

COMMON WINTER-CRESS *Barbaris vulgaris* Height up to 80cm
Upright, hairless perennial of damp ground. Widespread but commonest in the S. Leaves are dark green and shiny. Lower ones are divided, the end lobe large and oval; upper stem leaves entire. Flowers are 7–9mm across and appear May–August.

WATER-CRESS *Nasturtium officinale* Height up to 15cm
Usually creeping perennial of shallow streams and ditches; widely cultivated in S England. Pinnately divided leaves persist through winter. White flowers appear May–October and are 4–6mm across. Seed pod is 18mm long. Widespread and common.

HAIRY BITTER-CRESS *Cardamine hirsuta* Height up to 30cm
Widespread and abundant annual; only slightly hairy. Forms a basal rosette of pinnately divided leaves, the lobes of which are rounded. Upright stem carries a few leaves and a head of white flowers, 2–3mm across. Flowers throughout year.

CUCKOOFLOWER *Cardamine pratensis* Height up to 50cm
Variable perennial of damp, grassy places. Also known as lady's smock. Has basal rosette of pinnately divided leaves; the lobes are rounded. Pale lilac or white flowers appear April–June and are 12–20mm across. Widespread and locally common.

SEA RADISH *Raphanus raphanistrum ssp maritimus* Height up to 60cm
Robust, roughly hairy annual. Widespread on stabilised shingle, sand dunes and coastal grassland but commonest in S and W. Lower leaves pinnately divided but upper ones narrow and entire. Yellow flowers appear May–July. Seed pods beaded.

WILD CABBAGE *Brassica oleracea* Height up to 1.25m
Tough perennial found on coastal chalk cliffs and near seabird colonies, mainly SW England and W Wales. Lower leaves grey-green, large and fleshy; often ravaged by larvae of large white butterfly. Yellow flowers 10–20mm across; appear April–August.

BLACK MUSTARD *Brassica nigra* Height up to 2m
Robust, greyish annual which is locally common in England and Wales; often seen on sea cliffs and river banks. Leaves stalked, the lower ones pinnately lobed. Yellow flowers 12–15mm across; appear May–August. Pods pressed close to stem.

WILD CANDYTUFT *Iberis amara* Height up to 30cm
Local on calcareous grassland in S England. Favours disturbed soil, often beside rabbit burrows. Much branched. Toothed, spoon-shaped leaves become smaller up stem. White or mauve flowers appear July–August, two petals longer than other two.

SWEET ALISON *Lobularia maritima* Height up to 20cm
A hairy perennial, familiar as a garden plant but also widely naturalised as an escape. Leaves are narrow, entire and grey-green. Sweet-smelling white flowers appear June–October and are 5–6mm across. Small, oval seed pods on long stalks.

SHEPHERD'S-PURSE *Capsella bursa-pastoris* Height up to 35cm
Widespread and often common annual of arable land, tracks and waysides. Leaves vary from lobed to entire; upper ones are toothed. Flowers are found all year; they are 2–3mm across and white. Seed pods are green and triangular in outline.

COMMON WHITLOWGRASS *Erophila verna* Height up to 20cm
Common and widespread annual of dry, bare places. Narrow, toothed leaves form a basal rosette, from the centre of which arises leafless flowering stems. White flowers are 3–6mm across and comprise four deeply notched petals; appear March–May.

FIELD PENNY-CRESS *Thlaspi arvense* Height up to 45cm
Common and widespread annual of arable land with an unpleasant smell. Narrow, arrow-shaped leaves clasp the upright stem; no basal rosette. White flowers are 4–6mm across and appear May–September. Rounded seed pods have a terminal notch.

FIELD PEPPERWORT *Lepidium campestre* Height up to 50cm
Widespread grey-green hairy annual, locally common on dry, bare soil, especially in the S. Basal leaves are oval and untoothed. Stem leaves are arrow-shaped and clasping. Flowers 2–3mm across; appear May–August. Seed pods oval and notched.

COMMON SCURVYGRASS *Cochleria officinalis* Height up to 50cm
Locally common perennial of saltmarshes, coastal walls and cliffs, and mountains inland. Has kidney-shaped basal leaves but arrow-shaped upper ones clasping the dark stem. White flowers are 8–10mm across; appear April–October. Seed pods round.

THALE CRESS *Arabidopsis thaliana* Height up to 50cm
Distinctive annual of dry, sandy soils, often on paths. Broadly-toothed, oval leaves form a basal rosette; upright flowering stems bear a few small leaves. White flowers are 3mm across; appear March–October. Pods cylindrical and long.

SWINE-CRESS *Coronopus squamatus* Usually prostrate
Creeping annual or biennial. Common in S and E England but scarce elsewhere. Leaves are pinnately divided and toothed, sometimes forming a dense mat on the ground. Compact clusters of 2–3mm diameter white flowers appear June–September.

LESSER SWINE-CRESS *Coronopus didymus* Usually prostrate
Similar to swine-cress but flowers even smaller, sometimes completely lacking petals, and more finely divided leaves. An annual or biennial which favours dry, disturbed soil and wasteground; common only in S and SW. Flowers June–October.

GARLIC MUSTARD *Alliaria petiolata* Height up to 1m
A familiar wayside plant, common and widespread in most parts. Leaves are fresh green, heart-shaped and toothed. They are borne up the stem and smell of garlic when crushed. Clusters of white flowers appear April–June and are 6mm across.

SEA ROCKET *Cakile maritima* Height up to 25cm
Straggling, fleshy annual found on sandy and shingle beaches. Widespread and locally common around coasts of Britain and Ireland. Leaves shiny and lobed. The flowers are pale lilac, 6–12mm across; appear June–September in dense clusters.

SEA-KALE *Crambe maritima* Height up to 50cm
Robust perennial. Forms domed and expansive clumps on shingle and sandy beaches. Leaves are fleshy and have wavy margins; lower ones 25cm long and long-stalked. White flowers appear June–August in flat-topped clusters. Seed pods are oval.

WELD *Reseda luteola* Height up to 1.2m
Widespread biennial of disturbed calcareous ground, commonest in S and SE. Has basal rosette of narrow leaves in first year only. Tall flower spike appears in second year with narrow stem leaves; yellowish, 4-petalled flowers appear June–August.

WILD MIGNONETTE *Reseda lutea* Height up to 70cm
Biennial of disturbed calcareous ground; widespread but absent from N Scotland. Similar to weld but shorter and with pinnately divided leaves; yellow-green 6-petalled flowers carried in more compact spikes; appear June–August. Stem solid.

ROUND-LEAVED SUNDEW *Drosera rotundifolia* Height up to 20cm
Widespread insectivorous plant of boggy heaths and moors. Rosette of reddish, rounded leaves are covered with long sticky hairs which trap insects; curl inwards to digest victims. Upright spike of white flowers appear June–August.

OBLONG-LEAVED SUNDEW *Drosera intermedia* Height up to 20cm
Reddish leaves are narrow and oblong; these form a basal rosette. Upright spike of white flowers appears June–August and arises from below rosette. Widespread insectivorous perennial of wet heaths and moors. Locally common throughout.

NAVELWORT *Umbilicus rupestris* Flower spike up to 15cm tall
Distinctive perennial, widespread in W Britain and Ireland. Leaves are rounded and fleshy, with a depressed centre above leaf stalk. Spikes of whitish flowers appear June–August. Grows on walls and stony banks, often in partial shade.

ROSE-ROOT *Rhodiola rosea* Height up to 30cm
Characteristic plant of mountain ledges and sea cliffs. Locally common in W Wales, N England, Scotland and Ireland. Robust stems bear succulent, overlapping oval leaves. Terminal, rounded clusters of yellow flowers appear May–July.

ORPINE *Sedum telephium* Height up to 50cm
Perennial of shady woodland and scrub, found locally in England and Wales. The reddish stems carry green, fleshy leaves which are oval and irregularly toothed. Rounded terminal heads of reddish purple, 5-petalled flowers appear July–August.

ENGLISH STONECROP *Sedum anglicum* Height up to 5cm
Widespread and locally common mat-forming perennial of rocky ground, shingle and old walls. Fleshy, 3–5mm long leaves are often tinged red; borne on wiry stems which are topped with white, 5-petalled, star-shaped flowers June–September.

BITING STONECROP *Sedum acre* Height up to 10cm
Mat-forming perennial. Widespread and locally common on well-drained ground such as sand dunes. Crowded, fleshy leaves are pressed close to stem and taste hot. The bright yellow, star-shaped flowers appear May–July and are 10–12mm across.

GRASS-OF-PARNASSUS *Parnassia palustris* Height up to 25cm
Perennial of peaty grassland, marshes and moors. Locally common in N Britain and Ireland. Heart-shaped basal leaves are stalked. White, 5-petalled flowers are 15–30mm across and appear June–September; borne on stalks with clasping leaves.

MEADOW SAXIFRAGE *Saxifraga granulata* Height up to 45cm
Attractive perennial of grassy meadows; local and commonest in E England. Leaves are kidney-shaped with blunt teeth; bulbils produced at leaf bases in autumn. Sprays of white, 5-petalled flowers appear April–June and are 20–30mm across.

STARRY SAXIFRAGE *Saxifraga stellaris* Height up to 25cm
Streamside and damp ground perennial found in uplands of N Wales, N Britain and Ireland. Oblong, toothed leaves form a basal rosette from which the flower stalk arises. Flowers comprise five white petals with red anthers; appear June–August.

MOSSY SAXIFRAGE *Saxifraga hypnoides* Height up to 20cm
Upland perennial, locally common in N England and Scotland; scarce in Wales and Ireland. Pointed 3-lobed leaves give plant a moss-like appearance. White flowers appear in small clusters May–July. Plant forms mats on rocks and bare ground.

YELLOW SAXIFRAGE *Saxifraga aizoides* Height up to 20cm
Colourful perennial of streamsides and damp ground in mountains; locally common in N England, Scotland and N Ireland. Plant forms clumps comprising masses of narrow, fleshy leaves. Yellow flowers appear June–September; 10–15mm across.

PURPLE SAXIFRAGE *Saxifraga oppositifolia* Creeping
Mat-forming perennial found on mountain rocks. Locally common in Scotland and N England. Plant comprises trailing stems bearing opposite pairs of small, dark green leaves. Purple flowers appear mainly March–April and are 10–15mm across.

OPPOSITE-LEAVED GOLDEN-SAXIFRAGE *Chrysosplenium oppositifolium*
Height up to 12cm. Patch-forming perennial of shady stream banks and damp woodland flushes. Locally common, mainly in the N and W. Rounded, stalked leaves are carried in opposite pairs. Yellow flowers lack petals and appear March–July; they are 3–5mm across.

MEADOWSWEET *Filipendula ulmaria* Height up to 1.25m
Striking perennial of damp meadows, marshes and stream margins. The dark green leaves comprise 3–5 pairs of oval leaflets with smaller leaflets between. Sprays of creamy flowers appear June–September, each 4–6mm across. Common throughout.

DROPWORT *Filipendula vulgaris* Height up to 50cm
Similar to meadowsweet but smaller and characteristic of calcareous grassland. Leaves comprise 8–20 pairs of larger leaflets with smaller leaflets between. The creamy white flowers are borne in flat-topped sprays and appear May–August.

AGRIMONY *Agrimonia eupatoria* Height up to 50cm
Widespread and common perennial of grassy places and roadsides. Best known for its upright spikes of yellow, 5-petalled flowers that appear June–August. Leaves comprise 3–6 pairs of oval, toothed leaflets with smaller leaflets between.

GREAT BURNET *Sanguisorba officinalis* Height up to 1m
Local and declining perennial of damp grassland and river banks; common only in C and N England. Easily recognised when crimson, ovoid heads of flowers appear June–September. Pinnately divided leaves comprise 3–7 pairs of oval leaflets.

SALAD BURNET *Sanguisorba minor* Height up to 35cm
Locally common perennial of calcareous grassland; absent from N Scotland. The pinnate leaves comprise 4–12 pairs of rounded, toothed leaflets; basal leaves in a rosette. Rounded flower heads appear May–September; green with red styles.

LADY'S-MANTLE *Alchemilla vulgaris agg* Height up to 30cm
Grassland perennial, usually associated with upland areas. Easily recognised by palmately lobed leaves; leaf shape variation can be used to separate different species within this aggregate. Yellowish green flowers appear May–September.

PARSLEY-PIERT *Aphanes arvensis* Creeping
Easily overlooked downy annual. Widespread and often common on dry, bare ground, often beside paths. Fan-shaped leaves are deeply divided into three lobes and are parsley-like. Clusters of tiny green, petal-less flowers appear April–October.

MOUNTAIN AVENS *Dryas octopetala* Height up to 6cm
Locally common on basic soils. Occurs on mountains in N Wales, N England and Scotland; down to sea level in N Scotland and W Ireland. Dark green leaves are oblong and toothed. White flowers comprise eight or more petals; appear June–July.

DOG-ROSE *Rosa canina* Height up to 3m
Scrambling shrub of hedgerows and scrub whose long, arching stems bear curved thorns. Widespread in most parts although commonest in S. Leaves comprise 5–7 hairless oval leaflets. Pale pink flowers appear June–July. Red hips in autumn.

FIELD ROSE *Rosa arvensis* Height up to 1m
Clump-forming hedgerow shrub whose trailing, purplish stems carry curved thorns. Widespread and common in S England, Wales and Ireland; becoming scarce in the N. Leaves have 5–7 oval leaflets. White flowers appear July–August; 3–5cm across.

BURNET ROSE *Rosa pimpinellifolia* Height up to 50cm
Clump-forming shrub of sand dunes, calcareous grassland and heaths. Stems armed with straight thorns and stiff bristles. Leaves comprise 7–11 oval leaflets. Creamy white flowers appear May–July; 3–5cm across. Ripe hips purplish black.

BRAMBLE *Rubus fruticosus agg* Height up to 3m
Includes hundreds of microspecies of scrambling shrubs whose arching stems are armed with variably shaped prickles and which root when they touch the ground. White or pink flowers (A) appear May–August. Blackberries (B) mature in autumn. Widespread.

CLOUDBERRY *Rubus chamaemorus* Height up to 20cm
Creeping perennial of upland moors. Locally common in N England and Scotland; scarce in N Wales and N Ireland. Stems lack prickles. Plant has up to three leaves, each with 5–7 lobes. Solitary white flowers June–August. Mature berry is orange.

WILD STRAWBERRY *Fragaria vesca* Height up to 30cm
Low perennial with long, rooting runners. Common and widespread on dry, grassy ground. Leaves comprise three oval leaflets, with undersides hairy. 5-petalled white flowers appear April–July and are 12–18mm across. Fruits are tiny strawberries.

MARSH CINQUEFOIL *Potentilla palustris* Height up to 40cm
Favours marshes and damp meadows. Widespread but local; common only in N England and Ireland. Greyish leaves divided into 3–5 toothed, oval leaflets. Star-shaped flowers comprise five reddish sepals and smaller purple petals; appear May–July.

TORMENTIL *Potentilla erecta* Height up to 30cm
Widespread and abundant creeping perennial of grassy places, heaths and moors. Unstalked leaves are trifoliate but appear 5-lobed because of two large leaflet-like stipules at base. 4-petalled flowers appear May–September; 7–11mm across.

CREEPING CINQUEFOIL *Potentilla reptans* Creeping
Creeping perennial whose trailing stems root at the nodes. Leaves are 5–7 lobed and are borne on long stalks. The 5-petalled yellow flowers are 17–25mm across and appear June–August. Widespread and common on grassy places including verges.

SILVERWEED *Potentilla anserina* Creeping
Creeping perennial of damp grassy places and bare ground. Widespread and common throughout. Leaves are divided into up to 12 pairs of silvery leaflets with tiny ones between them. Flowers are 5-petalled and 15–20mm across; appear May–August.

WOOD AVENS *Geum urbanum* Height up to 50cm
Widespread and common hairy perennial of shady hedgerows and woodland; also known as herb bennet. Basal leaves are pinnate. Flowers soon droop and comprise five yellow petals; they are 8–15mm across. Fruits armed with hooked red styles.

WATER AVENS *Geum rivale* Height up to 50cm
Perennial of damp meadows, mostly on base-rich soils. Widespread and locally common except in S England. Basal leaves pinnate but stem leaves trifoliate. Bell-shaped, flowers comprise dark red sepals and pink petals; they appear May–September.

COMMON GORSE *Ulex europaeus* Height up to 2m
Spiny, evergreen shrub. Common and widespread in Britain and Ireland, usually on acid soils on heaths. Leaves trifoliate when young. Spines are straight, 15–25mm long and grooved. The flowers appear mainly February–May and smell of coconut.

WESTERN GORSE *Ulex gallii* Height up to 1.5m
Dense, spiny and evergreen shrub. Similar to common gorse but restricted mainly to W Britain and Ireland. Locally abundant on coasts, sometimes covering slopes. Spines are 25mm long and almost smooth. Yellow flowers appear July–September.

DWARF GORSE *Ulex minor* Height up to 1m, often smaller
Spreading evergreen shrub with 10mm long, rather soft spines. The leaves are trifoliate when young and the yellow flowers appear July–September. Favours acid soils and usually found on heaths. Local and restricted mainly to SE and E England.

BROOM *Cytisus scoparius* Height up to 2m
Deciduous shrub with ridged, 5-angled green twigs. Common throughout on heaths and in hedgerows but favours acid soils. Leaves usually trifoliate. The flowers are 20mm long; appear April–June. Hairy black pods explode on dry, sunny days.

DYER'S GREENWEED *Genista tinctoria* Height up to 1m
Spineless grassland shrub, widespread and locally common in England, Wales and S Scotland. Leaves are narrow and sometimes downy. The broom-like flowers are 15mm long; appear June–July on leafy, stalked spikes. Pods are oblong and hairless.

PETTY WHIN *Genista anglica* Height up 1m
A rather spindly, hairless shrub, armed with strong spines. Favours heaths and moors and rather local; absent from Ireland. Leaves are narrow, hairless and waxy. Flowers are 15mm long; borne in terminal clusters and appear April–June.

PURPLE MILK-VETCH *Astragalus danicus* Height up to 30cm
Spreading perennial of dry calcareous grassland. Local and rather scarce in E Britain; rare in Ireland. Hairy, pinnate leaves comprise 6–12 pairs of oval leaflets. Clusters of purple flowers appear May–July, each flower 15–18mm long.

TUFTED VETCH *Vicia cracca* Height up to 2m
Widespread and common scrambling perennial. Favours grassy places, hedgerows and scrub. Leaves comprise up to 12 pairs of narrow leaflets and end in a branched tendril. Spikes of bluish purple flowers, up to 4cm tall, appear June–August.

WOOD VETCH *Vicia sylvatica* Height up to 1.5m
Straggling perennial of shady woods and steep, coastal slopes. Widespread but local; commonest in the W. Leaves comprise 6–12 pairs of oblong leaflets ending in branched tendrils. Spikes of purple-veined white flowers appear June–August.

BUSH VETCH *Vicia sepium* Height up to 1m
Scrambling perennial of rough, grassy places and scrub. Common and widespread throughout. Leaves comprise 5–9 pairs of leaflets ending in branched tendrils. Groups of 2–6 pale lilac flowers appear April–October; each flower 12–15mm long.

COMMON VETCH *Vicia sativa* Height up to 75cm
Widespread and fairly common scrambling annual of grassy places and hedgerows. Leaves comprise 3–8 pairs of oval leaflets and end in tendrils. Groups of one or two pinkish purple flowers appear April–September. When mature, the pods are black.

SMOOTH TARE *Vicia tetrasperma* Height up to 50cm
Easily overlooked scrambling annual of grassy places. Common only in England and Wales. Leaves comprise 2–5 pairs of narrow leaflets and end in tendrils. 1–2 pinkish lilac flowers appear May–August. Pods smooth, usually with four seeds.

Hairy Tare *Vicia hirsuta* Height up to 60cm
Slender, scrambling annual of grassy places. Widespread and mostly common; less so in N and Ireland. Leaves comprise 4–10 pairs of leaflets and end in branched tendrils. 1–9 pale lilac flowers appear May–August. Pods hairy and 2-seeded.

Meadow Vetchling *Lathyrus pratensis* Height up to 50cm
Perennial with long, angled stems scrambling among and over vegetation. Common and widespread throughout, favouring grassy places. Leaves comprise single pair of narrow leaflets and have tendrils. Groups of 4–12 flowers appear May–August.

Yellow Vetchling *Lathyrus aphaca* Height up to 80cm
Scrambling annual. Local and restricted mainly to chalk grassland in S England. Angled stems carry pairs of grey-green, leaf-like stipules; leaves reduced to tendrils. Solitary yellow flowers borne on long stalks and appear June–August.

Sea Pea *Lathyrus japonicus* Height up to 12cm
Spreading grey-green perennial with stems up to 1m long. Found exclusively on coastal shingle and sand; local and restricted to S and E England. Leaves with 2–5 pairs of oval leaflets. Groups of bluish purple flowers appear June–August.

Sainfoin *Onobrychis viciifolia* Height up to 75cm
Perennial of dry, calcareous grassland. Possibly native in parts of SE England but introduced to other parts of England and Wales. Leaves comprise 6–14 pairs of oval leaflets. Conical spikes of red-veined pink flowers appear June–August.

Common Restharrow *Ononis repens* Height up to 70cm
A robust, creeping perennial with hairy stems. Locally common throughout on calcareous soil. Stickily-hairy leaves usually trifoliate with oval leaflets. Clusters of pink flowers appear July–September; each flower is 10–15mm long.

Ribbed Melilot *Melilotus officinalis* Height up to 1.5m
Widespread biennial of grassy places, locally common and native in England and Wales but scarce and introduced elsewhere. Leaves comprise three oblong leaflets. Yellow flowers borne in tall spikes and appear June–September. Ripe pods brown.

White Melilot *Melilotus alba* Height up to 1m
Distinctive biennial of grassy places and disturbed soil. Introduced but locally established in parts of S and E England. Leaves comprise three oblong leaflets. The white flowers are borne in tall spikes and appear June–August. Ripe pods brown.

Kidney Vetch *Anthyllis vulneraria* Height up to 30cm
Silky hairy perennial. Widespread and locally common in calcareous grassland and on coastal slopes. Leaves comprise pairs of narrow leaflets. Flowers are yellow, orange or red; borne in paired, kidney-shaped heads, 3cm across, May–September.

Horseshoe Vetch *Hippocrepis comosa* Height up to 10cm
Spreading perennial. Restricted to calcareous grassland; locally common only in England. Leaves comprise 4–5 pairs of narrow leaflets and end leaflet. Circular flower heads appear May–July. Ripe pods crinkled into horseshoe-shaped segments.

Common Bird's-foot-trefoil *Lotus corniculatus* Usually creeping
Perennial with trailing stems. Widespread and common in grassy places. Leaves comprise five leaflets but appear trifoliate since lower pair sited at stalk base. Yellow or orange flowers appear May–September. Pods arranged like a bird's foot.

Greater Bird's-foot-trefoil *Lotus uliginosus* Height up to 50cm
Perennial of damp grassland and fens. Widespread and locally common throughout in suitable habitats. Grey-green, downy leaves comprise five leaflets but appear trifoliate. Heads of yellow flowers carried on long stalks; appear June–August.

LUCERNE *Medicago sativa ssp sativa* Height up to 75cm
Downy perennial. Often cultivated but also widely naturalised in grassy places. Leaves are trifoliate with narrow, toothed leaflets which broaden towards the tip. Spikes of purple flowers appear June–September; each flower is 7–8mm long.

BLACK MEDICK *Medicago lupulina* Height up to 20cm
Widespread and rather common downy annual of short grassland and waste places. Leaves are trifoliate, each leaflet bearing a point at the centre of its apex. Dense, rounded heads of yellow flowers appear April–October. Ripe pods black.

BIRD'S-FOOT *Ornithopus perpusillus* Height up to 30cm
An often trailing, downy annual of dry, sandy places. Locally common in England and Wales but scarce elsewhere. Leaves comprise 5–13 pairs of leaflets. Red-veined, creamy flowers appear May–August. Ripe pods arranged like a bird's foot.

HOP TREFOIL *Trifolium campestre* Height up to 25cm
Generally common and widespread hairy annual of dry grassland but rather local in N and Ireland. Leaves alternate and trefoil. Compact, rounded heads of yellow flowers appear May–October. The pale brown dead flower heads resemble tiny hops.

RED CLOVER *Trifolium pratense* Height up to 40cm
Familiar grassland perennial which is widespread and common throughout. Leaves trefoil, the oval leaflets each bearing a white crescent-shaped mark. Pinkish purple flowers borne in unstalked heads, 3cm across, and appear May–October.

WHITE CLOVER *Trifolium repens* Height up to 40cm
Common grassland perennial which is widespread and common throughout. Leaves are trefoil, the rounded leaflets often bearing white marks. Flowers creamy white, becoming brown with age. Borne in rounded heads, 2cm across; appear May–October.

HARE'S-FOOT CLOVER *Trifolium arvense* Height up to 25cm
Annual of dry grassland, covered in soft hairs. Widespread and generally common but absent from N Scotland. Trefoil leaves comprise narrow leaflets. The pale pink flowers are borne in oval or cylindrical heads, appearing June–September.

ROUGH CLOVER *Trifolium scabrum* Height up to 15cm
Downy annual of bare grassland, often on gravelly soils. Locally common in S England and S Wales but mainly coastal. Trefoil leaves have oval leaflets with obvious lateral veins. White flowers are borne in unstalked heads, May–July.

WOOD SORREL *Oxalis acetosella* Height up to 10cm
Charming, creeping perennial. Widespread and locally common; an indicator of ancient woodlands and hedgerows. Trefoil leaves, which fold down at night, are borne on long stalks. Lilac-veined flowers carried on stalks; appear April–June.

FAIRY FLAX *Linum catharticum* Height up to 12cm
Delicate annual, also known as purging flax. Found in both wet and dry grassland often on calcareous soil. Slender stems carry opposite pairs of narrow, 1-veined leaves. Loose, terminal clusters of small white flowers appear May–September.

COMMON STORK'S-BILL *Erodium cicutarium* Height up to 25cm
Stickily-hairy annual of bare, grassy places. Widespread and locally common, especially in SE England and around coasts. Leaves finely divided and feathery. Pink flowers appear May–August; petals easily lost. Fruit is long and beak-like.

MEADOW CRANE'S-BILL *Geranium pratense* Height up to 75cm
Perennial of roadside verges and meadows, mostly on base-rich soils. Widespread and locally common, mainly in C and N England and Scotland. Lower leaves deeply divided into 5–7 lobes. Bluish violet flowers 3–5cm across; appear June–August.

WOOD CRANE'S-BILL *Geranium sylvaticum* Height up to 60cm
Showy perennial of upland meadows and open woodlands, usually found on base-rich soils. Absent from much of S England but locally common elsewhere. Leaves deeply cut into 5–7 lobes. Reddish purple flowers are 20–30mm across; appear June–August.

BLOODY CRANE'S-BILL *Geranium sanguineum* Height up to 25cm
Spreading or clump-forming perennial found on calcareous grassland and limestone pavements. Locally common in Britain but absent from the SE; also in W Ireland. Leaves deeply cut into 5–7 lobes. The reddish purple flowers appear June–August.

HERB ROBERT *Geranium robertianum* Height up to 30cm
Straggling, hairy annual of shady hedgerows, rocky banks and woodlands. Common and widespread throughout. Hairy leaves deeply cut into three or five lobes. Loose clusters of pink flowers appear April–October; each flower is 12–15mm across.

DOVE'S-FOOT CRANE'S-BILL *Geranium molle* Height up to 20cm
Spreading, very hairy annual of dry, grassy places including roadside verges. Common and widespread, especially in the S. Leaves hairy and rounded but margins cut into 5–7 lobes. Pairs of pink flowers, 5–10mm across, appear April–August.

CUT-LEAVED CRANE'S-BILL *Geranium dissectum* Height up to 45cm
Hairy annual which is widespread and common throughout, favouring disturbed ground and cultivated soils. Leaves are deeply dissected into very narrow lobes. Pinkish flowers, 8–10mm across, appear May–September; petals sometimes notched.

SHINING CRANE'S-BILL *Geranium lucidum* Height up to 30cm
Almost hairless annual of shady banks and rocky slopes, mostly on limestone. Widespread but local. Shiny leaves are green, sometimes tinged red; they are rounded but with margins cut into 5–7 lobes. Pink flowers appear April–August.

WOOD SPURGE *Euphorbia amygdaloides* Height up to 80cm
Downy perennial, found in woodland and scrub. Common in S England and Wales but scarce or absent elsewhere. Upright stems carry unstalked, dark green, 6cm long leaves. Umbels of yellow flowers, lacking petals and sepals, appear April–June.

SEA SPURGE *Euphorbia paralias* Height up to 60cm
Sand dune plant, widespread and locally common around the coasts of S and W England, Wales and Ireland. Upright stems carry close-packed, grey-green, fleshy leaves. Yellowish flowers, which lack petals and sepals, appear June–October.

SUN SPURGE *Euphorbia helioscopia* Height up to 50cm
Widespread and common hairless annual found on disturbed ground and cultivated soils. Unbranched, upright stems carry an array of spoon-shaped leaves, broadest near the tip. Yellow flowers, lacking petals and sepals, appear May–November.

PETTY SPURGE *Euphorbia peplus* Height up to 30cm
Upright, hairless annual which is common and widespread on cultivated ground and arable land. Branched stems carry oval, blunt-tipped and stalked leaves. These are topped by umbels of greenish flowers, comprising oval bracts, April–October.

IRISH SPURGE *Euphorbia hyberna* Height up to 55cm
Attractive tufted perennial restricted to shady wooded slopes in SW England and SW Ireland. Upright stems carry stalkless, tapering leaves and are topped by striking yellowish flowers which lack petals and sepals; these appear May–July.

DOG'S MERCURY *Mercurialis perenne* Height up to 35cm
Widespread and generally common perennial of woodlands of most kinds; scarce in N Scotland and Ireland. Upright stems carry oval, toothed leaves. Clusters of insignificant male and female flowers borne on separate plants, February–April.

COMMON MILKWORT *Polygala vulgaris* Height up to 30cm
Trailing or upright perennial. Common and widespread in grassland on all but the most acid of soils. Leaves are alternate, narrow and pointed. The flowers may be blue, pink or white; borne in loose, terminal clusters and seen May–September.

HIMALAYAN BALSAM *Impatiens balsamifera* Height up to 2m
Introduced from Himalayas but widely naturalised along riverbanks and on damp waste-ground. Upright, reddish stems carry leaves in whorls of three or opposite pairs. Pink-purple flowers, 30–40mm long, appear July–October. Seeds explosive.

MUSK MALLOW *Malva moschata* Height up to 75cm
Perennial of dry, grassy places. Widespread and locally common in England and Wales but scarce elsewhere. Leaves rounded and 3-lobed at base but increasingly dissected up the stem. Pale pink flowers, 30–60mm across, are seen July–August.

COMMON MALLOW *Malva sylvestris* Height up to 1.5m
Upright or spreading perennial of grassy verges and disturbed ground. Leaves are rounded at base but 5-lobed on stem. Purple-veined pink flowers, 25–40mm across, appear June–October. Widespread and common in S Britain but scarce elsewhere.

TREE MALLOW *Lavatera arborea* Height up to 3m
Imposing woody biennial which favours rocky ground near the coast, often near seabird colonies. Locally common on W coast of Britain and S and W Ireland. The leaves are 5–7 lobed. Dark-veined pinkish purple flowers appear June–September.

MARSH MALLOW *Althaea officinalis* Height up to 2m
Attractive downy perennial of coastal wetlands, often found on upper reaches of salt-marshes. Locally common on S coasts of Britain and Ireland. The leaves are triangular and slightly lobed. The pale pink flowers appear August–September.

TUTSAN *Hypericum androsaemum* Height up to 80cm
Upright, semi-evergreen shrub. Locally common in shady woods and hedgerows, mainly in S and W Britain and Ireland. Oval leaves are borne in opposite pairs. Yellow flowers, 15–25mm across, appear June–August. Berries ripen red to black.

PERFORATE ST JOHN'S-WORT *Hypericum perforatum* Height up to 80cm
Upright perennial, found in grassland, scrub and open woodland; usually on calcareous soils. Widespread but commonest in the S. 2-lined stems carry paired unstalked, narrow leaves with translucent dots. Flowers appear June–September.

SLENDER ST JOHN'S-WORT *Hypericum pulchrum* Height up to 80cm
Upright perennial of dry, grassy places and heaths, mostly on acid soils. Common and widespread throughout. Paired, oval leaves have translucent dots. Flowers comprise five yellow petals with black dots along their margins; seen July–August.

MARSH ST JOHN'S-WORT *Hypericum elodes* Height up to 20cm
Creeping, hairy perennial of peaty ground and marshes on acid soils. Rather local and confined mainly to SW Britain and W Ireland. The rounded, grey-green leaves clasp the stem slightly. Yellow flowers, 15mm across, appear June–August.

TRAILING ST JOHN'S-WORT *Hypericum humifusum* Creeping
Hairless perennial favouring bare ground on heaths and moors with acid soils. Widespread but commonest in W Britain and W Ireland. The leaves have translucent dots and are borne in pairs on trailing stems. Flowers appear June–September.

MEZEREON *Daphne mezereum* Height up to 2m
Deciduous shrub favouring woods and shady scrub on calcareous soil. Local and scarce, mainly in CS England. Dark green leaves are leathery and shiny. Pink flowers appear February–April, just before leaves. Berry-like fruit is red.

SPURGE LAUREL *Daphne laureola* Height up to 1m
Evergreen shrub found in woods on calcareous soils. Widespread but extremely local in England and Wales. Dark green, shiny leaves are oval and clustered at top of stem. Clusters of yellowish, trumpet-shaped flowers appear January–April.

SWEET VIOLET *Viola odorata* Height up to 15cm
Perennial herb of woods and hedgerows, mostly on calcareous soils. Widespread and locally common in England and Wales. Long-stalked leaves rounded in spring; larger and heart-shaped in summer. Violet or white flowers appear February–May.

COMMON DOG-VIOLET *Viola riviniana* Height up to 12cm
Familiar perennial herb of woodland rides and grassland. Widespread and locally common throughout. Long-stalked leaves are heart-shaped. Bluish violet flowers have a blunt, pale spur and are 15–25mm across; they appear mainly March–May.

MARSH VIOLET *Viola palustris* Height up to 10cm
Perennial of bogs and acid wetlands. Local but widespread although absent from much of E England. Long-stalked leaves are round or kidney-shaped. Dark-veined, pale lilac flowers are 10–15mm across with a short spur; appear April–June.

WILD PANSY *Viola tricolor* Height up to 12cm
Widespread and common annual or perennial of grassy areas. Subspecies *tricolor* has yellow and violet flowers and grows inland while subspecies *curtisii* with yellow flowers is mainly coastal. Flowers 10–25mm across; appear April–October.

MOUNTAIN PANSY *Viola lutea* Height up to 30cm
Perennial of upland calcareous grassland. Locally common in N Wales, N England and Scotland. Leaves lanceolate with palmate stipules at leaf bases. Flowers are 15–30mm across and vary from yellow to yellow and violet; appear May–August.

FIELD PANSY *Viola arvensis* Height up to 15cm
Widespread and common annual of arable land and cultivated ground generally. Commonest in E and S England. Has deeply toothed stipules. Flowers are 10–15mm across and creamy white with orange flush on lower petal; appear April–October.

COMMON ROCK-ROSE *Helianthemum nummularium* Height up to 40cm
Spreading undershrub, found in dry grassland on calcareous soils. Widespread and locally common in SE and E England but becoming scarce further N and W. Paired leaves narrow and oblong. Flowers with five crinkly petals appear June–September.

ROSEBAY WILLOWHERB *Epilobium angustifolium* Height up to 1.5m
Familiar perennial of wasteground, cleared woodland and riverbanks. Widespread and common throughout. Lanceolate leaves arranged spirally up stem. Pinkish purple flowers, 20–30mm across, appear July–September. Pods contain cottony seeds.

GREAT WILLOWHERB *Epilobium hirsutum* Height up to 2m
Imposing perennial of damp habitats such as fens and riverbanks. Widespread and common throughout except the far N. Unstalked hairy leaves borne on hairy stems; topped by pinkish purple flowers, 25mm across, with pale centres; appear July–August.

MARSH WILLOWHERB *Epilobium palustre* Height up to 50cm
Slender perennial of damp habitats, particularly on acid soils. Widespread and locally common throughout. Rounded stems carry opposite pairs of narrow leaves. Pale pink flower is 4–7mm across and has club-shaped stigma; seen July–August.

AMERICAN WILLOWHERB *Epilobium adenocaulon* Height up to 50cm
Introduced perennial from N America but now widely naturalised on wasteground and damp ground in England and Wales. Hairy stems bear opposite pairs of oval leaves. Pink flower has notched petals and club-shaped stigma; seen June–August.

ENCHANTER'S-NIGHTSHADE *Circaea lutetiana* Height up to 65cm
Delicate perennial of shady woodlands. Widespread and common except in the far N. Upright stems are sometimes slightly hairy and carry opposite pairs of oval, pointed leaves. White flowers borne in loose spikes above leaves, June–August.

COMMON EVENING-PRIMROSE *Oenothera biennis* Height up to 1.25m
Downy biennial, introduced from N America but now established locally in many parts on dry ground including sand dunes and railway sidings. Lanceolate leaves have red veins. Flowers, 4–5cm across, comprise four petals; seen June–September.

PURPLE-LOOSESTRIFE *Lythrum salicaria* Height up to 1.5m
Downy perennial of damp habitats such as riverbanks and fens. Widespread and common except in the N. Upright stems carry opposites pairs of narrow, unstalked leaves. Reddish purple, 6-petalled flowers borne in tall spikes, June–August.

DWARF CORNEL *Cornus suecica* Height up to 15cm
Creeping perennial of upland moors. Scattered in N England and locally common in parts of Scotland. Leaves are ovate and pointed with three main veins either side of midrib. Four white bracts topped by dark umbel of flowers, appear June–August. Fruit red.

MARSH PENNYWORT *Hydrocotyle vulgaris* Creeping
An atypical umbellifer, best known for its round, dimpled leaves found among low vegetation on damp, mostly acid, ground. Widespread and locally common although commonest in W. Tiny pinkish flowers are hidden by leaves; appear June–August.

SLENDER HARE'S-EAR *Bupleurum tenuissimum* Height up to 50cm
Slender annual umbellifer. Entirely restricted to coastal grassland and found only around coasts of S and E England. Leaves are narrow and pointed. Yellow umbels of flowers are 3–4mm across and produced in leaf axils, July–September.

SANICLE *Sanicula europaea* Height up to 50cm
Slender, hairless perennial of deciduous woodland, mostly on neutral or basic soils. Widespread and common, but becoming scarce in the N. Basal leaves have 5–7 lobes. Small umbels of pinkish flowers borne on reddish stems, May–August.

SEA-HOLLY *Eryngium maritimum* Height up to 60cm
Distinctive perennial of coastal shingle and sand. Widespread around the coasts of England, Wales and Ireland; absent from N and E Scotland. Grey-green leaves are spiny and holly-like. Globular umbels of blue flowers appear July–September.

ALEXANDERS *Smyrnium oleraceum* Height up to 1.25m
Distinctive biennial, introduced but now established on wasteground and verges. Widespread and locally common near coasts of England, Wales and Ireland. Leaves three times divided into dark green, shiny lobes. Yellowish flowers seen March–June.

COW PARSLEY *Anthriscus sylvestris* Height up to 1m
Downy perennial herb. Widespread and common throughout on roadside verges and along lanes. Upright, hollow and ridged stems carry two or three times pinnately divided leaves. Umbels of white flowers lack lower bracts and appear April–June.

UPRIGHT HEDGE-PARSLEY *Torilis japonica* Height up to 1m
Familiar white hedgerow umbellifer which flowers July–August, after the similar cow parsley has finished. Solid, hairy stems carry leaves which are two or three times pinnately divided. Umbels have upper and lower bracts. Widespread and common.

PIGNUT *Conopodium majus* Height up to 25cm
Delicate perennial, locally common in open woodland and grassland, mainly on dry acid soils. Finely divided basal leaves soon wither. Stem leaves divided into narrow lobes. Small umbels, 30–60mm across, of white flowers appear April–June.

SWEET CICELY *Myrrhis odorata* Height up to 1.5m
Upright perennial which smells of aniseed when bruised. Widely naturalised and locally common in N England and S Scotland. Fern-like leaves are two or three times pinnately divided. Umbels of white flowers with unequal petals appear May–June.

HOGWEED *Heracleum sphondylium* Height up to 2m
Robust perennial of open, grassy places including roadside verges. Common and widespread throughout. Broad, hairy and pinnate leaves borne on hollow, hairy stems. Large umbels of off-white flowers with unequal petals seen May–August.

GIANT HOGWEED *Heracleum mantegazzianum* Height up to 4m
Huge biennial or perennial; causes blisters if touched in sunlight. Introduced but established in scattered locations. Hollow stem ridged and purple-spotted. Leaves are pinnate and large. Large umbels of white flowers appear June–July.

COWBANE *Cicuta virosa* Height up to 1m
Local and rather scarce perennial of damp habitats including fens and marshes. Hollow, ridged stems carry dark green leaves, two or three times pinnately divided into narrow leaflets. Domed umbels of white flowers seen July–August. Poisonous.

HEMLOCK *Conium maculatum* Height up to 2m
Distinctive and highly poisonous biennial of damp wayside ground. Widespread and locally common throughout. Leaves are up to four times pinnately divided into fine leaflets. Stems are purple-blotched. Umbels of white flowers appear June–July.

WILD ANGELICA *Angelica sylvestris* Height up to 2m
Robust perennial of damp meadows and woods. Widespread and common. Purplish stem hollow. Lower leaves two or three times pinnate; upper leaves smaller but bases form inflated sheaths. Umbels of white flowers, 15cm across, seen July–September.

BURNET-SAXIFRAGE *Pimpinella saxifraga* Height up to 70cm
A locally common perennial of dry, calcareous grassland; widespread but absent from NW Scotland. Lower leaves pinnate with round leaflets; upper leaves finely divided with narrow leaflets. Loose umbels of white flowers seen June–September.

FENNEL *Foeniculum vulgare* Height up to 2m
Distinctive grey-green perennial with feathery leaves comprising thread-like leaflets. Widespread but mainly coastal in England, Wales and Ireland, favouring grassy, disturbed ground. Open umbels of yellow flowers appear July–October.

GROUND-ELDER *Aegopodium podagraria* Height up to 1m
Pernicious weed of cultivated, damp ground. Possibly introduced but established in most parts of Britain and Ireland. The basal leaves are two times trifoliate and triangular in outline. Compact umbels of white flowers appear June–August.

SCOTS LOVAGE *Ligusticum scoticum* Height up to 80cm
Perennial of stabilised grassland around the coasts of Scotland and N Ireland. The bright green, shiny leaves are two times trifoliate with oval leaflets. Flat-topped umbels of white flowers are borne on reddish stems; appear June–August.

WILD PARSNIP *Pastinaca sativa* Height up to 1m
Downy perennial found mainly in dry, calcareous grassland. Widespread and fairly common in S Britain but scarce or absent elsewhere. The pinnate leaves comprise oval, lobed leaflets. Bractless umbels of yellowish flowers seen June–September.

ROCK SAMPHIRE *Crithmum maritimum* Height up to 40cm
Grey-green perennial, characteristic of rocky habitats and stabilised shingle around the coasts of S and W Britain and Ireland. The leaves are divided into narrow, fleshy lobes. Umbels of greenish yellow flowers appear June–September.

HEMLOCK WATER-DROPWORT *Oenanthe crocata* Height up to 1.25m
Distinctive, poisonous perennial of damp meadows and ditches. Leaves are 2–4 times pinnately divided and are borne on the hollow, ridged stem. Domed umbels of white flowers appear June–August and have both upper and lower bracts. Widespread.

TUBULAR WATER-DROPWORT *Oenanthe fistulosa* Height up to 50cm
Perennial of marshes and damp ground. Widespread but only common in S and E England. Hollow stems appear inflated. Leaves have inflated stalks; leaflets of lower ones oval, tubular in upper ones. Umbels of white flowers appear July–September.

FOOL'S PARSLEY *Aethusa cynapium* Height up to 50cm
Delicate annual found in gardens and other areas of disturbed ground. Common in S England but scarce or absent elsewhere. Leaves two times pinnate and triangular in outline. Umbels of white flowers have long upper bracts; appear June–August.

PEPPER-SAXIFRAGE *Silaum silaus* Height up to 1m
Slender grassland perennial. Common in England but scarce or absent elsewhere. Leaves are 2–4 times pinnate and comprise narrow, pointed leaflets. Umbels of yellowish flowers have upper bracts; appear July–September. Fruit egg-shaped.

WILD CARROT *Daucus carota* Height up to 75cm
Widespread, hairy perennial of rough grassland. Commonest around coasts. Leaves are 2–3 times pinnate with narrow leaflets. Dense umbels are pinkish in bud but white in flower, central flower red; appear June–September. Umbels concave in fruit.

WILD CELERY *Apium graveolens* Height up to 1m
Biennial smelling strongly of celery. Favours rough, often saline, grassland and distribution mainly coastal; absent Scotland and commonest S England. Leaves 1–2 times pinnate. Umbels of greenish white flowers are 40–60mm across; appear June–August.

FOOL'S WATER-CRESS *Apium nodiflorum* Height up to 20cm
Creeping perennial of ditches and wet hollows. Widespread but commonest in the S and absent from the far N. Shiny leaves comprise oval, toothed leaflets and are rather similar to water-cress. Loose umbels of white flowers appear July–August.

PRIMROSE *Primula vulgaris* Height up to 20cm
Familiar perennial of woods, hedgerows and shady meadows. Widespread and common throughout. Oval, tapering leaves, up to 12cm long, form a rosette. The solitary flowers, 20–30mm across, are borne on long, hairy stalks; appear February–May.

COWSLIP *Primula veris* Height up to 25cm
Locally common perennial of unimproved grassland, often on calcareous soils. Widespread but scarce in Scotland. Wrinkled, hairy leaves form a basal rosette. Heads of 10–30 orange-yellow, bell-shaped flowers borne on stalks, April–May.

OXLIP *Primula elatior* Height up to 20cm
Attractive woodland perennial, locally common only in parts of E Anglia. Rather similar to primrose but the basal rosette comprises long-stalked oval leaves. 10–20 flowers, each 15–25mm across, borne in 1-sided, dropping heads, appear March–May.

BIRD'S-EYE PRIMROSE *Primula farinosa* Height up to 12cm
Charming perennial, restricted to limestone grassland in N England. Spoon-shaped leaves, mealy on the underside, form a basal rosette. Terminal clusters of pink flowers, each 8–10mm across, are borne on tall mealy stems and appear June–July.

YELLOW LOOSESTRIFE *Lysimachia vulgaris* Height up to 1m
Softly hairy perennial of damp ground, often beside rivers and in fens. Common and widespread throughout, except in the far N. The upright stems carry narrow, ovate leaves in whorls of 3–4. Clusters of yellow flowers appear July–August.

Creeping Jenny *Lysimachia nummularia* Creeping
Low, hairless perennial of damp grassy ground. Locally common in England; scarce or absent elsewhere. The rounded or heart-shaped leaves are carried in opposite pairs. Bell-shaped yellow flowers, 15–25mm across, borne on stalks, appear June–August.

Yellow Pimpernel *Lysimachia nemorum* Creeping
Evergreen, hairless perennial, similar to creeping jenny but more delicate. The oval or heart-shaped leaves are carried in opposite pairs along creeping stems. Yellow, star-like flowers, 10–15mm across, are borne on slender stalks, May–August.

Sea Milkwort *Glaux maritima* Height up to 10cm
Generally a creeping perennial, found on upper reaches of saltmarshes and on sea walls. Locally common around most coasts. Trailing stems carry opposite pairs of succulent leaves. Flowers comprise five pink sepals; these appear May–September.

Water Violet *Hottonia palustris* Aquatic
Delicate perennial of still or slow-flowing water. Local in S and E England but scarce or absent elsewhere. Has feathery floating and submerged leaves, divided into narrow lobes. Lilac flowers, 20–25mm across, appear on emergent stems, May–June.

Scarlet Pimpernel *Anagallis arvensis* Prostrate
Hairless annual of cultivated ground. Widespread and generally common although scarce in Scotland. Opposite pairs of unstalked, oval leaves borne on trailing stems. Flowers on slender stalks are borne May–September. Usually red but sometimes blue.

Bog Pimpernel *Anagallis tenella* Creeping
Delicate perennial of damp ground, such as bogs and dune-slacks, mostly on acid soils. Trailing stems carry opposite pairs of short-stalked, rounded leaves. The pink, funnel-shaped flowers are borne on slender, upright stalks, June–August.

Chickweed Wintergreen *Trientalis europaea* Height up to 20cm
Spreading perennial of mature conifer forests, mainly in Scotland but rarely in N England; sometimes also occurs on moors. Ovate leaves mostly borne in whorl at top of stem. One or two long stalked, 7-petalled white flowers appear June–July.

Ling *Calluna vulgaris* Height up to 50cm
Dense undershrub, characteristic of acids soils on heaths and moors; also known simply as heather. Widespread and locally abundant. The short, narrow leaves are borne in four rows along stems. The small pink flowers, 4–5mm long, appear July–October.

Bell Heather *Erica cinerea* Height up to 50cm
Hairless undershrub of dry acid soils on heaths and moors. Widespread but most common in N and W. Narrow leaves are borne in whorls of three up wiry stems. Bell-shaped, purplish red flowers, 5–6mm long, appear in groups along stems, June–September.

Cross-leaved Heath *Erica tetralix* Height up to 30cm
Downy, grey-green undershrub. Favours damp, acid soils; typical of boggy-margins on heaths and moors. Widespread and locally common. Narrow leaves in whorls of four along stems. Pink flowers, 6–7mm long, borne in terminal clusters, June–October.

Cornish Heath *Erica vagans* Height up to 80cm
Impressive undershrub of dry, heathy areas. Very locally common in SW England, particularly Lizard Peninsula, and SW Ireland. Narrow, dark green leaves in fours or fives. Pink or lilac flowers are borne in sub-terminal leafy clusters, July–September.

Bilberry *Vaccinium myrtillus* Height up to 75cm
Deciduous shrub of heaths, moors and open woodland on acid soils. Widespread but commonest in Scotland. Bright green, oval leaves borne on green, 3-angled stems. Greenish pink flowers appear April–June; ripen to edible, purplish fruits in autumn.

COWBERRY *Vaccinium vitis-idaea* Height up to 20cm
Small, evergreen shrub found on acid soils in woods and on moors. Locally common only in N England and Scotland. Leaves are leathery, dark green and oval. Pink, bell-shaped flowers, 5–6mm long, appear May–July; red berries ripen in autumn.

CRANBERRY *Vaccinium oxycoccos* Height up to 12cm
Creeping, evergreen shrub of bogs. Locally common only in N Wales, N England and E Ireland. Trailing stems carry small, dark green leaves with inrolled margins. Flowers with pink, reflexed petals and protruding stamens, May–July. Fruit red.

CROWBERRY *Empetrum nigrum* Height up to 10cm
Mat-forming, heather-like shrub found on upland moors; common only in N Britain. Reddish stems carry narrow, dark green leaves with inrolled margins. The pink, 6-petalled flowers appear April–June. The black berries ripen in late summer.

COMMON WINTERGREEN *Pyrola minor* Height up to 20cm
An evergreen perennial of woods and moors, often on calcareous soils. Locally common only in N England, Scotland and N Ireland. Oval, toothed and stalked leaves form a rosette. White, rounded flowers, 5–6mm across, seen June–August.

ROUND-LEAVED WINTERGREEN *Pyrola rotundifolia* Height up to 15cm
Perennial of damp, calcareous ground such as fens and coastal dune-slacks. The rounded, long-stalked leaves form a rosette. White, bell-shaped flowers, 8–12mm across, are borne in upright spikes, May–August. The S-shaped style protrudes.

YELLOW BIRD'S-NEST *Monotropa hypopitys* Height up to 10cm
Bizarre plant of beech and conifer woods; also in dune-slacks. Widespread but local. Lacks chlorophyll and appears creamy yellow; food obtained from soil leaf mould. Leaves scale-like and flowers are borne in nodding spike, June–September.

THRIFT *Armeria maritima* Height up to 20cm
Cushion-forming, coastal perennial, often carpeting cliff slopes. Widespread and locally common. Leaves dark green, long and narrow. Dense, globular heads of pink flowers are borne on stalks, 10–20cm long, and appear mainly April–July.

COMMON SEA-LAVENDER *Limonium vulgare* Height up to 30cm
Widespread perennial of saltmarshes around the coasts of England and Wales; most common in the S. Leaves are stalked and spoon-shaped. Clustered, pinkish lilac flowers borne in branched, flat-topped heads as arching sprays, July–September.

BOGBEAN *Menyanthes trifoliata* Height up to 15cm
Aquatic perennial found in shallow water as well as damp peaty soil in marshes and bogs. Widespread and locally common. Emergent leaves trifoliate and resemble those of broad bean. Clusters of star-shaped, pinkish white, fringed flowers, March–June.

FRINGED WATER-LILY *Nymphoides peltata* Floating
Aquatic perennial of still or slow-flowing water. Locally common in S England and naturalised elsewhere. Leaves are floating, rounded or kidney-shaped and 3–8cm across. Flowers, 30–35mm across, comprise five fringed petals; appear June–September.

LESSER PERIWINKLE *Vinca minor* Height up to 20cm
Trailing perennial of woods and hedgerows. Widespread and possibly native in S England but undoubtedly naturalised elsewhere. Evergreen leaves are leathery and oval. The 5-lobed flowers are bluish violet and 25–30mm across; appear February–May.

JACOB'S-LADDER *Polemonium caeruleum* Height up to 80cm
Upright perennial of rocky slopes and open woods on limestone. Locally native to N England but naturalised elsewhere. Pinnate leaves divided into 6–12 pairs of narrow leaflets. Bluish purple flowers, 20–30mm across, in spikes, June–August.

Common Centaury *Centaurium erythraea* Height up to 25cm
Upright annual of dry, grassy places, especially sand dunes in the N. Widespread and common throughout. Has basal rosette of oval leaves and opposite pairs of leaves on stems. Clusters of pink, 5-petalled flowers appear June–September.

Lesser Centaury *Centaurium pulchellum* Height up to 15cm
Slender annual, similar to common centaury but without basal rosette of leaves. Favours damp, grassy places. Distribution mainly coastal in England and Wales. Clusters of dark pink flowers are 5–8mm across; appear June–September.

Yellow-wort *Blackstonia perfoliata* Height up to 30cm
Upright, grey-green annual of short, calcareous grassland. Locally common in C and S England, Wales and W Ireland. Leaves form basal rosette; appear up stem in opposite pairs, fused at base around stem. Flowers 6–8 petalled, June–October.

Marsh Gentian *Gentiana pneumonanthe* Height up to 30cm
Scarce perennial of bogs and wet heaths on acid soils. Has scattered sites in England and Wales. Narrow leaves are carried up stem in opposite pairs. Clusters of bright blue, trumpet-shaped flowers, each 25–45mm long, appear July–October.

Spring Gentian *Gentiana verna* Height up to 7cm
Scarce perennial of limestone grassland in Upper Teesdale and the Burren in W Ireland. Oval leaves form a basal rosette and are borne in opposite pairs up the stem. Solitary, bright blue flowers, 1–2cm long, with five lobes, appear May–June.

Autumn Gentian *Gentianella amarella* Height up to 25cm
Biennial of dry, mostly calcareous grassland and dunes. Widespread and locally common. Leaves form a basal rosette in first year; wither before flowering stem appears in second year. Clusters of 4- or 5-lobed purplish flowers, appear July–October.

Field Gentian *Gentianella campestris* Height up to 10cm
Biennial, similar to autumn gentian but flowers are bluish and comprise four lobes. Favours grassland on neutral or acid soils. Locally common in N England and Scotland but scarce or absent elsewhere. Clusters of flowers seen July–October.

Hedge Bindweed *Calystegia sepium* Climbing, up to 2–3m
Perennial, twining around other plants to assist its progress. Favours hedgerows and woodland margins. Widespread and common in the S but scarce in the N. Leaves arrow-shaped and up to 12cm long. Flowers white, 30–40mm across, June–September.

Field Bindweed *Convolvulus arvensis* Creeping or climbing, up to 2–3m
Widespread and very common perennial of disturbed ground. Twists around other plants to assist its progress. Long-stalked, 20–50mm long leaves are arrow-shaped. The white-striped pink flowers are 15–30mm across and appear June–September.

Sea Bindweed *Calystegia soldanella* Creeping
Perennial of coastal sand dunes. Widespread and locally common on most suitable coasts except E England and Scotland where scarce or absent. Long-stalked leaves are kidney-shaped. White-striped pink flowers, 40–50mm across, appear June–August.

Common Dodder *Cuscuta epithymum* Climbing
Parasitic, leafless plant which lacks chlorophyll and gains its nutrition from host plants, which include ling, clovers and other herbaceous plants. Clusters, 7–10mm across, of pink flowers are borne on red, twining stems, July–September.

Field Madder *Sherardia arvensis* Creeping
Hairy annual of arable land and disturbed ground. Widespread; rather common in the S but becoming scarce further N. Narrow, oval leaves in whorls of 4–6 along stems. Heads of pinkish flowers, each one 3–5mm across, appear May–September.

SQUINANCYWORT *Asperula cynanchica* Height up to 15cm
Usually prostrate perennial of dry grassland, mainly on calcareous soil. Locally common only in S England. The 4-angled stems carry narrow leaves in whorls of four. Dense clusters of pink, 4-petalled flowers, 3–4mm across, appear June–September.

SWEET WOODRUFF *Galium odoratum* Height up to 25cm
Upright, hairless perennial of shady woodlands, mostly on basic soils; smells of hay. Locally common and widespread. Square stems carry lanceolate leaves in whorls of 6–8; leaf margins with prickles. Clusters of 4-lobed flowers May–June.

LADY'S BEDSTRAW *Galium verum* Height up to 30cm
Branched perennial of dry grassland. Widespread and common throughout. 4-angled stems carry narrow leaves with rolled margins in whorls of 8–12 and blacken when dry. The only yellow flowered bedstraw; dense clusters appear June–September.

HEDGE-BEDSTRAW *Galium mollugo* Scrambling, up to 1.5m
Widespread and generally common perennial, except in the far N. Favours hedges and scrub. Stems smooth and square; oval leaves, with single vein and pointed tips, borne in whorls of 6–8. Clusters of 4-lobed flowers appear June–September.

COMMON CLEAVERS *Galium aparine* Height up to 1.5m
Sprawling annual of disturbed ground. Widespread and common. Backward-pointing prickles secure plant in its scrambling progress through vegetation. Leaves in whorls of 6–8. Tiny white flowers appear May–September. Fruits with hooked bristles.

COMMON MARSH-BEDSTRAW *Galium palustre* Height up to 60cm
Rather delicate, straggling plant of damp, grassy ground. Widespread and common throughout. The narrow leaves are borne in whorls of 4–6 and are not spine-tipped. Open clusters of white flowers, each 3–4mm across, appear June–August.

CROSSWORT *Cruciata laevipes* Height up to 50cm
Attractive perennial of grassy woodland rides, hedgerows and verges, mainly on calcareous soils. Widespread; commonest in N and E England. Oval, hairy leaves borne in distinct whorls of four. Clusters of yellow flowers appear April–June.

BORAGE *Borago officinalis* Height up to 30cm
Widely cultivated in gardens and sometimes found naturalised as an escape, often on disturbed ground. Entire plant is bristly. Lower leaves are stalked, upper ones clasp the stem. 5-petalled flowers, 20–25mm across, appear April–September.

BUGLOSS *Anchusa arvensis* Height up to 50cm
Roughly hairy annual of disturbed, often sandy, soil. Widespread and locally common in E England. Narrow leaves have wavy margins; lower ones stalked, upper ones clasping stem. Sprays of blue flowers, 5–6mm across, appear May–September.

OYSTER PLANT *Mertensia maritima* Prostrate
Trailing perennial of coastal shingle. Rare in N England; more frequent further N in Scotland. Oval, fleshy, blue-green leaves borne on reddish stems. Leafy, long-stalked clusters of flowers appear June–August; pink, turning blue-purple.

RUSSIAN COMFREY *Symphytum x uplandicum* Height up to 1m
Fertile hybrid, now widely naturalised and often common in hedgerows, grassland and verges. Stems slightly winged. Oval leaves softly hairy, upper ones forming wings down stem. Blue-purple flowers are borne in curved clusters, May–August.

COMMON COMFREY *Symphytum officinalis* Height up to 1m
Hairy perennial of damp ground, often found beside rivers. Widespread but common only in C and S England. Stems prominently winged. Oval leaves hairy, upper ones clasping stem. Curved clusters of pink-purple or cream flowers appear May–June.

HOUND'S-TONGUE *Cynoglossum officinale* Height up to 75cm
Downy biennial smelling strongly of mice. Favours dry, grassy places, often near the coast, and commonest in SE England. Narrow, hairy leaves are stalked near the base of the plant. Clusters of maroon, 5-lobed flowers appear June–August.

COMMON GROMWELL *Lithospermum officinale* Height up to 50cm
Downy perennial of woodland margins and rides, usually on calcareous soils. It is locally common in S England and Wales but rare or absent elsewhere. Leaves narrow and alternate. Clusters of white, 5-petalled flowers appear June–July.

EARLY FORGET-ME-NOT *Myosotis ramosissima* Height up to 12cm
Downy annual of arable fields, bare grassy places and open woodland. Widespread and common in most parts except the far N. Leaves ovate, basal ones forming a rosette. Clustered spikes of blue, 5-lobed flowers, 5mm across, appear April–October.

WATER FORGET-ME-NOT *Myosotis scorpioides* Height up to 12cm
Creeping perennial with upright flowering shoots. Found in watery habitats on neutral and basic soils. Common and widespread throughout. Leaves narrow and oblong. Curved clusters of sky-blue flowers, each 10mm across, appear June–September.

WOOD FORGET-ME-NOT *Mysotis sylvatica* Height up to 50cm
Hairy, leafy perennial of woodland rides and margins. Locally common in SE and E England but scarce or absent elsewhere. Plant has spreading hairs on stems and narrow, oval leaves. Curved clusters of blue flowers, 6–10mm across, appear April–July.

GREEN ALKANET *Pentaglottis sempervirens* Height up to 75cm
Roughly hairy perennial of hedgerows and roadside verges. Widely naturalised as a garden escape and commonest in the SW. Leaves large, oval and pointed; basal ones stalked. Clusters of bright blue flowers, 2–3mm across, appear April–July.

VIPER'S-BUGLOSS *Echium vulgare* Height up to 80cm
Roughly hairy biennial of dry grassland, mainly on sandy or calcareous soils and often near the coast. Leaves are narrow and pointed; basal leaves stalked. Dense spikes of bright blue funnel-shaped flowers, 15–20mm long, appear May–September.

BUGLE *Ajuga reptans* Height up 20cm
Familiar perennial of woodland rides and verges. Widespread but commonest in the S. The leafy, creeping runners root at intervals and bear ovate, stalked leaves. The pale blue flowers, 15mm long, appear on upright flowering stems April–June.

SKULLCAP *Scutellaria galericulata* Height up to 40cm
Often hairy perennial of damp ground in marshes and river banks. Widespread and locally common throughout. Stems square and leaves oval, stalked and toothed. Blue-violet flowers, 6–10mm long, are borne on upright, leafy stems June–September.

WOOD SAGE *Teucrium scorodonia* Height up to 40cm
Downy perennial of acid soils along woodland rides, heaths and coastal cliffs. Widespread and locally common throughout. Leaves heart-shaped and stalked. The paired, yellowish flowers are borne in leafless spikes and appear June–September.

SELFHEAL *Prunella vulgaris* Height up to 20cm
Creeping, downy perennial of short grassland and woodland rides on calcareous or neutral soils. Widespread and common throughout. Leaves are paired and oval. The blue-violet flowers are borne in dense clusters, on leafy stems, June–October.

GROUND-IVY *Glechoma hederacea* Height up to 15cm
Softly hairy, strong-smelling perennial with creeping stems that root at regular intervals. Found in woodland, hedgerows and grassland; widespread and common. Leaves kidney-shaped and stalked. Violet flowers in whorls of 2–4, appear March–June.

WHITE DEAD-NETTLE *Lamium album* Height up to 40cm
Downy-stemmed perennial of verges and disturbed ground. Widespread and common throughout except far N. Heart-shaped leaves are nettle-like but lack stinging hairs. White flowers, 20–25mm long, borne in whorls and appear March–November.

RED DEAD-NETTLE *Lamium purpureum* Height up to 30cm
Branched, downy annual of disturbed ground and cultivated soil. Widespread and common throughout. Leaves are heart-shaped, toothed and stalked. Purplish pink flowers, 10–17mm long, are borne in whorls on upright stems, March–October.

HENBIT DEAD-NETTLE *Lamium amplexicaule* Height up to 20cm
An often trailing annual of cultivated soil and disturbed ground. Widespread but commonest in the S. Similar to red dead-nettle but leaves are unstalked, rounded and clasp stem in pairs. The pinkish purple flowers appear March–November.

COMMON HEMP-NETTLE *Galeopsis tetrahit* Height up to 50cm
Hairy-stemmed annual of arable land and disturbed ground. Widespread and common throughout. Leaves are ovate, stalked and toothed. Stems are swollen at leaf nodes. Pinkish flowers are borne in whorls, July–September. Sepal tubes persist.

LARGE-FLOWERED HEMP-NETTLE *Galeopsis speciosa* Height up to 50cm
Bristly-hairy annual or arable land, found mostly on peaty soils. Widespread but commonest in the N. Leaves are ovate, stalked and toothed and stems are swollen at leaf nodes. Large yellowish flowers have purple on lower lip and appear July–September.

BASTARD BALM *Melittis melissophyllum* Height up to 60cm
Hairy, strong-smelling perennial of woodland rides and shady hedgerows. Local and rather scarce in S England. Leaves are ovate, toothed and stalked. Flowers are white or pinkish purple, sometimes both; 25–40mm long, appearing May–July.

YELLOW ARCHANGEL *Lamiastrum galeobdolon* Height up to 45cm
Hairy perennial of woodland rides and hedgerows, mostly on basic soils. Locally common in England and Wales but scarce or absent elsewhere. Nettle-like leaves toothed and oval. Yellow flowers are borne in whorls up flowering stems, May–June.

BLACK HOREHOUND *Ballota nigra* Height up to 50cm
Unpleasant-smelling, hairy perennial of disturbed ground and roadside verges. Widespread and common in England and Wales; scarce or absent elsewhere. Ovate or heart-shaped leaves are stalked. Whorls of pink-purple flowers appear June–September.

BETONY *Stachys officinalis* Height up to 50cm
Perennial of grassland and open woods on sandy or chalky soil. Common in England and Wales; scarce or absent elsewhere. Lower leaves heart-shaped and stalked; narrower up stem. Dense spikes of reddish purple flowers appear June–September.

HEDGE WOUNDWORT *Stachys sylvatica* Height up to 75cm
Roughly hairy perennial with unpleasant smell. Found in hedgerows and widespread and common throughout. Heart-shaped leaves are toothed and long-stalked. Spikes of flowers appear June–October; reddish purple with white markings on lower lip.

MARSH WOUNDWORT *Stachys palustris* Height up to 1m
Non-smelling perennial of damp ground such as marshes and ditches. Widespread and locally common throughout. Leaves are narrow-oblong and mostly unstalked. Pinkish purple flowers with white markings are borne in spikes, June–September.

COMMON CALAMINT *Calamintha sylvatica* Height up to 50cm
Branched, hairy perennial, smelling of mint. Locally common in dry grassland, mostly on calcareous soil, in S England, Wales and S Ireland. Rounded leaves are long-stalked. Whorls of pink-lilac flowers borne in leaf axils, June–September.

MEADOW CLARY *Salvia pratensis* Height up to 1m
Downy perennial of calcareous grassland. Rare native in S England, naturalised locally elsewhere. Lower leaves oval, toothed and long-stalked. The blue-violet flowers, 20–30mm long, are borne in tall, whorled spikes and appear June–July.

WATER MINT *Mentha aquatica* Height up to 50cm
Strongly mint-scented perennial of damp ground, sometimes even growing in water. Oval, toothed leaves borne on reddish, hairy stems. Lilac-pink flowers carried in dense terminal heads 2cm long and appear July–October. Popular with insects.

CORN MINT *Mentha arvensis* Height up to 30cm
Mint-scented perennial of damp arable land, paths and disturbed ground. Common and widespread throughout. Toothed, oval leaves are short-stalked. Lilac flowers borne in dense whorls at intervals along stem, not terminally, May–October.

SPEARMINT *Mentha spicata* Height up to 75cm
Popular, strongly-scented garden mint but also widely naturalised as an escape on damp ground. Leaves are narrow-ovate, toothed and unstalked. The pale lilac flowers are borne in whorls forming long, terminal spikes; appear July–October.

PENNYROYAL *Mentha pulegium* Height up to 30cm
Often creeping perennial of damp hollows on grazed, grassy heaths. Very local, only in S England, especially New Forest. Leaves oval and toothed. Pink-lilac flowers in separated whorls without distinct terminal spike; appear August–October.

GIPSYWORT *Lycopus europaeus* Height up to 75cm
Hairy perennial of damp ground such as ditches and pond margins. Widespread and common in C and S England but scarce or absent elsewhere. Leaves deeply cut into lobes or pinnately divided. Whorls of whitish flowers appear July–September.

WILD BASIL *Clinopodium vulgare* Height up to 35cm
Aromatic, hairy perennial of dry grassland, mostly on calcareous soils. Locally common in S and E England, scarce or absent elsewhere. Leaves ovate and toothed. Whorls of pinkish purple flowers, with bristly bracts, appear July–September.

MARJORAM *Origanum vulgare* Height up to 50cm
Hairy perennial of dry grassland on calcareous soil. Widespread and common in the S but scarce or absent elsewhere. Oval, pointed leaves are borne in pairs on reddish stems. Dense, terminal clusters of pink-purple flowers, appear July–September.

WILD THYME *Thymus praecox* Height up to 5cm
Aromatic, creeping and often mat-forming perennial of dry grassland and heaths. Widespread and common throughout. Ovate, short-stalked leaves borne in pairs along stems. Dense terminal heads of pink-purple flowers appear June–September.

GROUND-PINE *Ajuga chamaepitys* Height up to 20cm
Hairy annual of bare, dry ground and arable fields on calcareous soil. Now rare and found only in S England. Stem leaves are deeply divided into three narrow lobes which smell of pine when crushed. Yellow flowers borne at leaf nodes May–August.

BITTERSWEET/WOODY NIGHTSHADE *Solanum dulcamara* Height up to1.5m
Scrambling perennial. Found in hedgerows and on shingle beaches; widespread and common except in N and Ireland. Oval leaves have narrow basal leaflets or lobes. Purple flowers with yellow stamens, May–September. Berries red and poisonous.

DEADLY NIGHTSHADE *Atropa belladonna* Height up to 1m
Branched perennial of scrub and open woods on calcareous soils. Locally common in S and E England but scarce or absent elsewhere. Leaves oval and pointed. The flowers are purplish and bell-shaped and appear June–August. Berries black and poisonous.

HENBANE *Hyoscyamus niger* Height up to 75cm
Branched, stickily-hairy and strong smelling plant of disturbed ground, often near the sea. Locally common in S and E England but scarce or absent elsewhere. Leaves oval and pointed. Dark-veined yellow flowers, 20–30mm across, appear June–August.

GREAT MULLEIN *Verbascum thapsus* Height up to 2m
Robust perennial covered in white, woolly hairs. Common on dry, grassy ground. Widespread and common except in N. Leaves form rosette in first year. Tall, leafy stalks in second year; flowers, 20–30mm across, appear in terminal spikes, June–August.

DARK MULLEIN *Verbascum nigrum* Height up to 1m
Ridged-stemmed plant of verges and disturbed ground on calcareous or sandy soil. Locally common in S and E England; scarce or absent elsewhere. Leaves dark green and oval. Yellow flowers, 1–2cm across, with purple stamens, appear June–August.

WATER FIGWORT *Scrophularia auriculata* Height up to 70cm
Upright perennial of damp woods and water margins. Has characteristic 4-winged stems. Widespread and common throughout, except in Scotland. Leaves blunt-tipped with rounded teeth. Maroon and green, 2-lipped flowers appear June–September.

COMMON FIGWORT *Scrophularia nodosa* Height up to 70cm
Upright perennial of damp woodlands and verges. Widespread and common except in N Scotland. Stems are square in cross section but not winged. Leaves are oval and pointed with sharp teeth. Maroon and green flowers appear June–September.

ROUND-LEAVED FLUELLEN *Kickxia spuria* Prostrate
Creeping, stickily-hairy annual of cultivated soil and arable fields. Locally common in S and E England; scarce or absent elsewhere. Rounded leaves borne on trailing stems. Spurred, yellow and purple flowers, 7–9mm long appear July–October.

COMMON TOADFLAX *Linaria vulgaris* Height up to 75cm
Grey-green perennial of hedgerows and grassland. Widespread and locally common throughout. Upright, often branched stems bear very narrow leaves. Long-spurred, orange-centred yellow flowers, 15–25mm long, seen June–October in tall clusters.

PALE TOADFLAX *Linaria repens* Height up to 75cm
Greyish perennial found in dry, often bare places in grassland. Possibly native; rather local in England and Wales. Several upright flowering shoots, bearing narrow leaves, arise from rhizome. Dark-veined, lilac flowers appear June–September.

IVY-LEAVED TOADFLAX *Cymbalaria muralis* Trailing
Perennial of rocks and walls. Originally a garden plant but widely naturalised throughout. The long-stalked, ivy-shaped leaves are 5-lobed and are borne on long reddish stems. Yellow-centred lilac flowers, 8–10mm long, appear April–November.

THYME-LEAVED SPEEDWELL *Veronica serpyllifolia* Height up to 20cm
Mostly creeping perennial of grassy places and cultivated ground. Widespread and common throughout. Thyme-like leaves are small and oval. Flowers, 5–6mm across and blue, are borne on upright stalks in loose spikes; appear April–October.

GERMANDER SPEEDWELL *Veronica chamaedrys* Height up to 20cm
Grassland perennial. Widespread and common throughout. Oval leaves are toothed and hairy. Prostrate stems root at nodes. Upright stems with two lines of hairs. The white-centred, blue flowers are 10–12mm across and appear April–June.

BLUE WATER-SPEEDWELL *Veronica anagallis-aquatica* Height up to 25cm
Hairless perennial of water margins and marshy ground. Widespread and locally common except in Scotland. Upright stems carry oval and pointed leaves. Pairs of pale blue flowers, arising from leaf axils, are borne in spikes June–August.

Heath Speedwell *Veronica officinalis* Height up to 10cm
Mat-forming perennial of grassland and woodland rides. Widespread and generally common throughout. Prostrate stems root at nodes and are hairy all round. The pale bluish lilac flowers, 6–8mm across, are borne in upright spikes May–August.

Common Field-speedwell *Veronica persica* Prostrate
Sprawling, hairy annual of arable land and cultivated soils. Probably not native but now widespread and common throughout. Pairs of pale green, toothed oval leaves are borne on reddish stems. Solitary blue flowers, 8–12mm across, seen all year.

Brooklime *Veronica beccabunga* Height up to 30cm
Hairless perennial of shallow water and damp soil. Widespread and locally common throughout. Oval, fleshy leaves have short stalks. Stems creeping, then upright. Blue flowers, 7–8mm across, are borne in pairs from leaf axils, May–September.

Monkeyflower *Mimulus guttatus* Height up to 50cm
Perennial of damp ground, often beside streams and rivers. Introduced from N America but now widely naturalised in many parts. Oval leaves in opposite pairs. Showy, yellow flowers, 25–45mm across, have red spots in throat; June–September.

Foxglove *Digitalis purpurea* Height up to 1.5m
Tall, greyish biennial or perennial of woods, moors and sea cliffs. Downy, oval leaves, 20–30cm long, form rosette in first year. In second year, tall spikes arise bearing succession of pink-purple, tubular flowers, 40–50mm long, June–September.

Red Bartsia *Odontites verna* Height up to 40cm
Straggly, branched downy annual of disturbed ground, tracks and verges. Common and widespread throughout. Narrow, toothed leaves borne in opposite pairs. Pink-purple flowers, 8–10mm long, appear in spikes June–September. Plant often tinged red.

Yellow Bartsia *Parentucellia viscosa* Height up to 40cm
Stickily-hairy, unbranched annual of damp, grassy places, mostly near the sea and often in dune-slacks. Very local in SW Britain and W Ireland. Leaves are lanceolate and unstalked. Bright yellow flowers, 15–25mm long, appear June–October.

Common Cow-wheat *Melampyrum pratense* Height up to 35cm
Straggly annual of woodland rides and grassy heaths, found mostly on acid soils. Widespread and locally common throughout. Narrow, shiny leaves borne in opposite pairs. Pairs of yellow flowers, 10–18mm long, arise from axils, May–September.

Eyebright *Euphrasia officinalis* Height up to 25cm
Variable, branched annual, semi-parasitic on roots of other plants. Widespread and common on bare, grassy places. Leaves oval in outline but sharply toothed; often purplish. Purple-veined, whitish flowers, 3–10mm long, seen May–September.

Yellow-rattle *Rhinanthus minor* Height up to 45cm
Semi-parasitic annual of undisturbed meadows and dunes. Widespread and common throughout. Stems are black-spotted. Oblong leaves have rather rounded teeth. Yellow flowers, 10–20mm long, are borne in leafy, terminal spikes, May–September.

Lousewort *Pedicularis sylvatica* Height up to 20cm
Branched, spreading perennial of damp heaths and moors. Widespread and locally common on suitable habitats throughout. Feathery leaves are divided into toothed leaflets. The pink flowers, 20–25mm long, have 2-toothed upper lips; appear April–July.

Marsh Lousewort *Pedicularis palustris* Height up to 50cm
Hairless, branched annual of boggy heaths and marshes. Widespread and locally common; less so in E England. Feathery leaves are deeply divided into toothed lobes. Leafy spikes of pinkish purple flowers, 20–25mm long, seen May–September.

TOOTHWORT *Lathraea squamaria* Height up to 25cm
Wholly parasitic plant on roots of woody plants, especially hazel. Widespread but local; absent from N Scotland and W Ireland. Leaves reduced to pinkish white scales, borne on lilac stem. Tubular lilac flowers, in 1-sided spike, April–May.

COMMON BROOMRAPE *Orobanche minor* Height up to 40cm
Parasitic annual on the roots of clovers and other herbaceous plants. Locally common C and S England, Wales and S Ireland. Lacks chlorophyll; leaves reduced to brownish scales. Purple-veined, pinkish yellow flowers seen June–September.

KNAPWEED BROOMRAPE *Orobanche elatior* Height up to 70cm
Imposing root parasite, mainly of knapweeds. Locally in S and E England, mostly on calcareous soils. Stem is robust and yellowish with brown, scale-like leaves. Yellow-brown flowers are borne in a tall, dense spike which appears June–July.

THYME BROOMRAPE *Orobanche alba* Height up to 25cm
Root parasite of thyme and other related plants; usually has an overall reddish appearance. Local, restricted to coastal grassland in Cornwall, W Scotland and W Ireland. Leaves scale-like. Fragrant flowers borne in a loose spike, May–August.

MOSCHATEL *Adoxa moschatellina* Height up to 10cm
Charming perennial of woodland and shady places. Locally common in Britain, especially in the S. Long-stalked, twice 3-lobed basal leaves form a carpet. 3-lobed stem leaves in opposite pairs. Stalked heads of five flowers seen April–May.

RED VALERIAN *Centranthus ruber* Height up to 75cm
Grey-green perennial of rocks, broken ground and walls. Locally common in SW Britain; scarce or absent elsewhere. Ovate, untoothed leaves in opposite pairs. Pink, red or sometimes white flowers are borne in terminal clusters May–September.

COMMON CORNSALAD *Valerianella locusta* Height up to 30cm
Branched annual of dry, bare places on grassland and dunes. Widespread but only locally common. Lower leaves spoon-shaped, upper ones oblong. Pale lilac flowers are borne in flat-topped clusters with leafy bracts beneath; seen April–August.

TWINFLOWER *Linnaea borealis* Height up to 7cm
Delicate, creeping perennial of native Scottish pinewoods. Rare and extremely local. Opposite pairs of oval or rounded leaves on wiry stems often form a mat. Pairs of pink, bell-shaped flowers are borne on slender stalks, June–August.

COMMON BUTTERWORT *Pinguicula vulgaris* Height up to 15cm
Carnivorous perennial of bogs and damp flushes; rosette of yellow-green, sticky leaves can trap and digest insects. Widespread and fairly common in Ireland and NW Britain; scarce elsewhere. Violet, spurred flowers, 10–15mm long, seen May–August.

GREATER PLANTAIN *Plantago major* Height up to 20cm
Persistent perennial of lawns and disturbed grassy places. Widespread and common throughout. Broad, oval leaves, up to 25cm long, have 3–9 veins and form a basal rosette. The flowers are borne in long, stalked spikes and appear June–October.

BUCK'S-HORN PLANTAIN *Plantago coronopus* Height up to 15cm
Downy, grey-green perennial of disturbed ground and rocky sites, mainly near the sea. Widespread and common around coasts of Britain and Ireland. The deeply cut, pinnately divided leaves form a rosette. Stalked flower heads seen May–October.

SEA PLANTAIN *Plantago maritima* Height up to 15cm
Characteristic coastal plant which is tolerant of salt spray and occasional immersion. Widespread and common around shores of Britain and Ireland. Strap-like leaves form a rosette. Flower heads borne on long stalks, June–September.

RIBWORT PLANTAIN *Plantago lanceolata* Height up to 15cm
Perennial of disturbed grassland, cultivated ground and tracks. Widespread and common throughout. Leaves lanceolate and up to 20cm long; form a spreading basal rosette. Compact, ovoid flower heads borne on furrowed stalks, April–October.

SHOREWEED *Littorella uniflora* Creeping
Hairless aquatic perennial, often found growing on the drying margins of ponds and lakes. Widespread in N and W but local in S Britain. Narrow, fleshy leaves form a basal rosette. Tiny flowers, with minute petals, appear June–August.

SEA ARROWGRASS *Triglochin maritima* Height up to 50cm
Plantain-like tufted perennial of saltmarshes. Widespread and common throughout. Leaves are long, narrow and unveined. The flowers are 3-petalled, 2–3mm across and borne in a long, narrow spike which itself is long-stalked; appear May–September.

SMALL SCABIOUS *Scabiosa columbaria* Height up to 65cm
Branching perennial of calcareous grassland. Locally common only in England and Wales. Pinnately lobed basal leaves form a rosette. Stem leaves are divided into narrow lobes. Bluish violet flower heads, 20–30mm across, appear June–September.

FIELD SCABIOUS *Knautia arvensis* Height up to 75cm
Robust, hairy biennial or perennial of dry grassland. Widespread and common but absent from N Scotland. Spoon-shaped, lobed basal leaves form rosette; those on stem are less divided. Bluish violet flower heads, 30–40mm across, seen June–October.

DEVIL'S-BIT SCABIOUS *Succisa pratensis* Height up to 75cm
Perennial of damp grassland, woodland rides and marshes. Widespread and common throughout. Basal leaves are spoon-shaped; those on stem are narrow. Blue-purple flowers are borne in rounded heads, 15–25mm across, and appear June–October.

TEASEL *Dipsacus fullonum* Height up to 2m
Biennial of damp grassland on heavy, often disturbed, soils. Produces rosette of spine-coated leaves in first year. In second year, conical heads of purple flowers are borne on tall, angled and spined stems, July–August. Dead heads persist.

SMALL TEASEL *Dipsacus pilosus* Height up to 1.25m
Branched plant of damp ground or shady places. Occurs locally in England and Wales. Oval, long-stalked basal leaves form rosette. Oval stem leaves sometimes have two basal lobes. Whitish flowers are borne in rounded heads July–September.

ROUND-HEADED RAMPION *Phyteuma tenerum* Height up to 50cm
Perennial of dry grassland on calcareous soil. Local and restricted to sites on chalk downs in S England. Leaves oval at base but narrow and unstalked on stem. Blue-violet flowers borne in rounded, untidy heads, 10–25mm across, June–August.

SHEEP'S-BIT *Jasione montana* Height up to 30cm
Spreading biennial of dry, grassy places on acid soils, commonest near the sea. Widespread but local. Wavy-edged, hairy basal leaves form rosette; stem leaves narrow. Blue flowers are borne in rounded heads, 30–35mm across, May–September.

HAREBELL *Campanula rotundifolia* Height up to 40cm
Attractive, delicate perennial of dry, grassy places, on both calcareous and acid soils. Widespread and mostly common. Rounded basal leaves soon wither; stem leaves narrow. Clusters of nodding blue flowers, 15mm long, seen July–October.

CLUSTERED BELLFLOWER *Campanula glomerata* Height up to 25cm
Downy perennial of calcareous grassland. Locally common S and E England; scarce or absent elsewhere. Basal leaves long-stalked and heart-shaped; narrower and clasping on stem. Clusters of violet-blue flowers, 15–20mm long, appear June–October.

NETTLE-LEAVED BELLFLOWER *Campanula trachelium* Height up to 75cm
Roughly-hairy perennial of hedgerows and open woodland. Locally common in S and E England only. Basal leaves stalked and heart-shaped; nettle-like stem leaves oval and toothed. Leafy spikes of blue-violet flowers, 30–40mm long, seen July–August.

IVY-LEAVED BELLFLOWER *Wahlenbergia hederacea* Creeping
Trailing perennial of damp, shady ground on moors and heaths. Locally common in SW England and Wales; scarce or absent elsewhere. Ivy-shaped leaves carried on long stems. Pale blue flowers, 5–10mm long, borne on long stalks, appear July–August.

WATER LOBELIA *Lobelia dortmanna* Aquatic
Perennial of clear, acid waters of upland lakes with gravelly bottoms. Locally common in N Wales, N England, Scotland and N Ireland. Narrow, fleshy leaves form basal rosette on lake bed. Lilac flowers borne on emergent stalks, June–August.

HEATH LOBELIA *Lobelia urens* Height up to 50cm
Slender, hairless perennial of grassy heaths and woodland rides on acid soils. Local and scarce, restricted to sites in S England. Dark green leaves oval near base but narrow up stem. Bluish purple flowers in loose heads, seen July–September.

HEMP AGRIMONY *Eupatorium cannabinum* Height up to 1.5m
Tall perennial of damp grassland and marshes. Widespread and common in England, Wales and Ireland; rare in Scotland. Trifoliate leaves borne in opposite pairs up stem. Heads of dull pink flowers form terminal inflorescences July–September.

GOLDENROD *Solidago virgaurea* Height up to 75cm
Variable perennial found in woods and grassland, and among rocks. Widespread and locally common. Stalked basal leaves are spoon-shaped; stem leaves are narrower and unstalked. Flower heads, 5–10mm across, in branched spikes, June–September.

CANADIAN GOLDENROD *Solidago canadensis* Height up to 1m
Familiar garden perennial which is widespread as a naturalised escape, mostly in damp wayside places. Leaves are oval, toothed and 3-veined. Flower heads are borne on crowded, arching, 1-sided sprays in branching clusters, July–October.

DAISY *Bellis perennis* Height up to 10cm
Familiar perennial of lawns and short grass. Widespread and common throughout. Spoon-shaped leaves form prostrate rosettes from which flower stalks arise, each bearing single flower heads, 15–25mm across; yellow disc and white ray florets.

SCENTLESS MAYWEED *Matricaria perforata* Height up to 75cm
Scentless, hairless perennial of disturbed ground and cultivated soil. Common and widespread throughout. Leaves are much-divided and feathery. Clusters of long-stalked, daisy-like flower heads, 20–40mm across, appear April–October.

CHAMOMILE *Chamaemelum nobile* Height up to 25cm
Creeping, aromatic perennial of short, often grazed, grass on sandy soils. Local and restricted to sites in S England and S Wales. Leaves are finely divided and feathery. The daisy-like flower heads are 18–24mm across and appear June–August.

PINEAPPLEWEED *Chamomilla suaveolens* Height up to 12cm
Bright green perennial of disturbed ground, paths and tracks; smells strongly of pineapple when crushed. Leaves are finely divided and feathery. Rounded-oval flower heads comprise yellowish green disc florets only and appear May–November.

SEA ASTER *Aster tripolium* Height up to 75cm
Salt-tolerant perennial of saltmarshes and cliffs. Locally common around coasts of Britain and Ireland. Leaves are fleshy and narrow. Clusters of flowers, 10–20mm across, comprising yellow disc and blue ray florets, appear July–September.

BLUE FLEABANE *Erigeron acer* Height up to 30cm
Annual or biennial of dry, grassy places. Widespread and common only in England and Wales. Stems reddish and hairy. Basal leaves stalked and spoon-shaped; stem leaves narrow, unstalked. Flower heads, 12–18mm across, in clusters, June–August.

MARSH CUDWEED *Gnaphalium uliginosum* Height up to 20cm
Grey-green, woolly, branched annual of damp, disturbed ground and tracks. Common and widespread throughout. Leaves narrow and up to 40cm long. Flowers comprise yellow disc florets and brown bracts; shrouded by leaves and seen July–October.

COMMON CUDWEED *Filago vulgaris* Height up to 25cm
Upright, woolly annual of dry, often sandy, grassland. Very locally common in S England and S Wales but scarce or absent elsewhere. Usually branched near tip. Leaves narrow. Rounded clusters of 20–35 flower heads are seen July–August.

SMALL CUDWEED *Logfia minima* Height up to 20cm
Slender, woolly annual of grassy heaths on sandy, acid soils. Locally common in England and Wales; scarce or absent elsewhere. Leaves lanceolate and 10mm long. Clusters of conical or ovoid flower heads, 3–4mm long, appear July–September.

PLOUGHMAN'S-SPIKENARD *Inula conyza* Height up to 1m
Perennial of dry grassland on calcareous soils. Locally common only in England and Wales. Stems red and hairy. Oval lower leaves resemble those of foxglove; stem leaves narrower. Rayless, yellow flower heads are borne in clusters, July–September.

GOLDEN SAMPHIRE *Inula crithmoides* Height up to 75cm
Tufted perennial of saltmarshes, shingle and sea cliffs. Widespread and locally common around coasts of SW Britain and Ireland. Upright stems with bright green, narrow, fleshy leaves. Flower heads, 15–30mm across, are seen in clusters, July–September.

COMMON FLEABANE *Pulicaria dysenterica* Height up to 50cm
Woolly perennial of damp meadows and ditches, mostly on heavy soils. Widespread and common in C and S Britain and Ireland. Basal leaves soon wither; stem leaves heart-shaped and clasping. Flower heads, 15–30mm across, appear July–September.

YARROW *Achillea millefolium* Height up to 50cm
Strong-smelling wayside perennial. Widespread and common throughout. Dark green leaves finely divided and feathery. Flat-topped clusters of flower heads, 4–6mm across, comprise yellowish disc and pinkish white ray florets; appear June–November.

SNEEZEWORT *Achillea ptarmica* Height up to 60cm
Upright, downy perennial of damp ground in woods and meadows. Locally common throughout. Leaves narrow and finely toothed. Open clusters of flower heads, 1–2cm across and comprising yellowish disc and white ray florets, seen July–September.

CORN MARIGOLD *Chrysanthemum segetum* Height up to 50cm
Hairless annual of cultivated ground, mostly on acid, sandy soils. Widespread and locally common although much reduced in range and abundance. Leaves narrow and deeply lobed. Bright yellow flowers, 30–60mm across, appear June–October.

TANSY *Tanacetum vulgare* Height up to 75cm
Aromatic, downy perennial of waysides and disturbed land. Widespread and common throughout. Pinnately divided leaves have deeply cut lobes. Yellow flower heads, 7–12mm across, form flat-topped clusters up to 12cm in diameter; appear July–October.

FEVERFEW *Tanacetum parthenium* Height up to 50cm
Aromatic, downy perennial of disturbed ground and walls. Introduced but widely naturalised in many places. Yellowish leaves are pinnately divided. Daisy-like flowers, 1–2cm across, comprise yellow disc and white ray florets; appear July–August.

OXEYE DAISY *Leucanthemum vulgare* Height up to 60cm
Perennial of dry, grassy meadows and disturbed ground. Widespread and common throughout. Spoon-shaped, toothed basal leaves form a rosette; smaller stem leaves are pinnately lobed. Solitary flower heads, 3–5cm across, seen May–September.

BUTTERBUR *Petasites hybridus* Height up to 50cm
Perennial of damp ground, often beside rivers. Widespread and locally common except N Scotland. Robust flowering spikes appear March–May, before leaves, with pink-red flower heads. Heart-shaped leaves, up to 1m across, appear in summer.

WINTER HELIOTROPE *Petasites fragrans* Height up to 20cm
Spreading perennial of damp or shady hedgerows. Introduced but naturalised as a garden escape in many areas. Rounded leaves, 20cm across, are present all year. Flowering stems appear December–March with fragrant, pink-lilac flower heads.

MUGWORT *Artemisia vulgaris* Height up to 1.25m
Aromatic perennial of roadside verges and wasteground. Widespread and common throughout. Stems reddish. Pinnate leaves dark green above but silvery-downy below. Small, reddish flower heads are borne in branched spikes July–September.

WORMWOOD *Artemisia absinthium* Height up to 80cm
Highly aromatic perennial of disturbed coastal grassland and wayside places. Locally common in England and Wales only. Pinnate leaves are silvery-hairy on both surfaces. Yellowish flower heads are slightly nodding; seen July–September.

SEA WORMWOOD *Artemisia maritima* Height up to 65cm
Aromatic perennial of saltmarshes and sea walls. Locally common around coasts of S and E Britain; scarce or absent elsewhere. Stems woody, downy-white. Pinnate leaves downy on both sides. Yellow flower heads in leafy spikes appear August–October.

COLT'S-FOOT *Tussilago farfara* Height up to 15cm
Creeping perennial of bare, often disturbed, ground. Widespread and common in most parts. Yellow flowers appear February–April, before the leaves; they are borne on scaly stems. Leaves are rounded or heart-shaped and 10–20cm across.

COMMON RAGWORT *Senecio jacobaea* Height up to 1m
Poisonous biennial or perennial of grazed grassland and verges. Widespread and common throughout. Leaves are pinnately divided with a blunt end lobe. Flat-topped clusters of yellow flower heads, 15–25mm across, appear June–November.

GROUNDSEL *Senecio vulgaris* Height up to 40cm
Annual weed of cultivated soil and disturbed ground. Widespread and very common throughout. Leaves are pinnately-lobed; lower ones stalked, upper ones clasping stem. Open clusters of small, rayless flower heads can be found almost all year.

OXFORD RAGWORT *Senecio squalidus* Height up to 50cm
Branched annual or perennial of wasteground, verges and railway tracks. Widely naturalised. Leaves are pinnately lobed and end in a pointed lobe. Open clusters of bright yellow flower heads, each 15–20mm across, appear April–November.

FIELD FLEAWORT *Senecio integrifolius* Height up to 65cm
Rather slender perennial, found on grazed calcareous grassland. Oval, toothed basal leaves form a rosette; stem leaves are infrequent, narrow and clasping. Orange-yellow flower heads, 15–25mm across, borne in few-flowered clusters, May–July.

GREATER BURDOCK *Arctium lappa* Height up to 1m
Branched biennial of woodland, scrub and verges. Locally common in England and Wales; scarce or absent elsewhere. Leaves large, downy and heart-shaped. Egg-shaped flower heads, 3–4cm across, are borne in open clusters, July–September.

CARLINE THISTLE *Carlina vulgaris* Height up to 60cm
Spiny biennial of dry, calcareous grassland. Locally common throughout except N Scotland. Oblong leaves have wavy margins and spiny lobes. Brown, rayless flower heads surrounded by golden bracts; July–September. Dead flower heads persist.

MUSK THISTLE *Carduus nutans* Height up to 1m
Upright biennial of dry grassland. Locally common only in England and Wales. Winged stems spiny and cottony. Leaves are pinnately lobed and spiny. Rayless, nodding flower heads, 30–50mm across, appear June–August, fringed by spiny bracts.

SLENDER THISTLE *Carduus tenuiflorus* Height up to 1m
Biennial of dry, grassy places, mostly near the sea. Locally common around most coasts except N Scotland. Stems are winged and spiny to the top. Spiny leaves are cottony below. Clusters of pinkish flower heads, 8–10mm across, appear June–August.

SPEAR THISTLE *Cirsium vulgare* Height up to 1m
Biennial of disturbed ground. Widespread and common. Pinnately lobed leaves are spiny. Stems are cottony, winged and spiny between leaves. Flower heads, 20–40mm across, comprise purple florets topping ball of spiny bracts, seen July–September.

MELANCHOLY THISTLE *Cirsium helenoides* Height up to 1m
Unbranched perennial of damp meadows. Locally common in N England and Scotland only. Stems are cottony, spineless and unwinged. Oval, toothed leaves are barely spiny, green above but white below. Flower heads, 30–50mm across, appear June–August.

MEADOW THISTLE *Cirsium dissectum* Height up to 75cm
Perennial of damp meadows. Locally common in S and C England, Wales and Ireland. Stem is unwinged, downy and ridged. Oval, toothed leaves are green and hairy above and white cottony below. Flower heads, 20–25mm across, appear June–July.

STEMLESS THISTLE *Cirsium acaulon* Height up to 5cm
Creeping, flattened perennial of short, calcareous grassland. Locally common in S and E England and S Wales. Extremely spiny, pinnately lobed leaves form basal rosette. Usually stalkless flower heads, 30–50mm across, appear June–September.

CREEPING THISTLE *Cirsium arvense* Height up to 1m
Creeping perennial with upright, unwinged stems. Widespread and very common on disturbed ground and in grassland. Leaves are pinnately-lobed and spiny. The pinkish lilac flower heads, 10–15mm across, appear in clusters June–September.

WOOLLY THISTLE *Cirsium eriophorum* Height up to 1.5m
Distinctive biennial of calcareous grassland. Local in S and E England and S Wales only. Pinnately divided leaves have lobes with two segments, one pointing up, the other down. Woolly flower heads spherical, 40–70mm across; seen July–September.

MARSH THISTLE *Cirsium palustre* Height up to 1.5m
Branched biennial of damp grassland. Widespread and common throughout. Stems are spiny-winged and cottony. Leaves are pinnately-lobed and spiny. Leafy clusters of reddish purple flower heads, each 10–15mm across, appear July–September.

COMMON KNAPWEED *Centaurea nigra* Height up to 1m
Hairy perennial of grassy places. Widespread and common. Grooved stems branch towards the top. Leaves narrow, slightly lobed near base of plant. Flower heads 20–40mm across and with brown bracts and purple florets, appear June–September.

GREATER KNAPWEED *Centaurea scabiosa* Height up to 1m
Downy perennial of dry grassland, mostly on calcareous soils. Common in parts of S and E England; scarce or absent elsewhere. Oblong leaves are deeply pinnately lobed. Flower heads, 30–50mm across, have enlarged outer florets; seen June–September.

SAW-WORT *Serratula tinctoria* Height up to 75cm
Delicate, spineless perennial of damp meadows and woodland rides. Locally common only in SW Britain. Leaves vary from undivided to deeply lobed but edges always saw-toothed. Open clusters of flower heads, 15–20mm long, appear July–October.

CHICORY *Cichorium intybus* Height up to 1m
Branched perennial of bare, grassy places and verges, often on calcareous soils. Locally common only in S England. Lower leaves stalked and lobed, upper ones narrow and clasping. Sky blue flower heads, 30–40mm across, appear June–September.

GOAT'S-BEARD *Tragopogon pratensis* Height up to 60cm
Perennial of grassy places. Locally common in England and Wales. Leaves narrow, clasping or sheathing at base. Flower heads, 30–40mm across, are fringed by bracts and close on dull days and by midday; seen May–August. Fruit a large white 'clock'.

SMOOTH SOW-THISTLE *Sonchus oleraceus* Height up to 1m
Annual of disturbed and cultivated ground. Widespread and common in lowlands. Broken stems exude milky sap. Pinnate leaves have toothed margins and pointed basal lobes. Pale yellow flower heads, 20–25mm across, in clusters May–October.

PERENNIAL SOW-THISTLE *Sonchus arvensis* Height up to 2m
Perennial of damp, grassy places and disturbed ground. Widespread and common throughout. Grey-green leaves have rounded lobes and bases, and clasp the stem. Yellow flower heads, 40–50mm across, appear in branched clusters, July–September.

COMMON DANDELION *Taraxacum officinale* Height up to 35cm
Perennial which embraces a large number of 'micro-species'. Lobed, spoon-shaped leaves form a basal rosette. Flower heads, 30–60mm across, borne on hollow stems yielding milky sap if broken; appear March–October. Fruits form familiar white 'clock'.

MOUSE-EAR HAWKWEED *Hieraceum pilosella* Height up to 25cm
Spreading perennial of dry grassy places. Common throughout. Spoon-shaped leaves are green and hairy above, white downy below; form a basal rosette. Solitary flower heads, 20–30mm across, are pale yellow with red stripes below; seen May–October.

BRISTLY OXTONGUE *Picris echioides* Height up to 80cm
Branched, bristly-stemmed perennial of dry, disturbed ground. Locally common in S Britain only. Narrow, clasping leaves covered with swollen-based bristles and pale spots. Pale yellow flower heads, 20–25mm across, are borne in clusters, June–October.

HAWKWEED OXTONGUE *Picris hieracioides* Height up to 70cm
Bristly-stemmed perennial of rough grassland, often near coasts. Locally common only in SE England. Resembles bristly oxtongue but narrower, toothed leaves have bristles without swollen bases. Flower heads are 20–25mm across; appear June–October.

ROUGH HAWKBIT *Leontodon hispidus* Height up to 35cm
Roughly-hairy perennial of dry grassland, mostly on calcareous soils. Locally common except N Scotland. Hairy, wavy-lobed leaves form basal rosette. Leafless, unbranched stalk arises with single flower head, 25–40mm across; appears June–October.

COMMON CAT'S-EAR *Hypochoeris radicata* Height up to 50cm
Perennial of dry grassland. Widespread and common throughout. Lanceolate, hairy leaves with lobed edges form a basal rosette. Flower heads, 25–30mm across, are borne on branched stalks which have a few purple-tipped bracts; seen June–September.

SMOOTH CAT'S-EAR *Hypochoeris glabra* Height up to 20cm
Perennial of dry grassland, mostly on sandy soils. Locally common only in S and E England; scarce or absent elsewhere. Lanceolate leaves are glossy and usually hairless; form basal rosette. Flower heads, 10–15mm across, appear June–October.

SMOOTH HAWK'S-BEARD *Crepis capillaris* Height up to 1m
Hairless annual or biennial of dry grassy places. Common in lowlands throughout. Lower, lobed leaves form a basal rosette; stem leaves arrow-shaped and clasping. Flower heads, 15–25mm across, borne in branched clusters and appear May–July.

COMMON WATER-PLANTAIN *Alisma plantago-aquatica* Height up to 1m
Aquatic perennial of margins and shallows of ponds and lakes. Locally common except in N Scotland and SW England. Oval, long-stalked leaves have parallel veins. Pale lilac flowers, 10mm across, borne in branched whorls, June–September.

ARROWHEAD *Sagittaria sagittifolia* Height up to 80cm
Aquatic perennial of still and slow-flowing water. Locally common in S Britain; scarce or absent elsewhere. Arrow-shaped emergent leaves, oval floating leaves and narrow submerged ones. 3-petalled flowers, 20mm across, appear July–August.

FLOWERING RUSH *Butomus umbellatus* Height up to 1m
Attractive perennial found in vegetated margins of still or slow-flowing water. Rush-like leaves are 3-angled, very long and arise from the base of the plant. Clusters of pink flowers, each 25–30mm across, borne on tall stems, July–August.

WATER-SOLDIER *Stratiotes aloides* Aquatic
Bizarre aquatic plant, submerged for much of year but rising to the surface to flower in summer months. Plant comprises rosette of 30–40cm long, narrow leaves which are spiny-edged. Solitary, 3-petalled white flowers appear June–August.

LILY-OF-THE-VALLEY *Convallaria majalis* Height up to 20cm
Creeping perennial of dry woodland, usually on calcareous soils. Occurs locally in England and Wales; sometimes naturalised as a garden escape. Oval leaves in pairs. Nodding, white flowers are borne on leafless, 1-sided spikes, May–June.

SNAKE'S-HEAD FRITILLARY *Fritillaria meleagris* Height up to 30cm
Perennial of undisturbed water meadows. Very locally abundant, S England. Grey-green leaves narrow and grass-like. Nodding, bell-shaped flowers on thin stems April–May; colour variable, usually pink-purple with dark chequered markings.

BOG ASPHODEL *Narthecium ossifragum* Height up to 20cm
Tufted perennial of boggy heaths and moors. Locally common on suitable peaty soils but absent from much of C and E England. Narrow, iris-like leaves borne in a flattened fan. Spikes of flowers appear June–August; turns orange in fruit.

YELLOW STAR-OF-BETHLEHEM *Gagea lutea* Height up to 15cm
Perennial of damp woodland, often on calcareous soils. Local, almost confined to E England. The single, narrow basal leaf has a hooded tip. Leafless stems, with two leaf-like bracts, are topped with clusters of flowers, 20mm across, April–May.

WILD TULIP *Tulipa sylvestris* Height up to 40cm
Grassland perennial, introduced and widely but locally naturalised, mainly in S England. Grey-green leaves are narrow and up to 25cm long. Flowers usually solitary and 30–40mm across when petals open fully and spread; appear May–June.

RAMSONS *Allium ursinum* Height up to 35cm
Bulbous perennial which smells strongly of garlic. Often forms extensive carpets in damp woods, mainly on calcareous soils. The leaves are ovate and all basal. The leafless flower stems carry clusters of up to 20 white flowers, April–May.

CROW GARLIC *Allium vineale* Height up to 50cm
Perennial of dry grassland and roadside verges. Fairly common in S Britain but scarce further N. Leaves grey-green, narrow and hollow; easily overlooked when plant not flowering. Heads rounded, few-flowered with a papery bract; seen June–July.

BLUEBELL *Hyacinthoides non-scripta* Height up to 50cm
Familiar bulbous perennial, often carpeting whole woodland floors if management regime suits its requirements; also found on coastal cliffs. Common throughout. Leaves narrow and all basal. Bell-shaped flowers in 1-sided spikes, appear April–June.

SPRING SQUILL *Scilla verna* Height up to 5cm
Compact perennial of dry grassland near the sea. Locally common on coasts of W Britain and E Ireland. Produces 4–6 wiry, curly leaves in spring. Flowers appear subsequently on short stalk, April–June. They are lilac-blue and 10–15mm across.

COMMON SOLOMON'S-SEAL *Polygonatum multiflorum* Height up to 60cm
Perennial of dry woodland, often on calcareous soils. Mainly restricted to S England but there locally common. Arching stems carry alternate, ovate leaves and hanging clusters of 1–3, bell-shaped flowers, May–June. Berry is black.

MEADOW SAFFRON *Colchicum autumnale* Height up to 10cm
Bulbous perennial of meadows and grassy woodland rides. Local in C England and scarce or absent elsewhere. Long, ovate leaves appear in the spring but die back by summer. The pinkish purple flowers are borne on pale stalks, August–October.

HERB-PARIS *Paris quadrifolia* Height up to 35cm
Perennial of damp woodland, often on basic soils. Widespread but locally common only in C and S England. Upright stem bears four oval leaves topped by flower with narrow petals and sepals and a dark ovary; May–June. Fruit is a black berry.

STAR-OF-BETHLEHEM *Ornithogalum umbellatum* Height up to 25cm
Bulbous perennial of dry grassland. Possibly native in parts of SE England but widely naturalised elsewhere. Narrow leaves have a conspicuous white stripe down the centre. White, star-like flowers, 30–40mm across, in open clusters, May–June.

BATH ASPARAGUS *Ornithogalum pyrenaicum* Height up to 80cm
Upright perennial of open woodland, also known as spiked star-of-Bethlehem. Very local, distribution centred around Bath. Grey-green, narrow leaves all basal and soon wither. Greenish white flowers in tall, drooping-tipped spikes, May–July.

BUTCHER'S-BROOM *Ruscus aculeatus* Height up to 1m
Branched, shrubby, evergreen perennial of shady woods, often on calcareous soil. Leaves minute but branches flattened to form oval, leaf-like structures, upper surfaces of which bear solitary flowers, January–April. Fruit is a red berry.

WILD DAFFODIL *Narcissus pseudonarcissus* Height up to 50cm
Bulbous perennial of open woods and meadows. Locally common in parts of England and Wales, often flourishing after woodland coppicing. Leaves grey-green, narrow and all basal. Familiar daffodil flowers, 50–60mm across, appear March–April.

SNOWDROP *Galanthus nivalis* Height up to 25cm
Familiar spring flower. Possibly native to damp woodlands in S Britain but also widely naturalised in many areas. Leaves are narrow, grey-green and all basal. Upright stem carries single, drooping white flower, 15–25cm long, January–March.

YELLOW IRIS *Iris pseudacorus* Height up to 1m
Familiar, robust perennial of pond margins, marshes and river banks. Widespread and common throughout. Grey-green leaves are sword-shaped and often wrinkled. Clusters of 2–3 yellow flowers, each up to 10cm across, appear May–August.

STINKING IRIS *Iris foetidissima* Height up to 60cm
Tufted perennial of scrub and woods, mostly on calcareous soils. Locally common only in S England and S Wales. Sword-shaped leaves are dark green and have an unpleasant smell. Purplish flowers, 70–80mm across, May–July. Seeds bright orange.

WILD GLADIOLUS *Gladiolus illyricus* Height up to 80cm
Perennial of open woods and heath. Only in the New Forest, but there locally common, often under bracken. Grey-green, narrow, grass-like leaves are easy to overlook when flowers absent. 3–8 pink-purple flowers, 30–40mm across, in spikes June–July.

LORDS-AND-LADIES *Arum maculatum* Height up to 50cm
Perennial of woods and hedgerows. Locally common S Britain and S Ireland; scarce further N. Leaves arrow-shaped and shiny, sometimes purple-spotted. Flowers with purple, rod-like spadix shrouded by cowl-like spathe; April–May. Berries red.

BEE ORCHID *Ophrys apifera* Height up to 30cm
Locally common in dry grassland, mostly on calcareous soils in England, Wales and S Ireland; scarce or absent further N. Leaves form a basal rosette and two sheathing leaves appear up stem. Flowers, 12mm across, comprise pink sepals, green upper petals; expanded, furry lower petal maroon with pale yellow markings giving it a fanciful resemblance to a bumblebee. Borne in spikes, June–July.

FLY ORCHID *Ophrys insectifera* Height up to 40cm
Intriguing, rather slender plant of dry grassland, open woodland and scrub on calcareous soils. Locally common in England and Wales, rare in Ireland and absent from Scotland. Oval, glossy leaves appear as a basal rosette and up stem. The superficially insect-like flowers comprise greenish sepals and thin, brown and antennae-like upper petals; lower petal is elongated with two side lobes and is maroon with a metallic blue patch. Flowers borne in open spikes, May–June.

EARLY-PURPLE ORCHID *Orchis mascula* Height up to 40cm
Widespread and locally common orchid of woodland, scrub and grassland, doing especially well on neutral or calcareous soils. Rosettes of glossy, dark green leaves with dark spots, appear from January onwards from which the flower stalk arises later in spring. The pinkish purple flowers are borne in tall spikes, April–June; the lower lip is 3-lobed, 8–12mm long, and there is a long spur.

GREEN-WINGED ORCHID *Orchis morio* Height up to 40cm
Locally common plant of undisturbed grassland, found in C and S England, S Wales and C Ireland. Unmarked glossy green leaves form a basal rosette and sheathe the flowering stem. The flowers are borne in a compact spike, April–June, and vary from pink-purple to almost white. Upper petals in particular are marked with dark veins and often suffused green; the lip has red-dotted, pale central patch.

BURNT ORCHID *Orchis ustulata* Height up to 15cm
Scarce plant, locally common only on chalk downland in S England. The dull green oval leaves form basal rosette and sheathe flower stem. Flowers, which appear May–June, are borne in compact, somewhat cylindrical spikes; they are maroon in bud, at tip, but whitish when open. The result is a burnt look, reminiscent of intact cigarette ash. In close-up, flowers have maroon hood and red-spotted white lip.

LADY ORCHID *Orchis purpurea* Height up to 75cm
An impressive orchid of woods and scrub, mostly on chalk. Locally common in a few sites in Kent and very rare in locations elsewhere in S England. Broad, oval leaves form a basal rosette and loosely sheathe the flowering stem. Flower spike, 10–15cm tall, is cylindrical with flowers opening from the bottom. In close-up, flowers have a dark red hood and pale pink, red-spotted lip; appear April–June.

COMMON TWAYBLADE *Listera ovata* Height up to 50cm
Distinctive orchid of woodlands and grasslands on a wide range of soil types; it is widespread and generally rather common. A pair of broad, oval basal leaves appear well before the flowering stem, from March onwards. The yellowish green flowers are borne in a loose spike, May–July; the lower lip is deeply-forked.

MAN ORCHID *Aceras anthropophorum* Height 25cm
Scarce and very local orchid of calcareous grassland and scrub. Restricted to parts of SE and E England. Oval, fresh green leaves form a basal rosette and sheathe the lower part of the flowering stem. Unusual flowers have a pronounced green hood, comprising sepals and upper petals, and an elongated, 4-lobed yellow lower lip, fancifully resembling a man. Flowers borne in tall spikes May–June.

PYRAMIDAL ORCHID *Anacamptis pyramidalis* Height up to 30cm
Attractive orchid of dry grassland, usually on calcareous soils, and stabilised sand dunes. Locally common in parts of England, Wales and Ireland but commonest in the SE. The leaves are grey-green, lanceolate and usually carried upright, partially sheathing the flower stem. The flowers are deep pink with a 3-lobed lip and a long spur; borne in dense, conical or domed flower heads, June–August.

FRAGRANT ORCHID *Gymnadenia conopsea* Height up to 40cm
Robust orchid found on both dry and damp grassland, mostly on calcareous soils. Locally common in many parts of the region but commonest in the S and SE. Short leaves are found at the base of the plant and a few, very narrow leaves are borne up the stem. The highly fragrant flowers are usually pink although plants can vary from purple to almost white; the lip is 3-lobed and there is a long spur. They are produced in tall spikes, up to 15cm long, and appear June–July.

FROG ORCHID *Coeloglossum viride* Height up to 20cm
An often rather short and compact orchid of calcareous grassland, sometimes in upland areas. Widespread and very locally common throughout. Broad, oval leaves form a basal rosette and narrower leaves partially sheathe the lower part of the stem. The sepals and upper petals form a green hood and the lip is 6–8mm long and yellow-brown. The flowers are borne in an open spike and appear June–August.

COMMON SPOTTED-ORCHID *Dactylorhiza fuchsii* Height up to 60cm
Robust and familiar orchid of grassland, woodland rides and roadside verges, mostly on calcareous or neutral soils. The green, glossy leaves are indeed dark-spotted and appear as a rosette long before the flower stalk is produced; narrower leaves sheathe the lower part of the stalk. The flowers range from pale pink to pink-purple but are marked with darker streaks and spots on the lip which has three even-sized lobes and is 10mm across; in tall spikes, June–August.

HEATH SPOTTED-ORCHID *Dactylorhiza maculata* Height up to 50cm
Superficially rather similar to common spotted-orchid but restricted to damp, mostly acid soils on heaths and moors. The leaves are lanceolate and dark-spotted, those at the base of the plant being largest and broadest; narrower leaves sheathe the lower part of the stalk. The flowers are usually very pale, sometimes almost white, but have darker streaks and spots; the lower lip is broad and 3-lobed but unlike common spotted-orchid, the central lobe is smaller than the outer two. Flowers borne in open, spikes, May–August.

EARLY MARSH-ORCHID *Dactylorhiza incarnata* Height up to 60cm
Orchid of damp meadows, often on calcareous soils but also acid conditions. The leaves are unmarked, yellowish green and narrow-lanceolate. Flowers are usually flesh-pink but can range from almost white to purple. The 3-lobed flower lip is strongly reflexed along the mid-line. Flowers borne in open spikes, May–June.

SOUTHERN MARSH-ORCHID *Dactylorhiza praetermissa* Height up to 70cm
Robust orchid of water meadows, fens and wet dune-slacks, mostly on calcareous soils. Widespread and locally common in S and C England and S Wales only. Glossy leaves are dark green, unmarked and broadly lanceolate; largest ones appear at the base of plant, narrower leaves partially sheathing the stem. Flowers borne in tall, dense spikes, May–June; pinkish purple with a broad, 3-lobed lip. Replaced in N Britain by counterpart the northern marsh-orchid *D.purpurella*.

Greater Butterfly-orchid *Platanthera chlorantha* Height up to 50cm
Found in undisturbed woodland, scrub and grassland, mostly on calcareous soils. Locally common throughout. Has a single pair of large, oval leaves at base of plant and a few small stem leaves. Greenish white flowers have long, narrow lip, long spur and pollen sacs forming an inverted V; in open spikes, June–July.

Lesser Butterfly-orchid *Platanthera bifolia* Height up to 40cm
Favours undisturbed grassland, moors and woodland. Locally common throughout. Has a single pair of broad, oval leaves at base and smaller, scale-like leaves up stem. Flowers are greenish white with a long, narrow lip, a long spur and pollen sacs that are parallel; borne in rather open spikes and appear May–July.

White Helleborine *Cephalanthera damasonium* Height up to 50cm
Attractive orchid, locally common in S England in woods and scrub on calcareous soils, often under beech. Leaves are broad and oval at base of plant but become smaller up stem. Creamy flowers are 15–20mm long, each with a leafy bract; they are borne in terminal spikes and appear May–July. Flowers never open completely.

Sword-leaved Helleborine *Cephalanthera longifolia* Height up to 50cm
Distinctly local plant of woods and scrub on calcareous soils, commonest in S England. Superficially similar to white helleborine but leaves are long and narrow, largest at base of plant. Each flower appears with a leafy bract, is pure white and up to 20mm long; they are borne in spikes and appear May–June.

Marsh Helleborine *Epipactis palustris* Height up to 50cm
Attractive plant of marshes, fens and dune-slacks. Very locally common in S England, S Wales and S Ireland but scarce or absent elsewhere. Leaves are broad and oval towards base but smaller and narrower up stem. Stem and flower stalks reddish. Flowers with reddish sepals and pale, frilly lip; appear July–August.

Broad-leaved Helleborine *Epipactis helleborine* Height up to 75cm
Purple-tinged, clump-forming orchid of woods and scrub. Locally common in most parts except N Scotland. Downy stems bear broadly-oval, strongly-veined leaves. Flowers greenish, tinged with purple; borne in tall, loose spikes, July–August.

Autumn Lady's-tresses *Spiranthes spiralis* Height up to 15cm
Charming little orchid of dry grassland. Locally common in S England, Wales and S Ireland. Rosette of oval leaves appears early summer; withers before flowering stems appear August–September. Tiny white flowers borne in spiral row up stem.

Bird's-nest Orchid *Neottia nidis-avis* Height up to 35cm
Brownish fungal parasite which entirely lacks chlorophyll. Found in undisturbed woodland, often under beech. Occurs throughout except N Scotland, but locally common only in S England. Flowers, with hood and 2-lobed lip, appear May–July.

Lizard Orchid *Himantoglossum hircinum* Height up to 1m
Impressive orchid of grassland and scrub; smells of goats. Local and rare in S and E England only. Oval basal leaves soon wither. Grey-green, reddish-streaked flowers have a very long, twisted lip; borne in tall, stately spikes May–July.

Musk Orchid *Herminium monorchis* Height up to 15cm
Delicate orchid of dry, calcareous grassland. Locally common only in S England. Leaves are oval at base of plant but small and bract-like up stem. Flowers are yellowish green with narrow lobes to the lip; borne in open spikes, June–July.

Bog-orchid *Hammarbya paludosa* Height up to 8cm
Delicate, yellowish green orchid found among bog moss in floating bogs. Fairly widespread in Scotland; very local in Wales and S England, perhaps commonest in New Forest. Small, oval leaves at base. Yellowish flowers appear July–September.

WATER-MILFOIL *Myriophyllum aquaticum* Aquatic
Freshwater plant, widespread in lowland areas, favouring still waters of lakes, drainage ditches and canals. Submerged stems carry whorls of feathery, 4-times pinnately divided leaves. Emergent flower stalks with tiny flowers, June–July.

CANADIAN PONDWEED *Elodea canadensis* Aquatic
Freshwater plant, introduced from N America but now widely naturalised in ponds, lakes and canals throughout. Submerged, rather brittle stems carry narrow, back-curved, unstalked leaves in whorls of three. The flowers are tiny and seldom seen.

MARE'S-TAIL *Hippuris vulgaris* Aquatic
Widespread freshwater plant favouring ponds and lakes but avoiding acid waters. Submerged part of plant produces upright, emergent stems which carry very narrow leaves in whorls of 6–12; appearance somewhat horsetail-like. Flowers minute.

GREATER BLADDERWORT *Utricularia vulgaris* Aquatic
Intriguing freshwater plant, widespread but commonest E England in still waters. Long submerged stems with finely divided leaves and small, flask-shaped bladders which trap tiny invertebrates. Yellow flowers on emergent stems, appear July–August.

COMMON DUCKWEED *Lemna minor* Aquatic
Floating, perennial freshwater plant which often forms a carpet over the surface of suitable ponds and lakes. Widespread and locally common throughout. Leaf-like thallus, up to 5mm across, has a single, dangling root. Multiplies by division.

BROAD-LEAVED PONDWEED *Potamogeton natans* Aquatic
Freshwater plant which is widespread and often common in still or slow-flowing waters throughout. Floating leaves are dark green, broadly-oval, 10–12cm long and borne on long stems. Emergent, plantain-like flower spikes, appear May–September.

BOG PONDWEED *Potamogeton polygonifolius* Aquatic
Widespread and locally common freshwater plant, favouring boggy pools and acid waters. Has both floating and submerged, oval leaves; sometimes forms dense carpet over surface of suitable habitats. Emergent flower spikes appear May–October.

WATER HORSETAIL *Equisetum fluviatile* Height up to 1m
Grows in marshes and margins of ponds and lakes. Widespread and locally common in Britain and Ireland. Tall, unbranched stems jointed and thin with whorls of narrow, jointed branches. Spores in cone-like structures at ends of some stems.

FIELD HORSETAIL *Equisetum arvense* Height up to 75cm
The commonest horsetail, forming spreading patches in dry, grassy places and on wasteground. Produces sterile shoots with ridged stems; these carry whorls of unbranched branches. Fertile stems appear in early spring and ripen in May.

WOOD HORSETAIL *Equisetum sylvaticum* Height up to 50cm
Elegant horsetail of shady woodland and moors. Widespread but commonest in N Britain. Sterile stems resemble the growing tips of conifers, carrying whorls of slender branches which are themselves branched. Fertile stems ripen in May.

WATER FERN *Azolla filiculoides* Aquatic
Surface-floating fern. Introduced from N America but naturalised in areas of still water in S England. Fronds are yellowish green but often tinged with red and comprising small, overlapping leaves. Thread-like roots dangle below frond.

FLOATING LIVERWORT *Riccia fluitans* Aquatic
Native, surface-floating liverwort found locally in still waters of ditches and canals. Sometimes forms dense mats in suitable habitats. The fronds are narrow and regularly forked with internal air chambers affording the plant buoyancy.

SHARP RUSH *Juncus acutus* Height up to 1.5m
Robust rush found on sandy ground, including dune-slacks, around the coasts of Britain and Ireland; rare inland. The tall, narrow leaves end in a sharp spine. Clusters of reddish brown flowers are also topped by a sharp spine, June–July.

TOAD RUSH *Juncus bufonis* Height up to 40cm
Tufted annual of damp, bare ground including wheel ruts along tracks and the margins of ponds. Widespread and locally common throughout. Narrow leaves arise at the base of the plant. The flowers are borne in branched clusters, May–July.

HARD RUSH *Juncus inflexus* Height up to 1m
Perennial of damp ground. Widespread and locally common in England, Wales and Scotland. Grey-green stems are leafless and ridged. The brown flowers are borne in a loose cluster, May–July, and this is topped by a narrow, pointed bract.

COMPACT RUSH *Juncus conglomeratus* Height up to 1m
Perennial of damp, often grazed, grassland, mostly on acid soils. Widespread and common in Britain; scarce in Ireland. Ridged stems bear brown flowers in rounded clusters, May–July, topped by long bract appearing as a continuation of stem.

SALTMARSH RUSH *Juncus gerardii* Height up to 50cm
Characteristic rush of saltmarshes around the coasts of Britain and Ireland, often covering extensive areas. The dark green leaves arise at the base of the plant and on the stems. Flowers in a loose cluster flanked by shortish bracts.

SOFT RUSH *Juncus effusus* Height up to 1.5m
Tall perennial of overgrazed grassland, mostly on acid soils. Widespread and locally common throughout. Stems green and smooth-looking. Pale brown flowers are borne in a loose, rounded cluster topped by a narrow bract; seen May–July.

FIELD WOOD-RUSH *Luzula campestris* Height up to 25cm
Tufted perennial with grass-like leaves that are fringed with long white hairs. Widespread and locally common in short grassland, especially on calcareous soil. Rounded, yellow-brown flower heads are borne in clusters and appear April–May.

GREAT WOOD-RUSH *Luzula sylvatica* Height up to 75cm
Tufted, clump-forming perennial found in damp woodlands. Widespread but most common in N and W Britain and Ireland. Grass-like leaves are fringed with long white hairs. Reddish brown flowers are borne in branched clusters, April–June.

COMMON SPIKE-RUSH *Eleocharis palustris* Height up to 50cm
Creeping perennial of marshes and pond margins. Widespread and locally common throughout. Green, leafless stems arise in tufts and are topped by brown, egg-shaped spikelets which contain the flowers, May–July. Fruits are yellow-brown.

SEA CLUB-RUSH *Scirpus maritimus* Height up to 1.25m
Creeping perennial found growing at the margins of brackish water near the sea. The stems are rough and triangular in cross-section and are topped by clusters of brown spikelets, flanked by leaf-like bracts. Leaves are rough and keeled.

FLOATING CLUB-RUSH *Scirpus fluitans* Aquatic
Widespread and locally common in still or slow-flowing, usually acid, water. The narrow stems and leaves form rather tangled, floating and submerged mats. Pale, stalked and egg-shaped spikelets are borne on long, emergent stalks, May–July.

BLACK BOG-RUSH *Schoenus nigricans* Height up to 50cm
Tufted perennial of bogs, dune-slacks and marshes, usually on base-rich soils. Commonest in N and W Britain and Ireland. Long, green leaves arise at base of stems which carry flower heads comprising black spikelets flanked by long bract.

WHITE BEAK-SEDGE *Rhynchospora alba* Height up to 40cm
Tufted perennial of bogs and wet heaths on acid soils. Very local in S Britain but widespread Scotland and W Ireland. Pale green leaves arise at base of plant and on stems. Flowers comprise clusters of pale brown spikelets; seen June–September.

LESSER POND SEDGE *Carex acutiformis* Height up to 1.5m
Creeping, tuft-forming sedge which forms extensive carpets in marshes and around the margins of ponds. Widespread but commonest in C and SE England. Leaves long, blue-grey and rough. Flowers comprise 2–3 male spikes above 3–4 female spikes.

SAND SEDGE *Carex arenaria* Height up to 35cm
Creeping perennial of sand dunes and locally common on most coasts. Progress of underground stems detected by aerial shoots which appear in straight lines. The leaves are wiry and the inflorescence comprises pale brown spikes, May–July.

COMMON YELLOW SEDGE *Carex demissa* Height up to 40cm
Tufted plant of damp ground, usually on acid soils. Widespread but commonest in the N and W. Leaves narrow, curved and longer than the stems. The inflorescence comprises a terminal, stalked male spike above small clusters of female spikes.

GLAUCOUS SEDGE *Carex flacca* Height up to 50cm
Common grassland sedge, often on calcareous soils. Widespread and locally common throughout. Leaves are pale green and stiff. 3-sided stems carry inflorescence which comprises 1–3 brown male spikes above 2–5 female spikes in April–May.

COMMON SEDGE *Carex nigra* Height up to 50cm
Variable, creeping sedge of damp grassland and marshes. Common throughout. Long, narrow leaves appear in tufts. 3-sided stems rough and taller than leaves. The inflorescence has 1–2 thin male spikes and 1–4 female spikes with black glumes.

FALSE FOX SEDGE *Carex otrubae* Height up to 80cm
Tufted sedge of damp ground. Locally common in S England, mostly on heavy soils. Leaves are stiff, upright and 5–10mm wide. Robust stems are rough and 3-sided. Inflorescence comprises a dense head of greenish brown spikes and a long bract.

GREATER TUSSOCK SEDGE *Carex paniculata* Height up to 1m
Distinctive plant of marshes and fens, easily recognised throughout the year by the large tussocks that it forms. Widespread and fairly common in S Britain. The leaves are long and narrow and the inflorescence comprises pale brown spikes.

PENDULOUS SEDGE *Carex pendula* Height up to 1.5m
Clump-forming sedge of damp woodlands on heavy soils. Locally common in parts of S and E England. Leaves long, yellowish and up to 20mm wide. Tall, 3-sided and often arched stems carry 1–2 male spikes above 4–5 long, drooping female spikes.

WOOD SEDGE *Carex sylvatica* Height up to 50cm
Tufted sedge of damp woodlands. Widespread but least common in N Britain. Leaves are pale green, 3–6mm across and often appear rather drooping. The inflorescence comprises one terminal male spike and 3–5 slender, long-stalked female spikes.

PILL SEDGE *Carex pilulifera* Height up to 25cm
Tufted sedge of heaths and dry grassland on acid soils. Widespread but local except in the N and W. Leaves yellowish green, narrow and wiry. Flower head with one male spike above cluster of egg-shaped female spikes with a long lower bract.

GREAT FEN SEDGE *Cladium mariscus* Height up to 2.5m
Imposing plant which sometimes forms dense stands in fens and around the margins of lakes. Locally common only in parts of E Anglia and NW Ireland. Leaves long, saw-edged; often bent at an angle. Flower head with clusters of brown spikelets.

GALINGALE *Cyperus longus* Height up to 1.5m
Tall perennial of damp ground, marshes and dune-slacks. Local and restricted to sites in S and SW Britain. Leaves are long, rough-edged and up to 10mm across. Tall, 3-sided stems carry umbel-like inflorescence of branched flower clusters.

COMMON REED *Phragmites communis* Height up to 2m
Familiar perennial of damp ground, marshes and freshwater margins which often forms vast stands. Common throughout. Robust stems carry broad leaves and large, terminal clusters of flowers. Plants turn brown and persist through the winter.

BRANCHED BUR-REED *Sparganium erectum* Height up to 1m
Sedge-like perennial found in still and slow-flowing freshwater. Locally common throughout. The bright green, linear leaves are keeled and triangular in cross-section. The spherical flower heads are borne in branched spikes, June–August.

GREAT REEDMACE *Typha latifolia* Height up to 2m
Impressive sedge-like plant of freshwater margins. Widespread and common. The leaves are grey-green, long and up to 20mm wide. Flower spikes comprise a brown, sausage-like array of female flowers and a narrow spire of males; seen June–August.

COMMON COTTON-GRASS *Eriophorum angustifolium* Height up to 75cm
Distinctive perennial when in fruit. Favours very boggy ground with peaty, acid soils and locally common throughout. The leaves are dark green and narrow. The inflorescence comprises drooping, stalked spikelets. Fruits have cottony hairs.

HARE'S-TAIL COTTON-GRASS *Eriophorum vaginatum* Height up to 50cm
Tussock-forming perennial of moors and heaths on acid, peaty soil. Widespread and locally common in N and W Britain and Ireland. Leaves very narrow. Upright, stalked flower spike emerges from inflated sheath. Fruits with cottony hairs.

PURPLE MOOR-GRASS *Molinia caerulea* Height up to 80cm
Tussock-forming perennial, usually associated with damp ground on acid heaths and moors. Widespread and locally common. The leaves are grey-green and 3–5mm wide. Purplish green flowers are borne in long, narrow spikes, July–September.

BLACK BENT *Agrostis gigantea* Height up to 1.5m
Widespread perennial of wasteground, verges and arable fields. Commonest in C and S England. Leaves dark green, up to 6mm across with long ligules. Numerous 1-flowered, purplish brown spikelets borne in branching clusters, July–August.

BRISTLE BENT *Agrostis setacea* Height up to 50cm
Tufted perennial of heaths and moor, almost confined to SW Britain where locally common. The leaves are grey-green and hair-like and have pointed ligules. Flower heads tall and dense and comprise yellow-green spikelets which flower June–July.

CREEPING BENT *Agrostis stolonifera* Height up to 1m
Creeping perennial whose stems run along ground before becoming upright. Found on grassland and in waste places; widespread and common, especially in the S. Leaves have pointed ligules. Purplish 1-flowered spikelets appear June–August.

MARRAM GRASS *Ammophila arenaria* Height up to 1m
Familiar and widespread perennial of coastal dunes. Colonises and stabilises shifting sands by means of its underground stems. Leaves are tough, grey-green and rolled. Dense flower spikes, comprise 1-flowered spikelets; seen July–August.

SWEET VERNAL GRASS *Anthoxanthum odoratum* Height up to 50cm
Widespread and common perennial of grassland throughout the region; aromatic when dried. Leaves are flat and relatively broad. The inflorescence comprises a relatively dense, spike-like cluster of spikelets which flower April–July.

FALSE OAT-GRASS *Arrhenatherum elatius* Height up to 1.5m
Tall perennial of disturbed grassland, roadside verges and waysides generally. Widespread and very common throughout, except in uplands. Leaves are broad and long with a blunt ligule. The inflorescence is open and comprises numerous 2-flowered spikelets, one floral element of which has a long awn; seen May–September.

WILD OAT *Avena fatua* Height up to 1m
Distinctive annual weed of arable crops and also found growing on wasteground. Widespread and fairly common throughout. The leaves are dark green, broad and flat. The inflorescence is an open array of stalked, dangling spikelets each of which is shrouded by the glumes and has a long awn; flowers June–August.

QUAKING GRASS *Briza media* Height up to 40cm
Distinctive plant when in flower. Favours grassland, often on calcareous soils, and locally common in England and Wales. The pale green leaves form loose tufts. Narrow, wiry stalks carry the inflorescence of flowers, June–September; this comprises dangling spikelets which resemble miniature flattened hops or cones.

COCKSFOOT *Dactylis glomerata* Height up to 1m
Tufted, tussock-forming perennial of grassland and woodland rides. Widespread and often extremely common in most parts. Leaves rough with slightly inrolled margins. Easiest to identify in flower, May–July: inflorescence has purplish, rounded stalked flower heads which spread and fancifully resemble a bird's foot.

TUFTED HAIR-GRASS *Deschampsia caespitosa* Height up to 1.5m
Tufted, clump-forming perennial of damp grassland, woodland rides and marshes. Widespread and locally common throughout. The leaves are dark green, wiry and narrow with rough edges. The inflorescences are borne on tall stems, June–July, and comprise spreading clusters of 2-flowered, silvery-purple spikelets.

WAVY HAIR-GRASS *Deschampsia flexuosa* Height up to 1m
Tufted perennial of dry ground on heaths and moorland, usually on acid soils. Widespread and locally common in Britain; scarce in Ireland. Leaves are inrolled and hair-like. Inflorescence has open clusters of purplish spikelets, June–July.

LYME GRASS *Elymus arenarius* Height up to 1.5m
Blue-grey perennial of sand dunes and sandy beaches. Widespread and common on the E coast of Britain but more local near coasts elsewhere. Leaves up to 15mm across; margins are inrolled. Grey-green spikelets in tall spikes, June–August.

RED FESCUE *Festuca rubra* Height up to 50cm
Clump-forming grass found in grassy places throughout the region and often very common. Dark green leaves are narrow, wiry and stiff. Inflorescence comprises spikelets which are 7–10mm long and are usually reddish; flowers May–July.

VIVIPAROUS FESCUE *Festuca vivipara* Height up to 40cm
Tufted plant of grassy places on moors and mountains. Locally common only in Scotland. The leaves are thread-like and green. Instead of having flowers, stems produce tiny plantlets which develop leaves and fall off to colonise new ground.

FLOATING SWEET-GRASS *Glyceria fluitans* Floating
Aquatic grass of still and slow-flowing freshwater in lowland regions. Locally common throughout. Broad, green leaves usually seen floating on water's surface. Emergent inflorescence comprises an open array of narrow spikelets, May–August.

REED SWEET-GRASS *Glyceria maxima* Height up to 2m
Impressive plant of shallow water and marshy ground; often forms large patches. Locally common only in SE England. Bright green leaves are long and 20mm across. Inflorescence is large and much-branched with narrow spikelets; appears June–August.

YORKSHIRE FOG *Holcus lanatus* Height up to 1m
A tufted perennial which is grey-green and downy both on its leaves and stems. Widespread throughout the region and generally very common, favouring meadows, woodland rides and wasteground. Flower head tightly packed at first but then spreads; comprises reddish-tipped, grey green, 2-flowered spikelets; seen May–August.

CREEPING SOFT-GRASS *Holcus mollis* Height up to 60cm
Superficially rather similar to Yorkshire fog but more slender and has stems which are hairy only at the pale joints. Found along woodland rides and on bare ground and heaths, usually on acid soils. Widespread and common in most parts. Flower head is purplish green and compact at first but spreads; appears June–August.

WOOD MELICK *Melica uniflora* Height up to 50cm
A rather delicate, creeping perennial of dry, shady woodland, often on chalk and under beech. Widespread and locally common in England and Wales but scarce or absent elsewhere. The leaves are pale green and rather lax. The inflorescence is loose and open with brown spikelets along the side branches; flowers May–July.

SAND CATSTAIL *Phleum arenarium* Height up to 30cm
A distinctive tufted annual grass of stabilised sand and shingle. Rather scarce and found very locally around the coasts of Britain and Ireland. The leaves are grey-green and flat. The inflorescence, which is borne on a long, straight and narrow stem, is a dense head of purplish or green spikelets; flowers May–June.

LESSER CATSTAIL *Phleum bertelonii* Height up to 60cm
Similar to timothy and considered by some authorities to be a subspecies of this grass. Favours bare, grassy places, often on calcareous soils. Widespread and locally common except in the far N. The leaves are flat and grey-green. The inflorescence is a cylindrical head of spikelets, 60–80mm long; flowers June–July.

TIMOTHY *Phleum pratense* Height up to 1.5m
Extremely common tufted perennial of meadows, agricultural land and waysides generally. Found throughout the region except in the far N and often cultivated as a fodder plant. Leaves are grey-green and flat. Inflorescence 15–20cm long, dense and cylindrical; borne on a tall, slender stem and flowering June–August.

ANNUAL MEADOW-GRASS *Poa annua* Height up to 25cm
Extremely common annual or short-lived perennial grass found in bare grassland and on disturbed ground. Widespread throughout the region. The leaves are pale green, blunt-tipped and often wrinkled. Inflorescence is triangular in outline and comprises branches with oval spikelets at their tips; flowers all year.

BLUE MOOR GRASS *Sesleria albicans* Height up to 45cm
A distinctive blue-green, tufted perennial found on dry grassland on limestone soils, sometimes forming large patches. Locally common only in N England, S Scotland and W Ireland. Leaves are rather narrow. The inflorescence comprises a tightly-packed, ovoid head of blue-green spikelets which flower April–June.

SMALL CORD-GRASS *Spartina maritima* Height up to 75cm
A tufted perennial of mudflats and saltmarshes in S England. The leaves are grey-green and tough and the inflorescence comprises an elongated cluster of 2–3 flower heads; flowers July–September. Common cord-grass *S.anglica* is a hybrid between this and an introduced American species; taller and more widespread.

DEERGRASS *Scirpus cespitosus* Height up to 35cm
Tufted perennial which sometimes forms small tussocks on damp heaths and moors, favouring acid, peaty soils. Locally common in N and W Britain. The stems are dark green and rounded with a short, bract-like leaf at the base. Inflorescence comprises a single egg-shaped, brown spikelet at tip of stem; flowers May–June.

BRACKEN *Pteridium aquilinum* Height up to 2m or more
The commonest fern in the region; carpets woodland floors and covers hillsides. Favours dry, acid soils. Compact, curled-tipped fronds appear in spring. Mature fronds are green and 3-times pinnate. Spore cases borne around leaf margins.

BRITTLE BLADDER FERN *Cystopteris fragilis* Frond length up to 40cm
A delicate fern which grows in tufts arising from crevices in rocks and stone walls, mostly on limestone. Locally common in NW England and NW Scotland. The leaves are 2–3 times pinnate and appear April–October. Spore cases are rounded.

BROAD BUCKLER FERN *Dryopteris dilitata* Frond length up to 1m
Robust fern, widespread and common in Britain and Ireland, favouring damp woods, heaths and mountain slopes, usually on acid soils. Fronds are dark green and 3-times pinnately divided, the stalks with dark-centred scales; April–November.

HAY-SCENTED FERN *Dryopteris aemula* Frond length up to 50cm
Locally common only in SW England, W Scotland and W Ireland. Favours W-facing slopes and damp valleys. Fresh green fronds smell of hay when crushed; remain green through winter; 3-times pinnately divided with pale brown scales on stalk.

MALE FERN *Dryopteris filix-mas* Frond length up to 1.25m
Large, clump-forming fern of woods and banks. Common and widespread throughout. Fronds remain green through winter; broadly oval in outline, 2-times pinnately divided and with pale brown scales on stalk. Spore cases round, August–October.

SCALY MALE FERN *Dryopteris affinis* Frond length up to 1m
Locally common in N and W Britain and Ireland. Favours shady woods, usually on acid soils. The yellow-green fronds do not overwinter. Stalks have orange-brown scales; margins of smaller frond lobes look as though cut neatly with scissors.

HARD FERN *Blechnum spicant* Frond length up to 60cm
Distinctive fern of woods and shady heaths on acid soils which is locally common throughout. Bright green, sterile, overwintering fronds are 1-pinnate and form spreading clumps. Fertile fronds are borne upright and have very narrow lobes.

HARTSTONGUE *Phyllitis scolopendrium* Frond length up to 60cm
Evergreen fern of damp, shady woods and banks. Fairly widespread but commonest in W of Britain and Ireland. Fresh green, undivided fronds are strap-like and form clumps. Dark brown spore cases are borne in rows on underside of fronds.

LADY FERN *Athyrium filix-femina* Frond length up to 1.5m
Large but rather delicate fern, forming large clumps in damp woods and on banks and hillsides. Widespread and fairly common throughout. Fronds are pale green and 2-times pinnately divided. The spore cases are curved and ripen in autumn.

PARSLEY FERN *Cryptogramma crispa* Frond length up to 25cm
Parsley-like fern which grows among rocks on mountain slopes, mostly on acid rocks. Widespread and mostly scarce but locally common in Snowdonia and Lake District. Pale green fronds form clustered tufts; stalks have basal scales.

COMMON POLYPODY *Polypodium vulgare* Frond length up to 50cm
Characteristic fern of damp, shady gorges and banks in woods and valleys, mostly on acid soils. Widespread, commonest in W Britain and Ireland. The dark green, leathery fronds are 1-pinnate on slender stalks. Appear in May and overwinter.

RUSTYBACK *Ceterach officinarum* Frond length up to 20cm
Distinctive fern of stone walls and rocks. Widespread but common only in SW England, W Wales and Ireland. The dark green fronds are pinnately divided into rounded lobes and form tufted clumps; underside covered in rusty-brown scales.

MAIDENHAIR SPLEENWORT *Asplenium trichomanes* Frond length up to 15cm
Charming and distinctive fern walls and rocks. Grows in tufts, and fronds comprise black, thread-like midrib bearing numerous pairs of small, oval leaflets. Widespread in Britain and Ireland but most common in W.

WALL-RUE *Asplenium ruta-muraria* Frond length up to 12cm
Delicate little fern found growing on stone walls and rocks, often in areas of limestone. Widespread but commonest in W Britain and Ireland. Evergreen fronds dull green and 2-times pinnately divided into oval lobes with spores beneath.

ADDERSTONGUE *Ophioglossum vulgatum* Height up to 20cm, often shorter
Intriguing fern found growing in damp, undisturbed grassland and dune-slacks. Widespread but local and seldom common. Frond is bright green, oval and borne upright on a short stalk. Spores are borne terminally on a tall fertile spike.

MOONWORT *Botrychium lunaria* Height up to 20cm
Unusual fern of grassy moors, mountain slopes and undisturbed meadows which is widespread but seldom common. The single stalk bears a solitary frond, pinnately divided into 3–9 rounded lobes. Spores are borne on a divided, fertile spike.

STAGSHORN CLUBMOSS *Lycopodium clavatum* Height up to 10cm
Creeping evergreen with long, trailing stems; these and the branched, fancifully antler-like, upright stems cloaked in pointed, scale-like leaves. Cones borne on long stalks. Found on moors and mountains in N Wales, N England and Scotland.

FIR CLUBMOSS *Huperzia selago* Height up to 10cm
Tufted, upright clubmoss with stems cloaked in green, needle-like leaves giving it more than a passing resemblance to a young conifer. Spore cases borne on stem. Favours dry, grassy moors and upland slopes, common only in Scotland.

Dicranella heteromalla Height up to 3cm
A widespread and often extremely common moss found on bare ground on tracks and along woodland rides; favours neutral to acid soils. The leaves are narrow, slightly curved and pointed. The ripe capsule is brown and held at an angle

Caligeron cuspidatum Height up to 4cm
Widespread and common moss of both dry, chalk grassland and in damp ground such as lawns. Typically appears yellow-green and has pointed tips to the shoots. Leaves, pressed together when young, can give it a rather bedraggled appearance.

CATHERINE'S MOSS *Atrichium undulatum* Height up to 5cm
Common and widespread moss of woodlands, found on most soil types except chalk. The long, narrow leaves are dark green and have wavy, toothed-edged margins. The curved, brown spore capsules are borne on long stalks and are held at an angle.

Eurhynchium praelongum Spreading
An extremely common moss of shady woodlands in most parts; often found growing at the base of tree trunks or on ancient banks. Forms tangled, spreading mats with much-branched stems. Yellowish leaves larger on main stems than near tips.

Brachythecium rutabulum Height up to 4cm
Extremely common lawn moss on damp ground but also found growing in woodland and on banks. Branching stems are covered with shiny, oval, pointed leaves; usually dark green but are sometimes tinged yellow. Capsule curved and long-stalked.

Bryum capillare Height up to 3cm
A common and widespread moss which forms compact and distinctive cushions on roofs and walls. The oval leaves are tipped with a fine point. The elongate-ovoid spore capsules are long-stalked and drooping; green ripening to brown.

Fissidens taxifolius Height up to 2cm
A widespread and fairly common moss of damp, shady places. Forms rather tangled and straggly masses. The stems carry oval, pointed-tipped leaves which are usually more-or-less in one plane, giving the shoots a superficially yew-like appearance. Narrow spore capsules are borne on stalks arising near plant base.

Grimmia pulvinata Height up to 3cm
A distinctive moss which is common and widespread in many parts of the region, especially in limestone areas. Forms compact cushions which are found on walls and roofs. The leaves are narrow and grey green; the greyish, pointed tips can sometimes give whole cushion a silvery appearance, especially in dry weather.

Homalothecium sericeum Height up to 2cm
A common and widespread moss, found growing in a wide range of sites including old brick and stone walls and at the base of tree trunks. The stems are much-branched and mat-forming, covered with narrow, finely-tipped leaves with have a rather glossy appearance. In dry weather, the plant stems curl and turn brown.

Hypnum cupressiforme Spreading
An extremely common and widespread moss found in most parts of the region. It typically forms flattened clusters or mats at the base of tree trunks but also occurs on walls and boulders. The stems are covered with overlapping, curved leaves which are oval and pointed. The spore capsule is borne on a short stalk.

WHITE FORK MOSS *Leucobryum glaucum* Height up to 4cm
An extremely distinctive moss of damp woodland and moors. It often forms large cushions on the ground which are, unfortunately, easily dislodged. Leaves are narrow and grey-green but become almost white in dry weather. Larger specimens of cushions may become eroded towards the centre, exposing older, dead parts.

Polytrichum commune Height up to 20cm
A comparatively large, upright moss found on moorland and in damp woodland, mostly on acid soils. The narrow, needle-like leaves are pointed and held almost at right-angles to the stems, giving plant a rather clubmoss-like appearance. Box-shaped spore capsules are brown when ripe and held on tall, slender stems.

WOOLLY HAIR MOSS *Rhacomitrum lanuginosum* Height up to 2cm
An important and locally dominant moss of mountain tops. Where not trampled, it is a spreading plant which sometimes forms deep carpets covering surprisingly large areas. Long, branched stems are covered with narrow, grey-green leaves which are tipped with a white, hair-like point. Spore capsules seldom produced.

BOG MOSS *Sphagnum recurvum* Height up to 5cm
One of several closely related, and difficult to distinguish, species of bog mosses, most of which favour wet, peaty ground. This species is typical of the wetter parts of heathland bogs. It can sometimes be picked out at a distance by the fresh green colour of its leaves. The leaf tips become recurved when dry.

Thuidium tamariscinum Spreading
A very distinctive moss whose fresh green fronds are 3-times pinnately divided, in one plane, giving them a feathery or fern-like appearance. The main stems are dark. Typically found in woodlands, where it grows beside fallen branches and among leaf-litter, and on shady banks; widespread and common in most parts.

Tortula muralis Height up to 1cm
A widespread and often extremely common moss. It is found growing on old brick walls and on rocks where it forms low, but spreading, cushions. Oval, rounded-tipped leaves end in a fine point. Spore capsules are narrow and held upright, borne on long, slender stalks; they are yellow when young but ripen brown.

Lophocolea heterophylla Spreading
A superficially moss-like liverwort which is found growing on the bark of living trees and fallen branches. Widespread and common in deciduous woodland habitats throughout. Stems branching and trailing, up to 2cm long. Leaves in two forms, the smaller leaves being almost hidden by larger, toothed-tipped, overlapping ones.

Anthoceros laevis Spreading
A common and widespread liverwort of damp ground, often found on shady banks beside woodland streams and ditches. The plant comprises a broad and flattened thallus with lobed margins; it is often divided with the lobes overlapping one another and the surface is minutely pitted. Attached by rootlets to the ground.

Conocephalum conicum Spreading
A large, carpeting liverwort which is widespread and common on damp rocks and stones, often in or beside woodland streams and rivers. The plant comprises a broad or narrow fleshy thallus which is dark green, sometimes up to 15cm long; lobes often overlap. On close inspection, thallus surface marked with pale dots.

Marchantia polymorpha Spreading
A common and widespread liverwort found typically on the shady banks of streams and rivers but also frequently found growing on well-watered compost of potted garden centre plants. It comprises a divided, dark green thallus the lobes of which often overlap one another. Surface bears shallow cups and umbrella-shaped reproductive structures: female stalked and rayed and male toadstool-like.

Metzgeria furcata Spreading
A common and widespread liverwort, found growing on tree trunks, rocks and walls in shady places. Plant comprises a long, narrow thallus barely 2mm wide. Only one cell thick except for the midrib which is thickened, resembling a miniature seaweed.

Plagiochila asplenioides Spreading
A delicate, leafy liverwort which is found growing on damp, shady banks; it is widespread and fairly common. Oval, overlapping leaves are borne in two rows on a thickened stem; plant resembles a miniature version of maidenhair spleenwort.

Pellia epiphylla Spreading
Familiar, patch-forming liverwort of damp, shady banks, often beside streams. Common and widespread. The broad, flattened and branched thallus has a thickened midrib. Round, black and shiny capsules, on green stalks, appear in spring.

Caloplaca marina Encrusting
Bright orange lichen forming irregular patches up to 50mm across on rocks around high-water mark on the seashore. Tolerant of salt spray and brief immersion in seawater. Widespread around coasts of Britain and Ireland; commonest in the W.

Cladonia floerkeana Spreading
Familiar lichen of bare peaty ground on heaths and moors. Widespread and locally common. Forms an encrusting patch of greyish white scales from which granular, scale-encrusted stalks arise, topped with bright red, spore-producing bodies.

Cladonia impexa Spreading
A common lichen of heaths and moors. Comprises a tangled network of hollow, branched stems which sometimes form dense, thick cushions or mats where not trampled. These are found growing in amongst the stems of plants such as ling.

Lobaria pulmonaria Spreading
Large, lobed lichen of woodlands in areas of high rainfall and low pollution; mainly SW and W coasts of Britain. Grows attached to the bark of trees and forms spreading sheets, pitted with depressions. Sometimes known as tree lungwort.

Graphis scripta — Up to 15mm across

A distinctive, encrusting lichen found on the bark of deciduous trees including hazel and ash. It forms an irregularly rounded patch which is blue-grey or green-grey in colour. Over the surface of this are spore-producing structures in the form of black lines and scribbles which, on close inspection, are slit-like.

Hypogymnia physodes — Up to 25mm across

A common lichen in most parts of Britain and Ireland. Often found growing on twigs and branches but also on rocks and walls. Although much-branched, forms an encrusting, irregularly rounded patch, smooth and grey on the upper surface.

BLACK SHIELDS *Lecanora atra* — Spreading

A patch-forming lichen which is found encrusting boulders and rocks on the seashore, at and just above the high-tide mark; not surprisingly, it is tolerant of salt spray. Also grows on walls inland. The surface is knobbly and grey while the spore-producing structures are rounded and black with pale grey margins.

CRAB'S-EYE LICHEN *Ochrolechia parella* — Spreading

Encrusting, patch-forming lichen found on walls and rocks; mainly in uplands and W Britain. Surface is greyish with a pale margin. Clusters of raised, rounded and flat-topped spore-producing structures give rise to its common English name.

Parmelia caperata — Spreading

An encrusting lichen which is found growing on the bark of mature trees. Although widespread, it is commonest in those parts of S Britain that are relatively free from air pollution. Patches are grey-green and comprise rounded, often overlapping lobes; surface has brown, flat-topped, spore-producing discs.

Placynthium nigrum — Spreading

An encrusting, patch-forming lichen which is found growing on limestone as well as on weathered concrete. The surface is black and granular, and often faintly cracked in places. This species' colour and irregular shape give it a passing resemblance to a splash of black paint. It is widespread and locally common.

SEA IVORY *Ramalina siliquosa* — Tufts up to 3cm long

A tufted and branched lichen which is found on coastal rocks and stone walls. It grows well above the high-tide mark but is still very tolerant of salt spray. Widespread around most coasts but particularly abundant in W Britain. The branches are flattened and grey, and bear disc-like spore-producing bodies.

MAP LICHEN *Rhizocarpon geographicum* — Spreading

An aptly-named, encrusting lichen found on rocks in uplands and mountains. The surface is yellowish and etched with black spore-producing bodies. When two neighbouring colonies meet, the boundaries between them are defined by their black margins, creating a map-like appearance. The effect is further enhanced if map lichen colonies adjoin lichen species whose surfaces are a different colour.

YELLOW SCALES *Xanthoria parietina* — Spreading

Arguably the most familiar and certainly most colourful coastal lichen which forms bright orange-yellow patches on rocks, walls and brickwork near the sea. The surface of the encrustation comprises leafy, narrow scales which are rather wrinkled. Yellow scales is widespread around coasts of Britain and Ireland.

Verrucaria maura — Spreading

An encrusting lichen which is found growing on rocks and stabilised shingle around the coasts of Britain and Ireland. It is often found just above the barnacle zone and is tolerant of periodic immersion in seawater as well as salt spray. The surface is sooty black and covered with a delicate network of cracks. As a sad indictment of modern times, this species is sometimes mistaken for oil.

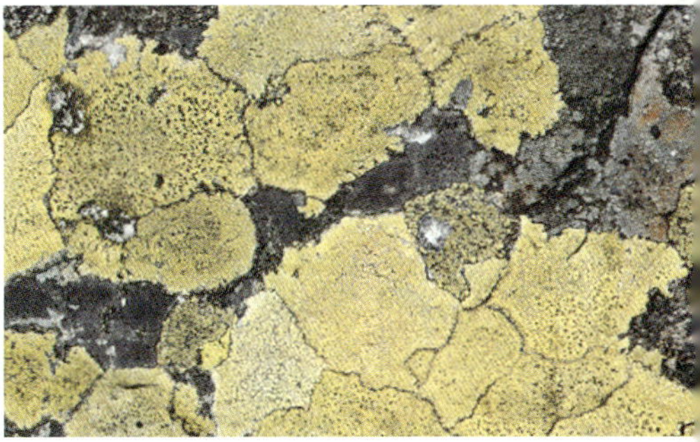

EGG WRACK OR KNOTTED WRACK *Ascophyllum nodosum* Length up to 150cm
Found on sheltered rocky shores where it grows between the upper- and middle shore levels. Widespread around the coasts of Britain and Ireland and is sometimes abundant in suitable habitats. The long, greenish stems are tough, leathery and flat. Air bladders are found at regular intervals along the stems which also branch repeatedly. The yellowish green reproductive bodies resemble sultanas.

GUTWEED *Enteromorpha intestinalis* Length up to 75cm or more
An aptly-named seaweed found in sheltered estuaries, brackish lagoons and rock pools on the upper shore. The fronds are membranous and green, and comprise long tubes which soon become inflated; these are occasionally constricted along their length, adding to their already gut-like appearance. Sometimes attached to the substrate by a holdfast but often detached and then forming floating masses.

SERRATED WRACK *Fucus serratus* Length up to 65cm
Common and widespread seaweed around the coasts of Britain and Ireland which grows attached to rocks on the lower middle shore. Fronds are greenish brown and flattened, but with a distinct midrib; they branch regularly along their length and have margins which are diagnostically toothed or serrated. Air bladders are absent. The reproductive bodies are found in pitted, swollen tips to the fronds.

SPIRAL WRACK *Fucus spiralis* Length up to 35cm
A familiar seaweed found growing attached to rocks on the upper shore. Common and widespread around the coasts of Britain and Ireland but absent from the most exposed shores. The frond branches regularly along its length and is typically twisted in a spiral fashion towards the tip; the margin is not serrated and the species lacks air bladders. Rounded reproductive bodies are found at frond tips.

BLADDER WRACK *Fucus vesiculosus* Length up to 1m
A tough seaweed which is found growing, attached to rocks, on the middle shore. It is widespread and common around the coasts of Britain and Ireland although often absent from the most exposed sites. The frond is olive- or greenish brown and branches regularly. Air bladders are found in groups of two or three along the seaweed's length and spongy reproductive bodies occur at the tips of the fronds.

THONGWEED *Himanthalia elongata* Length up to 2m
A distinctive seaweed which starts life as a short button-shaped structure found growing from the holdfast attached to rocks on the lower shore. Later in the season, a long, slightly flattened and strap-like frond develops, this being forked only towards the tapering tip; the frond colour is olive-green. Thongweed is widespread and common on the S and W coasts of Britain and around Ireland.

KELP OR OARWEED *Laminaria digitata* Length up to 1m
An impressive seaweed which often forms dense beds on the lower shore with only the floating fronds and not the stipe exposed at most low tides. It is olive-brown and comprises a branched and tough holdfast, home to small marine animals, a robust, flexible stipe, and a broad blade, divided into strap-like fronds.

CHANNELLED WRACK *Pelvetia canaliculata* Length up to 15cm
A distinctive seaweed which forms a zone on the upper shore around rocky coasts. Fronds are olive-brown and much branched. Inrolled margins help conserve water when seaweed is exposed to air for long periods at neap tides. The species lacks air bladders; reproductive bodies at frond tips. Widespread and mostly common.

SEA-LETTUCE *Ulva lactuca* Length up to 40cm
Delicate green and membranous seaweed which is found growing attached to rocks on sheltered shores; often thrives in rock pools on upper and middle shores, even if detached from substrate. The seaweed's precise shape can be difficult to determine because of its often tattered appearance. Tolerates brackish water.

ORANGE PEEL FUNGUS *Aleuria aurantia* Up to 8cm across
Extremely distinctive fungus which comprises a wavy-edge, saucer-shaped disc. Upper surface is bright orange and smooth while the lower surface is greyish orange and rather powdery. Grows on bare ground, September–November. Widespread.

WHITE HELVELLA *Helvella crispa* Height up to 15cm
Unusual-looking fungus with a strangely convoluted and distorted cap resembling melted plastic. Cap is creamy white and is usually slightly paler than the stem which is greyish white and deeply furrowed. Found on rides and verges in autumn.

CANDLE SNUFF FUNGUS *Xylaria hypoxylon* Height up to 5cm
Widespread and common fungus in deciduous woodlands. Flattened, antler-shaped stems arise from dead wood; they start off white but gradually blacken as they mature. Usually found in clusters on stumps. Can be found throughout the year.

KING ALFRED'S CAKE *Daldinia concentrica* Up to 5cm across
Forms hard, knobbly balls on the bark of dead and dying branches of deciduous trees, particularly on ash. Surface is usually shiny black and the fungus is brittle. Concentric rings revealed in cross-section. Widespread. Found all year.

CORAL-SPOT FUNGUS *Nectria cinnabarina* Up to 2mm across
Tiny but distinctive fungus which form clusters of orange-pink inflated cushions and cinnabar-red lumps on the dead and dying twigs and branches of deciduous trees. It is widespread and often very common; can be found throughout the year.

BIRCH POLYPORE *Piptoporus betulinus* Up to 20cm across
Familiar bracket fungus which is found exclusively on the trunks of birch trees. The fungus is semi-circular and up to 4cm thick. The upper surface is buffish brown while the underside is white with tiny pores. Widespread. Found all year.

MANY-ZONED POLYPORE *Coriolus versicolor* Up to 7cm across
Extremely common bracket fungus which grows on dead stumps and fallen branches of deciduous trees, often in tiers. Each bracket is semi-circular; upper surface is zoned with concentric rings of different colours. Widespread. Found all year.

CHANTERELLE *Cantharellus cibarius* Height up to 10cm
Well-known autumn fungus. Edible and delicious, smelling of apricots. The cap is bright yellow and rounded at first but becoming funnel-shaped with age. Gill-like ribs run down stem which is short and tapering. Locally common in woodland.

BLUSHING BRACKET *Daedaleopsis confragosa* Up to 18cm across
Widespread and common bracket fungus on dead branches of willow, sallow and birch. Upper surface is concentrically zoned with brown and buff. Underside has white pores which bruise reddish and darken with age. Found September–November.

DRYAD'S SADDLE *Polyporus squamosus* Up to 50cm across
Imposing and often massive polypore fungus which forms tiered brackets on ash, elm and other deciduous trees. Appears June–September. Upper surface is creamy buff, covered in dark brown scales. Lower surface creamy white with large pores.

HOOF FUNGUS *Fomes fomentarius* Up to 30cm across
Tough and rigid fungus which looks surprisingly like a hoof. It is found growing on the trunks of birch trees and is more-or-less confined to the Highlands of Scotland. The grey surface bears darker, horizontal ridges. Found all year.

HAIRY STEREUM *Stereum hirsutum* Up to 4cm across
Forms irregular tiers of rubbery but tough brackets which have wavy margins and are about 1mm thick. Although variable, lower surface colour is usually orange-yellow; upper surface greyish and hairy. Widespread on dead wood. All year.

Crepidotus variabilis Up to 3cm across
Widespread and fairly common woodland fungus which forms kidney-shaped brackets on fallen twigs and other debris from deciduous trees. The upper surface is pale cream and downy while the lower surface has pale gills which become pink-buff.

OYSTER FUNGUS *Pleurotus ostreatus* Up to 13cm across
Edible and delicious fungus which forms tiers of brackets on the trunks of beech and other deciduous trees. The upper surface is greyish buff and smooth while the lower surface has whitish gills. Widespread and locally common in autumn.

HONEY FUNGUS *Armillaria mellea* Height up to 15cm
Widespread and common woodland fungus found on tree stumps; also parasitises living trees, sometimes killing them. Cap brown and slightly scaly; domed but expands and flattens with age. Gills pale buff. Stem has a ring. Appears autumn.

WOOD BLEWIT *Lepista nuda* Height up to 8cm
Edible fungus found in deciduous woodlands and hedgerows. The cap is smooth and buffish lilac; conical at first but expands and flattens irregularly with age. The gills are lilac-purple and the stem is streaked lilac. Widespread in autumn.

CLOUDED AGARIC *Clitocybe nebularis* Height up to 12cm
Widespread and common fungus of deciduous woodland; appears October–November. Cap is blue-grey, usually paler towards the edges, rounded at first but flattens with age. The gills are creamy and decurrent and the stem expands towards base.

THE DECEIVER *Laccaria laccata* Height up to 8cm
Variable fungus found among leaf litter in deciduous and coniferous woodlands, July–October. Widespread and common. Cap usually orange-brown and irregularly rounded. Gills pinkish buff and stem twisted, fibrous and concolorous with cap.

AMETHYST DECEIVER *Laccaria amethystea* Height up to 9cm
Attractive fungus of deciduous woodland leaf litter which is wholly lilac or purple. Widespread and locally common. Cap domed at first; expands and flattens irregularly with age. Gills widely spaced. Twisted stem has white basal hairs.

BUTTER CAP/GREASY TOUGH SHANK *Collybia butyracea* Height up to 8cm
Most easily identified by cap's greasy, buttery texture. Widespread and common in both deciduous and coniferous woodland. Gills and flesh are whitish. Tough stem is pale brown, tapers upwards and is bulbous at the base. Appears autumn.

FAIRY-RING CHAMPIGNON *Marasmius oreades* Height up to 10cm
Typical ring-forming fungus, these being found on lawns and grassland. Cap is usually pale buffish tan but is sometimes stained darker. Gills white and widely spaced and flesh is white. Stem concolorous with cap. Widespread in autumn.

PORCELLAIN FUNGUS *Oudemansiella mucida* Up to 7cm across
Distinctive fungus which is white, slimy and translucent. Found growing on dying and fallen branches of deciduous trees, mainly beech; attached by slender stem of variable length. Gills are widely spaced. Widespread, September–November.

FLY AGARIC *Amanita muscaria* Height up to 20cm
Our most familiar toadstool. Widespread and common, always associated with birch and found on heaths and in mixed woodland. Red cap is covered with white flecks. Gills white and stem white with a ring. In troops, August–November. Poisonous.

FALSE DEATH CAP *Amanita citrina* Height up to 8cm
Widespread and fairly common fungus of deciduous woodland, often under beech. Cap is whitish or yellowish but often bears tatty remains of veil. Gills white and flesh white, smelling of raw potatoes. Stem has ring and is swollen at base.

Tawny Grisette *Amanita fulva* Height up to 12cm
Distinctive autumn fungus which is found growing in deciduous woodlands, often under oaks. Tawny brown cap is sometimes marked with radial streaks around the margin. Gills and flesh white. Stem, which has no ring, is tall. Widespread.

Death Cap *Amanita phalloides* Height up to 10cm
Highly poisonous fungus. Appears September–November in deciduous woods, mainly under beech or oak. Has a sickly sweet smell. Cap is tinged green. Gills and flesh white. White stem has ring; base surrounded by sac-like volva. Widespread.

The Blusher *Amanita rubescens* Height up to 15cm
Widespread and common fungus of deciduous woodland which appears August–October. Cap is pale buffish brown and covered with pinkish grey fragments of veil. Gills white. Stem has a ring and usually flushes pinkish buff, especially near base.

Volvariella speciosa Height up to 12cm
Superficially like *Agaricus* species. Locally abundant on manure-enriched fields and other fertile sites, July–September. Cap is sticky when wet; domed at first but flattens with age. Gills are pink and stem has a swollen base. Widespread.

Parasol Mushroom *Lepiota procera* Height up to 30cm
Large and familiar fungus, found in grassy places July–October. Cap is pale buff and marked with brown scales; egg-shaped when young but flattens with age. Gills white and stem brown with scale-like patterns. Edible and good. Widespread.

Lepiota mastoidea Height up to 25cm
Similar to closely related parasol mushroom but stem cleaner-looking. Widespread but rather scarce, found in grassy woodland rides and field edges. Pale cap is marked with brown scales, densest at centre. Gills white. Appears in autumn.

Wood Mushroom *Agaricus silvicola* Height up to 10cm
Edible and delicious mushroom found in both deciduous and coniferous woodland, September–November. Smells of aniseed. Cap smooth and white but bruises yellow. Gills and flesh are pinkish. Stem has ring and bulbous base. Locally common.

Field Mushroom *Agaricus campestris* Height up to 8cm
Familiar mushroom of pastures and grassland generally, appearing July–October. Cap is pale buffish brown and gills pink at first but darken brown. Flesh smells mushroomy. Stem has ring which is easily lost. Widespread and locally common.

Shaggy Ink Cap *Coprinus comatus* Height up to 30cm
Distinctive fungus, seen in troops on roadside verges and other grassy places, August–October. At first, cap egg-shaped and whitish with shaggy fibres; shrouds stem. Expands with age and, together with gills, blackens and liquefies. Common.

Sulphur Tuft *Hypholoma fasciculare* Height up to 8cm
Extremely common and widespread fungus, found growing in often large clumps on the dead stumps and fallen branches of deciduous trees. Appears June–November. Cap sulphur-yellow, darker in centre. Gills and flesh yellow. Stem often curved.

Panaeolus sphinctrinus Height up to 10cm
Widespread and locally common fungus found growing on dung or manure-enriched ground. Appears almost throughout the year. Cap is conical and grey-brown but pale buff when dry; margin fringed with veil 'teeth'. Stem slender and brown.

Cortinarius crocolitus Height up to 18cm
Impressive fungus. Widespread and locally in deciduous woodland, usually under birch. Cap yellow with small scales at centre and sometimes feels sticky. Gills white but mature buff. Stem yellow and robust with bulbous base. August–October.

CEP *Boletus edulis* Height up to 25cm
Edible and delicious fungus, found in deciduous woodland, usually under oak or beech, August–November. Cap is brown and often dimpled and lobed. Pores are white at first, becoming creamy or yellow. Stem is fat and bulbous. Widespread.

RED-CRACKING BOLETE *Boletus chrysenteron* Height up to 10cm
Distinctive fungus of deciduous woodland which is widespread and locally common August–November. The cap is buffish brown at first but soon cracks, especially around the margins, to reveal red flesh. Pores buffish yellow. Stem flushed red.

BAY BOLETE *Boletus badius* Height up to 15cm
Widespread and fairly common fungus of both deciduous and coniferous woodland. Appears September–November. Cap colour ranges from tan to buff. Pores are yellow but bruise bluish green. White flesh flushes blue when cut. Stem often tapers.

ORANGE BIRCH BOLETE *Leccinum versipelle* Height up to 25cm
Impressive fungus, almost always associated with birch and seen August–November. Cap is orange-brown and domed, margin sometimes overlapping pores which are greyish white. Flesh white but blackens when cut. Stem white with dark scales.

Suillus variegatus Height up to 12cm
Widespread and locally common fungus, restricted to conifer woodlands; appears September–November. Cap is brown and domed at first but flattens irregularly with age; slightly scaly but slimy when wet. Pores dark brown. Stem yellowish.

COMMON YELLOW RUSSULA *Russula ochroleuca* Height up to 10cm
Colourful and very common fungus, mostly in deciduous woods throughout lowland Britain. Cap is uniformly ochre-yellow; domed at first but flattening with age. Gills and flesh are white. Stem white and straight. Appears September–November.

BRIGHT YELLOW RUSSULA *Russula claroflava* Height up to 9cm
A very common fungus, found on damp ground in deciduous woods, mostly associated with birch. Cap is bright yellow and smooth but margins sometimes grooved. Gills and stem are off-white, flesh is white. Widespread, appearing August–November.

BLACKISH-PURPLE RUSSULA *Russula atropurpurea* Height up to 9cm
Widespread and common fungus of deciduous woodland, found mostly under oak or beech. Cap colour usually grades from almost black in centre to reddish purple around edge. Gills off-white; stem and flesh white. Appears September–November.

THE SICKENER *Russula emetica* Height up to 8cm
Colourful fungus of conifer woodlands which, as its name suggests, is poisonous. Widespread and locally common, appearing September–November. Cap is bright red; domed at first but flattened later. Gills creamy white; stem and flesh white.

STINKING RUSSULA *Russula foetans* Height up to 14cm
Widespread and common fungus, found in conifer and deciduous woodland, August–November. Cap is dirty yellow and extremely slimy and sticky when young. Often has debris stuck to cap. Creamy gills often blotched; stem stout. Rancid smell.

ROSE RUSSULA *Russula rosea* Height up to 7cm
An attractive fungus found growing in deciduous woodland, appearing September–November. Cap is pale rose-pink, the margins lined in older specimens. The gills are creamy white. Flesh and stem are whitish. Widespread and generally common.

CHARCOAL BURNER *Russula cyanoxantha* Height up to 9cm
A rather variable fungus whose cap is usually greyish lilac but often blotched with black and reddish purple. It grows in deciduous woodland and is widespread and common, July–November. Gills are white and feel slightly greasy. Stem white.

BROWN ROLL-RIM *Paxillus involutus* Height up to 12cm
Common and widespread fungus of deciduous woods, usually associated with birch. Cap colour tan to dirty brown; flattened then funnel-shaped but with margin inrolled. Gills brown and decurrent down brown stem. Appears September–November.

BLACKENING WAX-CAP *Hygrocybe nigrescens* Height up to 5cm
Widespread and common grassland fungus which appears August–October. Cap conical when young; becomes rounded with age, retaining pointed apex. Cap colour changes from orange-red to black with age. The gills and stem are yellowish orange.

WOOLLY MILK-CAP *Lactarius tomentosus* Height up to 8cm
Orange cap is marked with darker concentric rings and covered with a peach-coloured coat of woolly fibres. Widespread and common in deciduous woods, mostly under birch. Gills white. Yields white milk. Widespread and common in autumn.

Lactarius pyrogalus Height up to 6cm
Widespread and often common under hazel, especially where this is managed for coppice. The cap is buffish brown, rounded at first but funnel-shaped with age. Gills yellowish and stem pale brown. Milk white and acrid. Appears in autumn.

STINKHORN *Phallus impudicus* Height up to 15cm
Unmistakable fungus of deciduous woodland; appears May–November. Seen initially as soft, white ball, 50–60mm across, from which phallus-like fruit body emerges. Stalk's oval tip coated with stinking, spore-containing mucus; attracts flies.

COMMON PUFFBALL *Lycoperdon perlatum* Height up to 7cm
Distinctive, club-shaped fruit bodies are found in clusters growing on dead and part-buried decaying wood, September–November. Fruit body is off-white with dark spines when young; mature specimens brown and wrinkled. Widespread and common.

COMMON EARTH-STAR *Geastrum triplex* Up to 10cm across
Extraordinary-looking fungus found in woodlands, September–November. Initially, fruit body resembles an onion. Outer layer splits into 4–7 segments which fold back eventually lifting central orb off ground. Spores expelled via pore. Local.

WITCHES' BUTTER *Exidia glandulosa* Up to 4cm across
The fruit bodies comprise black, gelatinous blobs which appear in brain-like clusters on the twigs and branches of deciduous trees, especially oak. The fungus is widespread and generally common, and can be found throughout the year.

YELLOW BRAIN FUNGUS *Tremella mesenterica* Up to 8cm across
Often very distinctive, appearing as it does in winter, usually December–March. Fruit bodies are bright orange-yellow and jelly-like, forming convoluted, brain-like masses on dead twigs of deciduous trees. Widespread and generally common.

EAR FUNGUS *Hirneola auricula-judae* Up to 5cm across
Bizarre fungus with a strangely ear-like appearance. Found in clusters or tiers on dead branches of deciduous trees and shrubs, especially elder. Fruit body is reddish brown, translucent with wrinkles resembling veins. Widespread in winter.

YELLOW STAGSHORN FUNGUS *Calocera viscosa* Height up to 7cm
Distinctive fungus. Bright yellow and much-branched, the result fancifully like antlers; its colour darkens with age. Widespread and fairly common in conifer woodlands. Grows on dead stumps and part-buried fallen timber, October–November.

Ramaria stricta Height up to 7cm
Stiffly upright, highly branched fungus, found locally in deciduous and conifer woodland throughout; warm buff but often paler at tips of branches. It grows on rotting stumps and part-buried, decaying timber; appears September–November.

GLOSSARY

ABDOMEN: hind section of an insect's body; usually appears segmented

ANNELID: a type of worm (see Plant and Animal Groups)

ANNUAL: a plant that lives for a single growing season

ANTENNAE: slender, paired sensory organs on the head of an insect

ANTHER: pollen-containing structure in a flower, located on the end of the male reproductive structure, the stamen

ARBOREAL: tree-dwelling

AWN: bristle found in flowers of many grasses

AXIL: angle where upper surface of a leaf meets the stem on a plant

BALEEN: fibrous plates in the mouths of certain whale species; used for filtering food from water

BERRY: fleshy fruit containing several seeds

BIENNIAL: a plant that takes two years to complete its life cycle

BIVALVE: mollusc whose shell comprises two halve

BRACT: a small leaf- or scale-like structure beneath a flower

BULB: fleshy, underground structure found in certain plants and comprising leaf bases and next years bud

BULBIL: small, bulb-like structure

CAP: structure seen in fungi under which spore-bearing structures, usually gills or pores, are suspended

CAPSULE: structure within which seeds are formed in flowering plants and spores develop in mosses and liverworts

CARAPACE: hard, upper surface of a crustacean's shell

CARPAL: area on a bird's wing corresponding to the 'wrist' joint

CATERPILLAR: larval stage of butterfly or moth

CATKIN: flowering structure of certain trees and shrubs

CEPHALOTHORAX: fused head and thorax found in spiders

CERCI: paired appendages at hind end of an insect's body

CHLOROPHYLL: green pigment found in plant tissue and essential for photosynthesis

COMPOUND EYE: eye structure typical of insects and some other invertebrates comprising numerous cells and lenses not a single lens

CONE: structure bearing reproductive elements of conifers

CONIFER: tree which bears its reproductive structures in cones

DECIDUOUS: woody plant which sheds its leaves in winter

DISC FLORETS: small flowers found at centre of inflorescence of members of daisy family

DORSAL: upper surface

DIURNAL: active during daylight

ELYTRA: hardened forewings of a beetle

EVERGREEN: plant which retains its leaves throughout the year

FERAL: having returned to the wild

FLORET: small flower

FROND: leaf-like structure found in some lower plants

FRUIT: seeds together with their surrounding tissues

GALL: plant growth induced by another organism, often a gall wasp

GLUME: stiffened bract found on a grass flower

HAEMOGLOBIN: red pigment in blood which absorbs oxygen

HOLDFAST: root-like structure which anchors seaweeds to rocks

HYBRID: offspring from different parent species

INFLORESCENCE: combination of a flower, its bracts and flowering stems

INSECTIVORE: an organism which feeds on insects

JUVENILE: newly fledged bird which has not yet acquired adult plumage

LANCEOLATE: lance-shaped

LARVA: soft-bodied, pre-adult stage in the life-cycle of certain insect species

LEAFLET: small, separate segment of a leaf

LEK: communal display area used by certain bird species

LIGULE: membranous leaf sheath found in grasses

MELANIC: showing dark pigmentation

MIGRANT: bird which spends the summer and winter in different areas

MOULT: process seen in birds during which old feathers are lost and replaced by new ones

MUCUS: slimy, viscous fluid secretion

NOCTURNAL: active after dark

NODE: part of stem at which leaves arise

NUT: dry and often hard fruit containing a single seed

OPERCULUM: plate found in some molluscs and used to seal off entrance to shell

OVATE: roughly oval in outline

OVOID: egg-shaped

OVIPOSITOR: egg-laying structure found at the tail-end of some female insects

NEEDLE: narrow leaves found in conifers

NYMPH: pre-adult stage in certain insects, notably bugs, which has some characters in common with its adult stage

PALPS: sensory appendages found around the mouth in insects and crustaceans

PALMATE: leaf divided into lobes which fancifully resemble a hand

PARASITE: organism which lives on or in another organism, relying on it entirely for its nutrition

PASSAGE MIGRANT: bird species seen mostly on migration and which does not necessarily breed in Britain

PERENNIAL: plant which lives for more than two years

PETAL: often colourful inner row of structures surrounding reproductive part of a flower

PINNATE: leaf divided into more than three leaflets, these being arranged in pairs on either side of stem

PLANARIAN: a flatworm (see section on Plant and Animal groups)

POLLEN: minute grains produced by anthers and containing male sex cells

PRONOTUM: hardened dorsal plate covering the thorax of an insect

PUPA: stage in an insect's life-cycle between the larva and adult; also called the chrysalis

RAY FLORETS: small flowers found on the outer fringe of the inflorescence in flowers of the daisy family

RHIZOME: underground stem

ROSETTE: radiating arrangement of leaves

RUNNER: creeping stem which occurs above ground and may root at nodes or tip

SEPAL: outer row of structures surrounding the reproductive part of a flower

SOLE: underside of the foot in molluscs

SPADIX: upright spike of florets, found in arums

SPATHE: large bract surrounding spadix in arums

SPECIES: unit of classification defining animals or plants which are able to breed with one another and produce viable offspring

SPECULUM: species-specific patch of colour seen on ducks' wings

SPIKE: simple, branched inflorescence

SPIKELET: inflorescence arrangement in grasses and sedges etc

SPORE: tiny reproductive body that disperses and gives rise to a new organism

STAMEN: male reproductive structure of a flower

STIGMA: receptive tip of female part of flower, the style

STIPULE: leaf-like or scale-like structure at base of leaf stalk

STYLE: female reproductive structure of a flower

SUBSPECIES: sub-division of a species, members of which are able to breed with other subspecies but seldom do so because of geographical isolation

TENDRIL: slender, modified leaf or stem structure which assists climbing in some plants

THALLUS: unspecialised vegetative body of a lower plant

THORAX: middle section of an insect's body

TRAGUS: pointed inner ear outgrowth found in some bat species

TRIFOLIATE: leaf divided into three sections

UMBEL: umbrella-like inflorescence

VENTRAL: lower surface

FURTHER READING

Mammals

F.E. van den Brink, *A Field Guide to the Mammals of Britain and Europe*. Collins.
David MacDonald and Priscilla Barrett, *Collins Field Guide to Mammals of Britain and Europe*. HarperCollins.

Birds

Haken Delin and Lars Svensson, *Photographic Guide to the Birds of Britain and Europe*. Hamlyn.
Hermann Heinzel, Richard Fitter and John Parslow, *Pocket Guide Birds of Britain and Europe with North Africa and the Middle East*. HarperCollins.
Peter Lack, *The Atlas of Wintering Birds in Britain and Ireland*. T & AD Poyser.
Paul Sterry, F*ield Guide to the Birds of Britain and Europe*. The Crowood Press.
Paul Sterry and Jim Flegg, *A Photographic Guide to the Birds of Britain and Europe*. New Holland.
David Wingfield Gibbons, James Reid and Robert Chapman, *The New Atlas of Breeding Birds in Britain and Ireland: 1988-1991*. T & AD Poyser.

Other Vertebrates

Nicholas Arnold and John Burton, *Field Guide to the Reptiles and Amphibians of Britain and Europe*. HarperCollins.
Bent Muns and Preben Dahlstrom, *Collins Guide to the Freshwater Fishes of Britain and Europe*. HarperCollins.
Peter Maitland and Keith Linsell, *The Hamlyn Guide to Freshwater Fishes of Britain and Europe*. Hamlyn.
Peter Miller and James Nicholls, *Handguide to the Fishes of Britain and Europe*. HarperCollins.

Butterflies and Moths

L.G. Higgins and N.D. Riley, *Field Guide to the Butterflies of Britain and Europe*. HarperCollins.
Bernard Skinner and David Wilson, *Colour Identification Guide to Moths of the British Isles*. Viking.
Paul Sterry, *A Photographic Guide to the Butterflies of Britain and Europe*. New Holland.

Other Invertebrates

J. D'Aguilar, J-L. Dommanget and R. Prechac, *Field Guide to Dragonflies of Britain, Europe and North Africa*. Collins.
Michael Chinery, *Field Guide to the Insects of Britain and Western Europe*. HarperCollins.
Heiko Bellman, *A Field Guide to the Grasshoppers and Crickets of Britain and Northern Europe*. HarperCollins.

M.P. Kerney, R.A.D. Cameron and G. Riley, *Field Guide to the Land Snails of Britain and North-west Europe*. HarperCollins.
Michael Tweedie and John Wilkinson, *Handguide to the Butterflies and Moths of Britain and Ireland*. HarperCollins.

THE SEASHORE

Peter Hayward, Tony Nelson-Smith and Chris Shields, *Collins Pocket Guide to the Seashore of Britain and Northern Europe*. HarperCollins.

TREES

Andrew Cleave, *Field Guide to the Trees of Britain, Europe and North America*. The Crowood Press.
Alan Mitchell and John Wilkinson, *Pocket Guide Trees of Britain and Northern Europe*. HarperCollins.
Paul Sterry and Bob Press, *A Photographic Guide to the Trees of Britain and Europe*.
Alan Mitchell, *Alan Mitchell's Trees of Britain*. HarperCollins.

WILD FLOWERS

Richard Fitter, Alistair Fitter and Marjorie Blamey, *Pocket Guide Wild Flowers of Britain and Northern Europe*. HarperCollins.
Bob Gibbons and Peter Brough, *The Hamlyn Photographic Guide to the Wild Flowers of Britain and Northern Europe*. Hamlyn.
Paul Sterry and Bob Press, *A Photographic Guide to the Wild Flowers of Britain and Europe*. New Holland.

LOWER PLANTS

Hans Martin Jahns, *Photoguide to the Ferns, Mosses and Lichens of Britain and Northern and Central Europe*. HarperCollins.

FUNGI

R. Courtecuisse and B. Duhem, *Field Guide to Mushrooms and Toadstools of Britain and Europe*. HarperCollins.
Paul Sterry, *A Photographic Guide to the Mushrooms of Britain and Europe*. HarperCollins.

The Collins **New Naturalist** Series has titles which cover most aspects of British natural history.

PICTURE CREDITS

The copyright for the photographs in this book belong to Nature Photographers Ltd and have all been taken by Paul Sterry with the exception of:

Frank B. Blackburn: 77h, 101g, 105e, 109b, 113c, 117f, 125g, 127d, 189g, 225d, 231k, 291l, 305b, 339j, 345h
S. C. Bisserot: 53(a, b, c, d, e, g, h), 137(a, f, g), 143c, 153i, 155j, 185m, 189(i, j, m), 191(f, j, k, l), 207d, 211c, 221(b, f)
T. D. Bonsall: 101e, 169e, 189f
Idris Bowen: 189h, 311c
L. H. Brown: 79c
Nicholas Phelps Brown: 155k, 169(c, f), 185(a, c, d, f, j, n), 197c, 213i, 219(f, k)
Brinsley Burbidge: 225b, 227e, 247(e, h), 251e, 253d, 257l, 275c, 281k, 285i, 287e, 313l, 325b, 333i, 337b
Robin Bush: 44, 117a, 143a, 145(e, g, h, l), 147(h. i. j), 149(k, n), 151i, 231b, 241e, 247a, 251(a, d), 253g, 255(f, l), 277l, 281l, 283l, 287(d, f), 297b, 303j, 305k, 307i, 309d, 311(e, l), 319c
N. A. Callow: 177h, 179(h, i), 181l, 185b, 187(a, e, i, k), 191(a, b, c, d, h), 195(e, j), 197(d, g), 199a, 201a, 213c, 329b
Kevin Carlson: 51c, 63d, 73a, 77(d, e, i, j), 85b, 109c, 111b, 113a, 115a
Colin Carver: 51h, 55e, 105b, 109d, 111h, 113h, 115(b, d, e), 119(a, d), 129c, 131(b, f)
Bob Chapman: 165c, 301c
Hugh Clark: 75a, 107 (b, c, d), 167e, 169b, 185k, 189b
Andrew Cleave: 5, 19, 85f, 95f, 209(c, i), 211(d, f, i, j), 215(c, d, g, h), 217b, 221(a, e, i), 223(b, c, d), 225(a, g, i), 227(a, b, c, d, g, h, j, l), 229(b, c, e, f, h, i, k, l), 231(f, i, l), 233(b, g, l, m), 235(e, f), 237(a, d, h), 239(f, k), 241d, 247(f, i, k, l), 249l, 251(f, j), 253(a, e, h, k), 255g, 257j, 259h, 271d, 273g, 275(a, i), 277(d, g, j), 279c, 281(d, f), 285(e, j), 287i, 293(b, h), 295d, 299c, 301(d, f, g), 313(c, f), 319d, 321(i, j, l), 323(a, b, c, e, h, i, k, l), 325(c, d, e, i, j, l), 327(a, b, h, i, j, k, l), 329(a, d, h, j), 331(g, h), 333(g, h, k, l), 335(e, f), 337(c, d, g), 339(k, h), 341(c, d, e, f, j), 343(b, d, e, f, h)
Peter Craig-Cooper: 63e, 87f
Ron Croucher: 123b
Andrew Davies: 231a
Geoff du Feu: 35, 47b, 49i, 143i, 177f, 181k, 185(e, g), 187(c, g, j), 189l, 197k, 285b
David Elias: 239g, 325k, 329(f, i), 331(d, j)
Chris Gomersall: 97g, 157j
Michael Gore: 77a, 87b, 121f
Jean Hall: 321(a, f)
Michael J. Hammett: 135(d, e, g), 139(d, e, g, h), 141(a, j), 169g, 183(j, k), 211a, 221k, 223(a, f)
James Hyett: 273b
E. A. Janes: 47g, 49h, 51a, 51d, 55(f; g, h), 57(d, f), 69j, 75(e, f), 79k, 97b, 103(a, e), 119h, 121e, 129b, 143b, 169i, 187h, 245a, 249e, 281j, 283j, 305c, 321d, 337e, 345f, 347b
Len Jessup: 151(a, b), 159l, 205f
Chris Knights: 91f
Hugh Miles: 51f, 79g, 135I, 137(c, i)
Lee Morgan: 321c
Owen Newman: 47(a, d), 51(b, i), 53f, 59h, 289b
Philip Newman: 59(b, e), 75i, 77b, 79(d, e), 85a, 91b, 97f, 109e, 115c, 117e, 129a
David Osborn: 57e, 73b, 237l, 251b, 315l
Charles Palmar: 135f
W. S. Paton: 49e, 51(e, g), 77(c, f, k)
John Reynolds: 87c
Jim Russell: 231g, 315b
Tony Schilling: 225c, 249a
Don Smith: 49k, 77g, 209f, 211h, 221c, 223h
R. T. Smith: 59g, 111e, 113e
E. K. Thompson: 59a
Roger Tidman: 59(d, f), 63c, 75(c, d, j), 79j, 81f, 83(a, d), 85d, 89a, 95b, 97(a, d, i, j), 99e, 101b, 103 (b, c, d), 105f, 109a, 111c, 113(b, f, g), 123(c, e, g), 125c, 127(a, f), 129h, 175c, 275e
Jeff Watson: 325f
Andrew Weston: 271b, 311f
Keri Williams: 225f
Jon Wilson: 63b
Wolmuth (and Morten Muller): 75h

The letters after the page numbers refer to their relative position on the page, reading left to right and top to bottom.

INDEX

Abernethy forest, 30
Abraxas grossulariata, 164
Abrostola triplasia, 162
Acanthosoma haemorrhoidale, 178
Accipiter gentilis, 74
nisus, 74
Acer campestre, 230
pseudoplatanus, 230
Aceras anthropophorum, 316
Achillea millefolium, 302
ptarmica, 302
Acilius sulcatus, 192
aconite, winter, 244
Acrocephalus palustris, 112
schoenobaenus, 112
scirpaceus, 112
Acronicta leporina, 160
megacephala, 160
psi, 160
Actinia equina, 220
Actitis hypoleucos, 86
adder, 37, 130
adderstongue, 334
admiral, red, 32, 142
white, 27, 144
Adoxa moschatellina, 296
Aegithalos caudatus, 120
Aegopodium podagraria, 274
Aesculus hippocastanum, 228
Aeshna cyanea, 174
grandis, 174
Aethusa cynapium, 276
Agapetes fuscipes, 182
agaric, clouded, 346
fly, 346
Agaricus campestris, 348
silvicola, 348
Aglais urticae, 142
Agrimonia eupatoria, 256
agrimony, 256
hemp, 300
Agrostemma githago, 244
Agrostis exlamationis, 158
gigantea, 326
setacea, 326
stolonifera, 326
Aix galericulata, 68
Ajuga chamaepitys, 290
reptans, 286
Alauda arvensis, 108
Alca torda, 98
Alcedo atthis, 104
Alchemilla vulgaris agg, 256
Alcyonium digitatum, 222
alder, 228
alder-buckthorn, 232
Alectoris rufa, 78
Aleuria aurantia, 344
alexanders, 272
algae, features, 13
Alisma plantago-aquatica, 310
alison, sweet, 252
alkanet, green, 286
Alle alle, 98
Alliaria petiolata, 252
Allium ursinum, 310
vineale, 310
Alnus glutinosa, 228
Althaea officinalis, 268
Amanita citrina, 346
fulva, 348
muscaria, 346
phalloides, 348
rubescens, 348
Amaurobius similis, 198
Ammophila arenaria, 326
sabulosa, 190
amphibian, features, 11
Amphitrite johnstoni, 220
Anacamptis pyramidalis, 316
Anagallis arvensis, 278
tenella, 278
Anas acuta, 68
clypeata, 68
crecca, 68
penelope, 68
platyrhynchos, 68
querquedula, 68
strepera, 68
Anatis ocellata, 196
Anax imperator, 174
Anchusa arvensis, 284
Ancylus fluviatilis, 206
Andricus kollari, 188
quercuscalicis, 188
anemone, beadlet, 220
jewel, 220
snakelocks, 220
anemone, wood (flower), 26, 248
Anemone nemorosa, 248
Anemonia sulcata, 220
angelica, wild, 274
Angelica sylvestris, 274
Angerona prunaria, 166
angle shades (moth), 160
Anguilla anguilla, 134
Anguis fragilis, 130
Anodonta cygnea, 206
Anser albifrons, 66
anser, 66
brachyrhynchus, 66
fabilis, 66
ant, black garden, 190
red, 190
wood, 190
Anthoceros laevis, 338
Anthocharis cardamines, 142
Anthoxanthum odoratum, 326
Anthriscus sylvestris, 272
Anthus petrosus, 108
pratensis, 108
trivialis, 108
Anthyllis vulneraria, 262
Apatura iris, 144
Apeira syringaria, 164
Aphanes arvensis, 256
Aphantopus hyperantus, 146
aphid, black bean, 180

rose, 180
Aphis fabae, 180
Apis mellifera, 190
Apium graveolens, 276
nodiflorum, 276
Aplysia punctata, 210
Apodemus flavicollis, 48
sylvaticus, 48
apple, crab, 31, 230
Apus apus, 106
cancriformis, 212
Aquila chrysaetos, 74
Aquilega vulgaris, 248
Arabidopsis thaliana, 252
Araneus diadematus, 198
quadratus, 198
Araniella curcurbitina, 198
archangel, yellow, 288
Archidoris pseudargus, 210
Arctia caja, 158
Arctium lappa, 304
Ardea cinerea, 62
Arenaria interpres, 88
serpyllifolia, 240
Arenicola marina, 220
argus, brown, 150
Scotch, 41, 146
Argynnis paphia, 144
Argyroneta aquatica, 198
Arianta arbustorum, 204
Aricia agestis, 150
Arion ater, 202
distinctus, 202
subfuscus, 202
Armadillidium vulgare, 212
Armeria maritima, 280
Armillaria mellea, 346
Arne RSPB reserve, 38
Arrhenatherum elatius, 328
arrowgrass, sea, 298
arrowhead, 310
Artemisia absinthium, 304
maritima, 304
vulgaris, 304
arthropod, features, 12
Artogeia napi, 142
rapae, 142
Arum maculatum, 314
Arvicola terrestris, 46
ascidian, star, 222
Ascophyllum nodosum, 342
Asellus aquaticus, 212
ash, 25, 230
Asio flammeus, 102
otus, 102
asparagus, Bath, 312
aspen, 226
Asperula cyanchica, 284
asphodel, bog, 37, 310
Asplenium ruta-muraria, 334
trichomanes, 334
Astacus pallipes, 212
aster, sea, 300
Aster tripolium, 300
Asterias rubens, 222
Asterina gibbosa, 222
Astragalus danicus, 260
Athene noctua, 102
Athous haemorrhoidalis, 194
Athyrium filix-femina, 332
Atrichium undulatum, 334
Atriplex glabriuscula, 238
Atropa belladonna, 290
Atypus affinis, 198
auk, little, 98
Aurelia aurita, 220
Autographa gamma, 162
pulchrina, 162
Avena fatua, 328
avens, mountain, 39, 256
water, 24, 34, 258
wood, 258
avocet, 80
Aythya ferina, 70
fuligula, 70
marila, 70
Azolla filiculoides, 320

Babington's orache, 238
badger, 27, 50
Balaenoptera acutorostrata, 56
Ballota nigra, 288
balm, bastard, 288
balsam, Himalayan, 268
Barbaris vulgaris, 250
barnacle, 19
acorn, 216
bartsia, red, 31, 33, 294
yellow, 294
basil, wild, 290
bass, 138
Bass Rock, 60
bastard balm, 288
bat, Daubenton's, 51
greater horseshoe, 51
lesser horseshoe, 51
long-eared, 43, 52
Natterer's, 52
noctule, 52
pipistrelle, 43, 52
serotine, 51
beauty, brindled, 166
mottled, 166
oak, 166
bedstraw, common marsh-, 284
hedge-, 284
lady's, 284
bee, buff-tailed bumble, 190
honey, 190
leaf-cutter, 188
red-tailed bumble, 190
bee beetle, 194
bee-fly, 184
beech, 25, 228
beetles, 192–7
bellflower, clustered, 298
ivy-leaved, 300
nettle-leaved, 300
Bellis perennis, 300
Bempton Cliffs, 60
Bena prasinana, 162
bent, black, 326

bristle, 326
creeping, 326
Beta vulgaris ssp *maritima*, 238
betony, 288
Betula pendula, 226
pubescens, 226
Betws-y-Coed, 30
Bibio marci, 184
bilberry, 29, 278
Bilderdykia convolvulvus, 236
bindweed, black-, 236
field, 282
hedge, 282
sea, 282
Biodiversity Action Plan, 10
birch, 29
downy, 226
silver, 226
bird's-foot, 264
bird's-foot-trefoil, common, 262
greater, 262
bird's-nest, yellow, 280
birds, 11, 58–129
Biston betularia, 166
strataria, 166
bistort, 236
Alpine, 236
amphibious, 236
bithynia, common, 206
Bithynia tentaculata, 206
bitter-cress, hairy, 250
bittern, 23, 62
bittersweet, 290
black shields, 340
black-bindweed, 236
blackbird, 31, 43, 118
blackcap, 27, 31, 114
Blackstonia perfoliata, 282
blackthorn, 26, 31, 232
bladderwort, 23
greater, 320
Blakeney Harbour, 18
Blakeney Point, 20, 56
Blean Woods, 27
Blechnum spicant, 332
Blennius pholis, 140
blenny, common, 140
blewit, wood, 346
bloodworm, 184
bloody-nosed beetle, 196
blue damselfly, common, 176
blue, adonis, 34, 148
chalkhill, 148
common, 32, 148
holly, 44, 148
silver-studded, 37, 148
small, 148
blue-tailed damselfly, 176
bluebell, 26, 312
bluebottle, 186
blusher, the, 348
blushing bracket, 344
Boarmia repandata, 166
bog, habitat, 24–5
bog-rush, black, 322
bogbean, 23, 280
bolete, bay, 350
orange birch, 350
red-cracking, 350
Boletus badius, 350
chrysenteron, 350
edulis, 350
Bombus agrorum, 190
lapidarius, 190
terrestris, 190
Bombylius major, 184
Bonbycilla garrulus, 110
borage, 284
Borago officinalis, 284
Bosherton Ponds, 23
Botaurus stellaris, 62
Botrychium lunaria, 334
Botryllus schlosseri, 222
box, 232
Brachythecium rutabulum, 334
bracken, 29, 332
bracket, blushing, 344
bramble, 31, 258
brambling, 124
Branta bernicla, 64
canadensis, 64
leucopsis, 64
Brassica nigra, 250
oleracea, 250
Bridgwater Bay, 66
bright-eye, brown-line, 160
brimstone (butterfly), 142
brimstone moth, 166
brindled beauty (moth), 166
bristletail, 168
brittle-star, common, 222
Briza media, 328
brooklime, 294
broom, 260
broom moth, 158
broomrape, common, 296
knapweed, 296
thyme, 296
brown, meadow, 32, 34, 146
wall, 146
Bryonia cretica, 234
bryony, black, 31, 234
white, 31, 234
Bryum capillare, 334
Buccinium undatum, 210
Bucephala clangula, 70
buckthorn, 232
alder-, 232
sea-, 232
buddleia, 42, 43, 234
Buddleia davidii, 234
buff-tip, 156
Bufo bufo, 132
calamita, 132
bugle, 31, 286
bugloss, 284
viper's-, 286
bugs, 178–81
bulin, common, 204
bullfinch, 31, 124
bullhead, 22, 136
bumble bee, buff-tailed, 190

red-tailed, 190
bunting, cirl, 122
corn, 35, 122
reed, 23, 25, 122
sedge, 23
snow, 122
Bupleurum tenuissimum, 272
burdock, greater, 304
Burhinus oedicnemus, 90
burnet, 5-spot, 152
great, 256
salad, 256
burnet-saxifrage, 274
burnished brass, 162
bur-reed, branched, 326
bush-cricket, bog, 172
dark, 172
great green, 172
grey, 172
oak, 172
Roesel's, 172
speckled, 172
butcher's broom, 312
Buteo buteo, 74
Butomus umbellatus, 310
butter cap, 346
butterbur, 304
buttercup, bulbous, 246
celery-leaved, 246
corn, 246
creeping, 244
creeping, 43
hairy, 246
meadow, 33, 244
butterfish, 140
butterflies, 142–51
Butterfly Conservation, 10
butterwort, common, 24, 296
Buxus sempervirens, 232
buzzard, 27, 74
honey, 74

cabbage, wild, 250
caddisfly, 22, 182
Caerlaverock WWT Reserve, 64
Cakile maritima, 252
calamint, common, 288
Calamintha sylvatica, 288
Calidris alba, 84
alpina, 84
canutus, 84
ferruginea, 84
maritima, 84
pusilla, 84
temminckii, 84
Caligeron cuspidatum, 334
Calliphora erythrocephala, 186
Callistege mi, 162
Calliteara pudibunda, 156
Callophyrs rubi, 148
Calluna vulgaris, 278
Calocera viscosa, 352
Caloplaca marina, 338
Calopteryx splendens, 176
virgo, 176
Caltha palustris, 244
Calystegia sepium, 282
soldanella, 282
Campanula glomerata, 298
rotundifolia, 298
trachelium, 300
campion, bladder, 242
moss, 39, 242
red, 242
sea, 242
white, 244
Campyloneura virgula, 178
Cancer pagarus, 214
candytuft, wild, 250
Cantharellus cibarius, 344
capercaillie, 29, 78
Capra hircus, 54
Capreolus capreolus, 54
Caprimulgus europaeus, 100
Capsella bursa-pastoris, 252
Carcinus maenus, 214
Cardamine hirsuta, 250
pratensis, 250
carder-bee, common, 190
Cardiff Bay, 56
Cardium edule, 210
Carduelis cannabina, 126
carduelis, 124
chloris, 124
flammea, 126
spinus, 124
nutans, 306
tenuiflorus, 306
Carex acutiformis, 324
arenaria, 324
demissa, 324
flacca, 324
nigra, 324
otrubae, 324
paniculata, 324
pendula, 324
pilulifera, 324
sylvatica, 324
Carlina vulgaris, 306
carp, 136
carpet (moth), green, 164
silver ground, 164
Carpinus betulus, 228
carrot, 276
Carterocephalus palaemon, 150
Cassida rubiginosa, 196
Castanea sativa, 228
cat, domestic, 44
cat's-ear, common, 308
smooth, 308
catchfly, Nottingham, 244
Catocala nupta, 162
catstail, lesser, 330
sand, 330
celandine, greater, 248
lesser, 26, 246
Celastrina argiolus, 148
celery, wild, 276
Centaurea nigra, 306
scabiosa, 306
Centaurium erythraea, 282
pulchellum, 282

centaury, common, 282
lesser, 282
Centranthus ruber, 296
cep, 350
Cepaea hortensis, 204
nemoralis, 204
Cephalanthera damasonium, 318
longifolia, 318
Cepphus grylle, 98
Ceramica pisi, 158
Cerastium fontanum, 242
glomeratum, 242
Cercopis vulnerata, 180
Certhia familiaris, 122
Cerura vinula, 152
Cervus elaphus, 54
nippon, 54
Ceterach officinarum, 332
Cetonia aurata, 194
Cettia cetti, 112
chafer, rose, 194
chaffinch, 26, 30, 124
Chamaecyparis lawsoniana, 224
Chamaemelum nobile, 300
chamomile, 300
Chamomilla suaveolens, 300
champignon, fairy-ring, 346
chanterelle, 344
Chaoberus crystillinus, 184
char, 134
Charadrius dubius, 82
hiaticula, 82
morinellus, 82
charcoal burner, 350
charlock, 250
charr, Arctic, 134
chaser, broad-bodied, 174
Chelidonium majus, 248
Chelon labrosus, 138
Chenopodium album, 238
bonus-henricus, 238
rubrum, 238
cherry, bird, 230
wild, 230
Chesil Beach, 20
chestnut, horse-, 228
sweet, 228
Chew Valley Reservoir, 23
chickweed, common, 43, 240
water, 240
chicory, 308
chiffchaff, 112
Chirocephalus diaphanus, 212
Chironomus plumosus, 184
Chlidonias niger, 96
chlorophyll, 12
Chobham Common, 38
chocolate-tip, 156
Chorthippus albomarginatus, 170
brunneus, 170
parallelus, 170
vagans, 170
chough, 128
Chrysanthemum segetum, 302
Chrysaora isosceles, 220
Chrysis ignita, 188
Chrysomela menthastri, 196
Chrysoperla carnea, 182
Chrysops relictus, 184
Chrysosplenium oppositifolium, 256
Chthalamus stellatus, 216
chub, 22, 136
cicely, sweet, 274
Cichorium intybus, 308
Cicindela campestris, 192
Cicuta virosa, 274
Ciliata mustela, 138
Cimbex femoratus, 188
Cinclus cinclus, 110
cinnabar, the, 158
cinquefoil, creeping, 258
marsh, 258
Circaea lutetiana, 272
Circus aeruginosus, 76
cyaneus, 76
pygargus, 76
Cirsium acaulon, 306
arvense, 306
dissectum, 306
eriophorum, 306
helenoides, 306
palustre, 306
vulgare, 306
Cladium mariscus, 324
Cladonia floerkeana, 338
impexa, 338
Clangula hyemalis, 72
clary, meadow, 290
cleavers, common, 284
cleg-fly, 184
Clematis vitalba, 234
Clethrionomys glareolus, 46
click beetle, 194
cliff, habitat, 15–16
Clinopodium vulgare, 290
Clitocybe nebularis, 346
Cloeon dipterum, 168
Clossiana euphrosyne, 144
selene, 144
Clostera curtula, 156
cloudberry, 258
clover, hare's-foot, 264
red, 33, 264
rough, 264
white, 33, 264
club-rush, floating, 322
sea, 322
club-tailed dragonfly, 176
clubmoss, features, 13
fir, 334
stagshorn, 334
Clytus arietus, 196
coast, habitat, 15–16
Coccinella 7-punctata, 196
Coccothraustes coccothraustes, 126
Cochleria officinalis, 252
Cochlodina laminata, 204
cockchafer, 194
cockle, common, 210
cockroach, dusky, 178
cocksfoot, 328
coelenterate, features, 11

Coeloglossum viride, 316
coenagrion, common, 176
Coenagrion puella, 176
Coenonympha pamphilus, 146
tullia, 146
Colchicum autumnale, 312
Colias croceus, 142
Collembola, order, 168
Collybia butyracea, 346
Colocasia coryli, 160
Colostygia pectinataria, 164
colt's-foot, 304
Columba livia, 100
oenas, 100
palumbus, 100
columbine, 248
comfrey, common, 284
Russian, 284
Comibaena pustulata, 164
comma, 27, 32, 144
conehead, long-winged, 172
short-winged, 172
Conger conger, 138
conifers, 12, 28–30
Conium maculatum, 274
Conocephalum conicum, 338
Conocephalus discolor, 172
dorsalis, 172
Conopodium majus, 272
conservation, 9–10
Convallaria majalis, 310
Convolvulus arvensis, 282
coot, 23, 80
copper, small, 32, 34, 148
coppicing, 25
Coprinus comatus, 348
coral-necklace, 242
cord-grass, small, 330
Cordulegaster boltonii, 174
Cordulia aenea, 176
Coriolus versicolor, 344
Corixa punctata, 180
cormorant, 16, 60
corncockle, 34, 244
corncrake, 80
cornel, dwarf, 272
cornsalad, common, 296
Cornus sanguinea, 234
suecica, 272
Coronella austriaca, 130
Coronopus didymus, 252
squamatus, 252
Cortinarius crocolitus, 348
Corvus corax, 128
corone cornix, 128
corone corone, 128
frugilegus, 128
monedula, 128
corydalis, climbing, 248
Corydalis claviculata, 248
Corylus avellana, 228
Corynactes viridis, 220
Corystes cassivellaunus, 214
Cosmia pyralina, 160
cotton-grass, common, 24, 326
hare's-tail, 326
Cottus gobio, 136
Countryside Code, 10
cow-wheat, common, 294
cowbane, 274
cowberry, 29, 280
cowrie, common, 208
cowslip, 34, 276
crab, broad-clawed porcelain, 214
edible, 214
hermit, 19, 214
masked, 214
shore, 214
spider, 214
velvet swimming, 214
Crambe maritima, 252
cranberry, 280
crane's-bill, bloody, 266
cut-leaved, 266
dove's-foot, 266
meadow, 264
shining, 266
wood, 266
Crangon vulgaris, 216
Crategus monogyna, 232
crayfish, freshwater, 212
creeping jenny, 278
Crenilabrus melops, 138
Crepidotus variabilis, 346
Crepidula fornicata, 208
Crepis capillaris, 310
cress, lesser swine-, 252
swine-, 252
thale, 252
Crex crex, 80
cricket, dark bush, 32
field, 170
wood, 170
Cricklade, 35
Crithmum maritimum, 274
Crocallis elinguaria, 164
crossbill, common, 126
Scottish, 29
crosswort, 284
crow, carrion, 128
hooded, 128
crowberry, 39, 280
crowfoot, water-, 21
Cruciata laevipes, 284
crustaceans, 12, 212–17
Cryptogramma crispa, 332
cuckoo, 100
cuckooflower, 250
Cuculia umbratica, 160
Cuculus canorus, 100
cudweed, common, 302
marsh, 302
small, 302
Culex spp, 184
Cupido minimus, 148
Cupressocyparis x *leylandi*, 224
Curculio nucum, 196
curlew, 40, 88
stone-, 35
Cuscuta epithymum, 282
cushion-star, 222
Cyclopterus lumpus, 140

Cygnus columbarius, 64
cygnus, 64
olor, 64
Cylindrosulus punctatus, 218
Cymbalaria muralis, 292
Cynoglossum officinale, 286
Cyperus longus, 326
cyphel, 39
mossy, 240
cypress, leyland, 224
Cyprinus carpio, 136
Cystopteris fragilis, 332
Cytisus scoparius, 260

dace, 136
Dactylis glomerata, 328
Dactylorhiza fuchsii, 316
incarnata, 316
maculata, 316
praetermissa, 316
purpurella, 316
daddy-long-legs (insect), 184
daddy-long-legs (spider), 200
Daedaleopsis confragosa, 344
daffodil, wild, 312
dagger (moth), grey, 160
daisy, 300
oxeye, 31, 33, 304
Daldinia concentrica, 344
Dama dama, 54
damselflies, 22, 176
damselfly, blue, 176
blue-tailed, 176
large red, 176
dandelion, common, 308
Daphne laureola, 270
mezereum, 268
Daphnia sp, 212
darter, common, 174
ruddy, 174
Daucus carota, 276
Dawlish Warren, 18, 20
dead man's fingers, 222
dead-nettle, henbit, 288
red, 288
white, 288
Dean, Forest of, 27
death cap, 348
false, 346
deceiver, amethyst, 346
the, 346
Decticus verrucivorus, 172
deer, fallow, 54
muntjac, 54
red, 54
roe, 54
sika, 54
deergrass, 330
Delichon urbica, 106
Delphinus delphis, 56
demoiselle, banded, 176
beautiful, 176
common, 176
Dendrocopus major, 104
minor, 104
Deraeocoris ruber, 178
Deroceras reticulatum, 202
Deschampsia caespitosa, 328
flexuosa, 328
devil's coach-horse, 192
Diachrisia chrysitis, 162
Dianthus deltoides, 244
Diaphora mendica, 158
Dicentrachus labrus, 138
Dicranella heteromalla, 334
Dielephila elpenor, 154
porcellus, 154
Digitalis purpurea, 294
Dinocras cephalotes, 168
Diplolepis quercusfolii, 188
rosae, 188
dipper, 22, 110
Dipsacum fullonum, 298
Dipsacus pilosus, 298
Discus rotundatus, 204
diver, black-throated, 58
red-throated, 58
diving beetle, great, 192
dock, broad-leaved, 238
curled, 236
water, 238
wood, 238
dodder, common, 282
dog's mercury, 266
dog-rose, 258
dog-violet, common, 270
dogfish, lesser spotted, 138
dogwood, 31, 234
Dolomedes fimbriatus, 198
dolphin, bottle-nosed, 56
common, 56
Dolycoris baccarum, 178
Dorcus parallelipipedus, 192
dormouse, 46
edible, 46
dotterel, 82
Douglas-fir, 224
dove, collared, 100
rock, 100
stock, 100
turtle, 100
dragonflies, 174–7
Drepana falcataria, 162
drone-fly, 186
dropwort, 256
Drosera intermedia, 245
rotundifolia, 245
dryad's saddle, 344
Dryas octopetala, 256
Dryopteris aemula, 332
affinis, 332
dilitata, 332
felix-mas, 332
duck, long-tailed, 72
Mandarin, 68
ruddy, 72
tufted, 23, 70
duckweed, common, 320
Dugesia lugubris, 218
dune, habitat, 20
dung-fly, yellow, 186
dunlin, 18, 40, 84

dunnock, 31, 110
Durlston Head, 56
Dyer's greenweed, 260
Dysdera crocata, 198
Dytiscus marginalis, 192

eagle, golden, 41, 74
earth-star, common, 352
earthworm, common, 218
earwig, common, 178
Echinocardium cordatum, 222
echinoderm, features, 12
Echinus esculentus, 222
Echium vulgare, 286
Ectobius lapponicus, 178
eel, 134
conger, 138
egret, little, 62
Egretta garzetta, 62
eider, duck, 70
Eilema lurideola, 158
elder, 234
ground-, 43, 274
Elegug Stacks, 98
Eleocharis palustris, 322
Eligmodonta ziczac, 156
elm, 31
English, 228
wych, 228
Elminius modestus, 216
Elodea canadensis, 320
Elymus arenarius, 328
Emberiza cirlus, 122
citronella, 122
schoeniculus, 122
emerald, blotched, 164
downy, 176
large, 164
emperor, purple, 27, 144
emperor dragonfly, 174
emperor moth, 154
Empetrum nigrum, 280
Empis tesselata, 184
Ena obscura, 204
Enallagma cyathigerum, 176
enchanter's-nightshade, 272
Ennomos alniaria, 164
Ensis siliqua, 210
Enteromorpha intestinalis, 342
Ephemera danica, 168
vulgata, 168
Ephemeroptera, order, 168
Epilobium adenocaulon, 270
angustifolium, 270
hirsutum, 270
palustre, 270
Epipactis helleborine, 318
Eptesicus serotinus, 52
Equisetum arvense, 320
fluviatile, 320
sylvaticum, 320
Erannis defoliaria, 166
Eranthis hyemalis, 244
Erebia aethiops, 146
epiphron, 146
Eremophila alpestris, 108
Erica cinerea, 278
tetralix, 278
vagans, 278
Erigeron acer, 302
Erinaceous europaeus, 46
Eriophorum vaginatum, 326
Eristalis tenax, 186
Erithacus rubecula, 116
ermine (moth), white, 158
Erodium cicutarium, 264
Erophila verna, 252
Eryngium maritimum, 272
Erynnis tages, 150
Erysimum cheiranthoides, 250
Esox lucius, 134
estuary, habitat, 17–18
Euonymus europaeus, 232
Eupagurus bernhardus, 214
Eupatorium cannabinum, 300
Euphorbia amygdaloides, 266
helioscopia, 266
hyberna, 266
paralias, 266
peplus, 266
Euphrasia officinalis, 294
Euphydryas aurinia, 144
Eupithecia pulchellata, 164
Euproctis similis, 156
Eurhynchium praelongum, 334
Eutrigla gurnardus, 140
Exe estuary, 18, 80
Exidia glandulosa, 352
eyebright, 294

Fagus sylvatica, 228
Falco columbarius, 76
peregrinus, 76
subbuteo, 76
tinnunculus, 76
false death cap, 346
Fannia canicularis, 186
Farlington Marshes, 18
farmland, habitat, 33–5
Farne Islands, 16, 56, 96
fat hen, 238
Felix sylvestris, 50
fen, habitat, 24–5
fennel, 274
fern, adderstongue, 20
brittle bladder, 332
broad buckler, 332
features, 13
hard, 332
hay-scented, 332
lady, 332
male, 332
parsley, 332
scaly male, 332
water, 320
fescue, red, 328
viviparous, 328
Festuca rubra, 328
vivipara, 328
feverfew, 302
Ficedula hypoleuca, 116
field mushroom, 348

fieldfare, 31, 43, 118
figure of eighty (moth), 164
figwort, common, 292
water, 292
Filago vulgaris, 302
Filipendula ulmaria, 256
vulgaris, 256
fir, Douglas, 29, 224
firecrest, 8
Firth of Forth, 96
fish, features, 11
freshwater, 134–7
saltwater, 138–41
Fissidens taxifolius, 336
flax, fairy, 264
fleabane, blue, 302
common, 302
fleawort, field, 304
flesh-fly, 186
flies, true, 184–7
flounder, 140
fluellen, round-leaved, 292
fly, alder, 182
bee-, 184
caddis, 182
cleg-, 184
drone-, 186
flesh-, 186
scorpion, 182
snake, 182
snipe-, 186
St Mark's, 184
flycatcher, pied, 27, 116
spotted, 116
Foeniculum vulgare, 274
Fomes fomentarius, 344
footman, common, 158
rosy, 158
forest bug, 178
Forest of Dean, 27
Forficula auricularia, 170
forget-me-not, early, 286
wood, 286
Formica rufa, 190
fox, 27, 41, 50
foxglove, 294
foxglove pug (moth), 164
Fragaria vesca, 258
Frangula alnus, 232
Fratercula arctica, 98
Fraxinus excelsior, 230
freshwater, habitat, 21–3
Fringilla coelebs, 124
montifringilla, 124
Fritillaria meleagris, 310
fritillary, dark green, 144
Duke of Burgundy, 144
glanville, 144
heath, 144
high brown, 144
marsh, 144
pearl-bordered, 144
silver washed, 27, 144
small pearl-bordered, 144
fritillary, snake's-head (flower) , 310
frog, common, 23, 132
marsh, 132
froghopper, common, 180
Fucus serratus, 342
spiralis, 342
vesiculosus, 342
Fulica atra, 80
fulmar, 60
Fulmarus glacialis, 60
Fumaria officinalis, 248
fumitory, common, 248
fungi, 344–53
features, 13
fungus, candle snuff, 344
coral-spot, 344
ear, 352
honey, 346
hoof, 344
orange peel, 344
oyster, 346
porcellain, 346
yellow brain, 352
yellow stagshorn, 352
Furcula furcula, 152

gadwall, 68
Gagea lutea, 310
Galanthus nivalis, 312
Galeopsis speciosa, 288
tetrahit, 288
galingale, 326
Galium aparine, 284
mollugo, 284
odoratum, 284
palustre, 284
verum, 284
gall, cherry, 188
knopper, 188
marble, 188
spangle, 188
Gallinago gallinago, 90
Gallinula chloropus, 80
Gammarus pulex, 212
gannet, 16, 60
garden tiger, 158
garganey, 68
garlic, crow, 310
Garrulus glandarius, 128
Gasterosteus aculeatus, 136
Gastropacha quercifolia, 152
gatekeeper, 32, 146
Gavia arctica, 58
stellata, 58
Geastrum triplex, 352
Genista anglica, 260
tinctoria, 260
gentian, autumn, 34, 282
field, 282
marsh, 282
spring, 39, 282
Gentiana pneumonanthe, 282
verna, 282
Gentianella amarella, 282
campestris, 282
Geometra papilionaria, 164
Geranium dissectum, 266
lucidum, 266

molle, 266
pratense, 264
robertianum, 266
sanguineum, 266
sylvaticum, 266
Gerris lacustris, 180
Geum rivale, 258
urbanum, 258
ghost moth, 152
gipsywort, 290
gladiolus, wild, 314
Gladiolus illyricus, 314
glasswort, 17, 208, 240
Glaucium flavum, 248
Glaux maritima, 278
Glechoma hederacea, 286
Glis glis, 46
globeflower, 244
Glomeris marginata, 218
glow-worm, 32, 194
Glyceria fluitans, 328
maxima, 328
Glyphotaelius pellucidus, 182
Gnaphalium uliginosum, 302
goat, feral, 54
goat's beard, 308
Gobio gobio, 136
Gobius poaganellus, 140
goby, rock, 140
godwit, bar-tailed, 88
black-tailed, 88
goldcrest, 114
golden Y (moth), beautiful, 162
golden-ringed dragonfly, 174
golden-saxifrage, opposite-leaved, 256
goldeneye, 70
goldenrod, 300
Canadian, 300
goldfinch, 124
Gomphocerippus rufus, 170
Gomphus vulgatissimus, 176
Gonepteryx rhamnia, 142
good king henry, 238
goosander, 72
goose, barnacle, 64
bean, 66
brent, 18, 64
Canada, 64
greylag, 66
pink-footed, 66
white-fronted, 66
gooseberry, 232
goosefoot, red, 238
gorse, common, 37, 260
dwarf, 260
western, 260
goshawk, 30, 74
Graphis scripta, 340
Graphocephala fennahi, 180
grass, annual meadow-, 330
blue moor, 330
creeping bent, 33
creeping soft-, 330
deer, 39
false oat-, 328
features, 12
floating sweet-, 328
lyme, 328
marram, 20, 326
purple-moor, 39
quaking, 328
reed sweet-, 328
ryegrass, 34
small cord-, 330
sweet vernal, 326
timothy, 33, 34
tufted hair-, 328
wavy hair-, 328
well, 33
Yorkshire fog, 33, 330
grass-of-Parnassus, 254
grasshopper, common field, 32, 37, 170
common green, 170
heath, 170
large marsh, 37, 170
meadow, 170
mottled, 37, 170
rufous, 34, 170
stripe-winged, 34, 170
woodland, 170
grassland, habitat, 33–5
grayling, 134, 146
greasy touch shank, 346
grebe, black-necked, 58
crested, 23
great crested, 23, 58
little, 22, 58
red-necked, 58
Slavonian, 58
greenbottle, 186
greenfinch, 124
greenfly, 180
greenshank, 86
greenweed, Dyer's, 260
Greilada elegans, 210
grey dagger (moth), 160
Grimmia pulvinata, 336
grisette, tawny, 348
gromwell, common, 286
ground-elder, 274
ground-ivy, 286
ground-pine, 290
groundhopper, Cepero's, 172
common, 172
groundsel, 304
grouse, black, 40, 78
red, 78
Gryllus campestris, 170
gudgeon, 22, 136
guelder-rose, 234
guillemot, 16, 98
black, 98, 140
gull, black-headed, 20, 92
common, 92
glaucous, 94
great black-backed, 94
herring, 94
lesser black-backed, 94
little, 92
Mediterranean, 92
gurnard, grey, 140
gutweed, 342

Gymnadenia conopsea, 316

habitat, bog, 24–5
cliff, 15–16
coast, 15–16
estuary, 17–18
farmland, 33–5
fen, 24–5
freshwater, 21–3
grassland, 33–5
heathland, 36–8
hedgerow, 30–2
lake, 22–3
mire, 24–5
pond, 22–3
river, 21–2
roadside verge, 30–2
rocky shore, 19–20
saltmarsh, 17–18
stream, 21–2
types, 14–44
upland, 39–41
urban, 42–4
woodland, 25–30
Haematopota crassicornis, 184
pluvialis, 184
Haematopus ostralegus, 80
hair-grass, tufted, 328
wavy, 328
hairstreak, black, 148
brown, 148
green, 148
purple, 148
white-letter, 148
hairy stereum, 344
Halichoerus grypus, 56
Halichondria panicea, 222
Halimione portulacoides, 240
Hamearis lucina, 144
Hammarbya paludosa, 318
Haplophilus subterraneus, 218
hare, brown, 48
mountain, 48
hare's-ear, slender, 272
harebell, 298
harrier, hen, 30, 37, 40, 76
marsh, 23, 76
Montagu's, 76
hartstongue, 332
harvestmen, 32, 218
hawfinch, 26, 126
hawk, privet moth, 44
hawk's-beard, smooth, 310
hawkbit, rough, 308
hawker, brown, 174
southern, 174
hawkmoth, broad-bordered bee, 154
elephant, 154
eyed, 154
hummingbird, 154
lime, 154
pine, 154
poplar, 154
privet, 154
small elephant, 154
hawkweed, mouse-ear, 308
hawthorn, 26, 31, 43, 232
Hayle estuary, 18
hazel, 25–7, 31, 228
heart and dart (moth), 158
heath, Cornish, 278
cross-leaved, 37, 278
large, 146
small, 146
heather, bell, 37, 39, 278
heathland, habitat, 36–8
Hebrew character (moth), 160
Hedera helix, 234
hedge-parsley, upright, 272
hedgehog, 46
hedgerow, habitat, 30–2
Helianthemum nummularium, 270
heliotrope, winter, 304
Helix aspersa, 204
pomatia, 204
hellebore, green, 244
stinking, 244
helleborine, broad-leaved, 318
common, 31
marsh, 318
sword-leaved, 318
white, 318
Helleborus viridis, 244
Helophilus pendulus, 186
helvella, white, 344
Helvella crispa, 344
Hemaris fuciformis, 154
hemlock, 274
hemlock-spruce, western, 29, 224
hemp-nettle, common, 288
large-flowered, 288
henbane, 292
Hepialus humuli, 152
Heracleum mantegazzianum, 274
sphondylium, 274
herald (moth), the, 162
herb robert, 266
herb-paris, 312
Hermaness, 16, 98
Herminium monorchis, 318
heron, grey, 22, 62
Hesperia comma, 150
Hickling Broad, 25
Hieraceum pilosella, 308
Himanthalia elongata, 342
Himantoglossum hircinum, 318
Hipparchia semele, 146
Hippocrepis comosa, 262
Hippophae rhamnoides, 232
Hippuris vulgaris, 320
Hirneola auricula-judae, 352
Hirundo rustica, 106
hobby, 37, 76
Hofmannophila pseudospretella, 152
hogweed, 33, 274
giant, 274
Holcus lanatus, 330
mollis, 330
holly, 44, 230
sea-, 20, 272
Holy Island, 20
Homalothecium sericeum, 336

Homarus vulgaris, 214
honeysuckle, 27, 31, 234
Honkenya peploides, 240
hooktip, beautiful, 162
pebble, 162
hop, 31, 234
horehound, black, 288
hornbeam, 25, 228
horned-poppy, yellow, 20, 248
hornet, 190
horse-chestnut, 228
horse-fly, 184
horsetail, features, 13
field, 320
water, 320
wood, 320
Hottonia palustris, 278
hound's-tongue, 286
house moth, brown, 152
house-fly, common, 186
lesser, 186
Humulus lupulus, 234
Huperzia selago, 334
Hyacinthoides non-scripta, 312
Hyde Park, 43
Hydra fusca, 218
Hydrobates pelagicus, 60
Hydrobia ulvae, 208
Hydrocotyle vulgaris, 272
Hydrophilus piceus, 192
Hygrocybe nigrescens, 352
Hyloicus pinastri, 154
Hyoscyamus niger, 292
Hypericum androsaemum, 268
elodes, 268
humifusum, 268
perforatum, 268
pulchrum, 268
Hypholoma fasciculare, 348
Hypnum cupressiforme, 336
Hypochoeris glabra, 308
radicata, 308
Hypogymnia physodes, 340

Iberis amara, 250
iceplant, 42
Ilex aquifolium, 230
Illecebrum verticillatum, 242
Ilyocoris cimicoides, 180
Impatiens balsamifera, 268
Inachis io, 142
ink cap, shaggy, 348
insects, 142–97
Inula conyza, 302
crithmoides, 302
invertebrate, features, 11
iris, stinking, 312
yellow, 21, 24, 312
Iris foetidissima, 312
pseudacorus, 312
Ischnura elegans, 176
Isle of Man, 128
ivory, sea, 340
ivy, 31, 44, 234
ground-, 286

jackdaw, 128
Jacob's-ladder, 280
Jasione montana, 298
jay, 43, 128
jellyfish, common, 220
Juglans regia, 228
Juncus acutus, 322
bufonis, 322
conglomeratus, 322
effusus, 322
gerardii, 322
inflexus, 322
juniper, 29, 224
Juniperus communis, 224
Jynx torquilla, 104

kale, sea-, 20, 252
kelp, 19, 208, 342
Kenfig, 20
kestrel, 76
Kickxia spuria, 292
Kielder Forest, 30
king alfred's cake, 344
kingfisher, 22, 104
kite, red, 74
kittiwake, 16, 92
knapweed, common, 31, 33, 306
greater, 31, 34, 306
Knautia arvensis, 298
knawel, annual, 242
knot, 84
knotgrass, 236
knotweed, Japanese, 236

Laccaria amethystea, 346
laccata, 346
Lacerta agilis, 130
vivipara, 130
lacewing, 182
lackey (moth), the, 152
Lactarius pyrogalus, 352
tomentosus, 352
Ladoga camilla, 144
lady's-mantle, 256
lady's-tresses, autumn, 34, 318
ladybird, 14-spot, 196
7-spot, 196
eyed, 196
Lagopus lagopus ssp *scoticus*, 78
mutus, 78
lake, habitat, 22–3
Lamiastrum galeobdolon, 288
Laminaria digitata, 342
Lamium album, 288
amplexicaule, 288
purpureum, 288
Lampetra fluviatilis, 134
planeri, 134
lamprey, brook, 134
river, 134
Lampyris noctiluca, 194
Lanius collurio, 110
excubitor, 110
Laothoe populi, 154
lappet moth, 152
lapwing, 80

larch, European, 29, 224
Larix decidua, 224
lark, shore, 108
Larus argentatus, 94
canus, 92
fuscus, 94
hyperboreus, 94
marinus, 94
melanocephalus, 92
minutus, 92
ridibundus, 92
lasher, father, 140
Lasiommata megera, 146
Lasius niger, 190
Lasypeyria flexula, 162
Lathraea squamaria, 296
Lathyrus aphaca, 262
japonicus, 262
pratensis, 262
laurel, cherry, 232
spurge, 270
Lavatera arborea, 268
laver spire shell, 208
Lea Valley, 62
leafhopper, rhododendron, 180
Leander serratus, 216
leatherjacket, 184
Lecanora atra, 340
Leccinum versipelle, 350
Ledra aurita, 180
leech, fish, 218
Leighton Moss Reserve, 23, 62
Lemna minor, 320
Leontodon hispidus, 308
Lepadogaster lepadogaster, 140
Lepas anatifera, 216
Lepidium campestre, 252
Lepiota mastoidea, 348
procera, 348
Lepista nuda, 346
Leptidea sinapis, 142
Leptophyes punctatissima, 172
Lepus capensis, 48
timidus, 48
Leucanthemum vulgare, 304
Leuciscus leuciscus, 136
Leucobryum glaucum, 336
Libellula depressa, 174
lichen, crab's-eye, 340
features, 13
map, 340
lichens, 338–41
Ligia oceanica, 216
Ligusticum scoticum, 274
Ligustrum vulgare, 234
lilac beauty, 164
lily-of-the-valley, 310
Limax cinereoniger, 202
flavus, 202
marginatus, 202
maximus, 202
tenellus, 202
lime, common, 232
small-leaved, 232
Limnephilus elegans, 182
marmoratus, 182
rhombicus, 182
Limonium vulgare, 280
Limosa lapponica, 88
limosa, 88
limpet, blue-rayed, 208
common, 19, 208
river, 206
slipper, 208
Linaria repens, 292
vulgaris, 292
ling, 29, 37, 39, 278
Linnaea borealis, 296
linnet, 37, 126
Linum catharticum, 264
Liparis liparis, 140
Listera ovata, 314
Lithobius variegatus, 218
Lithospermum officinale, 286
Littorella uniflora, 298
Littorina littoralis, 208
littorea, 208
liverwort, features, 13
floating, 320
liverworts, 320, 338
lizard, common, 130
sand, 37, 130
Lizard Peninsula, 16, 37
loach, stone, 136
Lobaria pulmonaria, 338
dormanna, 300
urens, 300
lobelia, heath, 300
water, 300
lobster, common, 214
lobster moth, 152
Lobularia maritima, 252
Loch Garten Reserve, 23, 74
Locustella naevia, 112
Logfia minima, 302
Lonicera periclymenum, 234
loosestrife, purple-, 21, 272
yellow, 276
Lophocolea heterophylla, 338
lords-and-ladies, 314
Lotus corniculatus, 262
uliginosus, 262
louse, freshwater, 212
lousewort, 39, 294
marsh, 294
lovage, Scots, 274
Loxia recurvirostra, 126
Lucanus cervus, 192
lucerne, 264
Lucilia caesar, 186
lugworm, 220
Lullula arborea, 108
Lumbricus sp, 218
terrestris, 218
lumpsucker, 140
Lundy Island, 16, 20, 54
Luscinia megarhynchos, 118
Lutra lutra, 50
Luzula sylvatica, 322
Lycaena phlaeas, 148
Lychnis flos-cuculi, 244
Lycia hirtaria, 166

Lycoperdon perlatum, 352
Lycophotia porphyrea, 158
Lycopodium clavatum, 334
Lycopus europaeus, 290
Lymnaea pereger, 206
stagnalis, 206
Lymnocryptes minimus, 90
Lysandra bellargus, 148
Lysimachia nemorum, 278
nummularia, 278
vulgaris, 276
Lythrum salicaria, 272

Macroglossum stellatarum, 154
Macropipus puber, 214
Macropodia rostrata, 214
Macrosiphum rosae, 180
madder, field, 282
maggot, rat-tailed, 186
magpie, 128
magpie (moth), the, 164
Malacosoma neustria, 152
mallard, 22, 68
mallow, common, 268
marsh, 268
musk, 268
tree, 268
Malus sylvestris, 230
Malva moschata, 268
sylvestris, 268
mammals, 11, 46–57
Maniola jurtina, 146
maple, field, 26, 31, 230
maple prominent, 156
Marasmius oreades, 346
Marchantia polymorpha, 338
mare's-tail, 320
marigold, corn, 34, 302
marsh, 24, 33–4, 244
Marine Conservation Society, 10
marjoram, 31, 34, 290
marsh-bedstraw, common, 284
marten, pine, 29, 50
Martes martes, 50
Marthasterias glacialis, 222
martin, house, 106
sand, 106
Matricaria perforata, 300
mayfly, 22, 168
nymph, 168
mayweed, scentless, 300
meadow-grass, annual, 330
meadow-rue, common, 246
lesser, 248
meadowsweet, 256
Meconema thallasinum, 172
Meconopsis cambrica, 248
Medicago lupulina, 264
sativa ssp *sativa*, 264
medick, black, 264
Megachile centuncularis, 188
Melampyrum pratense, 294
Melanargia galathea, 146
Melanitta fusca, 70
nigra, 70
Meles meles, 50
Melica uniflora, 330
melick, wood, 330
melilot, ribbed, 262
white, 262
Melilotus alba, 262
officinalis, 262
Melittis melissophyllum, 288
Mellicta athalia, 144
Mellinus arvensis, 190
Mellitaea cinxia, 144
Meloe proscarabeus, 194
Melolontha melolontha, 194
Mentha aquatica, 290
arvensis, 290
pulegium, 290
spicata, 290
Menyanthes trifoliata, 280
Mercurialis perenne, 266
merganser, red-breasted, 72
Mergus albellus, 72
merganser, 72
serrator, 72
Merlangius merlangus, 138
merlin, 40, 76
mermaid's purse, 138
Mertensia maritima, 284
Mesoacidalia adippe, 144
Metellina merianae, 200
Metrioptera brachyptera, 172
roeselii, 172
Metzgeria furcata, 338
mezereon, 268
Micromys minutus, 48
Microtus agrestis, 46
midge, phantom, 184
mignonette, wild, 254
milfoil, water-, 320
Miliaria calandra, 122
milk-cap, woolly, 352
milk-vetch, purple, 260
milkwort, common, 268
sea, 20, 278
miller (moth), the, 160
miller's thumb, 136
millipede, flat-backed, 218
pill, 218
Miltochrista miniata, 158
Milvus milvus, 74
Mimas tiliae, 154
Mimulus guttatus, 294
mink, American, 50
minnow, 22, 136
Minsmere Reserve, 23, 80
mint, corn, 290
water, 290
mint leaf beetle, 196
Minuartia sedoides, 240
verna, 240
mire, habitat, 24–5
mistletoe, 236
Misumena vatia, 200
mole, 46
Molinia caerulea, 326
molluscs, 12, 202–11
monkeyflower, 294
Monodonta lineata, 208

Monotropa hypopitys, 280
Montia perfoliata, 238
  sibirica, 238
moonwort, 334
moor-grass, purple, 326
moorhen, 80
Morecambe Bay, 18
Mormo maura, 160
Morus bassanus, 60
moschatel, 296
moss, bog, 24, 37, 336
  Catherine's, 334
  features, 13
  white fork, 336
  woolly hair, 336
Motacilla alba ssp *yarellii*, 108
  cinerea, 108
  flava, 108
moth, emperor, 37
mother of pearl (moth), 152
mother-of-pearl, in shell, 210
mother shipton (moth), 162
moths, 152–67
mottled beauty (moth), 166
mottled umber (moth), 166
mouse, harvest, 31, 48
  house, 43, 48
  wood, 27, 31, 43, 48
  yellow-necked, 27, 48
mouse-ear, common, 242
  sticky, 242
mugwort, 304
Mull of Kintyre, 56
mullein, dark, 292
  great, 292
mullet, thick-lipped grey, 18, 138
Muntiacus reevesi, 54
Mus musculus, 48
Musca domestica, 186
Muscardinus avellanarius, 46
Muscicapa striata, 116
mushroom, field, 348
  parasol, 348
  wood, 348
muslin moth, 158
mussel, common, 210
  pea, 206
  swan, 206
mustard, black, 250
  garlic, 252
  hedge, 250
  treacle, 250
Mustela erminea, 50
  nivalis, 50
  putorius, 50
  vison, 50
Myosotis ramossissima, 286
  scorioides, 286
  sylvatica, 286
Myosoton aquaticum, 240
Myotis daubentoni, 52
  nattereri, 52
Myrica gale, 228
Myriophyllum aquaticum, 320
Myrmeleotettix maculatus, 170
Myrmica rubra, 190
Myrrhis odorata, 274
myrtle, bog, 37, 228
Mythimna conigera, 160
  pallens, 160
Mytilus edulis, 210
Myxocephalus scorpius, 140

Narcissus pseudonarcissus, 312
Nasturtium officinale, 250
Natrix natrix, 130
nature reserves, 10
navelwort, 254
Nectria cinnabarina, 344
Nemacheilus barbatus, 136
Nemobius sylvestris, 170
Nemoura cinerea, 168
Neomys fodiens, 46
Neottia nidis-avis, 318
Nepa cinerea, 180
Nereis diversicolor, 220
nettle, common, 42–3, 236
Neuroterus quercusbaccarum, 188
New Forest, 25, 27, 30, 38, 130, 198, 212
Newborough Warren, 20
newt, 23
  great crested, 132
  palmate, 132
  smooth, 132
Nicrophorus humator, 192
  vespilloides, 192
nightingale, 27, 118
nightjar, 37, 100
nightshade, deadly, 290
  enchanter's-, 272
  woody, 290
Noctua fimbriata, 158
  pronuba, 158
North Meadow NNR, 35
Northecium ossifragum, 310
Noss, 98
Notodonta dromedarius, 156
Notonecta glauca, 180
Nottingham catchfly, 244
Nucella lapillus, 210
Numenius arquata, 88
  phaeopus, 88
Nuphar lutea, 248
nut-tree tussock (moth), 160
nuthatch, 26, 122
Nyctalis noctua, 52
Nymphoides peltata, 280

oak, 25, 31
  English, 228
  galls, 188
  sessile, 228
  Turkey, 188
oak apple, 188
oak beauty (moth), 166
oarweed, 342
oat, wild, 328
oat-grass, false, 328
Ochlodes venatus, 150
Ochrolechia parella, 340
octopus, common, 208
Octopus vulgaris, 208

Odontites verna, 294
Oedemera nobilis, 194
Oenanthe crocata, 276
fistulosa, 276
oenanthe, 116
Oenothera biennis, 272
old lady (moth), 160
old man's beard, 31, 234
Omocestus rufipes, 170
viridulus, 170
Oniscus asellus, 212
Onobrychis viciifolia, 262
Ononis repens, 262
Operophtera brumata, 166
Ophioglossum vulgatum, 334
ophion, yellow
Ophion luteus, 188
Ophiothrix fragilis, 222
Ophrys apifera, 314
insectifera, 314
Opiliones, order, 218
Opisthographis luteolata, 166
orange moth, 166
orange tip butterfly, 27, 142
orchid, bee, 31, 34, 314
bird's-nest, 318
bog-, 318
burnt, 314
common spotted-, 31, 316
early marsh-, 24, 316
early-purple, 314
fly, 34, 314
fragrant, 316
frog, 34, 316
greater butterfly-, 318
green-winged, 314
heath spotted-, 316
lady, 314
lesser butterfly-, 318
lizard, 318
man, 34, 316
marsh, 20
musk, 34, 318
northern marsh-, 316
purple, 26
pyramidal, 31, 34, 316
southern marsh-, 24, 34, 316
Orchis mascula, 314
morio, 314
purpurea, 314
ustulata, 314
Orgyia antiqua, 156
Origanum vulgare, 290
oriole, golden, 110
Oriolus oriolus, 110
Orkney, 58, 94
Ornithogalum pyrenaicum, 312
umbellatum, 312
Ornithopus perpusillus, 264
Orobanche alba, 296
elatior, 296
minor, 296
orpine, 254
Orthetrum cancellatum, 174
Orthosia gothica, 160
Oryctolagus cunniculus, 48
osier, 226
osprey, 74
Ostrea edulis, 210
otter, 50
Oudemansiella mucida, 346
Ourapteryx sambucaria, 166
ouzel, ring, 118
owl, barn, 102
little, 102
long-eared, 102
short-eared, 30, 37, 40, 102
tawny, 102
Oxalis acetosella, 264
oxlip, 276
oxtongue, bristly, 308
hawkweed, 308
Oxychilus alliarius, 204
cellarius, 204
Oxyura jamaicensis, 72
oyster, common, 210
oyster plant, 284
oystercatcher, 80

Pagham Harbour, 18
painted lady, 142
pale prominent, 156
pale tussock, 156
Palomena prasina, 178
Panaeolus sphinctrinus, 348
Pandion haliaetus, 74
Panorpa communis, 182
pansy, field, 270
mountain, 39, 270
wild, 270
Panurus biarmicus, 120
Papaver rhoeas, 248
Papilio machaon ssp *britannicus*, 142
Pararge aegeria, 146
parasol mushroom, 348
Pardosa lugubris, 200
Parentucellia viscosa, 294
Parietaria judaica, 236
paris, herb, 26
Paris quadrifolia, 312
Parmelia caperata, 340
Parnassia palustris, 245
parsley, cow, 272
fool's, 276
upright hedge-, 272
parsley-piert, 256
parsnip, wild, 274
partridge, grey, 78
red-legged, 34–5, 78
Parus ater, 120
caeruleus, 120
cristatus, 120
major, 120
montanus, 120
palustris, 120
pasqueflower, 248
Passer domesticus, 126
montanus, 126
Pastinaca sativa, 274
Patella vulgata, 208
Patina pellucida, 208
Paxillus involutus, 352

pea, sea, 20, 262
peach blossom (moth), 162
peacock (butterfly), 43, 142
pear, wild, 230
pearlwort, procumbent, 242
pebble prominent, 156
Pedicularis palustris, 294
sylvatica, 294
Pellia epiphylla, 338
pellitory-of-the-wall, 236
Pelvetia caniculata, 342
penny-cress, field, 252
pennyroyal, 290
pennywort, marsh, 272
Pentaglottis sempervirens, 286
Pentatoma rufipes, 178
pepper-saxifrage, 276
peppered moth, 166
pepperwort, field, 252
peppery furrow shell, 208
Perca fluviatilis, 136
perch, 22, 136
Perdix perdix, 78
peregrine, 41, 76
Peridea anceps, 156
periwinkle (mollusc), 19
edible, 208
flat, 208
periwinkle, lesser (flower) , 280
Perla bipunctata, 168
Pernis apivorus, 74
Petasites fragrans, 304
hybridus, 304
Petrobius maritimus, 168
petty whin, 260
Phalacrocorax aristotelis, 60
carbo, 60
phalarope, grey, 90
red-necked, 90
Phalaropus fulicarius, 90
lobatus, 90
Phalera bucephala, 156
Phallus impudicus, 352
Phasianus colchicus, 78
pheasant, 78
pheasant's-eye, 34
Pheosia gnoma, 156
Philaenus spumarius, 180
Philomachus pugnax, 88
Phleum arenarium, 330
bertelonii, 330
pratense, 330
Phlogophora meticulosa, 160
Phoca vitulina, 56
Phoenicurus ochrurus, 116
Phoenicurus phoenicurus, 116
Pholas dactylus, 210
Pholcus phalangioides, 200
Pholidoptera griseoaptera, 172
Pholis gunnellus, 140
photography, 5–8
photosynthesis, 12
Phoxinus phoxinus, 136
Phragmatobia fuliginosa, 158
Phragmites communis, 326
Phryganea striata, 182
Phyllitis scolopendrium, 332
Phyllobius pomaceus, 196
Phylloscopus collybita, 112
sibilatrix, 112
trochilus, 112
Phyteuma tenerum, 298
Pica pica, 128
Picea abies, 224
sitchensis, 224
Picris echioides, 308
hieracioides, 308
viridis, 104
piddock, common, 210
Pieris brassicae, 142
pigeon, feral, 43, 100
pignut, 272
pike, 22, 134
pimpernel, bog, 278
scarlet, 278
yellow, 278
Pimpinella saxifraga, 274
pine, Caledonian, 28–9
Corsican, 29, 224
Scots, 29, 224
pineappleweed, 300
Pinguicula vulgaris, 296
pinion, lunar-spotted, 160
pink, maiden, 244
pintail, 68
Pinus nigra ssp *laricio*, 224
sylvestris, 224
pipefish, greater, 138
Pipistrellus pipistrellus, 52
pipit, meadow, 40, 108
rock, 108
tree, 29, 108
Piptoporus betulinus, 344
Pisaura mirabilis, 200
Piscicola geometra, 218
Placynthium nigrum, 340
Plagiochila asplenioides, 338
Plagodis dolabraria, 164
plane, London, 230
Planorbis corneus, 206
planorbis, 206
Plantago coronopus, 296
lanceolata, 298
major, 296
maritima, 296
plantain, buck's-horn, 296
greater, 296
ribwort, 298
sea, 296
Platalea leucorodia, 62
Platanthera bifolia, 318
chlorantha, 318
Platanus x *hispanica*, 230
Platichthys flesus, 140
Platycleis denticulata, 172
Plebejus argus, 148
Plecotus auritus, 52
Plectrophenax nivalis, 122
Pleuroptya ruralis, 152
Pleurotus ostreatus, 346
ploughman's-spikenard, 302
plover, golden, 40, 82

grey, 82
little ringed, 82
ringed, 20, 82
plume moth, white, 152
Pluvialis apricaria, 82
squatarola, 82
Poa annua, 330
pochard, 23, 70
Podiceps auritus, 58
cristatus, 58
grisegena, 58
nigricollis, 58
polecat, 50
Polemonium caeruleum, 280
Pollachius pollachus, 138
pollack, 138
Polydesmus angustus, 218
Polygala vulgaris, 268
Polygonatum multiflorum, 312
Polygonia c-album, 144
Polygonum amphibium, 236
aviculare, 236
bistorta, 236
hydropiper, 236
persicaria, 236
viviparum, 236
Polyommatus icarus, 148
Polypodium vulgare, 332
polypody, common, 332
polypore, birch, 344
many-zoned, 344
Polyporus squamosus, 344
Polytrichum commune, 336
pond, habitat, 22–3
pond skater, 180
pondweed, bog, 320
broad-leaved, 320
Canadian, 23, 320
poplar, hybrid black, 226
white, 226
poplar grey (moth), 160
poplar leaf beetle, 196
poppy, common, 248
Welsh, 248
yellow horned-, 20, 248
Populus alba, 226
tremula, 226
x canadensis, 226
Porcellana platycheles, 214
Porcellio scaber, 212
Potamogeton natans, 320
polygonifolius, 320
Potentilla anserina, 258
erecta, 258
palustris, 258
reptans, 258
prawn, common, 216
primrose, 276
bird's-eye, 39, 276
common evening-, 43
Primula elatior, 276
farinosa, 276
veris, 276
vulgaris, 276
privet, 234
prominent, great, 156
iron, 156
lesser swallow, 156
maple, 156
pale, 156
pebble, 156
Propylea 14-punctata, 196
Prunella modularis, 110
vulgaris, 286
Prunus avium, 230
laurocerasus, 232
padus, 230
spinosa, 232
Pseudoips fagana, 162
Pseudopanthera macularia, 166
Pseudoscorpiones, order, 218
Pseudotsuga menziesii, 224
ptarmigan, 41, 78
Pteridium aquilinum, 332
Pteropherus pentadactyla, 152
Pterostichus madidus, 192
Pterostoma palpina, 156
Ptilodonta cuculina, 156
puffball, common, 352
puffin, 16, 98
Puffinus puffinus, 60
Pulicaria dysenterica, 302
Pulsatilla vulgaris, 248
Pungitius pungitius, 136
Purbeck, 150
purslane, pink, 238
sea, 240
puss moth, 152
Pyrgus malvae, 150
Pyrochroa serraticornis, 194
Pyrola minor, 280
rotundifolia, 280
Pyronia tithonus, 146
Pyrrhocorax pyrrhocorax, 128
Pyrrhosoma nymphula, 176
Pyrrhula pyrrhula, 124
Pyrus communis, 230

Quercus petraea, 228
rober, 228
Quercusia quercus, 148

rabbit, 32, 48
radish, sea, 250
ragged robin, 244
ragworm, 220
ragwort, common, 304
Oxford, 43, 304
rail, water, 80
Raja clavata, 138
Rallus aquaticus, 80
Ramalina siliquosa, 340
Ramaria stricta, 352
rampion, round-headed, 298
ramshorn, great, 206
ramsons, 26, 310
Rana ridibunda, 132
temporaria, 132
Ranatra linearis, 180
Ranunculus acris, 244
aquatilis, 246
arvensis, 246

bulbosus, 246
ficaria, 246
flammula, 246
lingua, 246
omiophyllus, 246
peltatus, 246
penicillatus, 246
repens, 244
sardous, 246
scleratus, 246
Raphanus raphanistrum ssp *maritimus*, 250
Raphidia notata, 182
rat, brown, 48
rattle, yellow, 33
Rattus norvegicus, 48
raven, 128
ray, thornback, 138
razorbill, 16, 98
razorshell, pod, 210
Recurvirostra avosetta, 80
red admiral, 43–4
redpoll, 126
redshank (bird), 40, 86
spotted, 86
redshank (flower), 236
redstart, 27, 29, 116
black, 116
redwing, 31, 43, 118
reed, branched bur-, 326
common, 23, 326
reedmace, 23
great, 326
Regulus regulus, 114
reptiles, 11, 130–3
Reseda lutea, 245
luteola, 245
restharrow, common, 262
Reynoutria japonica, 236
Rhacomitrum lanuginosum, 336
Rhagio scolopacea, 186
Rhagium mordax, 1[illegible]
Rhagonycha fulva, 194
Rhamnus catharticus, 232
Rhinanthus minor, 294
Rhinolophus ferrumequinum, 52
hipposideros, 52
Rhizocarpon geographicum, 340
Rhodiola rosea, 245
rhododendron, 232
Rhododendron ponticum, 232
Rhynchospora alba, 324
Rhyssa persuasoria, 188
Ribes uva-crispa, 232
Riccia fluitans, 320
Richmond Park, 43
ringlet, 32, 146
mountain, 41, 146
Riparia riparia, 106
Rissa tridactyla, 92
river, habitat, 21–2
roach, 22, 136
roadside verge, habitat, 30–2
robin, 31, 43, 116
robin, ragged, 24, 34, 244
robin's pincushion, 188
rock-rose, common, 270
rocket, sea, 252
rockling, five-bearded, 138
rocky shore, habitat, 19–20
roll-rim, brown, 352
rook, 128
Rorippa palustris, 250
Rosa arvensis, 258
canina, 258
pimpinellifolia, 258
rose, burnet, 258
dog-, 31, 258
field, 258
rose-root, 39, 254
Rothiemurchus forest, 30
rowan, 43, 230
Rubus chamaemorus, 258
fruticosus agg, 258
ruby tiger, 158
rudd, 136
ruff, 88
Rumex acetosa, 238
acetosella, 238
crispus, 236
hydrolapathum, 238
obtusifolius, 238
sanguineus, 238
Ruscus aculeatus, 312
rush, black bog-, 322
common spike-, 322
compact, 322
field wood-, 322
floating club-, 322
flowering, 310
great wood-, 322
hard, 322
saltmarsh, 322
sea club-, 322
sharp, 322
soft, 322
toad, 322
russula, blackish-purple, 350
bright yellow, 350
common yellow, 350
rose, 350
stinking, 350
Russula atropurpurea, 350
claroflava, 350
cyanoxantha, 350
emetica, 350
foetans, 350
ochroleuca, 350
rosea, 350
rustyback, 332
Rutilus rutilus, 136
Rutland Water, 23

Sabella pavonia, 220
saffron, meadow, 312
sage, wood, 286
Sagina procumbens, 242
Sagittaria sagittifolia, 310
sainfoin, 262
St Abb's Head, 98
St John's-wort, marsh, 268
perforate, 268
slender, 268

trailing, 268
St Kilda, 60
Salicornia europaea, 240
Salix alba, 226
caprea, 226
chrysocoma, 226
cinerea, 226
fragilis, 226
pentandra, 226
viminalis, 226
sallow, 226
sallow kitten (moth), 152
Salmo salar, 134
trutta, 134
salmon, Atlantic, 134
Salsola kali, 240
Salticus scenicus, 200
saltmarsh, habitat, 17–18
saltwort, prickly, 240
Salvelinus alpinus, 134
Salvia pratensis, 290
Sambucus nigra, 234
samphire, golden, 17, 302
rock, 274
sand-hopper, 216
sanderling, 20, 84
sandpiper, common, 86
curlew, 84
green, 86
purple, 84
wood, 86
sandwort, sea, 20, 240
spring, 240
thyme-leaved, 240
Sanguisorba minor, 256
officinalis, 256
sanicle, 272
Sanicula europaea, 272
Sarcophaga carnaria, 186
Saturnia pavonia, 154
saucer bug, 180
saw-wort, 308
sawfly, birch, 188
Saxicola rubetra, 116
torquata, 116
saxifrage, meadow, 254
mossy, 256
opposite-leaved golden-, 256
pepper-, 276
purple, 39, 256
starry, 39, 254
yellow, 256
Saxifraga aizoides, 256
granulata, 245
hypnoides, 256
oppositifolia, 256
stellaris, 245
Scabiosa columbaria, 298
scabious, devil's-bit, 298
small, 298
scales, yellow, 340
scalloped oak (moth), 164
Scardinius erythropthalamus, 136
Scatophaga stercoraria, 186
scaup, 70
Schoenus nigricans, 322
Scilla verna, 312
Scirpus cespitosus, 330
fluitans, 322
maritimus, 322
Sciurus carolinensis, 48
vulgaris, 48
Scleranthus annuus, 242
Scoliopteryx libatrix, 162
Scolopax rusticola, 90
scorched wing, 164
scorpion, water, 180
scorpions, false, 218
scoter, common, 70
velvet, 70
Scots lovage, 274
Scrobicularia plana, 208
Scrophularia auriculata, 292
nodosa, 292
scurvygrass, common, 15, 252
Scutellaria galericulata, 286
Scyliorhinus canicula, 138
sea beet, 238
sea-blite, annual, 240
sea-buckthorn, 232
sea campion, 15
sea-hare, 210
sea-holly, 272
sea-kale, 252
sea-lavender, common, 17, 280
sea-lemon, 210
sea-lettuce, 342
sea-purslane, 17
sea-slater, 216
sea slugs, 210
sea-snail, common, 140
sea-spurrey, lesser, 242
rock, 15, 242
sea-urchin, common, 222
seal, common, 56
grey, 56
seashore, habitat, 19–20
spp, 138–41, 208–11, 214–17, 220–3
seaweeds, 342
sedge, common, 324
common yellow, 324
false fox, 324
glaucous, 324
great fen, 324
greater tussock, 324
lesser pond, 324
pendulous, 324
pill, 324
sand, 324
white beak-, 324
wood, 324
Sedum acre, 245
anglicum, 245
telephium, 245
Sehirus bicolor, 178
Selborne Hangers, 27
Selenia tetralunaria, 164
selfheal, 286
Semibalanus balanoides, 216
Senecio integrifolius, 304
jacobaea, 304
squalidus, 304

vulgaris, 304
Sericomyia silentis, 186
Serratula tinctoria, 308
Sesleria albicans, 330
shag, 60
shaggy ink cap, 348
shark (moth), the, 160
shearwater, Manx, 60
sheep's-bit, 298
shelduck, 18, 66
shepherd's-purse, 252
Sherardia arvensis, 282
Shetland Islands, 56, 94, 98
shield bug, green, 178
hawthorn, 178
pied, 178
Shingle Street, 20
shoreweed, 298
shoveler, 68
shrew, common, 31, 46
pygmy, 31, 46
water, 46
shrike, great grey, 37, 110
red-backed, 110
shrimp, common, 216
fairy, 212
freshwater, 212
Sialis lutaria, 182
sickener, the, 350
Silaum silaus, 276
Silene acaulis, 242
alba, 244
dioica, 242
maritima, 242
nutans, 244
vulgaris, 242
silver beetle, great, 192
silver lines (moth), green, 162
scarce, 162
silver Y (moth), 162
silverweed, 258
Sinapis arvensis, 250
Sinodendron cylindricum, 192
siskin, 124
Sisymbrium officinale, 250
Sitta europaea, 122
skater, pond, 180
skimmer, black-lined, 174
skipper, chequered, 150
dingy, 150
Essex, 150
grizzled, 150
large, 34, 150
Lulworth, 150
silver-spotted, 34, 150
small, 34, 150
Skomer Island, 60, 98
skua, Arctic, 94
great, 94
skullcap, 286
skylark, 108
slacks, 20
Slapton beach, 20
Slimbridge WWT Reserve, 64, 66, 72
sloe bug, 178
slow-worm, 37
slug, ashy-grey, 202
common garden, 202
dusky, 202
large red, 202
lemon, 202
leopard, 202
netted, 202
shelled, 202
tree, 202
yellow, 202
Smerinthus ocellata, 154
smew, 72
Smyrnium oleraceum, 272
snail, amber, 204
brown-lipped, 204
cellar, 204
copse, 204
garlic, 204
great pond, 206
plaited, 204
Roman, 204
rounded, 204
strawberry, 204
wandering, 206
white-lipped, 204
grass, 130
smooth, 37, 130
snake's-head fritillary (flower) , 310
sneezewort, 302
Snettisham reserve, 84
snipe, 25, 40, 90
jack, 90
snipe-fly, 186
snowdrop, 312
soft-grass, creeping, 330
Solanum dulcamara, 290
sole, 140
Solea solea, 140
Solidago canadensis, 300
virgaurea, 300
Solomon's seal, common, 312
Solway Firth, 18, 64
Somateria mollissima, 70
Sonchus arvensis, 308
oleraceus, 308
Sorbus aria, 230
aucuparia, 230
torminalis, 230
Sorex araneus, 46
minutus, 46
sorrel, common, 238
sheep's, 238
wood, 26, 264
sow-thistle, perennial, 308
smooth, 308
Sparganium erectum, 326
sparrow, house, 43, 126
tree, 126
sparrowhawk, 27, 74
Spartina maritima, 330
spearmint, 290
spearwort, greater, 246
lesser, 246
speckled wood (butterfly), 27
speckled yellow (butterfly), 166
spectacle (moth), the, 162

speedwell, blue water-, 292
common field-, 294
germander, 292
heath, 294
thyme-leaved, 292
Spergula arvensis, 242
Spergularia marina, 242
rupicola, 242
Sphaerium corneum, 206
Sphagnum recurvum, 336
Sphinx ligustri, 154
spider, daddy-long-legs, 200
garden, 198
house, 200
purse-web, 198
swamp, 38, 198
water, 198
zebra, 200
spike-rush, common, 322
Spilosoma lubricipeda, 158
spindle, 31
spindle-tree, 232
Spiranthes spiralis, 318
Spirorbis borealis, 220
spleenwort, maidenhair, 334
sponge, breadcrumb, 222
features, 11
spoonbill, 62
spring beauty, 238
springtail, 168
spruce, Norway, 224
sitka, 224
western hemlock-, 224
spurge, Irish, 266
petty, 266
sea, 20, 266
sun, 266
wood, 266
spurrey, corn, 242
Squalius cephalus, 136
squill, spring, 312
squinancywort, 284
squirrel, grey, 27, 48
red, 27, 29, 48
SSSI, 10
Stachys officinalis, 288
palustris, 288
sylvatica, 288
stag beetle, 192
lesser, 192
stagshorn fungus, yellow, 352
Staphylinus olens, 192
star, cushion-, 222
star-of-Bethlehem, 312
spiked, 312
yellow, 310
starfish, common, 222
spiny, 222
starling, 43, 110
statutory bodies, 10
Stauropus fagi, 152
Stellaria graminea, 240
holostea, 240
media, 240
Stenobothrus lineatus, 170
Stercorarius parasiticus, 94
skua, 94
stereum, hairy, 344
Stereum hirsutum, 344
Sterna albifrons, 96
dougallii, 96
hirundo, 96
paradisaea, 96
sandvichensis, 96
Stethophyma grossum, 170
stick insect, water, 180
stickleback, 22
nine-spined, 136
three-spined, 136
stinkhorn, 352
stint, little, 84
Temminck's, 84
stitchwort, greater, 240
lesser, 240
stoat, 50
Stodmarsh NNR, 23
stone-curlew, 90
stonechat, 37, 116
stonecrop, biting, 254
English, 254
stoneflies, 22, 168
stoneloach, 22
stork's-bill, common, 264
storm-petrel, European, 60
Strangalia maculata, 196
Stratiotes aloides, 310
strawberry, wild, 258
stream, habitat, 21–2
Streptopelia decaocto, 100
turtur, 100
Strix aluco, 102
Strymondia pruni, 148
w-album, 148
Studland Heath, 38, 62
Sturnus vulgaris, 110
Suaeda maritima, 240
Succinea putris, 204
Succisa pratensis, 298
sucker, Cornish, 140
Suillus variegatus, 350
sulphur tuft, 348
sundew, 24
oblong-leaved, 254
round-leaved, 254
swallow, 106
swallowtail, 142
swallowtailed moth, 166
swan, Bewick's, 64
mute, 22, 64
whooper, 64
sweet chestnut, 228
sweet-grass, floating, 328
reed, 23, 328
swift, 43, 106
swine-cress, 252
lesser, 252
sycamore, 230
Sylvia atricapilla, 114
borin, 114
communis, 114
curruca, 114
undata, 114

Sympetrum sanguineum, 174
striolatum, 174
Symphytum officinalis, 284
x uplandicum, 284
Syngnathus acus, 138
Syrphus ribesii, 186

Tabanus bromius, 184
Tachybaptus ruficollis, 58
Tadorna tadorna, 66
Talitris saltator, 216
Talpa europaea, 46
Tamus communis, 234
Tanacetum parthenium, 302
vulgare, 302
tansy, 302
Taraxacum officinale, 308
tare, hairy, 262
smooth, 260
tawny grisette, 348
Taxus baccata, 224
teal, 68
teasel, 298
small, 298
Tegenaria domestica, 200
tern, 20
Arctic, 96
black, 96
common, 96
little, 96
roseate, 96
sandwich, 96
Testacella scutulum, 202
Tethea ocularis, 164
Tetragnatha extensa, 200
Tetrao tetrix, 78
urogallus, 78
Tetrix ceperoi, 172
undulata, 172
Tettigonia viridissima, 172
Teucrium scorodonia, 286
Thalictrum flavum, 246
minus, 248
Thalpophila matura, 160
Thecla betulae, 148
thistle, carline, 306
creeping, 33, 306
marsh, 306
meadow, 306
melancholy, 306
musk, 306
slender, 306
spear, 306
stemless, 306
woolly, 306
Thlaspi arvense, 252
thongweed, 342
thorn, canary-shouldered, 164
purple, 164
Thorney Island, 62
thrift, 15, 280
thrush, mistle, 31, 118
song, 118
Thuidium tamariscinum, 336
Thursley Common, 38
Thyatira batis, 162
Thymallus thymallus, 134
thyme, 34, 290
Thymelicus acteon, 150
lineolus, 150
sylvestris, 150
Thymus praecox, 290
tiger (moth), garden, 44, 158
ruby, 158
tiger beetle, green, 192
Tilia cordata, 232
x vulgaris, 232
Timarcha tenebricosa, 196
timothy, 330
Tipula maxima, 184
paludosa, 184
tit, bearded, 23, 120
blue, 43, 120
coal, 120
crested, 29, 120
great, 43, 120
long-tailed, 31, 120
marsh, 120
willow, 120
toad, common, 23, 132
natterjack, 132
toadflax, common, 292
ivy-leaved, 292
toothwort, 296
topshell, toothed, 208
torgoch, 134
Torilis japonica, 272
tormentil, 39, 258
tortoise beetle, 196
tortoiseshell, small, 142
Tortula muralis, 336
Tragopogon pratensis, 308
trees, conifer, 28–30, 224
deciduous, 25–7, 226–35
treecreeper, 26, 122
trefoil, bird's-foot, 33
common bird's-foot-, 262
greater bird's-foot-, 262
hop, 264
Tremella mesenterica, 352
Trichia striolata, 204
Trichius fasciatus, 194
Trichoniscus pusillus, 212
Trientalis europaea, 278
Trifolium arvense, 264
campestre, 264
pratense, 264
repens, 264
scabrum, 264
Triglochin maritima, 298
Tringa erythropus, 86
glareola, 86
nebularia, 86
ochropus, 86
totanus, 86
triops, 212
Triturus cristatus, 132
helvetica, 132
vulgaris, 132
Trivia monacha, 208
Troglodytes troglodytes, 110
Trollius europaeus, 244

trout, 134
brown, 22
true lover's knot (moth), 158
Tsuga heterophylla, 224
tulip, wild, 310
Tulipa sylvestris, 310
Turdus iliacus, 118
merula, 118
philomelos, 118
pilaris, 118
torquatus, 118
viscivorus, 118
turnstone, 88
Tursiops truncatus, 56
Tussilago farfara, 304
tussock, pale, 156
tutsan, 268
twayblade, common, 314
twinflower, 29, 296
twite, 40
Typha latifolia, 326
Tyria jacobaeae, 158
Tyto alba, 102

Ulex europaeus, 260
gallii, 260
minor, 260
Ulmus glabra, 228
procera, 228
Ulva lactuca, 342
umber, mottled, 166
Umbilicus rupestris, 245
underwing, broad-bordered yellow, 158
large yellow, 158
red, 162
straw, 160
upland, habitat, 39–41
urban, habitat, 42–4
urchin, heart, 222
sea-, 222
Uria aalge, 98
Uroceras gigas, 188
Urtica dioica, 236
Utricularia vulgaris, 320

Vaccinium myrtillus, 278
oxycoccos, 280
vitis-idaea, 280
valerian, red, 296
Valerianella locusta, 296
Vanellus vanellus, 80
Vanessa atalanta, 142
vapourer, the, 156
Verbascum nigrum, 292
thapsus, 292
Veronica anagallis-aquatica, 292
beccabunga, 294
chamaedrys, 292
officinalis, 294
persica, 294
serpyllifolia, 292
Verrucaria maura, 340
vertebrate, features, 11
Vespa crabro, 190
Vespula germanica, 190
vetch, bush, 260
common, 260
horseshoe, 262
kidney, 262
kidney-, 31, 34
purple milk-, 260
tufted, 260
wood, 260
vetchling, meadow, 262
yellow, 262
Viburnum lantana, 234
opulus, 234
Vicia cracca, 260
hirsuta, 262
sativa, 260
sepium, 260
sylvatica, 260
tetrasperma, 260
Vinca minor, 280
Viola arvensis, 270
lutea, 270
odorata, 270
palustris, 270
riviniana, 270
tricolor, 270
violet, common dog-, 270
marsh, 270
sweet, 270
water, 278
viper's-bugloss, 286
Vipera berus, 130
Virginia Water, 27, 68
Viscum album, 236
vole, bank, 31, 46
short-tailed, 32, 41, 46
water, 46
Volucella bombylans, 186
Volvariella speciosa, 348
Vulpes vulpes, 50

wagtail, grey, 22, 108
pied, 108
yellow, 108
Wahlenbergia hederacea, 300
wainscot, common, 160
wall-rue, 334
walnut, common, 228
warbler, cetti's
Dartford, 37, 114
garden, 114
grasshopper, 112
marsh, 112
reed, 23, 112
sedge, 23, 112
willow, 27, 112
wood, 112
wartbiter, 172
Wash, The, 84
wasp, common, 190
field digger, 190
German, 190
giant wood, 188
ruby-tailed, 188
sand digger, 190
wasp beetle, 196
water beetle, 23
water boatman, 180

lesser, 180
water-cress, 21, 250
fool's, 276
water-crowfoot, chalk stream, 246
common, 246
pond, 246
round-leaved, 246
water-dropwort, hemlock, 276
tubular, 276
water-flea, 212
water-lily, fringed, 280
white, 23, 248
yellow, 248
water-milfoil, 320
water-pepper, 236
water-plantain, common, 310
water scorpion, 180
water-soldier, 310
wax-cap, blackening, 352
waxwing, 43, 110
wayfaring-tree, 234
weasel, 50
weevil, hazel, 196
weld, 254
Welney Wildfowl Refuge, 64
Wembury, 20
whale, minke, 56
wheatear, 116
whelk, common, 210
dog, 19, 210
whimbrel, 88
whin, petty, 260
whinchat, 116
white, green-veined, 27, 142
large, 44, 142
marbled, 32, 34, 146
small, 44, 142
wood, 142
white ermine (moth), 158
whitebeam, 43, 230
whitethroat, 114
lesser, 31, 114
whiting, 138
whitlowgrass, common, 252
Wicken Fen, 25
wigeon, 18, 68
wild service tree, 230
wildcat, 29, 50
willow, bay, 226
crack, 226
grey, 226
weeping, 226
white, 226
willowherb, American, 270
great, 21, 270
marsh, 270
rosebay, 270
winter moth, 166
winter-cress, common, 250
wintergreen, chickweed, 278
common, 29, 280
round-leaved, 280
witches' butter, 352
Woburn Park, 54
wood, speckled, 146
wood mushroom, 348
wood-rush, field, 322
great, 322
woodcock, 90
woodland, habitat, 25–30
woodlark, 37, 108
woodlouse, common, 212
pill, 212
woodpecker, 27
great spotted, 30, 43, 104
green, 104
lesser spotted, 104
woodpigeon, 43, 100
woodruff, sweet, 284
worm, ghost, 184
peacock, 220
planarian, features, 11
segmented, features, 12
slow, 130
wormwood, 304
sea, 304
wort, saw-, 308
yellow-, 34, 282
woundwort, hedge, 288
marsh, 288
bladder, 19, 342
channelled, 19, 342
egg, 19, 342
knotted, 342
serrated, 19, 342
spiral, 19, 342
wrasse, corkwing, 138
wren, 31, 110
wryneck, 104
Wye Downs, 35

Xanthoria parietina, 340
Xanthothoe montanata, 164
Xylaria hypoxylon, 344
Xysticus cristatus, 200

yarrow, 302
yellow (butterfly), clouded, 142
yellow-rattle, 294
yellow-tail (moth), 156
yellowcress, marsh, 250
yellowhammer, 31, 122
yew, 224
Yorkshire fog (grass), 33, 330

zonation, 19
Zygaena trifolii, 152